Sharing Common Ground

Sharing Common Ground

A Space for Ethics

Robert Harvey

Bloomsbury Academic
An imprint of Bloomsbury Publishing Inc

B L O O M S B U R Y
NEW YORK · LONDON · OXFORD · NEW DELHI · SYDNEY

Bloomsbury Academic
An imprint of Bloomsbury Publishing Inc

1385 Broadway	50 Bedford Square
New York	London
NY 10018	WC1B 3DP
USA	UK

www.bloomsbury.com

BLOOMSBURY and the Diana logo are trademarks of Bloomsbury Publishing Plc

First published 2017

© Robert Harvey, 2017

"Les Chantiers" (in *Des journées entières dans les arbres*) by Marguerite Duras © Editions Gallimard, Paris, 1954

All rights reserved. No part of this publication may be reproduced or transmitted in any form or by any means, electronic or mechanical, including photocopying, recording, or any information storage or retrieval system, without prior permission in writing from the publishers.

No responsibility for loss caused to any individual or organization acting on or refraining from action as a result of the material in this publication can be accepted by Bloomsbury or the author.

Library of Congress Cataloging-in-Publication Data
Names: Harvey, Robert, 1951- author.
Title: Sharing common ground : a space for ethics / Robert Harvey.
Description: New York : Bloomsbury Academic, 2017. | Includes bibliographical references and index.
Identifiers: LCCN 2016048836 (print) | LCCN 2017008620 (ebook) | ISBN 9781501329609 (hardback) | ISBN 9781501329593 (paperback) | ISBN 9781501329616 (ePDF) | ISBN 9781501329623 (ePUB)
Subjects: LCSH: Collective memory and literature. | Literature and morals. | Art and morals. | Literature--Philosophy. | BISAC: LITERARY CRITICISM / Semiotics & Theory. | PHILOSOPHY / Ethics & Moral Philosophy. | PHILOSOPHY / Epistemology.
Classification: LCC PN56.C618 H37 2017 (print) | LCC PN56.C618 (ebook) | DDC 809/.93353--dc23
LC record available at https://lccn.loc.gov/2016048836

ISBN:	HB:	978-1-5013-2960-9
	PB:	978-1-5013-2959-3
	ePub:	978-1-5013-2962-3
	ePDF:	978-1-5013-2961-6

Cover design: Eleanor Rose
Cover image © Getty Images

Typeset by Fakenham Prepress Solutions, Fakenham, Norfolk NR21 8NN

To find out more about our authors and books visit www.bloomsbury.com. Here you will find extracts, author interviews, details of forthcoming events, and the option to sign up for our newsletters.

Contents

Preface		vi
1	Construction Sites	1
2	Empathy and the Kantian Sublime	63
3	Of Spaces Otherwise	101
4	Zones of Indistinction	141
5	Foucault's Transgression	191
6	The Cleave Informs: René Char and the Hope of Heresy	243
Bibliography		293
Index		303

Preface

When imagination-fueled thinking about inhospitable environments—spaces that are rebarbative yet altogether *real*—becomes reflection *shared between two or more people*, the endeavor *in common* holds unique potential to move individuals into ethical dealings with each other. *Sharing Common Ground* examines this phenomenon through a number of examples that are historical, photographic, literary, filmic, and philosophical in nature.

Empathy is the premier interpersonal and social experience without which work toward an ethics proves futile. A gesture (and so much more), the empathetic move (I prefer the term "move" to affectless "action") takes place when one consciousness encounters another at a *site* that is as imaginary as it is real. I call such meeting-spaces for sensible emotion *common grounds*. Common ground is not so much a *place* as it is a *space*: common ground is only tenuously localizable in the real world, operating rather in our imagination, in our memory, in day-dreaming, where it best maintains its power to outstrip accepted reality, thus readying us to plan potentialities.

Sharing Common Ground describes and analyzes various *spaces*, then—topographies propitious for empathic construction, what Michel Foucault once termed "spaces otherwise" [*des espaces autres*]. Mapping tools borrowed from both literature and philosophy are deployed here, mobilizing figures, thinkers, with whose works I have been engaged—in teaching and in writing—over the past three years: Michel Foucault and Marguerite Duras primarily, but also Georges Didi-Huberman, Giorgio Agamben and a supporting cast including Eugène Atget, Immanuel Kant, Samuel Fuller, Jorge Luís Borges, Blaise Pascal, Étienne Balibar …

Sharing Common Ground comprises six chapters organized loosely in two parts with Duras, then Foucault, as successive guideposts. The point of departure for *Sharing Common Ground* is a close reading of "Construction Sites," a largely neglected and somewhat obscure short story by Marguerite Duras, written in 1954. "Construction Sites" stands as a heretofore hidden, yet crucial turning point in the prolific oeuvre of this major French author whose centenary fell in 2014. Because it is virtually unknown, an entirely new translation of "Construction Sites" is included in the book's first chapter.

It is commonly agreed that from the late 1950s onward, Duras's artistic enterprise reveals an increasingly insistent determination to "remember" the Shoah, albeit vicariously. In an unpublished letter where she attempted to explain the title she lent to *Green Eyes*—incongruously, but successfully a filmic, photographic, and literary work simultaneously—Duras wrote, "I see the end of the world through the green eyes of a girl, I also see an infinite laziness, and joy as well." In the first chapter of this book, I attempt to show that beyond, yet no doubt also with the help of, the melancholy of this vision, Duras was setting the groundwork for a post-genocide ethics that was already apparent in the bizarre 1954 story.

My study of "Construction Sites" also gives the reader the opportunity to discover two fascinating works by Duras—a novel and a poem—previously unpublished in English. I also revisit, under new light, her first two film scenarios: *Hiroshima mon amour* and *The Long Absence*. This chapter advances the thesis that Marguerite Duras constructed—through the literary imagination—a model for effectively mobilizing the work of memory in regard to humanity's crimes against itself.

The most prominent features of Duras's "Construction Sites" call for analysis under the light of Kant's "Analytic of the Sublime." While extending the initial exploration of the woman's trauma in *Hiroshima mon amour*, "Empathy and the Kantian Sublime" turns on a reintroduction of the endlessly fertile sections of Kant's *Critique of Judgement*. The part that the Enlightenment's conceptualization of the sublime plays in increasing our understanding of how empathy takes hold in consciousness may be illustrated by a number of the essays that Georges Didi-Huberman has included in the books Éditions de Minuit has published over the last decade under the series titled "The Eye of History." Showing how empathy grows out of *shared* experiences of the sublime will necessitate expansion of two of Didi-Huberman's studies in particular: one that examines Samuel Fuller's early film documenting the opening of the Flossenbürg concentration camp at Falkenau (now Sokolov, Czech Republic); the other on photographs taken inside Bram concentration camp (Languedoc, France) by Catalonian inmate Agustí Centelles. These artworks by Fuller and Centelles are passageways onto common ground and the sharing of such a space enables peaceful coexistence.

The resolute indeterminacy of Duras's 1954 story notwithstanding, what so profoundly disturbs the female character is the sight of a cemetery being extended. To her, this construction site (*chantier* in French) conjures the image of mass graves (*charniers* or "*chantiers de la mort*"). If all stories effect transformations, the object transformed by the plot of "Construction Sites" is a cemetery: by the end of her story, Duras has managed to mutate cemeteries from their usual status as spaces *of* death into that of spaces *between* life and death. In Chapter 3, I begin to introduce the other major figure of *Sharing Common Ground*: Michel Foucault. Already the new translation that I provide of the title of Foucault's celebrated essay, "Des espaces autres" as

"Of Spaces Otherwise" (instead of "Of Other Spaces"), will begin moving the reader—with a regrettable tardiness—to the limit experience enabled uniquely in such limit spaces—an experience that both Duras and Foucault advocate explicitly and, sometimes, implicitly.

Just as cemeteries are spaces between life and death, they are often—quite concretely—spaces on the outskirts of cities, in no-man's land, between the city and what city dwellers often consider the degraded form of existence of those who inhabit the suburban zone. Setting the stage for a critical examination of core claims in Giorgio Agamben's *Homo sacer*, in "Zones of Indistinction" I explore the ways in which photography, film, and literature imaged one particular slum: *la Zone* that encircled Paris from the mid-nineteenth through the mid-twentieth century. *La Zone* was captured by the lens of Eugène Atget, then documented by that of Georges Lacombe. These artists of the visual managed to capture for later contemplation the proudly intermedial being of *la Zone*'s inhabitants. This wasteland (one sense of the word *shoah*) was also explored in texts by authors as divergent as Louis-Ferdinand Céline and Raymond Queneau. It is perhaps even the inspiration for the devastated mental landscapes found in the work of Henri Michaux or of Samuel Beckett. More distantly, zones of indistinction, or mental common grounds, may be seen studied by writers as diverse as Herman Melville (the prison yard where Bartleby ended up), Walter Benjamin (the notion of "critical point" in the *Arcades Project*), and of course Giorgio Agamben (the camp as *nomos* in *Homo sacer*). These efforts to transform spaces otherwise into grounds for improved intersubjectivity are explored in the third chapter.

At the nexus between images of spaces otherwise and what I earlier referred to as our ability to think about them via the imagination lies the possibility of shared experience and, thus, a possible opening onto ethics. Michel Foucault's boldly transgressive linguistic inventiveness hit upon a word—and, thus, a concept—for that nexus. We know that the ironies exposed by Foucaldian archaeology trump, supplement, and surpass by surprise what we routinely call the ironies of history and that this is perhaps the major gift of that oeuvre to critical thinking. What we know less is how the beautifully bivalent word *partage*—*partage* as noun, but also *partage* in its avatars as verb, as adverbial component, as participle—was put to work by Foucault in order to convey those ironies linguistically. By the sheer frequency of its use under Foucault's pen, by dint of its appearance at nearly every crescendo culminating his demonstrations and abidingly (if not always consistently) from one end to the other of his work, the function of *partage* shows itself to be crucial, yet nearly illegible for the English-only reader of that work. Our way of translating *partage* into English demands adjustment, if not correction. Variously rendered in the extant translations as "division" and "sharing" or "share," *partage* is, in fact, sharing *and* division, division that *includes* sharing. Thus my study—in the chapter entitled "Foucault's Transgression"—of this term by means of a consistent new translation in "cleave," with its significantly meaningful polysemy, serves both to focus several of Foucault's most recalcitrant claims and heighten our understanding of them. The cleave figure lends function to spaces otherwise and its transgressive force is bolstered by the "point of heresy"—a notion which Foucault adopted and adapted from Pascal and introduced in *The Order of Things*. A point of heresy itself, the cleave is where we witnesses actively meet the gaze of the *Zone*'s denizen.

Transgression in Foucault's use of the concept is, unlike in Bataille, an *inclusive* disjunction. And it is in that very inclusiveness, despite all, that a modicum of optimism can be heard to murmur even in the darkest of the Foucaldian archaeologies. In the final chapter of this book, I maintain—against the current—that the literary function abided in Michel Foucault well beyond the cultural rupture of May '68 and continued to *inform* his thought to the end in June 1984. Trusting his own hypothesis that our relationship to language creates a viable "'cleave' of being," to borrow an expression from Gerard Manley Hopkins, Foucault negotiated that inclusive disjunction in himself by continuing to take inspiration from poetry without making the inspiration explicit by naming names.

Of all the creative voices that coursed through Michel Foucault, one of the most significant—and certainly one of the more unique ones in that it was the voice of a near contemporary as well as that of a poet—was René Char. There can be little doubt that Foucault assigned *partage*, or cleave, the major textual and rhetorical role that he did in homage to and imitation of René Char and his pivotal group of aphorisms, *Partage formel* (*Formal Cleave*). Not only had Foucault memorized and taught René Char's poems in the early years of his professional career, it is patent that he drew inspiration from them right up to his final work, *Le Souci de soi* (*The Care of the Self*) whose back cover bears, simply, a quote from the only poet for whom Martin Heidegger wrote poetry.

The admiration that both René Char and Michel Foucault shared for the Marquis de Sade is surpassed by their commitment to the lightning flash of *resistance*—whether recovered by History or lived to the last breath as fundamental *resistance for the sake of resistance* or, as Lyotard once put it, for "the honor of the name." That cleave in the stone of our sense of being nurtures not only the saxifrage[1] but also the glimmer of hope Foucault saw beyond the

---

[1] René Char adopted the saxifrage as emblematic of our fundamental impulse to resist the forces of what Michel Foucault would call biopolitics. The Oxford English Dictionary defines "saxifrage" as "[a]ny plant of the genus *Saxifraga*, esp. *S. granulata* (white meadow saxifrage). The numerous species are mostly dwarf herbs with tufted foliage and panicles of white, yellow or red flowers; many root in the clefts of rocks."

effacement of man in the sands of history. By invoking the survival of hope in face of Agamben's generalization of *homo sacer*, *Sharing Common Ground* ends, then, on a heretical note.

In and for the unfolding of this project, I owe the debt of thanks to Bernard Alazet, Étienne Balibar, Gabriela Basterra, Odile Baumgartner-Roman, Corinne Benestroff, Réda Bensmaïa, Sophie Bogaert, Edward S. Casey, Mary Ann Caws, Kimberly Coates, Tom Conley, Martin Crowley, Michel Deguy, Georges Didi-Huberman, Éditions Gallimard, Gregory Fabre, Thierry Gillyboeuf, Stuart Kendall, Nathalie Léger, Steve Light, Jean Mascolo, Haaris Naqvi, François Noudelmann, Florent Perrier, Thangam Ravindranathan, Sophie Raynard-Leroy, Gabriel Rockhill, Donna Sammis, Philippe Sellier, Nancy K. Squires, Mary Watkins, the twenty students in a Spring 2013 "Foucault Fundamentals" seminar during which the idea for the book coalesced, Hélène Volat, *bien sûr*, and last but far, far from least, Elise Woodard.

1

Construction Sites

"Common ground" is spoken of.

But perhaps, one might say, we use the expression too often. "It is commonly that we speak of 'common ground'" might be a better way to start. One way or the other, "common ground" is spoken of often enough for the expression to have long ago become a *commonplace*. When this happens to a locution, whatever power came with the moment of its invention, its catachresis—that first explosive and excitingly imperfect attempt at meaningfulness by coining—has long fizzled to nearly nothing.

So, what might we still be trying to convey today when we refer—often longing for it—to common ground: ground in common, that is, space shared in mind if not also in body, ground to which we might assign some common purpose, some purpose toward the building of community?

If we take the two lexical items making up the expression "common ground" and examine them separately, apart from each other, we quickly notice that together, as a phrase, they create redundancy, a truism of sorts. Whether used metaphorically or "literally," *ground* denotes the solid surface of the planet on which we dwell, the habitable and naked crust of earth on which we stand and are able—on condition that a few fundamental necessities gleaned from that self-same ground are available—to survive. As adjective, *common* refers to that which belongs to all—where "all" is usually understood as all those belonging to the species known by *homo sapiens* as *homo sapiens*. Ground would then always be common.

Truism or all-too-well-worn compound metaphor notwithstanding, I think that by "common ground" we still envision and project a space where two or more people would find themselves getting along. On such grounds people would manage to coexist peacefully, cooperate, live in a state of mutual aid and moral solidarity. Furthermore, there is, I think, understood to be some causal relationship between fundament and commonality. It is *because* this ground is *propitious* to agreement, harmony, peace, and so forth, that we credit it with a *power to unite*. Directly on the fundament of earth we place the foundations of our shelters and our dwellings. Our need and our urge to build result in constructions that enable and enhance our social interactions. As much as language, architecture binds us, grounds us in our commonality.

I have, however, gone somewhat far afield as I find myself already anticipating conclusions that we may draw from reading and analyzing discursive as well as figural elaborations of thought regarding common ground. Such readings and analyses of texts and images fill the propensity of the remainder of this book. But the first question that this study will consider is not the relationship between a cause (ground) and an effect (commonality), but the question of the geographical relationship of a given space to two or more subjects who seem to have found common ground mediated by that space or, more precisely, who are in the process of finding it. How do certain spaces facilitate the sharing of common ground? What turns a mere space into "space of interest"?

Upon uttering the expression "common ground," both speaker and interlocutor (sender and receiver) infer that the subjects who are moved to commonality find themselves occupying one very same space where they may thrive in love and care. But what of spaces that are elsewhere? What if the very ground most propitious to the vivifying possibilities for us were not "right here," where you and I are standing, but "over there"? And what of spaces that are not only elsewhere but otherwise than those habitually at my feet? What if the power of ground to create the multiplicity in harmony that we call "commonality" resided in a paradox consisting in the fact that we do not stand upon it, yet it is undeniably here, present, now?

There is, after all, ground—in both the literal and the metaphorical senses—other than the one on which I have my feet planted at the present moment. Such ground otherwise is nevertheless attestable today, in this nation, under these meteorological, political, economic conditions. Yet I may not experience this ground otherwise as *common* ground, because I am not presently in the situation of sharing a vision of *and* for those conditions with another soul. Allowing ground to slip, as it is wont to do, towards its metaphorical valence, there are, today, other conditions for the possibility of community that differ, to varying degrees, from the conditions that are available to me here and now. There are, in short, today—here and now—spaces other than this one *for* community.

The focus of this study is just such spaces. They are spaces elsewhere or—adjusting and correcting the extant English translation of "*Des espaces autres*," the title of one of Michel Foucault's most important short theoretical works—these spaces are not only "spaces apart," they are "*spaces otherwise.*" They exist in our world, but at a remove. And they act upon us altogether differently from the spaces that we complacently inhabit. They are spaces in relationship to which durable commonality among us may be kindled as an irrepressible impulse. Spaces otherwise coexist for me alongside the ground on which I stand. Spaces otherwise will be named thus because, although like the space I occupy, "my space," they too are in the present moment, *right now*, they are nevertheless *over there* with respect to the sensible world, the phenomenological world that I apprehend with my senses. They must be, if at all possible; we keep them at a distance for although they are propitious to ethical common ground, they are not particularly vivifying. Some, as a matter of fact, are downright death dealing. Thus, the spaces otherwise that this book will examine function upon us by dint of that part of experience with considerable powers that we call the imagination.

Here, without further ado, is a story that attests to those powers while presenting a paradigmatic example of a space otherwise that becomes common ground for disparate beings:

"Construction Sites" (1954)
by Marguerite Duras

translated from the French
by Robert Harvey

She had gone by in the lane, heading toward the man, and had passed him. Then, retracing her steps, she had passed by him again. She had proceeded along the lane in the opposite direction and had entered the woods—that woods into which the lane disappeared.

It was late: a little before dinnertime.

The man himself was stretched out on a chaise longue in the lane, halfway between the hotel's garden gate and the construction site and he had seen the girl emerge from the woods. Mechanically, his eyes had followed her. He thought she was on her way back into the hotel, but he saw her stop a few paces short of the gate opening onto the road, retrace her steps and, again enter the woods from which she'd come.

A few moments passed; it was dinnertime: the hotel's bell rang.

The man remained stretched out on his chaise longue. He wondered what on earth the girl could be doing at that hour in the woods.

When she went by first, then again, she had more than merely glanced at the man. She at first seemed in a hurry to go back into the hotel. But after having stopped before the gate when heading back off toward the woods, she had appeared as much in a hurry to get back into the woods that she'd just left. She had walked just as quickly in one direction as in the other as if some unknown force had her caged between the woods and the hotel gate. And, without looking at anything, without a glance at the man whose legs—since he and his chaise longue took up more than half the width of the lane—she had nevertheless almost had to brush up against.

Dinnertime had come without the man having seen her return.

The impression remained with him for a good while that the lane was so devoid of the girl that it was as if the woods had swallowed up her memory, even.

And then it was getting late. Dinnertime had long passed.

The man still waited for the girl to emerge from the woods.

It wasn't that she was remarkable or that he had noticed her before. But the lane disappeared into the woods, leading to a village several kilometers from the hotel. And she had to be there. And the man wondered what spectacle it was that could retain her or what she could have to do in that woods instead of returning to the hotel. As daylight waned and the shadows grew longer, he wondered about all this with increasing curiosity and lost more and more resolve to retire.

And, in the end, all this wondering caused him to arise and take a few steps in the direction she had taken. It would not have been natural to restrain himself from doing so after having wondered so insistently about what had become of her. A good half hour had gone by without him thinking about anything else.

No, he remembered well: she was not that pretty. Had it not been for that strange behavior—being alone in the woods and so late in the evening, all this at a time when it would have been normal for her to be elsewhere—at the hotel—No, all this aside, there would have been nothing remarkable about her.

He began walking down the lane and was approaching the construction site when he saw her come out of the woods. She too stepped into the lane, but soon stopped when she got to the construction site.

The man waited. Surely he hadn't been seen. They were each posted at extremities of the construction site. He had stopped in his tracks, turned towards her. She had turned toward the construction site and her light-colored dress stood out against the dark mass of the woods. It was almost nighttime. All he could make out was the vague profile of her body, arrested, facing the construction site. And so, even though he didn't know her better than any other hotel guest, as soon as he saw her—alone, apparently fascinated by the construction site, and so late—he understood that he was taking her by surprise, unwittingly, in one of the most intimate moments of her life and that to know her better might not have helped find her otherwise. They were alone and together, he and she, but separated one from the other, before this construction site.

And her still being unaware, perfectly unaware of the presence of this thief, of this violator, naturally made the man desire to be seen.

Behind them, on the highway separating them from the hotel, nearly continuously, cars passed by with their headlights on. It was between them, between this luminous and sonorous wall and that dark and silent wood that their meeting was situated.

The man waited a bit before showing himself. He remained still at the near extremity of the construction site and watched her. And when he decided to move forward, he moved so slowly that she didn't notice. The sound from the cars covered that of his steps. He was taking his time. She, on her side, let time pass. Still unaware that she was not alone. Perhaps she hadn't heard the hotel bell. Perhaps she had come from the hamlet located on the far side of the woods. Walking fast, she would have had the time to go there. It had been nearly three-quarters of an hour since she had gone off again toward the woods. But it didn't seem as though she had just been hurrying. And this was all the less probable for the fact that the lane didn't lead there directly; rather, a path that she no doubt knew nothing about and probably couldn't discover or find again [in any case] once night had fallen. No, it was the construction site that fascinated her. Altogether transfixed, she gazed at it or at least in its direction. Once he was right near her, he saw her petrified face in a state of immobile intensity and he was certain that it was indeed the construction site that she was staring at. This astonished the man. Hadn't she noticed it before this evening? Had he had the good fortune of being there at the moment she discovered it?

The construction site extended out, vacant, with its rather special emptiness, to be sure. But, then again, there was nothing particularly notable within its light-colored walls, nothing unexpected, in any case. Perhaps, after all, she was discovering it [only] this evening.

"Pardon me," went the man.

Startled, she turned and looked at him. Her gaze widened further, but now displaced onto the man.

"Pardon me, I'm at the hotel."

"Ah!" she went, mechanically, laughing at the same time. She came forward toward the man.

"Pardon me," he said, "I startled you."

Like her, he began laughing.

"That's alright," she said.

She appeared neither frightened nor disturbed that he had approached her in this manner. She appeared, rather, to think it natural.

"Had you already noticed this construction site?" the man asked.

"This is the first time," she said. "Until now, I thought it was something else. It's a funny idea…"

"A funny idea?"

"It's terrible," she said, "and so close to the hotel."

The man hesitated.

"I beg your pardon," he said at length. "I'd like to know… I noticed you already a while ago… Why did you retrace your steps after having passed by here?"

The girl turned her head away.

"I hadn't seen it well… I'd misunderstood. It's crazy, but I think I'll be leaving the hotel."

The man tried to see her face, but couldn't. She walked with her head turned the other way, distractedly. She probably hadn't looked at him. He was still laughing.

"The whole hotel knows about that construction site," said the man.

They'd gotten to the gate. He could see her face better in the light of the gas lamp under the hotel's porch.

"It's an everyday thing," the man said, laughing harder. "Sometimes they have to be made."

The girl laughed in turn. There was no irony, confusion or flirtatiousness in her laugh; just a certain uncertainty that clung—but how was one to know?—to these last words he'd pronounced.

This was how things started between them. This was three days before. Since then, he'd only seen her at a distance, at mealtimes.

In the first night following their encounter, the man believed she'd perhaps actually leave the hotel because of her discovery of the construction site. This fear was perhaps also, in a sense, an expectation. It wouldn't have displeased him to see her peculiarity extend to the point of leaving the hotel for no other reason than the proximity of that construction site.

The wish was contradictory and, had it been satisfied, there would have been little chance that the man would ever see her again. But at this stage, he was still able to imagine adjusting to the notion of her departure.

Already, the day following their encounter, he had started waiting for her in the lane. She didn't appear. At noon, he saw her at table again, as usual, and found that in appearance, at least, nothing—no hastiness, no disquiet on her face or in her gestures—indicated her intention to leave. He said to himself that what must have been painful for her was simply the sight of the construction site and that, following their encounter the evening before, she had probably decided to not return to that side of the valley. She was forcing herself not to go back. Since she hadn't left the hotel, since she didn't seem intent on cutting short her stay, she had undoubtedly succeeded in at least surmounting the thought of the construction site's proximity.

This success, this small victory over her fear might have lent her a certain banality in the man's eyes. Nothing of the kind occurred. Although he might have been a bit disappointed to see her at table the day after their encounter, this didn't last long. He said to himself that it was unlikely that she hadn't thought that anywhere else, in any peaceful setting where she might find herself, she might always encounter something like the construction site. She must nevertheless have realized that. To have understood once and for all that even if—and despite what he had said to her—this construction site were not something as usual as all that, there were enough things of the same nature in the world to make her flee from anywhere else she might go to hide. And, at bottom, her success proved that she knew this very well, that she had a certain familiarity with these things, and that she knew it would be childish and futile to flee them and to leave the hotel she was in now just on account of these things. Yet, was this courage? a form of steadfastness? lucidity? It was nothing. The banality of everything.

By the next day after their encounter, his desire to see her again had grown. He didn't see her in the lane where he waited for her as he had the day before, but only in the dining room, at mealtimes. And so, already, he admitted to himself that there was some good in this small victory over herself, without which he would have stood no chance of seeing her again. He realized that this pleased him. And even went as far as to tell himself, moreover, that if she hadn't overcome the distress that the sight of things analogous to that construction site caused her, she probably wouldn't have been able to survive until their encounter. There could be no doubt that had she continued to flee things like this, she would in the end have found no other refuge than in death itself.

No, there was a wisdom about her. And one truly had to agree that the possibility he had of seeing her again depended, in fact, on that part of her that he had deemed a bit regrettable when he'd seen her again at table the day after their encounter and that he'd felt he could call her imperfection.

And if something of that first slight disappointment remained nevertheless with him, her nature had also slightly changed. The fact that she was not altogether the one he had hoped she'd be the first day that had followed their encounter—that slight flaw—made her appear more peculiar to him, nearer, no doubt because more real. And, in the end, for this very reason, her existence became more astonishing. Thus for the man, this encounter ceased imperceptibly being an event in his mind and tended to become an event in his life. He had ceased seeing it as an exacting spectator demanding perfection when such perfection can only be had from art.

His desire to know her grew each day, each half day.

This resulted, simply, from his having had the courage to accept an initial disillusion, just as she had had the courage to accept the construction site. However, the ideal complicity that was born of this shared minor loss more than compensated for any disappointment. Or, rather, that was it: it was this disappointment itself which, from the start, had become encouragement. It was the fact of its being possible.

But as quickly as he'd come to see things this way, he continued to act as if he hoped to be able to witness, once again, the spectacle begun the other evening. He began waiting for her every morning and every afternoon in the lane facing the construction site. She didn't pass by. He was right: she'd surely decided to avoid the sight of the construction site. He persisted, notwithstanding, stretched out right before the construction site, as if, in the very décor where it had begun, to not lose a single chance of seeing the pursuit of the action begun previously. He proceeded, thus, for three days in a row and for three days he only saw her at mealtimes, from afar. Never did she appear in the lane.

The dining room tables were neatly arranged in six rows, four per row, in a vast square hall extended by a glass-enclosed space. This enclosure was a rotunda whose smaller tables were reserved for guests eating alone. They were arranged in concentric circles following the shape of the rotunda. It was at one of these tables that the girl was seated. The same for the man except that his, fortunately, was on the opposite side, facing inward. As a result, the girl, who was in full sunlight near the glass, was naturally inclined to look outdoors toward the tennis court spread out before the hotel, and could scarcely notice that she was being observed.

At the table next to the girl's was a single woman with her little boy. This mother almost never stopped by turns entertaining and reprimanding her capricious child in order to get him to eat. Yet sometimes, distracted, the child would start to eat on his own. The girl was so intent on observing the child's distraction that the man could observe her without taking precautions. Later, when the child got up to play among the tables, the girl completely lost interest.

Outside those moments, the man watched her such that it would have been difficult for her to notice. Moreover, the position of the tables they occupied put her in his line of sight and he could see her without turning his head. All he had to do was lift his eyes and she appeared to him in the background, in profile, between two other guests who hardly hindered his view of the girl. They faced her. They could thus not notice the look passing between them and only better served to protect it. He told himself that she wasn't really good at noticing the things that people usually noticed—like, for example, his gaze. For as skilled and protected as he was, anyone else would have noticed. Not she, though. He all the same took great precautions so that she would not yet notice the surveillance to which he was subjecting her.

Those meals were for him occasions to observe lots of things about her. To observe how she ate, for example. She ate with gusto, attentively, methodically. It pleased the man [to think] that she might have repelled the sight of the construction site [with] this [same] calm body that craved food with regularity. That this fear had made its way into this body, the alliance of its health and its refusal transported him. Each time he took stock of it again, at mealtimes, he gave himself over to the same ravishment, the same reassurance. Such a rare sensibility with such unbound strength at its disposal left him in wonderment. Thus her very fright, far from taking on some morbid quality, was like the most precious extension of that surge of animal vigor, of that avidness that she could also display.

Just as she ate insistently, avidly, so she sometimes truly looked with her body's eyes at what was happening around her in the dining room. Her gaze would light, then drift off, then light again, her eyes scrutinizing with a sort of sweetness that could lead one to believe that she was slightly near-sighted. But he was certain that it was only a sort of secondary look, following the first, which was, to the contrary, astoundingly pellucid. It was rather as if, as soon as she'd noticed something, she were in the habit of studying the intimate effect what she'd just seen had on herself. Then she'd turn her gaze outside, toward the tennis area, letting it drift there. Whatever scene or thing or face she had been watching, she would leave it before long and look out toward the tennis courts. There were six of these, grouped in threes, in a great quadrilateral enclosed by a fence. These courts were generally in use all morning and all afternoon, until late in the evening. However, sometimes, during lunch, a few die-hards would train. The dining room stood slightly above the courts and the players' impersonal and mechanical announcements could be heard—attenuated by distance, yet very clear. Uniformly dressed in white shorts and shirts, they could hardly be distinguished and, at that distance, melded into the endless back and forth of the balls, the flash of their rackets, and their apparently gratuitous gesticulations, their respective abilities cancelled each other out. There were always a few spectators at the fence. Rapt, they followed one or the other of the matches. But from the hotel, one only took in the spectacle as a whole. Before, like other hotel guests—especially those alone—the man occasionally gazed at the courts while eating. Now, too, he watched them. But while [before] he had only been sensitive to the absurdity of the spectacle, it now gave him pleasure to watch it. Always there at any hour of the day, absorbed in the exercise of a sort of lucid passion, the players naturally became part of the interminable and exalting duration of his wait.

Inside, it always seemed to him that when she wasn't watching the child, it was the men she watched—especially those whose table was under the glass enclosure. She hadn't seemed to notice him yet, however. His table was at the other end of the enclosure, a bit back toward the dining room's entryway and, although not within the shadowed area, it occupied the most discreet location within this luminous cage. He, nevertheless, was together with her there—he who was waiting for her and who was made for her. She was probably still oblivious to his having noticed her, that a man existed who found her suitable. The man was thrilled when she looked at other men. He knew none of them could quite do for her. And in order to have her understand this, all he would have to do is come forth in the glass enclosure, look at her and smile at her in such a way that she would grasp that this smile was the same as the one made the other evening near the construction site and that it had only ceased to appear on account of his own will to not let it appear, while in fact it had never ceased shuttling between them—invisible spring—since the first day. This apparently absolute oblivion about what had come to pass between them three days before on account of the construction site lent her the aura of a capacity for forgetting that struck him as an endearing naiveté that he alone could sense. She would have to come to know that he alone could sense it.

These observations comforted him. Each of the observations he made on those days, moreover, reassured him. They took him by surprise as well, since they all contributed to bringing her into convergence with the one he had desired she be already on the first day. She definitely was that one. She was that one as much as it were possible to be her without having fled the hotel.

Since their encounter, the man had not heard her voice. But the words she'd uttered in the lane, facing the construction site, and the order in which she had uttered them, often returned to his memory. He didn't stop to lend meaning in them: that was now useless. But he did spend time recollecting them saturated with her voice, her look, her body walking next to him as she uttered them. He'd had the good fortune to hear them because he'd been there, so near the construction site. For, had anyone else approached her the other evening, it would have been impossible for him to do otherwise. And she would have responded to anyone in the same spot who would have approached her. But just anyone would perhaps have not waited as he'd done the first evening and, especially, as he'd done since then to approach her again. He thus thought that she'd done well to confess to him what she'd confessed to him and that no one was better suited than he to receive such confessions.

Five nights and five days had passed since their encounter. When she'd go out after lunch, he didn't follow her. He only saw her at mealtimes. Nine times she had taken a seat at her table in the window and he'd observed her. No one else in the hotel seemed yet to have noticed her.

When he'd arrive at the dining room, she was already there. For five days, at each meal, she was there, and each time before him, always alone at her table. There was nothing particularly remarkable about her. She was not beautiful, precisely, and her behavior was not that of a woman who knows herself to be beautiful or who desires to appear as such. There were several other more beautiful women at the hotel and toward whom men gravitated. As for her, she watched those women and, like everyone else, probably found them beautiful, all the while ignoring the fact that he already found her more beautiful than the most beautiful of those she found beautiful. What was she like, then? Tall. She had black hair. Her eyes were light in color. Her movements were somewhat cumbersome, her body was robust—perhaps a bit hefty. She always wore light-colored dresses, as did the other women who'd come to spend their vacation on the lake.

Truth be told, he'd never seen her very well or near enough, except the first time, but that was in the dark. And all he could say for certain was that he'd seen her eyes once or, rather, her look just as she'd averted it from the construction site. He could no longer forget it. He said to himself that he didn't remember having seen anyone before her use the gaze so naturally. He didn't think he was mistaken. "And why not?" he said to himself. Why wouldn't that have been the first time?

Every morning, every afternoon, for several hours, he went out with a book in hand to watch the work's progress at the construction site. He still hoped she'd return to the lane, back to her fright. But she wasn't coming back yet.

The construction of new stretches of wall was advancing, but one could still see the inside of the site very well. One part was obviously old. There was, on the one hand, the old enclosure and its fully occupied space could easily be made out; on the other, the new enclosure with its yet untouched space with nothing to indicate that it had to be used one day except for the fact that, as days went by, it was more precisely delimited by the new walls with which the workers extended the old ones and which would obviously be closed in by a fourth one whose position nothing could yet allow one to predict with certainty.

It was a construction site like others, though one, it is true, with a particular purpose. It wonderfully illustrated the development of man's gift of foresight—a gift whose exercise was occurring, here, with a rather astounding placidity, all the same. The toiling workers behaved as naturally as if they'd been busy with just any earthwork and masonry job.

They were even rather gay and calm. Once in a while one of them would roll a cigarette and smoke while seated on a stone. These moments, along with lunchtime, were their only moments of respite in the day. Some moved sand and stones from the dried streambed along the lane; others poured cement. Some meticulously stretched lines. These appeared impelled by some mysterious will. Only they knew how far the new construction was to extend beyond the limits of the old construct. Workers then began digging along the lines set. Part of the meadow was already enclosed by the combination of walls, ditches, and lines. The construction site was delimited by these walls meant to forever enclose part of the meadow. The portion of the meadow that had been set aside for enclosure was about as big as that contained, up until now, by the old enclosure. The wall that had been knocked down allowed one to see that old part that was entirely utilized, with each of its square meters being utilized in the same way, gradually filled according to an unpredictable, but fatal rhythm.

To the man, it was altogether clear what the workers were doing and he felt no discomfort at watching them work. At most, a certain bitterness altered his tranquility when he realized how deeply calm he was. On account of his age and his experience, he was hardly to be troubled over such a trifle. But now, less than ever, would he have been so affected, for since his encounter with the girl this work no longer meant to him what it, in reality, was. He found no meaning in it outside her. More than anything else, it was the construction site that had disturbed her. The surveyors were his accomplices. The sound of their shovels was music to his ears and even the word—death—that it evoked, sang to him of her distress. The thought, in other words, that she could be disturbed to this degree by the calm sight of such a thing exalted the man more than he might ever again be put off by the sight of this construction site. Of course, he could have given the reasons for her distress: he knew them as well as he knew himself. He could have described them at length, for all these reasons were latent in him, as they probably were in every man in the slow day-in-day-out of his life. But that a being could exist who was afflicted by the impossibility of tolerating the sight of this site sheltered him from being tempted, had she not come along, to experience an impossibility of similar nature and to vainly rehash the reasons.

Her having seen it dispensed him of the obligation of seeing it himself. It was sheer delight, he told himself, to thus see something as someone else's vision.

The man, thus, lapsed into darkness. Slowly taking leave of the world of clear ideas and significations, he penetrated further each day into the red forest of illusion.

Freed of a reality which, had it only concerned him, would have subjected him to that reality, the man tended more and more to see mere signs in things. Everything became either sign of her or sign for her. Sign of her own indifference to herself or her indifference to things. He felt as if she were filtering, as it were, his days and nights which only came to him now transformed by the way he imagined she was living them.

For two days now, however, when he'd enter the dining room and she was already at her seat, not yet served, he'd see her mechanically turn her head toward him without, for all that, her gaze alighting on him. The indifference in this uncertain look gave him to understand that she saw no point in recognizing him. Did she recognize him, even dimly? Perhaps she hadn't seen him so clearly in the dark lane. Perhaps she'd not even conserved any memory of that encounter? Rather bizarrely, he was almost happy that she didn't recognize him. He thought that if she were to recognize him, it was perhaps preferable that it be on another occasion. She was ceding the initiative to him. She would recognize him when he wanted her to. And since he was sure that, sooner or later, she'd have to recognize him, he gave himself over to the somewhat frightening feeling that it was absolutely up to him that something altogether necessary take place. Some of his usual inertia dissipated.

Each time he'd penetrate the dining room, he'd fear she'd left the hotel in the meantime. But, each time, she'd be there and he'd think she might still stay for a while, since she'd only arrived a few days before their encounter. He was worried all the same. How much time did he still have?

The issue of this ever-possible departure came to him with particular clarity one certain evening. He thought of all the reasons she could have for leaving. There was the construction site's proximity. There was also the strain of facing that unease alone. The man reproached himself for not having approached her, for having thus prolonged the dubious pleasure he felt at deciding nothing. There was no reason for him to delay that moment: just the possibility of putting it off. When he thought of this that evening, he was frightened. At the thought that he might never get to know the girl, the ghost of his own solitary shape emerged from the shadows and he was afraid he'd hate himself if he came to a state of such total abandonment of his own choosing. He might have liked that fear to develop and become precise, but it played upon him and he failed. Perhaps the fear before the construction site which, thanks to her, he did not feel, was returning under another guise. Yes, this nocturnal fear might well be the same as the fear that she alone felt before the construction site.

In the end, he reassured himself. He told himself that she couldn't leave without something taking place between them, that this couldn't be delayed much longer, that the fear he'd just felt was precisely one sign that the moment was approaching. But it took him longer than usual to regain his calm.

It was the next day, after the midday meal, that he found himself not far from her in the smoking room. Usually she didn't tarry after a meal, but went back to her room or went out as soon as lunch was over. Was it some disease on this particular day that caused her to tarry for a few minutes?

She had her back to him. He saw that her black hair was tied up loosely at the base of her neck. This was the first time since their encounter that he'd been so close to her. The first time she'd been so close to him that he would only have had to reach out to touch her. He didn't give that gesture another thought. But he did think that upon leaving the smoking room, he could have got up, if he'd wanted, and brush up against her elbow resting on the arm of her chair. He didn't do that either. He remained seated where he was. He gazed at her, he looked at that untidy hair—hair that she neglected. He didn't believe her hair was particularly neglected on that day though. To the contrary, he thought that it must have always been thus. Always that hair must have been on the verge of coming undone. When she'd move her head a little the hair mass followed the movement and caressed her neck, which it only partially hid.

At a certain moment she leaned forward a bit and her hair lifted up. He could see that the inside of her blouse collar was lightly soiled from rubbing against her neck.

This suddenly touched off a very great emotion. The sight of that collar, soiled and wrinkled by that neck, that nape half hidden by that hair, that linen and that hair and that neck that could soil it, those things that he alone could see, that she didn't know he saw and that he saw better than she, made him relive the situation he'd known the evening of their encounter, facing the construction site. It was as if the two of them were living together in that body of hers, without her yet, at that moment, being aware.

During the following night, the memory of that minute took on the allure of desire. The sign of a carelessness coinciding with what he'd imagined about her was not all he read in that memory. This detail lent an immediate reality to her that she'd not had up to that point and the thought of which he realized he could no longer escape. He probably desired her since the first day, since the first moment, as soon as they'd both found themselves alone in the dark in the lane. But that desire was now immediately so intense that he found himself wishing she'd be still more oblivious than she had been of the life that lived in her. He would thereby, at the right moment, be able to surprise her even more completely, to more fully use her, to totally possess that body held until now in that state of sovereign negligence in which he had found it.

He had trouble sleeping that night. He considered his own body, wracked with desire, and seeing this was to see hers, as though her arms had slid into his. He let himself go. His body possessed the gifts of will and word: he calmly said that he wanted her. With more calmness than he himself would have anticipated. Then, as never before, under the effect of a reassured and placid violence, he felt at one with himself.

He wasn't so blinded that he didn't remember having had this feeling about other women. He was happy to learn he was still able to feel it and, this time, with a plenitude without equivalence in his memory—an equivalence he didn't care to look for, moreover. And it didn't displease him that he was still able to believe that he'd only known pale premonitions of what he was living through today.

That night, however, wasn't enough to make him make the decision to approach her. True: life in the hotel offered few occasions to do so. But he hadn't yet made up his mind. This was not his usual wishy-washiness. It's as if he'd suddenly tasted the philter of patience, its voluptuousness.

After lunch a good half of the guests gathered in the smoking room, where they stayed part of the afternoon. She too seemed now to have got into the habit of spending time there. But this place didn't seem propitious to the man for approaching her in a way appropriate to both of them. At the risk of losing her, he would not have run the risk equal, in his view, of approaching her in public and calling attention to her. No one yet in the hotel appeared yet to have paid attention to this girl who seemed to be the only one alone. It's true that nothing about her was apt to captivate the disinterested eye—nothing except that slight personal carelessness. But nothing about her indicated that she'd decided to rebuff all contact either. The rather incomprehensible undiscovered state she kept herself in reassured him concerning the perfectly secret character of the attraction she held for him and him alone. That she was so unremarkable to superficial observation was far from cause for him to doubt her. Then again, there was something strange about this sort of incognito, for not only was everyone else unaware of her existence, they were unaware that he knew her. Consequently, not only did he not dare break the sort of spell that allowed him—as though she were endowed with invisibility—to go unnoticed, but he found himself connected to her by an extraordinary complicity, given the scant relations they had had.

No, at the risk of losing her, he would never approach her in public.

As with places, rare were the times that the man found propitious for that encounter.

Certain hours of the night seemed to him more favorable. When the hotel was altogether silent, a few hours before dawn, when the strained bark of dogs entered through the window and made the night all the more uncertain. Although he still regularly waited for her in the lane part of the morning and afternoon, now it was the late hours of the night, the most deserted ones, that seemed best suited to him. At those instants, starting, wide awake, the man sometimes arose, thrown to his feet by nocturnal certainties. And, erect in the dark, half dressed, he regretted the impossibility of entering her room and telling her, "I beg your forgiveness but I'm that hotel guest, you know, who …".

Despite all the obstacles—imaginary or real—separating him from that second encounter, obstacles all the more insurmountable for their hinging, perhaps, he thought, simply on imaginings he knew well he could not help concocting, he didn't despair of succeeding. To the contrary, if he ceased thinking about it and second-guessing himself, he quickly found himself absolutely certain that each day brought him closer. At those times he knew that if he gave himself over to impatience, if he broke the spell, if he followed the nocturnal injunctions, he would upset the march of an otherwise ineluctable necessity that was working in his favor. But he only knew this at moments when he stopped thinking about it.

At the same time, curiously, the end of his very existence seemed to approach. Over the last few weeks, as he thought about it again, this end blended with the notion of a term—a term both further off and more certain—whereas now that end tended to become one with the moment when he would come to know her. That moment was near, but the term itself also become improbable. He ceased seeing what it might mean. Maybe, at that moment, relieved of all obligations and cares, he would begin simply lasting, surviving himself.

His future opened onto a sort of oceanic duration. And he even met this in that state of detachment from the obligation to hope that normally only dissipates at the moment of death. Hope probably doesn't matter one whit when one has the opportunity of losing one's life in death or in someone else. From the outside, one might have thought that he was really giving himself over to despair, that he had nothing before him but the end of all ends: death. He could only tolerate being alone. He fled the acquaintances he'd made at the hotel. He ate in a dream state. He spent whole days contemplating the construction site and upon his face the static grimace of mortal anguish was drawn. Or else was it because she had such great familiarity with death? The moment when he would finally reach her substituted itself in him for the true end that is death. That's probably also why, reciprocally, the moment when he'd reach her seemed to promise no future.

He still didn't know if she'd noticed him. Nothing in her attitude allowed one to think so. This uncertainty didn't really preoccupy him. He was sure that she wouldn't reject him, that she'd accept whoever wanted her imperiously. And, especially, given her horror of the construction site. About that, he was reassured. He believed her incapable of doing anything to attract attention to herself, but also believed her incapable of deciding. Like her terrors, her preferences would be sudden, passive, and insurmountable.

Now, evenings, when he'd go back to his room, he had fruitful days behind him. Every evening, he'd bring back something of her. He'd stay awake late.

Every night he'd invent her anew—sometimes from the howl of menacing dogs, sometimes from the redness of dawn or, simply, from that empty hand of his that lay inert, next to him, in bed.

He did nothing. He gave up reading. He no longer so much as cracked open the books he'd brought. He was incapable of dwelling for even an instant on anything other than this on-going event, his own story. The difference between this event and any other—the biggest, most vast, noblest—was insurmountable.

Even when he'd feel guilty about it, it would not be without a certain feeling of satisfaction. He had met her by chance on an evening like any other, and he'd been initiated to her drama at the instant it attained its strongest expression, in the greatest simplicity. Through a naiveté equal to the love he assumed, the antecedents of this drama shattered all others. But the drama also possessed that primacy of the least enunciated thing over the thing enunciated. He was powerless before that. Moreover, the pleasure he felt at realizing he was neglecting other dramas in favor of this one was also a pleasure in vengeance. And he even told himself, in the end, that the complacency with which he had heretofore concerned himself with the dramas of others was perhaps only due to the absence of drama in his own life.

What he knew about her—little, surprisingly little—had sufficed for him to know her. Because of that construction site there, next to the hotel, she had said to him what she'd had to say with the perfection of simple confessions. In truth, everything was simple. That's why he thought that when they'd meet again, the words they'd speak would be far less important than their gestures and their looks.

It was as he'd thought.

She passed again in the lane.

It was near noon. The workers hadn't yet left the job. She opened the gate and took the lane where the man had been waiting for her for ten days, every morning, every evening. When she appeared, he was certain he'd never doubted that she'd return. Since the first day, he knew that she wouldn't resist the need to see the construction site so close to the hotel once again. And, his reasoning notwithstanding, he finally understood why he'd persisted in waiting for her in the lane.

While she moved toward him, he remained sprawled on his chaise longue.

This time, it was she who stopped before him. She glanced at the workers and went no further. She gave the impression of someone straining to contain herself. Her expression was not the same as it had been the evening of their encounter: it was less directed, yet more intent, better controlled.

The weather was fine throughout the valley. The workers worked in the sun. Some were moving sand around, shirtless. Much progress had been made with the job. The wall foundations had been erected a few days earlier: all that was left was to finish them off, to raise them, and to consolidate them. The surveyors had left.

"They're still at it," said the girl.

At present, her voice sounded disappointed. The man didn't look at her. Like her, he was looking at the construction site. He no longer saw the new parcel of meadow enclosed by walls. This was something that was coming to a close, something that had taken its place in the valley. The linesmen's absence meant that this thing no longer stood as a problem to be resolved, a difficult question.

"They've removed at least twenty dumpers of soil," said the girl.

The man finally stopped looking at the construction site and turned toward her.

"The walls are too high, now," said the man. "You can't see anything any more."

The girl seemed to be trying to remember something. He figured out that she was forgetting the construction site. She tried to remember it [*lui*] precisely, as he remembered her. The man gazed at her, smiling. She too smiled and began to gaze at him, to look and to watch the man who remembered.

"That's true," said the girl.

She continued looking at him with exaggerated attention, while smiling. He too smiled and looked at her, but less directly. This was not his role and, besides, he would have been incapable of it. He knew that she was in the process of discovering that he remembered her perfectly. He thought he must have appeared a bit pale, that she noticed his pallor. While watching him, she seemed to be making an effort to understand why he remembered her with such intensity.

When she went out again, it was on the hotel side. She didn't go any further on along the lane. It was plain that she'd forgotten why she had come here: she had forgotten the construction site. The man felt the urge to catch up to her and shout to her that the existence of things like the construction site was good fortune, a joy. He did nothing of the sort. He could neither shout to her to stay nor rise to try to catch up to her. This incapacity also was strangely satisfying. His heart burned at each beat.

From that day forward, they greeted each other.

When he would enter the dining room, she'd smile at him with a slight nod of the head. However, she didn't approach his table; nor he hers.

She perhaps made this sign of recognition five times in the three days that followed their second encounter. Her smile was never the same. The first time he saw her again was in the dining room, as always, a few hours after her walk along the lane. She smiled at him. It was a shy smile. It beckoned encouragement to more smiling, which didn't come. It thus subsided and did not reoccur that day. He was sure that this first smile was meant to please and was, at the same time, somewhat awkwardly inquisitive. She must still have been uncertain of what had begun to course between them.

And in the smile she made to him that very evening at the door of the smoking room, the man noticed that the uncertainty had increased and had almost become dismay. He attempted to augment it further by showing her a certain aloofness. From the moment she knew—for she knew—his delay in approaching her wasn't the same as before: it was of another nature altogether. It was a delay he granted her to allow her, in turn, to become impatient and catch up to him in a slight exercise of impatience. But she would never be patient. She upset things. And he thought that whatever he did now, their final encounter was not far off.

The day after their second encounter, she smiled again at him when he entered the dining room. He instantly understood that she clearly knew where they were heading. If there was still any uncertainty in her, it must merely have been in the way he wished she'd appear before him. That day, she was as someone who doesn't know how to dance. She waited on the dance floor of his silence as he watched her perform, refusing to yet give her any tips on how to move.

Neither that day nor on the following did he try to help her. He no longer waited for her in the lane.

During meals, she appeared animated, a bit worried. She could have had no doubt, nevertheless, that she was attractive to him. She seemed happy. A fertile impatience buffeted her, raising her eyes toward the man with almost brutal impatience.

That day, he noticed that other men at the hotel had started to notice her.

On the third day, her smile was somber and a bit put on. It might have caused the man to believe that she was attempting to become the accomplice of his silence, for she had finally understood the slow power of his waiting and the pent-up flourishing that it harbored. But that smile on her face clouded over as soon as she'd noticed that no sign of approval was forthcoming from him.

It was at the end of the meal, which could have spelled defeat for her, that he finally looked at her in a manner so significant, with such serious insistence, that she could not fail to understand that it was henceforth pointless to smile at him in that way, that all efforts to please him were useless, futile, that their encounter now merely hinged a lapse of time that had not yet reached its term and whose course it would have been useless to interrupt because breaking it before the right time would have marked a defeat far worse than the one she'd just averted.

She no longer took the trouble to smile. She now just waited. And from that moment on, they took such care to ignore each other as though in this resort hotel, in the heart of summer, and despite the complete freedom they both had, their love were punishable by death.

She was nevertheless now only interested in him, obviously. She no longer looked at the child who had captivated her. She made no effort to hide from him that no one other than he interested her. Only the tennis courts did she still gaze at, but perhaps without seeing them.

He learned her room number. She was on the floor below his, but across from it, so he could only see her window by leaving the hotel and going around to the other side. And this is exactly what he did the very night he learned this. He remained outside until the moment the window went dark and he learned that she went to bed late. He had no hesitation in believing that her impatience was growing, that she couldn't go to sleep with her usual ease.

During those three days that followed their second encounter, the man didn't go back to the construction site. He didn't even think about it. The construction site might have had its use, but it was now at rest in an altogether swallowed up past. He didn't go back even a single time to the lane: he didn't want to know if she herself had gone back to look for him there. He left the hotel after having finished lunch and went off into the valley. During his walks, unconcerned, he'd think of her. A bit of snow fell those days on the mountains above the lake.

It was now the end: their wait was almost over. They both knew it. The only unknown was how it was going to end, how they'd emerge, where and when.

He slept very little. He'd lost weight and when he looked at himself in the mirror, he had trouble recognizing himself. He found himself handsome. Beneath his eyes spread great violet circles of expectation.

It was only on the fourth day that the wait ended.

It was very hot that day in the valley along the lake. The evening before, she'd arrived in the dining room clothed and coiffed differently. Her hair was down. He imagined her alone in her room inventing this touch, at the height of exasperation and sure of nothing, inventing it ahead of time, with an almost virile audaciousness. She had also put on a new dress: a red one.

It was thus that she stood before him, in the exact shape and color of the imminent event. This was their impatience, its explosion, their triumph.

He understood that their wait had come to an end.

It was still early. The man went out after dinner and started walking in the meadows along the lake past the tennis courts.

Suddenly there was, before the next day, time to live—a curiously extended time. For it was to be the next day: this single day of reckoning absorbed all the others, even the most distant ones.

From the path the man had taken, he could see, spread before him, a vast landscape of villages, mountains, and meadows. He also saw, for the last time, the construction site. The workers had finished their job. The lane was deserted. The four walls now stood at the same height. All that was needed was to whitewash them. They were done.

Time was up. The man dawdled. Night was falling. He had time to return. He felt disposed to live a long time outside all reason.

Once lunch was over, she came to sit before him in the smoking parlor. Her hair was still loose and she wore the same red dress as the day before. She sat down opposite him, they looked at each other, and it was she who let out the first low, long, indiscrete bit of laughter. It might have been the superior laughter of she who can finally, impassively, walk along the walls of all the construction sites in the world. But in that laughter, there was, more than anything, a disturbing vulgarity one might like to contain, but that had an undertone of cruel audacity. Her laughter up to this point had nothing to do with this laughter. He responded with a similar laugh.

The guests near them noticed that these two were laughing together without knowing each other and that their manner was far from ordinary. Some discomfort set in. Those nearest them stopped chatting.

The man looked out through the smoking room door. Bright, vertical sunlight fell on the road. He no longer wondered about anything. He got up, headed for the door, and found himself on the road. Then he set out. He passed the fun fair that had gone up that morning with barker cries and the unfurling of red tents. Lots of stands were already set up and, in the shade of the village square, people were dancing to a blaring turntable. Standing at a shooting gallery, youngsters aimed at plaster pigeons. And clouds of children contemplated open suitcases full of bullion spread out on the road before displays being erected on sawhorses. Shortly after passing the fun fair, about a hundred meters from the hotel, he could hear her footsteps. He turned, yet continued on his way. He laughed beneath his breath: he knew she was capable of following him.

He continued to walk and she to follow him, as was normal.

He made her walk a long time. He walked fast. She no doubt had a hard time following him. Sometimes he heard her quickened steps behind him. He quickened his, in turn. At the instant he might have thought she'd given up, he turned around without stopping. She'd stopped on the road and was watching him continue on. It was of no importance, for he knew where she'd go once she gave up following him. She had stopped precisely on the verge of the path where he'd decided to lead her. In stopping, she'd let him know that she knew that it was there that they were to meet. When he turned around a second time, he no longer saw her and he understood that she had turned. He retraced his steps to join her. He laughed.

It was near the lake, a creek almost completely hidden by fields of reeds. The lake waters saturated the earth and the only way to go on was to remove one's shoes. This soil was woven with intertwined reed roots and, upon this humus, other reeds and things of the water, drenched with water, grew. To reach the lake, the man had to make his way through the field. But in order to do so, all he had to do was follow the fresh trail marked by broken reeds and others, still bent over. When he got to the middle of the field, in the midst of reeds that were almost as high as he, he saw two other species of plants in flower. One reached half the height of the reeds and its yellow flowers brought out the vibrant violet of the others. The deep green of the reeds with their inky flowers produced a striking harmony between them. The yellow flowers spread a sort of sulfurous luminescence. Their stems were rigid and, unlike the other flowers, stayed still in the lake's breeze as if, with some curious lucidity, they were careful not to succumb to the indolence that menaced them, to this fresh water, to this lake of freshness, to this womb of water that had borne them. Next to these were rarer, supple violet flowers with velvety and flexible stems that flexed at the least assault of the breeze, bending to it—females. Yet it was in them that the brightness of the yellow flowers, in their ecstatic splendor, always ready to yield, died.

This floral harmony caused a violent tide of presence and memory to rise up in every corner of the man's body and he felt as though he were filled with knowledge.

He continued on his path.

On leaving the field of reeds, he saw her standing on the other side of the creek, watching him approach her.

To the extent that the two unnamed protagonists in this story reach—at long last and at the edge of a lake—some semblance of what we call "common ground," our initial question is: What have they *become* as a result? This is tantamount to asking the question thus: Where have they been geographically with respect to what we earlier called the "space of interest" that catalyzed their encounter? The consequences of our obvious and seemingly insignificant answer are far-reaching: At no moment in this story do either the young woman or the man who pursues her occupy the space of the construction site. Conversely—and this requires that we allow for a stretch in what we mean when we say that someone "occupies a space"—it is *because* both of these characters *invest* the space of the construction site *imaginatively* that they are able to come together. It is because the construction site becomes for both a preoccupation—an obsession for her first, then for him—that they find common ground.

The story we have just read is a largely neglected and, consequently, little known short story that Marguerite Duras included at the end of a collection entitled *Des journées entières dans les arbres*, or *Whole Days in the Trees*, published by Gallimard in 1954. Duras called the story "Les Chantiers." It was first translated as "Building Sites" by Anita Barrows and published in London by John Calder in 1984. Respecting many of Barrows' excellent solutions, I have nevertheless felt the need to retranslate it and center it for the launch of this book on the sharing of common ground.

Certainly the obsessive self-absorption that Duras has the man in the story display, coupled with the plot's almost total absence of action—at least in a sense traditionally associated with the novel and its subgenres—must account for the persistent resistance to readers' understanding of "Construction Sites." (This initial emergence into obscurity, by the way, matched that of another text of 1954 by another writer still exploring objects and yet to find the voice that we now identify with a name: Michel Foucault.[1]) Yet these are the very characteristics that will become recognized just a few years later as trademarks of a unique voice. Beginning with *Le Square* (1955), becoming emphatic with *Moderato cantabile* (1958), and arguably culminating with *Le Ravissement de Lol V. Stein* (1964), the restless and disturbing voice that we now equate with the name Marguerite Duras developed on the foundation of this altogether untimely text—"untimely" in the sense that Nietzsche meant the epithet, *unzeitgemäß*.[2]

What does "Construction Sites" present to our reflective consciousness? —Two characters who find themselves at some hotel near a lake. If not altogether bucolic, the countryside is nearby. The hotel is no doubt situated

---

[1] Michel Foucault, *Maladie mentale et personnalité*. In 1954 as well, Jean-François Lyotard published his first book: *La Phénoménologie*, in the booklet encyclopedia series "Que sais-je?" published still today by the Presses Universitaires de France.
[2] Cf. Friedrich Nietzsche, *Unzeitgemäße Betrachtungen* (1876). Translated as *Untimely Meditations* by Walter Kaufman.

in a small town. Is it a hotel for tourists? some sort of private residence? an upscale sanatorium? —Two characters: a man and a young woman. Both unnamed. Both nameless and faceless. And what transpires? —At the level of action, very little. Out of idleness, the man follows the woman and, when she stops walking, he observes her from some distance. She stands, apparently in stricken stupor, at the edge of some construction site not far from the hotel. Over the several days following this serial sight (hers of the site; his of her), the man, without being seen, apparently, starts observing the young woman from afar every chance he gets: in the vicinity of the construction site, in the hotel restaurant, everywhere he can. Then, one day, perhaps just before she checks out of the hotel, she ends up following him. When he becomes aware of her presence behind him, he sends somatic signals beckoning her to follow. They press on, not to the construction site, though, but to a cove in the lake where, in the reeds, we are led to understand, they give themselves one to the other. That's it. Yet certain aspects of this slim plot, certain of its ineffable passages leave the reader feeling creepy, as though something deeply unethical drives what little plot there is. This discomfort will guide us in our examination of this story of spaces and of the functions such spaces take on when they are reflected upon for sharing common ground.

With the plurality of its title heralding the enigmas harbored within, "Construction Sites" is generically at odds with the three other texts in the 1954 collection—a group of "short stories" that bizarrely carried the designator of "novel" in its original Gallimard edition. "Whole Days in the Trees," the lead piece, whose title was used for the volume, stages the encounter between an elderly mother who returns to Paris from an unnamed French colony to dote one last time on her wastrel of a son, a sociopath who robs her blind. The second story, "The Boa," is a parable about an adolescent girl whose old piano teacher thinks she's entertaining her by bringing her to the zoo to watch a boa digest a chicken. The third, rather more a novelette, "Madame Dodin," is a rambling and rambunctious urban epic laced with irony and featuring a concierge and an alcoholic street sweeper. For all its repetitive and hypnotically banal dialogue that almost makes its stage adaptation in 1965 redundant, "Whole Days in the Trees" is a conventional short story. "Construction Sites," on the other hand, is almost devoid of speech and, what little there is, could easily have been transposed into the same plodding narration that makes up the majority of its words. With its tone and its focus not on action, but on the minute "movements" of consciousness, "Construction Sites" even departs with such modernist ancestors as Woolf and Joyce. The closest we come to designating its genre is to assimilate it to the types of narratives (*récits*) that Duras would write later in her career—not dissimilar to those with which her close friend Maurice Blanchot is already experimenting.

"Construction Sites" also offers the reader what—within the continuum of the Durassian oeuvre—can only be characterized as a first expression of desire bordering on madness, desire at the zenith of intensity. For the reader of 1954 who already knew something of the writer's life and perhaps even for many of Duras's close friends, "Construction Sites" must have appeared to break altogether with the use of biographical material to fuel fictions such as *Un barrage contre le Pacifique* (*The Sea Wall*, 1950) or *Les Petits Chevaux de Tarquinia* (*The Little Horses of Tarquinia*, 1953). Furthermore, what, that reader might have asked herself, is a prose piece that consists in an ineffable dance of vision? —She is stared at, she searches with her eyes: both *voyeuse* and object of voyeurism, she envisions yet something other than the object of her scopic desire. But what? The emphatic "suppression of the explicit" which will, a few years later, become one of the hallmarks of Duras's narrative style, but which readers have yet to recognize as enticing in 1954, is already pervasive here, in this complex study of the gaze that might have intrigued Michel Foucault as much as *Las Meninas* did. This all renders "Construction Sites" simply too bizarre for the reader of 1954 to pay it much attention and, in sum, makes everything *before* it look quite traditional.[3] Its thematic choices will nevertheless often be taken up again as Duras nurtures the evolution of her art. Its narrative elements as well as setting will, in particular, be redeployed and reworked in the 1969 novel, *Détruire, dit-elle* (*Destroy, She Said*).

First and foremost among the highly allusive and barely implicit elements composing "Construction Sites" is, oddly enough, the construction site itself. But before the reader can even consider that enigmatic space, what is she to make of the title's plural? However veiled in mystery it might be, there is, after all, only *one* construction site in the story itself. What is the reader to do with the other construction sites implied by the title? From that one phenomenal, perceivable construction site situated out there, at some distance from the characters who contemplate it, we, the readers of that title, are led through all *chantiers* imaginable. Our mind inexorably wanders from sites where *building* takes place—whether of edifices or ships—through various depots, yards, holding areas, through certain camps, shambles, *shanties*, to sites for the *demolition* of all this. *Chantier* can thus both promise a future, and it can also warn of disaster. The scholar may be working vigorously on two books—*Elle a deux livres en chantier*—or his desk may be an indescribable

---

[3] Jirí Srámek, "Limites du roman durassien." *Études Romanes de Brno* 33 (24) (2003): 153.

mess—*Quel chantier!* The poet will no doubt bring the sound, spelling, and meanings of *chantier*[4] into proximity with those of *charnier*, or charnel house, in order to meditate on their interpenetrations, perhaps endeavoring to extricate one from the other but learning that separation impossible.

Chantiers—the plural noun for that space over which, about which, on the basis of which the two characters of the story end up uniting—suspends us as it suspends them between construction and destruction.

Within the diegesis of "Construction Sites" too, there would be reasons to think in terms of multiplicity. The site in the meadow that seemed to the man to have so shocked the young woman is thought to be perceived differently (or at least evaluated or *judged* differently) by everyone except her. "The whole hotel knows about that construction site," is as much as to say "It's just a construction site: it won't harm you." Edward S. Casey defines *site* as "the leveled-down, emptied-out planiform residuum of place and space eviscerated of their actual and virtual powers and forced to fit the requirements of institutions that demand certain very particular forms of building" (1997: 183). To the extent that the site Duras envisioned in the meadow wholly eludes the strictures Casey is correct in asserting that we usually impute to a site, *this* site also abhors singularity. Rather, it expands and multiplies like those sites for philosophical musing into which Denis Diderot transformed paintings by Claude-Joseph Vernet in his *Salon de 1767*.[5] In delighting his reader by holding back for some thirty pages before revealing that instead of a series of chatty strolls with his friend, he has been quite simply alone, contemplating seven paintings by Vernet, Diderot demonstrates the faculty of sites to maintain their concrete and imaginary functionality upon us simultaneously.

Early twenty-first century readers will not go very far in an exploration of the construction site located on the periphery of Duras's story before they pause to take stock – at least at a preliminary level of feminist examination – of this story's disturbing elements and what, from a perspective of seven decades beyond *The Second Sex*, is a rather unsavory gender politics that Duras's male character embodies. If an encounter with this text is to be motivated by some sense of its potential and not foreclosed by its ponderousness, its redundant awkwardness, and its heretofore neglect in the study of Duras's oeuvre, then what *might become* our experience of reading "Construction Sites"? One could foreground what the dominant descriptive position of the text imputes to the young woman's behavior:

---

[4] From Latin, *cantherius*, "*cheval hongre, mauvais cheval de charge*"; vitruve: "*support auquel on fixe la vigne.*"

[5] Denis Diderot, "*Salon de 1767.*" In *Œuvres. IV*, 594–635. Paris: Robert Laffont, 1996.

nervousness, oscillating indecision, obliviousness to nearly everything except the construction site. Inseparable from these seeming characteristics is the eerie fact that they are conveyed to us through the inner voice of a male protagonist whose desire to know and perhaps experience her experience ("he understood that he was taking her by surprise [...] in one of the most intimate moments of her life") leads to his being called a "violator."

The long toneless periods of "Construction Sites," its flat, banal, and colorless manner of barely moving the quasi absence of action forth are intercut—even before the story begins its crescendo—by melodramatic, hyperbolic turns. "He [...] went as far as to tell himself [...] that if she hadn't overcome the distress that the sight of things analogous to that construction site caused her, she probably wouldn't have been able to survive until their encounter." Not all readers today had also been readers in the 1960s and 1970s, so I wondered if the presumptuousness in this male voice "telling himself" such things and that Duras had created in an otherwise precocious text of 1954 would strike a "millennial" as hopelessly and abhorrently patriarchal.

Voluntarily rising to the occasion, one such reader indeed averred that she had experienced disappointment and, indeed, some anger at the gall of the man from whose viewpoint "Construction Sites" is told. But she was willing to read it again and consider two sets of questions: What difference—if any—does it make that the male protagonist was invented by a writer who is a woman? Does it make any difference to know that the writer in question was resolutely (and sometimes offensively) heterosexual? The second pair of questions I put to this reader eschewed biographical fact: Is it possible that a female writer who casts such a disturbing heterosexual male in a story that in no way critiques his behavior is performing an equally disturbing vicarious imposition of herself? If so, why? Or, if she is asserting her subjecthood elsewhere, by some other means, through some other medium, can she convey the same message? My reader began thus:

> I did not find myself offended by the author's depiction of this woman, this distant but alluring object of desire, until three-quarters into the text. I wasn't upset that she was represented as naïve, alluring, pursuable, and not very attractive. [...] Eventually, he stops trying to interpret her altogether, leaving her as a mysterious signifier, whose form he follows but does not know. He leaves her as a negative space, a reader who can interpret for herself, and as someone who can gesture autonomously.

But then, she wrote:

> Although his initial depictions of her at first seemed innocent to me, if not also flattering, they became offensive [when the narrator

says] "He was sure that she would want him. That she would want whoever imperiously wanted her." He also "didn't believe her capable of choosing." Whereas previously he stopped interpreting her and thus controlling her, now he "each night reinvent[s] her." Whereas before he was captivated by her mysteriousness, her autonomy, and her distance, these are all now dependent on him.

And, further reflecting on her balk, she wrote:

> I think it's interesting to note that this shift in depiction, [...] comes right after he decides to depart the world of clear ideas. He wants to be paralogical and attracted merely to the superficial; he even gives up reading books. This is traditionally how women have been depicted— irrational and too attracted to the sensuous world to understand Platonic forms.

At this point, I interrupted her report to ask if I was to understand that the man's attitude and actions become offensive when Duras "feminizes" him. My close reader continued:

> At this point, I found myself asking, "What is feminine in this text?" and "Who is feminine?" Does at least one aspect of femininity have to do with subtle control over the opposite sex? [...] I think it does make a difference that the male protagonist was created by a female. If femininity has, as I propose, an element of subtle power—a power that is delicate and overwhelming—then I think that Duras' narration is able to strengthen that power and take control of it. [...] Duras takes this power out of the body and turns it into words over which she does have control. The female is still able to construct desire but not because she has a helplessly attractive body. She can control her own "construction" and no longer be horrified when she arrives at the building site and sees how she has been depicted and molded.

Finally, her intellectual honesty ever at the fore, reiterating the caveat that she had still, at this point, only read three Duras texts at the most, she concluded: "In *The Lover*, [Duras] has a body that 'knows' even before she experiences, and in 'Construction Sites,' she depicts the male gaze in all of its potential violence without ever having been a man. Duras has a sort of *a priori* knowledge in both cases, and I think this *a priori* knowledge is related to what I have said about female nature."

This, to my view, is a hopeful reading. This is a reading with the potential to reinforce principles for sharing common ground. This is a reading blissfully oblivious of the diametrical oppositionality that so often made critique in the second half of the twentieth century into a caricature of critique. Polarized opinions like those that received *Hiroshima mon amour* when it premiered at the Cannes Film Festival in 1959, with Marcel Achard, the festival's president that year, pronouncing it "a piece of shit!" and Claude Chabrol's rebuttal in the form of a pronouncement that *Hiroshima* was "the most beautiful film [he'd] seen in five hundred years."[6] This, in sum, is a reading that proves that at least *some* twenty-first century readers have cleared themselves altogether of much of the identitary zhdanovism that marked and marred the feminism of the late twentieth century and that perpetuates itself in retrograde thought today.

Along with the emergence of a singularly recognizable voice, of which "Construction Sites" is a precocious sign, Duras's artistic enterprise begins in the late 1950s to reveal, in its steadily increasing diversification, what will soon be recognized as an explicit determination to "remember" the Shoah.[7] Archival residuum from *Hiroshima mon amour*'s preparatory stages that show Duras having once envisioned the film's anonymous Frenchwoman as Jewish is perhaps the earliest evidence of this memorial project. Lol V. Stein, the paradigmatic character first introduced in the eponymous 1964 masterpiece, and Stein, arguably the pivotal force in *Destroy, She Said*, are examples from her work published in the decade following. But before becoming even more explicit, with such filmic works as the *Aurélia Steiner* series, Duras's effort to perpetuate memory and reflection on the crimes of fascism was being carried out with increasing insistence at the level of implicitness. Common to both phases—implicit and explicit—of this politics of memory is that it is carried out vicariously. Duras and Duras's characters remember what should never be forgotten through the proxy of another consciousness. In a letter to a young researcher where she attempted to explain the title she lent to a work of 1980—*Les Yeux verts*, or *Green Eyes*—a work incongruously, but successfully at once film, photography, and literature—Duras wrote, "I see the end of the world through the green eyes of a girl, I also see an infinite

---

[6] Quoted in Edgar Schneider, "Bataille à Cannes autour d'*Hiroshima mon amour*," *France-Soir*, May 10, 1959.

[7] Despite its designation as the "World Holocaust Remembrance Center," Yad Vashem nevertheless rightly explains that "[t]he biblical word *Shoah* (which has been used to mean 'destruction' since the Middle Ages) became the standard Hebrew term for the murder of European Jewry as early as the early 1940s. The word *Holocaust*, which came into use in the 1950s as the corresponding term, originally meant a sacrifice burnt entirely on the altar. […] Many understand *Holocaust* as a general term for the crimes and horrors perpetrated by the Nazis; others go even farther and use it to encompass other acts of mass murder as well. Consequently, we consider it important to use the Hebrew word *Shoah* with regard to the murder of and persecution of European Jewry in other languages as well." http://www.yadvashem.org/yv/en/holocaust/resource_center/the_holocaust.asp (accessed December 19, 2016),

laziness, and joy as well."[8] Beyond (yet no doubt also with the help of) the apparent melancholy, here, Duras was setting the groundwork for a post-genocide ethics that was already apparent in the bizarre 1954 story.

Astonishing discoveries, rich revelations are to be made in relating the story we have just read to well known works by Duras. While seeking to identify some experience in a writer's life that likely nourished one of her literary creations is usually of limited hermeneutic importance, the tangential relationship of the unnamed characters in "Construction Sites" to a space corresponding to this title's referent is a paradigmatic function that drives a whole series of "famous" Duras creations ranging from the dialogue and screenplay for *Hiroshima mon amour* to *The Lover*. To pull only those two examples into preliminary parallels in advancing this point, the anonymous lovers of the 1959 film are to the city of Hiroshima as the anonymous pair in the 1954 story are to the unnamable (unspeakable) cemetery. So too are Duras writing as an old woman in the 1984 bestseller of herself as a European teenager in Indochina coupled with her rich Chinese lover with respect to colonial Saigon. Responsible criticism therefore dictates that we consider what—in her life—might have driven Duras to elaborate this exercise in circumlocution, this studied avoidance of referentiality.

Hiroshima mon amour is anything but accessory to this archaeology of "Construction Sites." At the behest (some might say the insistence) of her Japanese lover in 1958 peace-time Hiroshima, an equally unnamed French woman details what followed the death in Wehrmacht uniform of her German lover in 1945 Nevers while France was being liberated. Judged extrajudicially, as so many women were, of having aided the enemy occupier, she is publicly roughed up and humiliated, lapses into a sort of catatonia punctuated by hysteria, which leads to her parents' sequestering her in a damp cellar under their Nevers home. After a few months, toward the end of that summer, she is allowed to flee by bicycle to Paris in the middle of the night. The day she arrives was no ordinary day: the first atomic bomb had just been dropped on Hiroshima. It was August 6, 1945. In the film, following the famous match cut of twitching fingers, the lovers shower, and:

> He: What did Hiroshima mean for you, in France?
> She: The end of the war, I mean, really the end. Amazement ... at the idea that they had dared ... amazement at the idea that they had succeeded. And then too, for us, the beginning of an unknown fear. And then, indifference. And also the fear of indifference ...
> He: Where were you?
> She: I had just left Nevers. I was in Paris. In the street. (*OC II*, 30; 33)

[8] Letter to Colette Rondepierre, March 21, 1983. In M. Duras, *OC II*, 803.

And Duras, we might just as insistently ask? Where was she on that shocking day in August 1945? Here is what she writes in 1980 in *Green Eyes*—a collage of texts where she is also, frequently, intent on having the reader recognize her commitment to honoring the memory of the millions dead in the Shoah:

> I REMEMBER
>
> I remember August 6, 1945. My husband and I were in a home for deportees [*une maison de Déportés*] near Lake Annecy. I read the newspaper headline on the Hiroshima bomb. Then I rushed out of the boarding-house [*la pension*] and I leaned against the wall facing the road, as if suddenly I'd fainted standing up. Little by little I returned to my senses, I recognized life, the road. It was the same in 1945 while the German charnel houses [*charniers*] in the concentration camps were being discovered. I would station myself in railroad stations and in front of hotel entrances with photos of my husband and my friends and I would wait without any hope for the survivors' return, in a state close to the one I'd been in at Annecy. I wasn't weeping, outwardly I was the same as ever except that I could no longer talk at all.[9]

Further details of events during the weeks and months of Robert Antelme's convalescence in the months following his rescue *in extremis* by François Mitterrand and Dionys Mascolo will be provided by Marguerite Duras when she publishes *La Douleur*, or *The War: A Memoir*, in 1985. But those details are not required in order to recognize that the "home for deportees near Lake Annecy" where she and Antelme were staying in August 1945 when news of the atomic bomb reached them is altogether homologous with the hotel where two unnamed characters—a man and a woman—find solace in each other's company after coming to terms with the terrifying proximity of a cemetery under construction.

In writing out "I Remember"—echoing Georges Perec's then recently published *Je me souviens* (1978), itself an explicit tribute to Joe Brainard's poetic innovation, *I Remember* (1970)—Duras makes no reference to any construction site near the boarding-house but does, at the dramatic temporal turn at the center of her text, refer to the construction site's assonant neighbor, the *charnel house*, thus collapsing any distance there might otherwise be between the crime at Hiroshima and the crimes in the Auschwitz archipelago. If the order of Duras's discourse about trauma, here, is meant to mimic the ordering of her memory, then "I Remember" might go something like this: The state of conscious paralysis ("I'd fainted standing up") that news of mass murder in Japan put me in was just like the state of

---

[9] Translation slightly modified.

Construction Sites

Figure 1 Hôtel de la Poste, Saint-Jorioz, used as "*Centre de repos pour prisonniers de guerre et déportés de la Haute-Savoie*," date uncertain, private collection of Odile Baumgartner-Roman, by kind permission.

functional muteness that I had been in a few months earlier when I was hunting desperately for my husband who had been deported to Nazi concentration camps. What happened in late summer 1945 in Hiroshima brings me back to what was happening to me in springtime of that same year. "What did Hiroshima mean to you in France?" Shock and awe—the results of terror whatever its source—were to inspire a story perhaps not as fully thought-out as *Hiroshima mon amour* in which a young woman seems to remember the charnel house (*charnier*) when she sees a construction site (*chantier*).

In the aftermath of Occupation and Liberation, the provisional French government reassigned dozens of hotels located in quiet settings as temporary convalescent homes. The Hôtel de la Poste, in the pastoral alpine town of Saint-Jorioz, just one short kilometer from the shore of Lake Annecy, was one such establishment.

This is where Robert Antelme and Marguerite Duras were sojourning in August 1945. By then, Duras, who had published her first novel in 1943, had filled several notebooks with sketches and recollections that would feed much of her subsequently published work. She had also begun work on one novel, however: "Théodora," which was—with the exception of a fragment here and there—to never see the light of day. Duras's failure to craft this manuscript into what she deemed a publishable state occurred

Figure 2 Hôtel de la Poste and Café-Restaurant J. Cottet, Saint-Jorioz, date unkown, author's personal collection.

despite her several returns, at fairly regular intervals, to it right up to the end of her life in 1996. Already in the earliest drafts of "Théodora," vivid scenes are set in a certain "Hôtel Beauséjour" where, as the narrator writes, "boredom dominates. It filters in, even infiltrating one's sleep, affecting one's dreams. The people there dream, they dream in broad daylight of the nighttime to come, the night before the next day (yet another one). A whole population of daydreamers haunted by the grand illusion, these sleepwalkers of despair pursue the dream of boredom's end" (*OC IV*, 1185–6). One of the manuscript pages of "Théodora" in the archive at Institut Mémoire de l'Édition Contemporaine near Caen contains the text of a telegram Robert Antelme sent, announcing their return to Paris from Saint-Jorioz.

Over the course of those fifty years during which Marguerite Duras tried periodically to finish the "unfinished, unfinishable" "Théodora," she made her title character more and more explicitly Jewish. Taking up a key line from *Yann Andréa Steiner*, where Duras writes that "[p]erhaps Théodora Kats was something still unknown, a new *silence of writing*, the silence of women and Jews" (121; my emphasis), mimicking the discursive gesture that she notes in Duras of "frequent recourse to quite physical, almost bellicose metaphors," Sophie Bogaert comments that "To peer into the unfathomable void of the last century's martyrdom of the Jews, as this 'silence of writing' allows, is not to abide by it but, rather, to attempt to tackle it."¹⁰ To the extent that "Théodora" failed, in fact, to ever emerge from Duras's workshop, our glimpse into the void she struggled to portray can only come as a composite vision of the person she made herself into through a vicarious relationship to Jews. The trajectory of her existence may be simplified thus: Marguerite Donnadieu converted a very intimate, altogether individual core of unrequited desire into the very social, plural, and historical melancholy Marguerite Duras associated with Ashkenazim Jews because historical fact at the height of her adulthood had made this group the emblem of human mass persecution. Some of this existential conversion made its way into Duras's work; some of it did not.

One part of Duras's part in making *Hiroshima mon amour* has already helped us once; it can help us again—this time to begin to see how this slow but abiding Judaization of Marguerite Duras ties in with her exploration of common ground initiated publicly in "Construction Sites." So will Duras's second screenplay, *Une aussi longue absence*, that she co-wrote with Gérard Jarlot and that was made into a prize-winning film, distributed in the English-speaking world as *The Long Absence*,¹¹ by Henri Colpi in 1960, and that, finally, has regrettably been allowed to slip into obscurity. Duras did, as we have seen, deem "Construction Sites" publishable. So did Gallimard, obviously, since they decided to not bind *Whole Days in the Trees* before adding it at the end. One adverbial expression in French for an unfinished work is "*en chantier*." And *chantier* is without doubt the source for the English word, shanty—a type of dwelling that will have supreme importance among common grounds studied here.

As incongruous as it might seem today, Marguerite Duras had not been Alain Resnais's first choice for the 1959 screenplay. Duras no doubt got the job writing the dialogues for *Hiroshima mon amour* thanks to her old friend, Olga Wormser. Resnais had first tried tapping Françoise Sagan. But when the fêted author of *Bonjour tristesse* failed to show up at their first meeting, Resnais turned elsewhere. Simone de Beauvoir might have crossed his mind but he soon contacted Duras. A few short months after the release of the film, Resnais demonstrated his storied largesse by appearing to connect the hiring of Duras for *Hiroshima* to his admiration for her literary work: "For my own personal pleasure, I felt like filming *Moderato cantabile*

---

[10] "*Se pencher sur le vide abyssal que constitue le martyre juif au XXe siècle, ainsi que le permet ce 'silence de l'écriture', n'est pas s'y soumettre, mais bien plutôt tenter de le prendre à bras-le-corps*" (Bogaert, 196).

[11] *Such a Long Absence* would be a more accurate translation of the title and one more in keeping with the mood of the story. When she translated the scenario in 1966, Barbara Wright left the title in French.

in 16 mm. When I told the producer I was withdrawing from the deal, I jokingly added 'Although obviously if someone like Marguerite Duras were to be interested …' and they took me seriously."[12] In this version of the story, recounted during a January 7, 1960 session of a seminar on "film and cinema" at the Free University in Brussels, Resnais remains discreet about Duras not having been the first choice. His admiration and his playful "what if" notwithstanding, it is far more likely that Resnais came to Duras via Olga Wormser who had, along with Henri Michel, provided historical advice on *Nuit et brouillard* (*Night and Fog*). Wormser's qualifications for serving on Resnais's groundbreaking poetic documentary on the death camps were not only her status as historian, but also that of Resistance member. It was in that capacity that she had met Duras in 1944 after Robert Antelme had been deported.[13] Duras, under the *nom de guerre* of "Madame Leroy," figures prominently in Wormser's memoires of that period: "'Mme Leroy' is busy organizing a 'Hitler's Crimes and Penal Colonies' exhibit at the Grand Palais. Having miraculously escaped arrest, she waits for Robert and Marie-Louise A[ntelme]" (Wormser-Migot, 88) or "One can sense the rivalries—civil, for the moment—cropping up between all the organizations searching for the deported, the ministry, the C.O.S.O.R., the M.N.P.G.D. We share tips with Mitterrand and 'Mme Leroy' to whom I swore I'd give news of M. L. and R. A. whatever color they be. That promise […] will be a heavy one to carry" (140). This premonition is borne out by the news itself, with which we are familiar if we have read *La Douleur*, but which comes across with gripping difference in the words of Duras's comrade in resistance, Olga Wormser:

> From Dr. E's house in the suburbs, we phone the woman who's been waiting for Robert Antelme to tell her he was alive on 5 April [1945]. This is the first sign of him she's had. He'll return weeks later. He hadn't left Buchenwald on 5 April, but much earlier. Dr. E couldn't have met him, but he served as the messenger of his return. R. A. weighed 40 kilos, hadn't the strength to pick up a fork, and was waiting for news of Marie-Louise. About her, I once again had to serve as the conveyer of bad news. A British liaison officer brought back lists and hospital index cards. Evacuated from Ravensbrück by the Swedish Red Cross among those selected in March 1945, Marie-Louise died eight days later in a Danish hospital: "Dead, skeleton, shorn." (218)

---

[12] "Entretien avec Alain Resnais" (*"Tu n'as rien vu à Hiroshima!"*), 215.
[13] Certain elements of this story are recapitulated in Jean Vallier, *C'était Marguerite Duras*, II, Fayard, 2010, 295 and 368n.

Figure 3 "Cahier à Outa," front and back covers, IMEC DRS 18.1. By kind permission, Jean Mascolo.

That image of her sister-in-law as shorn cadaver will have begun to haunt Duras well before she saw *Night and Fog*. Wormser was thus ideally positioned to serve as go-between to initiate the soon-to-be-famous Resnais–Duras encounter that would lead to the creation of *Hiroshima mon amour*.[14]

The dialogue Marguerite Duras conceived for *Hiroshima mon amour* serves to advance a plot that might seem to hinge on very little: A French woman who travels to Hiroshima fourteen years after the atomic hecatomb to play in a film on the peace movement meets a Japanese architect with whom she has a torrid affair that lasts little more than a day. Alain Resnais and his screenplay writer had agreed, momentously, that the trauma wreaked upon Hiroshima's civilian population was to be conveyed through the erotic encounter between two characters who would remain anonymous. Regardless of whether this was actually Resnais's or Duras's idea, the effect of this absence of names is that the spectator is free to infer metonymically—or, rather, *metanonymously*—the applicability of the story to whole populations, rather than to specific, named individuals. Implication in events, accountability, in other words, were to be universal: the spectator was to become part and parcel of her story and history. This is an effect of anonymity whose radical consequences Duras had already experimented with a first time in "Construction Sites."

---

[14] Marguerite Duras alludes to this episode in a footnote to *Les Parleuses*, 228.

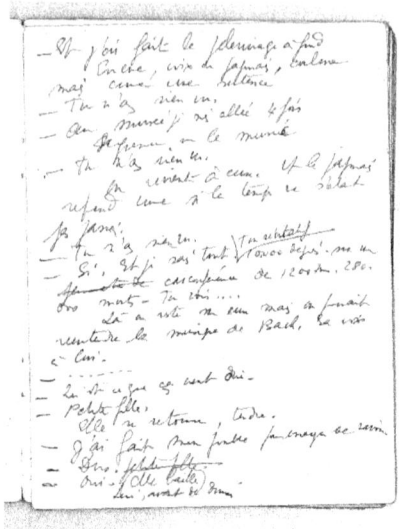

Figure 4 "Cahier à Outa," page with first draft of *Hiroshima mon amour* dialogue, IMEC DRS 18.1. By kind permission, Jean Mascolo.

"—*Tu n'as rien vu à Hiroshima.* —*J'ai tout vu. Tout.*" (OC II, 16; 15). Marguerite Duras laid down the essential dialogue extending from these famous initial lines of the screenplay at a fever's pitch—probably within a week—and in a school notebook she filched from her son, Jean Mascolo, who would have been eleven years old in that summer of 1958.[15]

While Duras had hit upon the key phrases for *Hiroshima mon amour*'s dialogue in a single burst of inspiration, she spent the next few weeks of late summer 1958 doing what she always did (and did with ever-increasing meticulousness)—incessantly revising, rewriting, fine-tuning, adjusting the conversation between She and He.

In doing so, Marguerite Duras took time out to write out in longhand an extremely important document. She probably didn't know that she was leaving this needle in a haystack for posterity. After recalling, in the "I Remember" recollection that Duras included in *Green Eyes* in 1980, that she and Robert Antelme were in a convalescent home in Saint-Jorioz when news of the Hiroshima bomb reached them and that she was gripped by a horror similar to that she experienced when the Nazi death camps were opened, she continues:

---

[15] The transcription of the "Cahier à Outa" by R. Harvey is in *OC II*, 105–12.

These are very exact, very clear memories; I had clearly become another person. Later, and this is what I'm getting to, later on in my life, I never wrote on the war, on those moments, never anymore, except a few pages, on the concentration camps. Similarly, if I had not been commissioned to do Hiroshima, I would not have written anything on Hiroshima either and when I did, you see, I compared the enormous number of the Hiroshima deaths with the story of the death of a single love that I had invented. Later, and this is what I'm getting to, [...] I never wrote on the war.

Well, of course, she would four years after *Green Eyes* when she offered *La Douleur*, or *The War: A Memoir* for publication by Paul Otchakovsky-Laurens (P.O.L.) in 1985. However, in the early autumn of 1958, just as she was about to turn over to Resnais her final version of the dialogues for *Hiroshima mon amour*, on the back of eight sheets of carbon copies pulled with apparent randomness from the sheaves, with a blue ballpoint pen, Duras painstakingly recounts in a markedly confessional mode those weeks of desperate search for news of her husband, Robert Antelme. What stands out, in reading this bit of archive found in the collection of the Institut Mémoire at the magical Abbaye d'Ardenne just north of Caen, are the words devoted to what those closest to her at the time judged to be a decidedly ambiguous relationship with a Gestapo agent she identifies here with the initials "A.D."

"I met A.D. fourteen years ago, at about this time of the year. I first had the desire to write out this story of that encounter thirteen years ago. Then, shortly afterwards, it was the firing squad for him. But, that desire has returned to me several times since." With no apparent relationship to the film script on the recto of these pages, Duras nevertheless adds: "A.D. is right at the cusp of memory and forgetting for me." And, it is "in order to snatch A.D. from this perilous situation" that she, Marguerite Duras, takes time out of her feverish work on the scenario to fill eight pages with careful script.

A.D., of course, is none other than Rabier, the Gestapo agent of the text in *La Douleur* entitled "Monsieur X, dit ici Rabier" and in which we may read passages such as these:

> I forgot to say that Rabier always arranges to meet me in open places with several exits: at corner cafes or intersections. The districts he likes best are the sixth arrondissement, Saint-Lazare, the République, Duroc.
> At first I was afraid he'd ask to come up for a moment after seeing me back to my door. But he never did. I know he thought of it as early as our first rendezvous in the park in the avenue Marigny.
> The last time I saw Rabier he asked me to go and have a drink with

him "in the studio of a friend who was out of Paris." I said, "Some other time," and escaped. But he knew that was the last time. He'd already decided to leave Paris that evening. What he wasn't sure of was what he would have done with me, how he would have seduced me, whether he would have taken me with him when he ran away, or if he would have killed me. (83)

[...]

I can't remember what restaurant it is—it was a black market restaurant, patronized by collaborators, members of the Militia, the Gestapo. It wasn't yet the restaurant in the rue Saint-Georges. He thinks that by inviting me out to eat he's keeping me comparatively healthy. In that way he saves me from despair; in his own eyes he's my good angel. What man would have resisted this role? He doesn't. These lunches are the worst part of the memory—restaurants with closed doors and "friends" knocking on them, butter on the tables, fresh cream overflowing in every dish, juicy meat, wine. I'm not hungry. He is in despair. (89)

With such passages that name and enumerate real places, while evoking imagined spaces, as well as the archival material from autumn 1958 echoing in our ears, we might ask ourselves: Did Marguerite Duras suddenly imagine, fourteen years after her ambiguous association with Charles Delval (A.D. in the story), that she had somehow risked meeting the same humiliating fate as the woman of *Hiroshima* had in Nevers? —Short of an answer, what we can say is that Duras's collaboration with the director of *Night and Fog* must have set off an intense return of memories of the Normandy Invasion, the atomic bombs, and everything that happened in her own life during the intervening year. And, in any case, the drive to violence against fascists that we see in so many texts contained in *La Douleur* would seem to have had those months in the late 1950s, when she was working with Alain Resnais on the scenario of *Hiroshima mon amour* as backdrop. —Quite a thing to forget when writing a piece entitled "I Remember."

Marguerite Duras never went to Japan during the gestation of *Hiroshima mon amour*. Alain Resnais decided that the production budget could only afford that long trip for himself, his script-girl, the incredibly talented, largely forgotten, yet crucial Sylvette Baudrot, and, of course, Emmanuelle Riva. So while imagining what that space named "Hiroshima" was for her character, Duras was moved to put down on paper the story—"right at the cusp of memory and forgetting for me"—of her relationship in 1945 to a Gestapo agent.

SHE: Oh! It's horrible. I'm beginning to remember you less clearly.
(He holds the glass and makes her drink. She's horrified by herself.)

SHE: ... I'm beginning to forget you. I tremble at the thought of having forgotten so much love ... (64)

Wrenching as it is, the scene is unforgettable: she and her lover are in a late-night bar after closing time; she is drunk, nearly delirious, beautiful but disheveled, nearly mad; the viewer too, raw as we are with intolerable velocity back and forth between the two spaces of Nevers-"then" and Hiroshima-"now." But the famous dialectic that drives the still more famous film of 1959 has its source not even in Marguerite Duras's secret striving to hold onto the memory of her Gestapo agent and their questionable (or, let us say "complex") relationship during the Liberation, but in "Construction Sites," where the pinnacle of the dialectic's bizarre possibilities occurs when the narrator reports:

> The girl seemed to be trying to remember something. He figured out that she was forgetting the construction site. She tried to remember it precisely, as he remembered her [*Elle essayait de se souvenir avec précision de lui comme lui se souvenait d'elle*]. The man gazed at her, smiling. She too smiled and began to gaze at him, to look and to watch the man who remembered.

More than Duras's first sustained and explicit experiment with the dialectic of memory and forgetting that would culminate with *Hiroshima mon amour*, in "Construction Sites," it is not a lost lover that the woman is about to forget but the construction site. We might wonder how it is possible to forget something that is right there within one's field of perception? Perhaps if by "forgetting" we mean "learning to not let it bother us," or if what is about to be forgotten is another construction site, elsewhere, in another time. Or, again, both of these simultaneously. But the "cusp of memory and forgetting" in "Construction Sites" is more complicated than in *Hiroshima mon amour* for two reasons: one is that contextually, the antecedent of the pronoun *lui* is the construction site, but Duras's aberrant usage references the man;[16] the other is that the man in the 1954 story remembers too. Not by substituting himself, as an actor might, for the German soldier of his lover's past, but directly. The man at the construction site remembers the same thing that the young woman he met there remembers.

Fusion between the Hiroshima lovers comes to a point of perfection wherein the woman, despite the capital importance of her first love, realizes that she begins to forget him yet, at the same time, realizes too that the experience she is living in the present is also, in turn, destined for the archive

---

[16] With the verbal expression *se souvenir de*, to remember something would be *s'en souvenir* and to remember someone would be *se souvenir de lui* or *se souvenir d'elle*.

of memory even before the experience itself is over. On the verge of a nervous breakdown, a slap in the face administered by her "analyst" draws her back to acknowledging that her most precious memory—however traumatic—is also on a verge: that of being forgotten definitively. Besides the paternalism, whose incidence in Duras's work does not, for some readers, diminish its reprehensibility, Julia Kristeva sees in such lessons a compulsively insistent melancholia that is potentially dangerous for Duras's unconditional fans.[17]

When Duras sketched out the essence of what would become *Hiroshima mon amour*'s scenario and dialogue in the school notebook she borrowed from her young son in the summer of 1958, she did so with the rapidity of someone who knew the story by heart ahead of time ("I brought a text back to Paris after two weeks"[18]). Sketches and drafts of "The Boa" and "Madame Dodin" may be found in a notebook that Duras started filling with script as early as 1943.[19] The title story, with its characters' obvious psychological and sociological parallels with Duras's eldest brother and her mother, was no doubt written as soon as Madame Donnadieu died in August 1956. There is no clear-cut preparatory manuscript in the archives for "Construction Sites" and, in a 1955 radio interview she infers that it had probably been written quickly, just before the publication of *Whole Days in the Trees*.[20] All seems to indicate that Duras wrote "Construction Sites" in a state of urgency not unlike the conditions under which she wrote *Hiroshima mon amour*.

Let us think through what we know of *Hiroshima mon amour* once again, but this time with "Construction Sites" there, firmly implanted on our minds. While we see, hear, and feel empathetically that the intensity of the desire that circulates between the two anonymous characters is of such magnitude that it stirs sharp recollections of her first great love in Nevers, during the Occupation, with the Wehrmacht soldier, Duras, however, summarizes the story differently. It's one, she said for example in an interview, in which "one woman's destiny is identical to that of Hiroshima. Like the city, she has been destroyed and we witness her arising out of the ashes."[21] In its published form, the film's screenplay is supplemented by a synopsis that takes up this

---

[17] Cf. the whole final chapter of Kristeva's *Black Sun* (1987), entitled "The Malady of Grief: Duras." In a nutshell, Kristeva argues that what she terms Duras's "discourse of dull pain" leads to "an aesthetics of awkwardness" and is potentially harmful to the reader because it forecloses any cathartic resolution.

[18] "L'auteur de *Hiroshima mon amour* vous parle." Interview with Alain Hervé, *Réalité* 206 (March 1963): 92.

[19] These two stories had both appeared in *Les Temps modernes*—the monthly journal founded by Jean-Paul Sartre—in the October 1947 and the May 1952 issues, thus prior to the publication of *Whole Days in the Trees*.

[20] Jean-Marc Turine, *Marguerite Duras. Le Ravissement de la parole*, INA/Radio France, 1997, 4 CDs.

[21] "'Non, je ne suis pas la femme d'Hiroshima.'" Interview by André Bourin, 1.

very equation, radicalizing it: "It is as if the disaster of a shorn woman of Nevers and the Hiroshima disaster echoed each other *exactly*" (*OC II*, 12; Duras's emphasis). Putting the destruction of tens of thousands of lives on the same moral scale as one single proscribed love affair—albeit swallowed by death and shame—scandalously defies established values. Other, that is, than what the author may also have at the back of her mind: the Nazi attempt to destroy the European Jews.[22] This is indeed what even the earliest—but ultimately rejected—versions of *Hiroshima mon amour* appear to show. In "Outa's Notebook," adopting the voice of the character Emmanuelle Riva will play in the film, Duras remarked, "My mother was Jewish and had left us in 1942," that is, the young woman of Nevers and her pharmacist father, "to live in a department in the south."

In the middle of the night, in bed with her lover, between bouts of love-making, the woman enumerates documents consulted, museums and hospitals visited, documentaries viewed, all meant to bolster her claim that she "saw everything" of the atomic holocaust—that she incongruously had been there. All the while, her Japanese lover retorts, flatly, insistently, that she "saw nothing. Nothing" (*OC II*, 19; 18). This sequence allows the viewer—early in the film—to learn what each of these "survivors" was doing and did, what happened to each on August 6, 1945. It also makes evident how inaccurate, absurd, how off-the-mark the term "survivor" can be in so many of the cases in which we use it. On August 6, 1945, state violence against civilian populations suddenly leapt to an unprecedented level of magnitude. The couple Duras and Resnais imagined in 1959 Hiroshima grapples with that moment of terror that endures like melancholia. But the spatiality of this coping is yet more poignant than its temporality. Her claim to have seen everything at Hiroshima notwithstanding, her space—the space that preoccupies her existence—is Nevers or, more precisely, as her Japanese lover puts it, "*Nevers en France*," meaning Paris too. Paris, where the spaces of Nevers and Hiroshima come to overlay one another. His putative authority to deny her claim at having been witness to Hiroshima notwithstanding, the space that preoccupies him, his space tends to be Nevers as well. But here—Nevers for him—can only be a space present to the extent of his ability to care, to experience empathy for her and "be" the dead German lover. This is a calculus Duras was obviously already rehearsing in "Construction Sites."

Nameless, thus both mysterious and generic, the two characters united in reconstructed Hiroshima circulate in places without character and from which they are proscribed or banished: dark and provincial Nevers,

---

[22] To honor the work of Raul Hilberg, I am using his terminology for the Shoah. Cf. *The Destruction of the European Jews*.

the soulless Hiroshima Hotel. She and He are generic too in that Duras has them function as emblematic or paradigmatic of all couples and, yet, these two at Hiroshima, like *those* two at the lakeside hotel, it is as if they are, if not exactly homeless, rootless, stateless. These couples form because each member is a nomad obsessed with some no-man's-land or another: Hiroshima flattened, a soulless France, *ein Vernichtungslager*, a cemetery in the making.

Alongside and along *with* her writing of *Hiroshima mon amour* and *The Long Absence* less than a year later, Marguerite Duras was also deeply involved with that space otherwise that was Algeria at war against colonial rule—what Pierre Guyotat would call that "tomb for 500,000 soldiers." With Robert Antelme, Dionys Mascolo, and Edgar Morin at her side, Duras gave herself body and soul to the activities in support of Algerian independence of the *Comité d'action des intellectuels contre la poursuite de la Guerre d'Algérie*. On the last pages of "Outa's Notebook," one finds three difficult to decipher pages concerning the protracted Algerian War, which culminate with these words written clearly and large: "Down with hypocrisy, Mr. President. Algeria. What would you do differently from what they're doing."[23] The Algerian uprising began in November 1954—the very month in which we presume that Marguerite Duras urgently elaborated that inscrutable parable focused on a hauntingly circumscribed no-man's-land. In November 1955, when that state without status that had been Algeria since 1834 won a French ally in the *Comité des intellectuels*, Duras immediately let it command her militant political caring. Duras's first piece of published journalism—"Les fleurs de l'Algérien"—was crafted in such a way as to invite the reader to the edge of a microcosmic space within everyday Parisian life where she had witnessed first-hand, nearly mad with outrage, an act of petty racism with its death-dealing repercussions.

"Construction Sites" experiments—perhaps awkwardly, perhaps too allusively for a public that hadn't yet been trained and attuned to Duras's voice—with the dialectical tensions at the heart of *Hiroshima mon amour*. These tensions, in both texts, are based upon a fundamental disagreement between ephemeral lovers as to the relationship between seeing and understanding: until the very end of both stories, they disagree (but without argument) over the possibility of *actually* seeing what has traumatized them both yet cannot be altogether experienced, since to experience the source of trauma at the place of trauma—Auschwitz, Hiroshima—is to perish. Told solely from the man's point of view and with very little speech coming from the young woman, this disagreement is largely tacit in "Construction Sites," though

[23] Unpublished manuscript DRS 18.1 at IMEC.

easily extrapolated from those parts of the man's narration through which we most clearly hear Duras's voice. These tensions are built on several dyads: memory and forgetting, recollection and amnesia, being "here" and being "there" simultaneously, the magnitude of destruction wrought by advanced techniques for dealing death and the psychic disintegration of which passion is capable. In sum, "Construction Sites," like *Hiroshima mon amour* five years later, stages a twentieth-century avatar of the ancient dialectic of love (or life) and death. These are all limned in the first minutes of the film, in those voices as if borrowed from an operatic recitative, whose tone could well be imagined as that adopted by the characters in "Construction Sites." What complicates this series of dialectical tensions in the rest of *Hiroshima mon amour* is the increasingly strident interference of the enigma of Nevers. In other words, what intervenes to disrupt straightforward dialectics is the woman's insistence on the madness of her youth in Nevers. The 1959 film becomes an early occasion for Duras to unabashedly posit an equivalency between a peculiarly feminine intelligence and what is "normally" considered unreason. When her Japanese lover asks her to describe her period of sequestration by her mother for having slept with the enemy, "You know, intelligence is like madness," she cannily responds (*OC II*, 35). This circular, "insane" logic where one learns to forget in order to remember and remember in order to forget is foregrounded elliptically in "Construction Sites": "No, there was a wisdom about her."

The love affair uniting the French woman and the Japanese man is haunted by an irrepressible return of initiatory love in the form of recollection. Personal, subjective temporality is brazenly superimposed on the temporality of events of global import: the woman's period of "madness" in Nevers establishes a bridge between her lover's murder while French territory was being liberated and the atomic conflagration meant ostensibly to bend imperial Japan to surrender occurred. Resnais made sure this link was locked tight by the demand that the dialogue be in the present tense.[24] Recollection—a particular form of remembering—is the successful return of an event to my space, this space, the space of my presence, to consciousness, in other words, from *that* space, that is, oblivion. Slightly different is the space remembered by the madwomen in these stories: just as Hiroshima on August 9, 1945 can *only* be present to me as a space otherwise, so the space of "the unthinkable" is metonymically present in the guise of the construction site that is apart, "over there."

---

[24] Alain Resnais will recall, in a 1966 radio interview with Michel Polac, how adamantly he had wished that everything be recounted in the present indicative and that even though two temporalities were to be rolled out, there would be no flashbacks. "Histoire sans images," September 3, 1966, Archives INA, reproduced on the DVD version of *Hiroshima mon amour*, EDV, 236.

The resurgence of recollections in the French woman of her reproved liaison with a German soldier in the last months of the war becomes inexorable. The inexorability of this tide of anamnesis is tied to the supposed "impossibility" of the liaison. But it was obviously anything but an impossible relationship, since it *happened*. Without its having happened, along with thousands of others like it, France might not have been moved to commit the dubious mass scapegoat punishment of shearing women and worse. Given that reprobation, condemnation, revenge, displacement of culpability onto a whole sector of patriarchal society would have been all but inevitable even under suspicion of having had such a liaison, the person tempted to engage in one might "reasonably" have checked herself by treating its possibility *as though it were* impossible. Reinforced, in any case, by the incantatory repetition of the word, "Nevers," the namelessness of the characters and the intensity of desire leads to the dead German lover being superimposed upon the live Japanese lover. (Is the latter really alive when he asks, "When you're in the cellar, am I dead?") This identification is anticipated and perhaps even suggested to the keen-eared Japanese man endowed with evenly suspended attention (what Freud called *die gleichschwebende Aufmerksamkeit*) when he hears the French woman say "I remember you" in the hypnotic drone she used in the initial recitative.

Certain passages from *Hiroshima mon amour*, that dialogue of disaster—to use a turn of phrase invented by Marguerite Duras's associate both in literature and politics, Maurice Blanchot—have become unforgettable. It is a dialogue of disaster impelled by and distilled from the narrative in the vicinity of the construction site. Years after the film was released, during her hours of interviews with Xavière Gauthier in 1973, Duras ties the famous ritornello, "*Tu me tues tu me fais du bien*" (OC II, 22; 25), to a whole series of her own texts—some contemporary with *Hiroshima* and others appearing in the intervening years. When she releases her lurid 1980 short story, *The Man Seated in the Corridor*, she hastens to add, "I had written it. But I never, never lived [that story]"[25]—double *nevers* through which we may read the undeniably telltale signs of denial, the same signs that can be read through the foreword to *The War*, in which she claims that she wrote out the raw material for the memoirs immediately following the war, stored them in a blue armoire, and completely forgot about them until the early 1980s. The archival remnant from 1958, of course, stands as clear refutation of this claim.

In those same interviews of 1973, she rather proudly declared that the "*Tu me tues tu me fais du bien*" refrain had been adopted by some of the strip

---

[25] *Les Parleuses*, 60.

clubs in Paris's tawdry Pigalle district.[26] Tawdriness, shady political commitments for the sake of erotic desire, denial that lets itself be read between the lines, between the blades of the venetian blinds: all this, Duras knew very well because she practiced it, repeatedly, in her private life which was always, also, partially public. At the very time she was making the dialogues for *Hiroshima mon amour* for Alain Resnais, she was sharing life—at least in its violently passionate dimension—with a certain Gérard Jarlot. Dashing, nine years her junior, Jarlot wrote for the tabloid weekly *France Dimanche* but cultivated literary aspirations. Her intense desire for Jarlot notwithstanding, clear divisions were erected from the start in this life shared intensely, then endured, then, ultimately, broken with. While Jarlot would collaborate on several of Duras's writing projects and she would agree to share space on those title pages with him, she displayed diffidence toward Jarlot's tendency to garishness in order to pander to popular taste. With Jarlot in her intimate vicinity, Duras's confidence in her own talent as an artist of writing only grew even though passion and jealousy were now driving her to the heavy drinking that would nearly kill her a couple of decades on. And while this raucous private and tense professional association with a journalist also renewed Duras's own journalistic activity, she exploited her own magazine articles and reportages to keep her literary and budding cinematic work in touch with preoccupations that were now finding voice: the poor, outsiders, criminals, the oppressed, Jews, Algerians, women ... others of all sort. The 1980 anthology that she aptly called *Outside* bears testimony to this practice. In sum, while Jarlot by no means shared with Duras the fact that while involved with her (and in addition to remaining married) he was promiscuously pursuing many other women (he would die "in the saddle" at age forty-three), Duras shared with Jarlot reluctantly and parsimoniously the literary universe she had created for herself—that imaginary realm of her own for working on the real world.

"Subterranean" is the stratum on which Duras maintained that realm in the late 1950s just as she was thinking more and more seriously about how film might stage construction sites. As inevitable and unforgettable as the dialogue of *Hiroshima mon amour* may be, the published text offers another major element absent from (or at least barely present in) the film, but gripping in its faculty for parting the veil on capital spaces—spaces of capital importance. Having picked up some cinematographic terminology from the film's all too underestimated script "girl," Sylvette Baudrot, and having absorbed some of the imagery that a filmmaker of Alain Resnais's keenness invents, Marguerite Duras came to alternately name this element

---

[26] Ibid., 196–7.

the film's "subterranean continuity" or its "nocturnal evidence." In a manner as covert as the continuity Resnais asked Duras to prepare for the psychological profiles of *Hiroshima*'s characters, Duras conceived Emmanuelle Riva's role as the concatenation of several women, the embodiment of several individuals at disparate moments in a single life: the girl shorn for shame in Nevers; Duras herself, flirting with a fascist; Duras, in person, again, seeking to free her husband from the "concentrationary universe"; Duras, yet again, with Robert Antelme in a rest home for former deportees; a married woman who "really likes guys" (*OC II*, 34; 35) and who gives herself over to an erotic adventure with a survivor of Hiroshima ... in Hiroshima. To a significant degree, we may consider that carefully wrought manuscript about her "adventure" with A.D. in 1945 as a deeper level of *Hiroshima*'s "subterranean continuity," perhaps, but certainly something akin to what Bob Dylan might have termed Duras's back pages.[27]

In any case, no sooner was *Hiroshima mon amour* released and fêted with near unanimity as a landmark work of both film and literature than Marguerite Duras would plunge into another film script with the space of the Second World War "over there," just beyond the space in which the protagonists of *The Long Absence* evolve. The writing styles of Marguerite Duras and Gérard Jarlot negotiate their near incompatibility into a script sufficiently workable as to help Henri Colpi's film win a prize before it gradually slipped into semi-oblivion.[28] When, fourteen years after the obliteration, her Japanese lover asks her, "What did Hiroshima mean for you, in France?", the woman reconstructs the young trollop ("*salope*") who had just arrived in Paris from Nevers, just as Duras, in "I Remember," sees herself in that same place, on that same day, in that space ... apart. She draws herself here, to the space where she *remembers* through the power of imagination. After "such a long absence," Thérèse, in Colpi's feature film of 1960, is convinced that a man living in a *shanty* in the no-man's-land *between* Paris and its suburbs—known then as *la Zone*[29]—who passes one day in front of her café in Suresnes is her husband. She will try to remember for him. Duras and Jarlot will stage the struggle between amnesia and anamnesis. But unlike the man in "Construction Sites," who lets the young woman nurture a relation to space otherwise, allowing her to forget as she remembers, when Thérèse attempts to force the opera-humming hobo to remember his "true place" and

---

[27] The refrain of Dylan's song from 1964, entitled "My Back Pages," well expresses a logic one sees Duras deploy from *Hiroshima mon amour* to *The Lover* (1984): "Ah but I was so much older then / I'm younger than that now."
[28] The film shared the Palme d'or with Luís Buñuel's *Viridiana* at Cannes that year and also garnered the Prix Louis-Delluc.
[29] *La Zone* will be explored in Chapter 4.

recall his identity as Albert Langois, disaster occurs: he runs out in front of a truck, the screen goes black. *Fin.*

In 1954, just as Duras, in a fit of anamnestic, memorial inspiration, was adding "Construction Sites" to her collection of short stories, a complete unknown named Michel Foucault described the relationship of the deranged mind to the category of space in these terms:

> As structure of the lived world, space lends itself to analyses that combine the noetic with the noematic. Distances, thus, may collapse, as with those maniacs who recognize right here people they know are elsewhere, or those hallucinated subjects who hear their voices not in the objective space from which sound emanates, but in a mythical space, a sort of quasi-space whose referential axes are fluid and mobile: right here, near themselves, all around and inside themselves, they hear the voices of persecutors which, at the very same time, they situate beyond the walls, far beyond the city and its limits. For transparent space in which each object has its geographic place and where perspectives articulate one with the other, an opaque space substitutes itself—one in which objects move to and fro, intermingling with immediate mobility, then shift without movement and, finally, fuse together on a horizon without perspective. (1954: 62–3)

To this madness, the scandal—as if it were somehow equivalent—of substituting for the destruction of the European Jews (Shoah) some personal trauma—however acute—or even Hiroshima, for that matter, can be seen as a close correlate in the realm of ethics. But we must remember that Foucault would come to repudiate his youthful introduction to Ludwig Binswanger's *Traum und Existenz* (1930) and find value in the tendency of the "abnormal" to embrace such "opaque space [...] in which objects move to and fro." W. G. Sebald presses this issue of the justice or injustice in the substitution of one world of disaster with another in reflecting, via Elias Canetti, on Hans Erich Nossack's 1948 *Interview mit dem Tode*. This passage, in which we immediately recognize the response to Adorno's injunction against the writing of poetry after Auschwitz is, moreover, a quintessential example of Sebald's deceptively meandering logic of presentation that, in its succinctness, is almost overwhelming:

> Elias Canetti, in an essay on the diary of Dr. [Michihiko] Hachiya from Hiroshima, asks what it means to survive such a vast catastrophe, and says that the answer can be gauged only from a text which, like Hachiya's observations, is notable for precision and responsibility. "If there were any point," writes Canetti, "in wondering what form of literature is essential

to a thinking, seeing human being today, then it is this." The same may be said of Nossack's account of the destruction of the city of Hamburg, which is unique even in his own work. The ideal of truth inherent in its entirely unpretentious objectivity, at least over long passages, proves itself the only legitimate reason for continuing to produce literature in face of total destruction. Conversely, the construction of aesthetic or pseudo-aesthetic effects from the ruins of an annihilated world is a process depriving literature of its right to exist. (Sebald e-book: 74)

We will have occasion to think further about Sebald's meditations on the "natural history of destruction" in the second half of *Sharing Common Ground*, but let us note that the characteristics that Sebald notes that Canetti noted in Hachiya are precisely those at the fore everywhere and always in the seminal witness work of Primo Levi.[30] Finally, this glance at Duras's 1960 filmic variant of her 1959 exploration of the imbrication of trauma and place with the dialectic of memory and forgetting should serve to reorient our attention to the seminal 1954 story and the necessity of bringing a certain Immanuel Kant into the picture, which we do in the next chapter.

After *The Viaducts of Seine-et-Oise* appeared in the summer of 1960, Duras told Madeleine Chapsal in an interview that: "Gérard Jarlot and I are working on a film called *Une aussi longue absence* whose subject matter is based on a news item from last year. You might remember that woman from Aubervilliers, Léontine Fourcade, who thought she'd seen her husband, who had been a prisoner at the Nazi camp at Buchenwald, pass by in the street."[31] The scenario for this film appears in the same series as *Hiroshima* at Gallimard in June 1961. The film itself, directed by Henri Colpi, had been released in theatres the previous month. Duras's former husband, Robert Antelme, had also been deported to Buchenwald (Bad Gandersheim, an auxiliary to Buchenwald, to be precise), before being transferred to the concentration camp at Dachau, where he had nearly died.

Conceived in the immediate wake of *Hiroshima mon amour*, at whose crux one also finds a dialectic of memory and forgetting, Henri Colpi's *The Long Absence*[32] would first appear in theatres on May 17, 1961. Jasmine Chasney, with whom Colpi had collaborated in this role for *Hiroshima mon amour*, did the montage. It was thus foreseeable that Marguerite Duras, heretofore a writer of fiction who was now taking increasing interest in filmmaking itself,

---

[30] For one discussion of these characteristics in Primo Levi, from *If This Be a Man* to *The Drowned and the Saved*, see Harvey, 2010, 19–29.

[31] Madeleine Chapsal, "Entretien avec Marguerite Duras," *L'Express*, June 30, 1960, 36.

[32] The film starred Georges Wilson as The Hobo and Alida Valli as Thérèse. For more information, see Harvey in Duras, *OC II*, 1657–63.

chose to adapt a true story among simple people in which amnesia plays a preponderant role. And given the thirty-odd articles Duras had given the weekly *France-Observateur* in the late 1950s and throughout the 1960s on a variety of social, political, and cultural issues involving real-life stories of unassuming working class individuals, immigrants and so forth, it is equally unsurprising that *The Long Absence* is based on a news item.

With *The Long Absence*, Marguerite Duras transposes for the cinema a quite unusual event lifted out of the life of altogether ordinary people. She had learned about the story of Léontine Bourgade (not "Léontine Fourcade," as she would remember it, defectively, less than a year later) while reading an article in the October 20, 1959 issue of *France-Soir*, in the "investigation" column run by Jacques Hussenet, dramatically titled: "She Thinks She Recognizes Her Husband: A Hobo." A photograph of Madame Bourgade and her husband on their wedding day illustrates the article:

> A woman who refuses to believe her husband died at Buchenwald in 1944 is convinced she's found him alive. She recognized him in the hobo who recently came to her café, asking for a glass of water.
>
> Madame Léontine Bourgade, 58, owns a café at 12 rue Daumesnil. Against all hope, she's been waiting for the return of her spouse, Adrien, born in Dégagnac (Lot), who was denounced by the Gestapo for passing patriots across the line of demarcation and deported. Official papers confirm his death in the Nazi camp.
>
> The widowed Bourgade continued to run the café the couple set up a year after their marriage in 1937.
>
> This past 17 July, Madame Bourgade thought she would faint. A hobo came into the café. She recognized him. It was Adrien. Overwhelmed, she served the vagabond in a woman's coat and who appeared to be in his sixties a glass of water. She said nothing.
>
> The hobo returned the following day. "Before leaving, he took on a strange look. I instantly knew it was Adrien. But he was not the same Adrien…"
>
> *The hobo tries on the dead man's suits*
>
> Adrien's ghost crossed the café's threshold a third time on 21 September. He'd just spent three months in hospital in Corbeil. Madame Bourgade gives it one last try: "Do you recognize anything here?" "No," the man answered dreamily, "yet…" Then Madame Bourgade unburdened her heart: "You're at home, here: I'm your wife."

The hobo didn't appear too surprised. He begged her pardon, spoke of doubles (spitting images), but agreed to go upstairs to Madame Bourgade's apartment and try on the dead man's suits and shoes. They fit him perfectly.

Madame Bourgade tried to recreate the atmosphere of yesteryear and invited the hobo to cook. With Adrien's expert gestures, he concocted the same dishes.

The ghost flees

After four days of this life, the hobo—who claims, though he has no ID, that his name is André Bourlier—announced, "I'm going to take a walk."

That was Sunday, 3 October. The ghost had still not returned the next day and Madame Bourgade learned from police headquarters that "Adrien" had been taken to the infirmary and, from there, admitted to Sainte-Anne [Psychiatric Hospital]. No arbitrariness in that move: in a fit of madness, the hobo had stationed himself with his arms folded on his chest in front of a bus.

Since then, Madame Bourgade makes regular visits to her hobo. She got him registered at Sainte-Anne under the name, Adrien Bourgade, and patiently awaits an administrative inquest that she hope will prove to her that her affection has not misled her.

Although Gérard Jarlot (who, as we have discussed, was also Duras's lover in the late 1950s and early 1960s) played a major part in the conceptualization and realization of the screenplay for *The Long Absence*—the rather obsessively abundant documentary details about the daily life of Parisian hobos, who were often ragpickers and used paper collectors—Robert Antelme, whom Duras had divorced in 1947 so that her son would carry the name of his biological father, Dionys Mascolo, reappears on the scene insistently concerned with details of the scenario and ensuing film. The Bourgade story resonates at multiple levels with what was happening with and between Duras and Antelme in 1945 and 1946. While Antelme, along with Dionys Mascolo, was intensely invested in everything Duras had written up until the early 1950s, that interest had either flagged or become diverted by Antelme's new family with his second wife, Monique. With apparent suddenness, however, Antelme takes a keen interest in *The Long Absence*.

Filmed in the autumn of 1960, a somewhat mediocre montage was projected to a few friends in October: Louis-René des Forêts, Robert and Monique Antelme were there. The day after, Robert writes a letter to

Marguerite summarizing the group's impressions: while there were some truly beautiful moments in the film, such as the sublime scene with the opera aria played out of the jukebox, the role of the hobo (played by George Wilson, whose theatrical prowess was no doubt adjudged to have been wasted on Colpi's film) is underdeveloped, and "a way for it all to give way to a true tragedy needs to be discovered." Duras's response will come indirectly, in the midst of a letter to Monique Antelme about other things as well—like summer vacation plans for the children of both households:

> I received, we received the long letter from Robert. We've used it as basis for further work. And we've even reworked some more, after having received the film. But we prefer that the story ends up opening onto total darkness [*le noir total*] rather than on a more or less expected tragedy. As Robert says, he chose silence, chose to be the way he is. We agree with everything Robert says, but that's *exactly* what we wanted to avoid. Pious silence, wisdom opted for as non-singularity which, in the end, is the worst kind of singularity possible.[33]

With its plot so close to the story of Robert Antelme's return from Dachau and of Duras patiently nursing him back to some semblance of health,[34] given *The Long Absence*'s many similarities with *Hiroshima mon amour*, during whose elaboration we now know Duras vividly recalled her troubling relationship to a Gestapo agent, writing this screenplay would no doubt have rekindled memories of that other place of memory and forgetting: the convalescent hotel in Saint-Jorioz. And that space otherwise, of course, inspired "Construction Sites" in 1954, which we now must consider a veritable theoretical text.

Recalling Edward S. Casey's definition of site, let us recognize that in "Construction Sites" we encounter one of the earliest examples in Duras's oeuvre of purified, stripped-down expressions of intense desire of the kind found in far more well-known later texts, like *The Ravishing of Lol Stein* (elevated to the status of paradigm by Jacques Lacan), *The Lover*, and *The Malady of Death*. This is Duras's first and best example of a *construction site of desire* where the reader may clearly take stock of how erotic charge, its augmentation, its intensity, its resolution (its "return to reason") follows a course reminiscent of the itinerary (or economy) of the sublime as Immanuel Kant described it in the *Critique of Judgement*. Through this

---

[33] These two letters were transcribed in the Marguerite Duras issue of *Les Cahiers de l'Herne*, 40–1.

[34] She recounted this story famously in *The War* (*La Douleur*), but also, anonymously, in an early feminist journal. "L'Horreur d'un pareil amour." *Sorcières* 4 (September 1976): 31–2.

experience, which I explore in further detail in the next chapter, the desiring subject enters a space that is foreign to her—akin in many ways to that state of being a "stranger to oneself" that Julia Kristeva, after Victor Shklovsky, after Arthur Rimbaud, made one of her hallmark notions.[35]

An essential condition for my becoming a stranger to myself—whether through desire or through the experience of the sublime—is a kind of ontological splitting that ultimately, nevertheless, fails to shatter me. The experience of the sublime gets under way when a sense perception shocks consciousness, thereby severing the understanding from itself. The subject stricken is suddenly beside herself with terror. A break of vital proportions would seem to have occurred. Almost immediately (an immediacy that feels like a lifetime), however, the imagination comes to the rescue of reason unmoored. But, in fact, the imagination had always been there, even in that darkest moment, sharing space with and clinging to the understanding adrift in a tempestuous sea. The subject then realizes that she is at a safe distance from the threat and the tranquility that sanity affords is restored in her. This adventure of the sublime operates not dissimilarly to the dual valences embodied in the word "*partage*"—a simultaneous sharing and division, a sort of cleft. A cleft, that is, that both cleaves *and* enables cleaving *to*. (Cleaving to, but not cloying.) Similarly, in the form of a parable, "Construction Sites" stages selves divided yet united—cleft but who yet cleave to one another. Gerard Manley Hopkins hit upon a term that perfectly encapsulates this cluster of meanings that *partage* carries. Elaborating on the image of "'*cleaves*' or exposed faces of [a] pomegranate [...] cut in all directions across" to describe the interrelationality of all possible worlds, Hopkins asserted that each "creature" is situated interrelationally as well within a "'*cleave*' of being."[36] Following Hopkins, then, *cleave* shall be our translation of *partage* and the name designating the function that construction sites activate in individuals. Cleaves unite while preserving difference. "Construction Sites" tells the tale of this union in preserved difference.

---

[35] In chronological order, the references here would be Rimbaud's famous "*Je est un autre* (I is another)" in his May 13, 1871 letter to Georges Izambard (one of the "*lettres du voyant*"); Victor Shklovsky's notion of остранения (defamiliarization) explained in his 1917 essay, "Art as Technique"; and Julia Kristeva, *Étrangers à nous-mêmes* (1988).

[36] "[...] God can always command if he chooses the free consent of the elective will, at least, if by no other way, by shutting out all freedom of field [...]. Therefore in that '*cleave*' *of being* which each of his creatures shews to God's eyes alone (or in its 'burl' of being/uncloven) God can choose countless points in the strain (or countless cleaves of the 'burl') where the creature has consented, does consent, to God's will in the way above shewn" (153–4; my emphasis). I regret that I was unable to discuss this passage with Peter Manchester before he died in July 2015.

"Two days before, in the morning, at the same hour of the day, when she arrived at the villa, he had noticed that she existed, brutally. She had understood this from his look" (*OC I*, 832). Telltale signs in Duras's previously published work of what she accomplishes with "Construction Sites" are limited to one or two sentences like this one from *The Little Horses of Tarquinia*, where nothing takes place except two looks—looks not exchanged but, rather, successive looks, followed by successive revelations. Nothing takes place, in other words, but the movement of desire: the unremarkable move of a man for a woman and the move—far more specific and anticipatory of the later "Duras"—that consists (whether to one's pleasure or displeasure) in being the object of a man's desire. The entirety of "Construction Sites," the fourth and final story in the 1954 collection, is devoted to the minute details of this "nothing": a man notices that a woman exists and he waits for the woman to seize upon the signification of his look—a look that simply means that he has noticed her existence.

For all its vagueness, a veritable lexicon for concerns more often found in philosophical treatises structures "Construction Sites" and an intricate temporal algebra underlies the eventual (re)union of the story's pair. For example, a multiplicity of meanings that may be ascribed to "nature" proliferate in this "atmospheric novel," as French critics would have labeled it in the mid-1950s. Any number of eighteenth-century thinkers—philosophers as disparate as Voltaire, Rousseau, Diderot, even Sade—might come to mind as we read. While the scenario plays itself out in a bucolic setting, what is at issue is also—or perhaps principally—the very "nature" of man and the "nature" of women. Beyond the effects of and constraints imposed by *homo sapiens*, indeed, how does the world—including the "human" animal—behave? What are its "laws"? Is it right that we distinguish and divide between actions deemed "natural" and those deformed by our customs, habits, rules, regulations, or do all our actions entail one another [*départager/partage*]. Leaving aside this primal question for a later chapter, the man of our story—this *particular* man, whose advantaged point of view makes him a stand-in for Duras, a woman[37]—decided that "it wouldn't have been natural for him to hold himself back" from following the girl when she left for the first time in the direction of the construction site. And, as though mimicking him (but from whose perspective?), a few paragraphs further, the girl "rather seems to find it natural" that he comes on to her.

---

[37] As Duras's art evolves, she will repeat this paradigm in key texts of which *The Ravishing of Lol Stein* (1964) and *The Vice-Consul* (1966) are prime examples.

As in most philosophical texts, "Construction Sites" presents precious little action or action that is so minimal that the reader, taken by tedium, succumbs to the repetition of infinitesimal, seemingly insignificant movements that take on the allure of rituals and that, together, form a sort of simple, repetitive, little music. Any autobiographical foundation that one could without much difficulty identify as such in prior Duras fictions (like the acclaimed 1950 novel *Un barrage contre le Pacifique* or even "Whole Days in the Trees," which opens this same collection) seems to have vanished or is, at least, undetectable by the lay reader. Moreover, whereas in any previous Duras text the reader readily equates the narrative point of view with that of the woman who signed the book as author, "Construction Sites" adopts the explicit and rather bold masculinist perspective that we have discussed. Driven by an overweening imagination, this male surrogate strives to capture the object of his desire by means of the look. He therefore incarnates, as we observed earlier, the quintessential voyeur. He also plans—albeit with endless ratiocinations transcribed in indirect discourse—an erotic conquest that might, in 1954, have been read as par for the course but unfailingly shocks today. Untimely (and perhaps failing) in 1954, Duras's deliberate provocation works today: it begs consideration on its own terms.

Duras uses *violeur* (violator) to qualify the man with the overly persistent gaze. Heavily tinged with rape (*viol*), the word necessarily gives pause. In the sentence where it appears, the violence of *violeur* builds on *voleur* (thief), recalling the man's principal activity as *voyeur*. This is no amateurish poetic hyperbole from a writer yet to fully master her art: a tidal wave of moral questions rush forth. It will be the task of this book to address them as we proceed. Just how does this particular voyeur in "Construction Sites" violate the object of his curiosity and his desire? Is a person who seeks to empathize, which the man in this story does, a voyeur and, therefore, a violator of the other's right to secrecy? Just as the nature of the construction site remains stubbornly ambiguous, so does the significance and moral charge of the man's look. Yet, knowing what we do about patriarchy and its complicity in mass crimes, must we not conclude that Duras's man's gaze is fundamentally malefic? Could it not just possibly be, on the contrary, that his gaze is somehow, despite all, a moral one—a gaze that is motivated by and imbued with empathy for an event unknown?

At this conjuncture, I can imagine a heated exchange between me and a reader who protests vehemently my having dared to suggest that a voyeur's desire for an individual tetanized with terror before a construction site because it reminds her of an extermination camp could possibly be driven by innate and irrepressible morality. To this reader's recoil, I would need to reply that while Duras's narrative takes great pains to mark *both* the construction site *and* the man's desirous look with extreme ambiguity, I would contend that it is *only* the look that might be otherwise than "sick"—indeed, that it is perhaps even underpinned by exemplary values. This possibility results from the two registers of the construction site's ambiguity: one, which we position on the side of reason, a commitment to reality, and a preference for verisimilitude, confirms in us the conviction that the site is that of an altogether conventional cemetery; the other, which culture tends to associate with unreason, abnormality, fantasy, and so forth, is the vision we receive from the *mnemonic imagination* of a young woman who—if we strictly abide by what the story published in 1954 tells us—is *perhaps* a camp survivor (or at least *imagined* as such by the man); it's a *charnier* or, if you will, it is *like* a *charnier*. "Like" or "as if" [*als ob*] in Kant's language is *as if it were*.

Bracketing for an instant the issue of the relative morality of the man's gaze and its relationship to empathy, it may be legitimate to ask if empathy itself—that relational positioning *vis-à-vis* the other consequent of a certain vicarious experience—is fundamentally immoral. But for now, we shall leave this question unanswered, as it will arise again through material presented in later chapters. If voyeurism is *prima facie* the act of looking without being caught, then what are we to make of the fact that the object of *this* story of voyeurism "still being [...] perfectly unaware of [him] naturally made the man desire to be seen"? And how do we deal with the fact that, as readers, just as "naturally," since we decipher the scene through his eyes, we become complicitous with his desire and desire to know. "[A]s soon as he saw her [...] he understood that he was taking her by surprise, unwittingly [*sans l'avoir voulu*], in one of the most intimate [*secrets*] moments of her life." The surprise is presumed to be hers, but the *unwitting* subject, here, is the thief, the so-called violator. This man we indict for sadism has realized that he has done something he didn't mean to do. Everything the sadist does is *wittingly*. *This* witness is unwitting. In other words, he seems to *understand* but falls short of *knowing*. He comes to understand that "he'd been initiated to her drama at the instant it attained its strongest expression, in the greatest simplicity" but also that in that instant "the drama [...] possessed that primacy of the least enunciated thing over the thing enunciated." By this, I understand Duras to be asserting that we attain a feeling for the trauma experienced by another at the moment we witness the words to express it falling miserably short. More than just philosophical discourse, what Duras wrote in this passage is the crux of ethics being presented to the reader's imagination-fueled reason. In that instant, all of the man's moral wherewithal is being summoned to the fore, for he understands, finally, that his desire for the woman is inextricable from his desire to help her get beyond being tetanized at the site of the construction site. And, in turn, our will to *feel we know* what gnaws at her at the sight of the construction site—yes: a certain will to knowledge—grows with his.

Nothing in the version of "Construction Sites" that found its way into *Whole Days in the Trees* in 1954 as the book's end piece can confirm that it is, in fact, Nazi extermination camps that the young girl has on her mind. There is no manuscript that we can affirm with absolute certainty helped Duras prepare the 1954 parable. The archive does, however, contain a highly enigmatic typescript, entitled "Les Chantiers de Monsieur Arié," whose date, while difficult to determine, is most probably posterior to that of the published parable.[38] While there remains the slight possibility that this short text served as a kind of preliminary sketch of "Construction Sites," its stylistic characteristics compel us to suppose that the poem is a later reformulation of the scenario, no doubt related to one of Duras's many attempts to breathe new life into the "Théodora" project begun in 1947. Most immediately important, however, for a thorough-going interpretation of "Construction Sites" is that "Les Chantiers de Monsieur Arié" is as close as poetry can get to being explicit regarding the woman's experience that the man can only guess at in the published version:

> Immobile intensity of your face when you say it to me:
> "Construction sites of death fill me with fright." (*OC I*, 1129)

Duras, here, has not only placed the word "death" in the mouth of the young woman, she has had her pronounce the expression, *chantiers de la mort*, which by the middle of the twentieth century had become the usual metaphor in French for the Nazi *Vernichtungslager*, or extermination camps. "Les Chantiers de Monsieur Arié," thus, solves the enigma of "Construction Sites": the published narrative indeed stages the spectacle of a woman attempting to gain mastery over the memory of horror. Actual horror, horror experienced in actuality. It stages that spectacle, but at a double remove. One remove—the first one—is that of the person who remembers, whose memory is so vivid that it can overpower and supplant the present of consciousness; the other remove is the one whose primary function is to drive the parable's plot (to the extent that a plot there is). This is the remove that consists of a man imagining he sees (and, thus, understands) that this is the spectacle of a woman attempting to gain mastery over the memory of horror—not terror, but horror. If she succeeds in mastering her residual fear it is, according to the solution Duras suggests, thanks to the voyeuristic maneuvering of a man fascinated with a woman's experience in the death camps—the "construction sites of death."

---

[38] The full text of "Les Chantiers de Monsieur Arié" may be found in *OC I*, 1129–30.

With "Les Chantiers de Monsieur Arié" in mind, and guessing—which is all we can do—at its date of fabrication, we might profitably return, once again, to "Théodora," the novel Marguerite Duras would resuscitate several times following its inception in 1947, reworking a story that so obviously haunted her, coming ultimately to recognize it as "unpublishable," leaving it shelved, unfinished, at her death five decades later. One of the novel's later titles is "Théodora Kats."[39] The story's décor and its characters who, as time passes, become explicitly Jewish, and some of whom are survivors of the Shoah, will form the kernel of various Duras works - notably *Destroy, She Said*, and *Yann Andréa Steiner*. But the *Urtext* underpinning "Théodora" is, most obviously, "Construction Sites," and the glacial yet unwavering evolution of the "unfinishable" "Théodora" into "Théodora Kats" reinforces our speculative understanding of what disturbs the young woman and fascinates her empathic, but disturbing, witness.

Nothing in "Construction Sites" even proves that the young woman is a survivor of the Nazi attempt to destroy the European Jews. Nothing on the body of the Shoah survivor – even the forearm tattoo – necessarily indicates that she survived the Shoah. Nothing somatic binds her, by the visual inspection of another, to having been at the place named Auschwitz during the Nazis' use of it as a factory for human extermination. To have survived Hiroshima, August 6, 1945, is to have been elsewhere. To have survived Auschwitz is to be *as if* (*als ob*) one had been elsewhere. Only a Hiroshima of the imagination draws the characters of *Hiroshima mon amour* toward fusion with each other. Only an Auschwitz of the imagination can draw the characters of "Construction Sites" toward each other. What gets built—not at the story's construction site, but on the basis of its direct and indirect sighting—is a caring relationship between the two characters: the ethical edifice that a plurality of individuals may share.

[39] Sophie Bogaert analyzes these manuscripts from the period 1990-2 (DRS 42.22 in the IMEC archive) in *OC IV*, 1525-9. But a much earlier hint that Duras thinks of Théodora as Jewish is in a note written in December 1946 that Dionys Mascolo "summarizes" ("*Je la résume ici*") in *Autour d'un effort de mémoire* (1987): "Madame Kats [une ami juive] voyageant dans le même compartiment que l'évêque de Lourdes [?] et de religieuses, en vient à leur dire: 'Ma fille est morte, gazée, en Allemagne. Si j'avais cru en Dieu, j'aurais cessé d'y croire.' Et les sœurs et l'évêque de lui exposer comment, Dieu laissand à chacun sa liberté, il est normal que ce soient les plus forts qui gagnet dans le monde. Les innocents sacrifiés le sont en somme dans le respect d'une règle du jeu, pour l'accomplissement d'un ordre, la neutralité de Dieu faisant loi. Mme Kats, rapportant cela, fait le rapprochement: 'Les hitlériens disaient la même chose.' La Providence, complice de l'âme SS, ou n'entrant pas en contradiction avec elle" (72-3). Mascolo does not say who the author of this note is. If not himself, it was either Robert Antelme or Marguerite Duras. In any case, Madame Kats must have been the "Jewish friend" of all three.

Since it is a function of site—a space otherwise for anyone who was never in Auschwitz, that is—the issue of what might be visible to me on the body of the traumatized other should be at least considered under the lens of Foucault's concept of the "docile body."[40] A subject's body is rendered docile as a function of its being situated in specific ways and in specific locations. Indeed, docility is requisite for the possessor of this body to become constituted as subject. "Thanks to the micropractices of disciplinary power, [...] bodies become 'docile bodies,'" Edward S. Casey writes in 1997, succinctly restating Foucault's thesis from *Discipline and Punish*, "bodies that exist only in sites and as a function of sites" (184). Casey reinforces this point in a footnote elsewhere in the same work, where he traces Foucault's thesis back to Merleau-Ponty in whose *Phenomenology of Perception*, as Casey puts it, "institutionally passive or 'docile' bodies inscribe and internalize the power-gaze of the other, [...] rob these bodies of the privacy and intimacy they might otherwise enjoy" (n. 215, 441). This, of course, is also a conclusion we are compelled to draw from Sartre's analysis of how I receive the gaze of the other in *Being and Nothingness*. In "Construction Sites," although Marguerite Duras situates her female protagonist in such a way—between a site that seizes her with fright and the insistent gaze of her male counterpart—that she should be a model of the "docile body," quite the opposite occurs. For once she finally espies the man, never within the temporal confines of the story to release him from her view, the young woman, *au contraire*, constitutes him as the compliant, complicitous, subjugated subject of her experience of the site.

According to Gaston Bachelard, the spaces that most entice and stimulate the imagination are subsets of the architecturally circumscribed space that we inhabit—"the place I call home." The expedition Bachelard invites us to follow in *The Poetics of Space* begins at home, then ranges through its most secret extremities—the basement and the attic—through nooks and crannies of various types, to end in the wondrous paradox of "intimate immensity." These are places of comfort, reassuring us in our illusion of wholeness and safety. They illustrate Casey's axiom, inspired by the first thinkers of place in Western thought, then reconfirmed by Bachelard and Martin Heidegger: "Both Archytas and Aristotle proclaimed that place is prior to space, and, more recently, Bachelard and Heidegger have re-embraced the conviction. All four thinkers subscribe to what I have called the Archytian Axiom: 'Place is the first of all things'" (2009: 319).

But as Marguerite Duras amply shows, a site is not a place in such a comforting sense. So while I would like to suggest that it is indeed through

---

[40] "*Les corps dociles*" is the first chapter of Part III, "Discipline," of *Discipline and Punish*.

our experience developing our spatial sensibilities in such primordial places as dwellings, our experience elaborating a personal somatic lexicon whose limits are place and space that each of us prepares to "read," analyze, and interpret certain spaces as common grounds, these sites, these spaces elsewhere and otherwise are the last places we would ever wish to dwell. In such a vocabulary for situating my body, spatialization would consist of this: place is "the first of all things" and spaces are *here*, whereas sites are over or out *there*. Indeed, it is *because* certain sites *should* be uninhabitable that we are free to use our imagination to come to ethical agreement with other dwellers.

Behind and through Hiroshima fourteen years after the atomic bomb, behind and through a cemetery expansion project that resembles a construction site, pairs of characters that sprang from the imagination of Marguerite Duras remember spaces elsewhere and otherwise: Hiroshima in August 1945, in the one case; Auschwitz under the Third Reich, in the other.[41] These are the spaces of horror brought to mind and recalled in places out of time. When members of such couples come simultaneously to the realization that they are not, in fact, *there then*, but *here now*, where the horror of that space is buffered by the force of imagination, the process of the pair's construction into a couple of lovers commences.

The first thing I decided to change from Anita Barrows' translation of "Les Chantiers" was the title entity: a building site is not the same as a construction site. Casey, again, is extremely helpful in this regard:

> Building [...] transforms pregiven places—"building sites"—into places for inhabitation. [...] Not only does such building identify the potential for dwelling found in certain unbuilt places; it also realizes this potential itself in the activity of construction, and it carries this potential into new ranges by an attentiveness to the micro-features as well as the macro-features of the given edifice. (2009: 175)

Eschewing the promise of future shelter, construction sites, as Marguerite Duras conceived them, beckon the imagination of two or more desiring subjects while remaining at a safe distance. It is by keeping "there" *there* that our shared aspirations for life can cohabit *here*, that the "activity of construction" *without* the promise of a building, that the ethical edification of protagonist-subjects can proceed *without* the promise of an edifice.

Construction sites thus constitute a category of spaces elsewhere that are conducive to or fertile for the convergence of ethical horizons *here and*

---

[41] This paradigm repeats itself in many other Duras texts: S. Thala in *The Ravishing of Lol Stein* and in the film, *La Femme du Gange*; Battambang in *The Vice-Consul*; Calcutta in *India Song*; etc.

now. At a remove, like spectacles of nature that instill paralyzing awe in the single subject, construction sites enable existential communion to occur in pluralities of subjects by virtue of combined forces of imagination, just as the imagination enables the recovery of reason in Kant's tale of the experience of the sublime. The parties involved occupy those spaces by virtue of imagination alone. Their *preoccupation* is the realization of terror's promise: living death. Such spaces carry neither the name "utopia" nor "dystopia" because although they are occupied or invested "merely" by means of the imagination, these spaces nevertheless *do exist now*, in the current phenomenal world. Or, as in the case of Duras's fiction which often references actual historical events, such spaces *have* existed. But to fail to occupy them by dint of imagination would be to fail to do justice to our innate moral impulses. Realizable, realized or not, utopia, as its etymology suggests, has no place on this construction site.

2

Empathy and the Kantian Sublime

'TIS pleasant, safely to behold from shore
The rowling Ship, and hear the Tempest roar:
Not that anothers pain is our delight;
But pains unfelt produce the pleasing sight.
Lucretius, De natura rerum, II (tr. John Dryden)

Dave 2 removed the large hand from Carol's forearm and placed it in the vague area of his heart. His great chin filled up with dimples and his cheeks creased as his long face took on an expression that was obviously intended to betoken deep sympathy, or even empathy ... yes empathy, for Dave 2, unchallenged by Carol, followed on: "I can identify with your hurt, Carol. I've felt as you have—utterly indifferent to the fate of someone I once thought I loved. Utterly indifferent."
Will Self, Cock and Bull

Gertrude Stein's most famous statement, after "a rose is a rose is a rose [...]," is: "There is no there there." She was referring to Oakland, where she ever regretted having been brought up. It's easy to guess that the perfectly plenary "there" over which she pined as a young girl was San Francisco, a half-hour ferry ride away. She would of course settle altogether elsewhere, in Paris—a true place "where it's at" or, more to the point of her dig at Oakland, a place with a "there" at its center if not in its heart.

As clever as Stein's double-"there" distancing from the site stripped of its oaks to build San Francisco may appear, she was wrong: as long as it's been called Oakland, that city on the eastern shore of the Bay, just like every other place in the world, has always been populated by selves—whether Ohlones or Oakies or Blacks—juxtaposed with other selves in tandem with whom they perceive spaces otherwise. The natural inclination of humans to be beside themselves from time to time and their tendency to imagine themselves, when that happens, inside someone else's shoes even extends to Oakland. For example, every time there is a major earthquake in that city right up the length of which runs the San Andreas Fault, everyone is instantaneously awed, petrified in fear, only to come to the realization, a few moments later, that most of us will have survived, that we will go on occupying that "there," however altered by destruction. We who will have survived proudly invest the "there" of Oakland not only to honor those who perished but because we care for our brothers and sisters who, like us, could have succumbed. Care for others, those individuals other than oneself, is born—even in Oakland—in that short lapse of time between paralyzing terror and the inkling of one's possible survival. Although I am now going to return to Duras through the lens of Kant's "Analytic of the Sublime," be forewarned, dear reader, that I haven't quite finished with Gertrude Stein—that recalcitrant Oaklander—and the consequences of her imperviousness to spaces otherwise.

As explained in the previous chapter, "spaces otherwise" is how I express in English what Michel Foucault called "*hétérotopies*" or, in deceptively simple terms, "*des espaces autres*" in the eponymous lecture he delivered in Tunisia in 1967. Oddly, this now famous lecture pointedly refrains from a precise definition of heterotopias. Instead, Foucault described how "[t]he space in which we live" not only "draws us out of ourselves" but "claws and gnaws at us," thus sketching a somewhat disconcerting scenario wherein the comforts of hearth and home are delusions, since "spaces otherwise" haunt and eat away at us without our ever having to *be there* (*DE I*, 1573–4; Miskowiec, 4). Heterotopias, then, would be spaces in which there occurs "a sort of simultaneously mythic and real contestation of the space in which we live" (1575; 4). Foucault's descriptions of "external spaces"—of which "spaces otherwise" constitute a subset—reveal an inevitable bleeding of strife into the assumed tranquility of routine existence, a rule wherein normality is necessarily "contaminated" by the *anormal* that begs for examination. Like the relationship between the characters in "Construction Sites," so, apparently, our relationship from home, *from here* to spaces otherwise: we believe that we are separated from them by a salutary cleft but, in fact, spaces otherwise cleave to us. The case of the cemetery—a paradigmatic "space otherwise" and the subject of our next chapter—will further that examination. Here, we begin our exploration of the operation that takes place in us when confronted with a space otherwise.

In his 2006 series of ruminations on places, entitled *Topographies*, philosopher John Sallis wrote that what he calls "the riddle of the sublime" is that "sublime nature both exceeds and yet is exceeded by the human who encounters it and that this double exceeding belongs to the encounter itself" (39). What makes an earthquake an example of "sublime nature," in the sense understood throughout eighteenth-century Europe and picked up again by late twentieth-century thinkers of the sublime, is that the *excess* allowing for survival following the event is not only a question of a certain distance from a terrible space, but excess is also a question of time. The time it takes for the imagination to recover enough reason from the rubble of its ruination to think of that other that I might have been just a moment before constitutes the temporal excess of survival. This is the time during which empathy gestates out of the raw need to reconnect: that other that I might have been could be, in principle, all others. Kant described it first and perhaps better than anyone else: the subject awed out of its mind strives immediately to regain its senses; it does so by moving back outside itself—beside itself, actually—seeking to recognize another just like him.

Kant's Third Critique—the *Critique of Judgement* (1790)[1]—not only throws instructive light on the economy of desire at work in "Construction Sites," it draws the narrative's enigma toward implications for the realm of moral philosophy. The experience of the sublime, according to Kant, occurs before certain spectacles of nature that are perceived as menacing to the perceiver. However, because the subject perceiving realizes more or less quickly that she is situated at a safe distance from the phenomenon, she settles down, experiences a certain pleasure ("pains unfelt produce the pleasing sight," as Lucretius wrote), and begins to draw rational consequences from the initial alarm. Initially seized by terror, the subject realizes that distance will preserve her from any real danger. Reassured, calmed, the mind and the soul "pull themselves together," as it were. They regain peace or, to paraphrase Jean-François Lyotard's close reading of "The Analytic of the Sublime," the imagination exceeds the initial dread, allowing the understanding to get a grip on itself, to take itself in hand and proceed with reason reinforced.[2] Paramount among those thoughts is one of humility and respect with regard to others. The universality of this experience and its federating features would lead Hannah Arendt to speculate that had Kant lived longer he would have elaborated a "critique of political judgment" based on the ethical repercussions from this part of the *Third Critique*.[3]

Unlike the experience of the beautiful which, as Kant writes, concerns "the form of the object," the sublime "is to be found in a formless object [*an einem formlosen Gegenstande zu finden*]," in objects, in other words, by whose "occasion" or encounter "*boundlessness* [*Unbegrenztheit*] is represented, and yet its totality is also present to thought" (§23, 82; Kant's emphasis). Much later in the "Analytic," he returns to this quality of

---

[1] *Kritik der Urteilskraft* in the original German, *Critique of the Power of Judgment* has also been suggested by Paul Guyer and Eric Mathews for as precise a translation of Kant's title as possible (New York: Cambridge University Press, 2000). For the quotes I introduce here, I nevertheless use J. H. Bernard's 1951 translation as the *Critique of Judgement*.
[2] Lyotard, *Lessons on the Analytic of the Sublime*, esp. §7, 159–91.
[3] Cf. Arendt, 1982.

formlessness inherent to whatever precipitates the feeling of the sublime: "But the sublime in nature [...] may be regarded as quite formless or devoid of figure [*als formlos oder ungestalt*], and yet as the object of a pure satisfaction." And he ends this point by adding—enticingly for the ethical extension he wants to lend aesthetic judgment—that the sublime "may display a subjective purposiveness in the given representation" (§30, 121). Since nowhere in Duras's parable is the specific nature of the construction site that fascinates the young woman made altogether explicit and since the word "thing" proliferates in the narrator's account, promiscuously standing in notionally for objects, feelings, events or even realizations of which the construction site is somehow the catalyst, formlessness (not to speak of undecidability) seems to reside at the heart of desire under construction. *Formlösigkeit*—unboundedness or, literally, formlessness—is a key characteristic of the perceptual events that give rise to the experience of the sublime in the *Critique of Judgement*.

The experience of the sublime, in Kant's description, differs further from that of the beautiful in that the latter "is always directly accompanied by a feeling of vital elevation," whereas any pleasure obtained from the sublime comes only *in extremis, indirectly*, and in a *diachronic* process—a process that *takes time*, however long or short that lag time may be. First, the subject has "the feeling of a sudden blockage of the vital forces, immediately followed by an even greater outflow of them" (ibid.). This two-part movement is echoed in the passage of "Construction Sites" where the girl's dismay [*frayeur*] is described as "the most precious extremity of her animal vigor" while the man, for his part, experiences *ravishment* at the sight of this indecipherable spectacle. Generating and facilitating community between the two characters, the construction site enables him to share vicariously in her experience of *shock and awe* and ultimately facilitate her recovery.[4] Fear, Duras appears to be teaching us, breeds empathy, so that although resulting from terror, empathy grows on the fertile grounds of dispelled dismay. With its conflicting contours, the consequence of this economy of reason bolstered by imagination is that the mind in the throes of the sublime is alternately attracted to and repulsed by the object of perception. Kant names the pleasure thus obtained "*negative Lust*" or negative pleasure.

We know how desperately Marguerite Duras sought—even to the point of seducing a Gestapo agent—to free her husband, Robert Antelme, from

[4] Yes, dear reader, "shock and awe," the military doctrine of "rapid dominance," just like the name U.S. armed forces gave the preemptive invasion of Iraq in 2003. Cf. Harlan K. Ullman and James P. Wade, *Shock and Awe: Achieving Rapid Dominance*. Washington, DC: National Defense University, 1996 and Harvey and Volat, 2006.

the Nazi camp archipelago before he died. We know this not only (and not least) because she tells us so in *The War*, or *La Douleur*, but because multiple witnesses, including Antelme himself, corroborate the story. And we also know the wrenching details of his convalescence, under her care, in the apartment in Rue Saint-Benoît, of the scrupulous feeding, of the cleansing of a body that would extrude only black excrement, of her empathic extension beyond herself. What *The War* elides is the couple's sojourn in an Alpine hotel that was temporarily converted, as hundreds of similar places were in the months following the return en masse of survivors, into a sanatorium. In that locale not only far from Paris, but far from the usual seaside or fluvial settings for her narratives, the author, while continuing to care for the man she would divorce so that he would not be legally considered the father of her child, Marguerite Duras conceived of a fable that we go on exploring, here, in light of the Kantian sublime—a parable centered on a no-man's-land that struck dread in the central character.

This is how the father of her child, Dionys Mascolo, remembered the sequence of events at Dachau concentration camp at the end of April 1945 that would clinch Robert Antelme's survival at the eleventh hour and his recovery under Marguerite Duras's self-reportedly meticulous care over the course of the remainder of that bittersweet year:

> I don't know how long I walked aimlessly down the alleys between the barracks, studying the faces, questioning those who could speak. The weather was fine. The most fit were standing or strolled in small groups. All the others—the quasi-totality of the camp population—were lying on the ground, side by side, aligned at a right angle to the barrack walls, along both sides of the alleys, leaving only the middle free. When from the right I hear a voice pronounce my name, I draw near and lean over only to hear—just as I see, right up close, the lips below a look that absorbs my attention forming the word—my name again. I recognized Robert by the gap in his upper incisors. (48; my translation)

This is an excruciatingly vivid recollection of having found a dying Robert Antelme in the camp or, rather, of a failing Antelme beckoning Mascolo to find him. That it was Mascolo who found this needle of a man in that haystack of the dead and dying fails, however, to find corroboration with Marguerite Duras's recounting of the same episode of recognition at the limit of an individual's life in her memoires covering the last months of the war in *La Douleur*:

> François Morland and Rodin were part of a mission organized by Father Riquet. They had gone to Dachau, and that was where they'd found

Robert L. They had gone into the prohibited area of the camp, where the dead and the hopeless cases were kept. And there, one of the latter had distinctly uttered a name: "François." "François," and then his eyes had closed again. It took Rodin and Morland an hour to recognize Robert L. Rodin finally recognized him by his teeth. (51; my translation)

And should the fictional dimension of some of what *La Douleur* conveys to us cast any doubt on its power to contradict Mascolo's rendition of the story of finding Antelme barely alive in Dachau, we have the testimony of François Mitterrand, known at the time by the *nom de guerre* of "Morland." Mitterrand had, by 1945, become a principal player in the resistance network to which Dionys Mascolo and Marguerite Duras belonged. In March of that year, when three disparate movements were forged into a single *Mouvement national des prisonniers de guerre et déportés* or M.N.P.G.D., the future president of France became that coalition's leader. As such, he was assigned by General de Gaulle to accompany General Lewis through the Dachau concentration camp on April 30, 1945, the day after it was liberated from the SS.

Le bureau de poste de la rue Dupin, et autres entretiens presents five conversations between Marguerite Duras and François Mitterrand organized between summer 1985 and spring 1986. The exchange that Mazarine Pingeot, the editor of the volume (and Mitterrand's daughter), chose for the book's title took place in Marguerite Duras's apartment on July 24, 1985. That apartment, located in the Saint-Germain-des-Prés neighborhood at 5, rue Saint Benoît, is a place of legend. But it was in another apartment, near the Sèvres–Babylone intersection, above the post office located on the ground floor of 3, rue Dupin and just around the block from the Hôtel Lutetia, where the *Abwehr* set up its headquarters in 1940, that on June 1, 1944 Robert Antelme and his sister, Marie-Louise, were arrested by the Gestapo.

The exchange between the French president and the woman who by 1985 was an amply famous author begins on the subject of elemental fear or fright—*la peur*. Imperious despite her awe at conversing on equal footing with a world leader, Marguerite Duras quickly orients their discussion to "a friend in common, Robert A..." A massive stroke in 1983 had left Robert Antelme paralyzed and his short-term memory dysfunctional. But he had nevertheless remembered a recent visit from Mitterrand during which his old friend, who had been elected to the presidency in 1981, had evoked older, more durable memories of their struggles together in the Resistance. After some words in honor of Antelme and comments about *La Douleur*, which he had of course read, Mitterrand recalls his mission to Dachau the day after its gates were flung opened by U.S. armed forces: "[...] I find myself there, witnessing the liberation of the camp at Dachau, the executions of SS officers—an insane spectacle—and I make my way into that field inside the camp where the dead and the dying are abandoned." At these words worthy of Dante, Duras spurs Mitterrand on, interjecting "*Une sorte de mouroir,*" using one of those French words only tenuously and inconveniently translatable into English. A *mouroir* is, as dictionaries will tell us, certainly a place where people are left to die. When referring to a concentration camp, as Duras was doing here, a *mouroir* is certainly *not* what dictionaries go on to tell us and what in English used to be called an "old people's home" or, today, with medically correct euphemism, a "palliative" care unit where efforts are deployed to take care of people as they die, or again, but with flowery euphemism, a "twilight home." No—SS camps were spaces where subjects transformed discursively into objects (*Figuren*), thus stripping them of the dignity coming with the term "human," were programmed to die more or less as quickly as possible. Efforts like Duras's to remember crimes perpetrated in such spaces otherwise, however, purposely restore the ethical bivalence inherent to terms like *mouroir* in order to perpetuate the survival of hope. Perhaps an English neologism for *mouroir* is in order: Dachau was, like every other site in the Auschwitz archipelago, a *space of and for death*—a *necrotopia*. Mitterrand continues:

> Yes, a space in which the dead and those who were not quite dead yet were tossed in together... And we traverse this field in order to get from one place to another within the camp and—not particularly here, but everywhere—we step over bodies ... And out of one visibly inert pile of those bodies, a voice arose, calling me by my first name... It was just incredible! It was a happy moment, but only later, not right away: I didn't know who it was ... [...]
> *Duras*: Who were you with, there?
> *Mitterrand*: I must have been with a young man we called Poirier ... and Bugeaud, a communist militant. I leaned down: I didn't know who had pronounced my name. We searched, and when we found it was him, we didn't recognize him...
> *Duras*: Didn't he start calling out again?
> *Mitterrand*: Yes, yes ... If not, we wouldn't have located him. Unrecognizable ... unrecognizable ... I went to see Lewis and told him, 'I've got to get one of the deportees back to Paris tonight.' They were nice, we conferred, we discussed things: how to circumvent the absolute prohibition—typhus was widespread and no one could leave without having been examined by a doctor. I went right back to Paris where I saw Mascolo, Bénet

and Beauchamp. In a print shop, we immediately fabricated false papers (a sort of permit) identical to the ones that had got me into the camp and, with those in hand, Mascolo and Beauchamp got themselves as quickly as possible to Dachau. (19–20; my translation)[5]

Are we thus to conclude that Dionys Mascolo recounted this story in bad faith?—No, certainly no more than Gertrude Stein whose best friend was Bernard Faÿ—director of the Bibliothèque nationale and Gestapo agent—and who was simply absurd about Oakland not having a "there." The gray zone between collaboration and resistance was (and is) vast and dark.[6] Nor was Mascolo any more disingenuous than anyone else in the ethical gray zone pervading that period in history: the Auschwitz survivor who misremembers factual details in the work of memory triumphing over trauma. In a powerful presentation of empirical evidence in support of the claim that the distortion of fact may nevertheless qualify as truthful testimony, psychoanalyst and collaborator in the Holocaust Trauma Project at Yale University, Dori Laub, boldly asserts that "[t]he victim's narrative [...] begin[s] with someone who testifies to an absence, to an event that has not yet come into existence, in spite of the overwhelming and compelling nature of the reality of its occurrence" (57). In the summer of 1945, when Robert Antelme related breathlessly, without pause, to his wife (Duras) and her lover (Mascolo) his experience surviving the Nazi slaughter, the Shoah—what Raoul Hilberg dubbed "the destruction of the European Jews"—had not yet come into existence as the unsurpassable event of that generation. But what *did* exist in 1945 between these three individuals who were so intimately intertwined that they could empathically experience occurrences lived by one or the other among them was a capacity, within each, to become the other without, nevertheless, foregoing her selfhood. Being beside oneself. "[T]he listener to trauma comes to be a participant and a co-owner of the traumatic event: through his very listening, he comes to partially experience trauma in himself" (Felman and Laub: 57).

The psychoanalyst explains how it came to be that he would "co-own" or *share in* survival at Auschwitz, even though he had never been in that space otherwise, that "there":

---

[5] Mitterrand recounts essentially the same story at p. 215 in another conversation, conducted by Jean-Pierre Saez, "In the Company of Robert Antelme: Interviews with George Beauchamp, Marguerite Duras, Dionys Mascolo, François Mitterrand, Edgar Morin, Maurice Nadeau, and Claude Roy" (tr. Jeffrey Haight), 209–24 in *On Robert Antelme's The Human Race: Essays and Commentary*.

[6] "The gray zone" of course derives from the work of Primo Levi and will be examined in Chapter 4.

Figure 5 Dionys Mascolo, Marguerite Duras, Robert Antelme, c. 1943. By kind permission, Jean Mascolo.

A woman in her late sixties was narrating her Auschwitz experience [...]. She was slight, self-effacing, almost talking in whispers, mostly to herself. Her presence was indeed barely noteworthy in spite of the overwhelming magnitude of the catastrophe she was addressing. She tread lightly, leaving hardly a trace.

She was relating her memories as an eyewitness of the Auschwitz uprising; a sudden intensity, passion and color were infused into the narrative. She was fully there. "All of [a] sudden," she said, "we saw four chimneys going up in flames, exploding. The flames shot into the sky, people were running. It was unbelievable." There was a silence in the room, a fixed silence against which the woman's words reverberated loudly [...]. (59)

Maimed as he had been by that very same inexorable SS killing machine, it is quite conceivable to imagine Robert Antelme too having made some similarly fantastic claim to Dionys Mascolo and Marguerite Duras in his reportedly loquacious narration of events in Gandersheim, then in Buchenwald, then in Dachau—the three successive camps into which he was shoved. The experience of survival testimony gatherers thus compels us to imagine the revered author of *The Human Species* making some claim or another reinforcing the veracity of his testimony of the Shoah (that event of events slowly taking historical shape after the fact, as in some *nachträglich* process) but a claim that is nevertheless defective and, therefore, subject to rejection by historians. Dori Laub continues:

Many months later, a conference of historians, psychoanalysts, and artists [...] watched the videotaped testimony of the woman, in an attempt to better understand the era. A lively debate ensued. The testimony was not accurate, historians claimed. The number of chimneys was misrepresented. Historically, only one chimney was blown up, not all four. (59)

Laub then recounts, in some detail, the disagreement that ensued between psychoanalysts such as himself and historians concerned with historical accuracy as the only rampart imaginable against revisionist discrediting. Throughout his justification for retaining this woman's testimony as not only valuable evidence of the Shoah's reality but as invaluable in conveying something to us about sheer survival, Laub repeatedly invokes the figure of the frame—the frame around a space and one's capacity to break out of that frame. By testifying to something that is so unbelievable that it in fact didn't exactly take place as recounted, the woman was nevertheless "bursting out of the very frame of Auschwitz"—a frame which holds as inconceivable, for example, that an uprising of Jews could ever have taken place there when, in fact, one did: the uprising of the "Canadian commando." Laub determines the contention that by her very testimony, the woman *imagines the unimaginable* act of bursting out of the space of Auschwitz: "She was testifying not simply to empirical historical facts, but to the very secret of survival and of resistance to extermination" (62).

If Dionys Mascolo wasn't purposely distorting the truth, then, what is the value of his skewed testimony? If Mascolo melded or conflated his own traumatized recollection of finding Robert Antelme alive with that of, say, François Mitterrand, this tells us volumes about how Mascolo and Duras's love for Antelme led them to seamlessly imagine—through the power of empathy—the unspeakably horrific acts perpetrated in that space literally or metonymically named Auschwitz that Antelme had survived. Just as Mascolo came to believe he'd come to recognize Antelme in among cadavers tossed aside by a facial feature—the gap in his front teeth—so Duras never knew Dachau except through Antelme's vivid testimony—wherever that witness-bearing would take him on the spectrum between truth and distorted fact or, as Goethe put it, between *Dichtung und Wahrheit*. Just as Duras was never in that space otherwise of August 1945 Hiroshima either, she nevertheless crafted some of the most eloquent thought experiments in empathic morality by sheer power of vicarious imagination from which we may draw lessons.

The vagueness of some "thing" or things in general, one's being situated in the midst of "nature"—nature in its rudimentary, generic sense—, finding oneself all of a sudden beside oneself with fear or desire or joy or grief or ravishment, the constitution of one's agreement with another of the same species—a meeting of minds by means of "sentiment"—, all these prominent features of "Construction Sites" substantiate our comparison to terms essential to Kant's "Analytic of the Sublime." While we need to extend the exploration already begun in the first chapter of the stakes underpinning the *Hiroshima* woman's trauma, our study should now let itself be inflected by that endlessly fertile part of Kant's critical project. But we have already rehearsed a few of the key moves in that well known (albeit often misunderstood) text. Let us now consider the "Analytic of the Sublime" through the lens of and read it *into* stark examples from historically attestable experience given recently by Georges Didi-Huberman.

The part that the "experience of the sublime" plays in the development of empathy in consciousness will be illustrated by a number of the essays that Didi-Huberman included in the substantial volumes Éditions de Minuit has published over the course of this decade under the series title, "The Eye of History." Showing how empathy grows out of shared experiences of the sublime may be illustrated by two of these studies in particular: one that examines Samuel Fuller's early film footage shot during the opening of the Flossenbürg concentration camp at Falkenau; the other on photographs taken inside Bram concentration camp by Catalonian inmate Agustí Centelles. These artworks by Fuller and Centelles open passageways into our common ground and Marguerite Duras, once again, provides theoretical impetus to our method for exploring these passageways.

In one of the pieces that she included in *Les Yeux verts* (*Green Eyes*), whose title poetically suggests eyes that are wide open (*les yeux ouverts*),[7] Duras speculates starting with the following question about certain photographs by Édouard Boubat: "If eyes saw the way Boubat's photography sees, could they stand it?" This might mean something like this: If someone were to shut her eyes at an awful sight would she yet be overcome by what she saw behind her eyelids? Duras then begins to explain: "I'm thinking of certain photographs of children. Of children who on suddenly realizing that they're being photographed are torn [*partagés*] between fear, wonder, the fundamental surprise that means 'Why us and not someone else?' or 'us rather than something else'" (*OC III*, 736).

Figure 6 "Lella" by Édouard Boubat, as reproduced in *Les Yeux verts* (*Cahiers du cinéma* 312–13, June 1980).

---

[7] Duras did something similar with *L'Amante anglaise*, the title of a novel of 1967. Literally, "the English lover," but suggesting, by homophony, both "English mint" (*la menthe anglaise*) and "the lover in clay" (*l'amante en glaise*), it is entirely understandable that Barbara Bray left the title untranslated in her 1968 translation of the text.

This is a portrait of Lella made by Boubat in 1948. Duras inserted it strategically, as she did dozens of other photographs, in *Green Eyes*. But instead of positioning it near her text on the photographer, she placed it between texts entitled "The Man Seated in the Corridor" and "Man Makes Do with Fear." In the first of these texts, Duras claims that she wrote the eponymous pornographic tale, published in 1980, while writing the scenario for *Hiroshima*; in the second, Duras gives voice to her extreme doubts about humanity's chances for establishing peace.

"Opening the Camps, Closing Eyes" (*Ouvrir les camps, fermer les yeux*), or perhaps, to convey both of the meanings brought out in what unfolds beneath it, "[...] Closing (One's) Eyes," is the title of the first of the two principal essays making up Georges Didi-Huberman's *Remontages du temps subi*, yet to be officially translated into English as, perhaps, *Going Back Over Time Undergone*.[8] The 56-page meditation turns on dignity and indignation: the dignity of the men in the U.S. 1st Infantry Division, to which Samuel Fuller belonged, making the citizens living in the vicinity of Falkenau treat the bodies of the dead with a modicum of respect; the indignation—those men's indignation, Fuller's indignation at those "respected citizens" having closed their eyes on what was happening right under their noses.

> On the other hand, there was the soldiers' indignation at the Nazis' unworthiness [*indignité*] and, nearly as much, their indignation at the indignity of the neighboring town's population—half of whom denounced each other, while the other half pretended that they knew nothing, even though the camp was only a few short meters from certain of the town's houses and, especially, since the intolerable smell of death reigned throughout the surrounding space. (2010: 36)[9]

Our indignation too, Didi-Huberman no doubt hopes, for even if we haven't seen Emil Weiss's montage of Fuller's footage, the author attempts through the presentation of his meditation to open the eyes of our imagination upon that space where the inconceivable happened.

---

[8] Yet other titles suggest themselves: *Redoing the Montage of Times Suffered*, etc. (2010: 11-67).

[9] In the documentary that a thirty-three-year-old Sam Fuller narrates while strolling through the ruins of Falkenau, he recalls the "stench," which he immediately degrades further to a "stink" of all that rots. Everyone who has been to whatever remains of certain SS camps and taken the time to inspect the perimeter cannot but be struck by this proximity and the criminal heights to which human hypocrisy can rise. These were thoughts that crossed my imagination on one sunny afternoon at Sachsenhausen where houses obviously built before the Shoah not only almost abut the two-meter-high walls, but whose upper stories overlook them.

In those studies where he explores the intricacies of empathy, Georges Didi-Huberman invariably conducts what in French is called *un état des lieux*—he takes stock of a situation. In anticipation of my attempt to demonstrate the wedding of empathy to the experience of the sublime, as described by Immanuel Kant, it is worth dwelling for a moment on this expression—*état des lieux*—and its possibilities for translation specific to the context of Didi-Huberman's studies of documentary work in film by Samuel Fuller and in photography by Agustí Centelles. We cannot but notice that for the French language, the situation taken stock of—*dont on dresse un état des lieux*—is, however metaphorically, a *place*. Although Flossenbürg concentration camp was located in a *place* (*lieu*) called Falkenau, now named Sokolov, in the Czech Republic, and although Bram concentration camp was located in a *place* (*lieu*) still called Bram in the Languedoc region of France, those places *become* for our gaze *today* at Fuller's film and Centelles' photographs perhaps—a gaze amplified by Didi-Huberman's meditations—*spaces* into which our imagination intervenes to come to the rescue of reason shocked by what we see. Under the heading of "the mathematically sublime," Kant tells us that, confronted with a space of inestimable magnitude, imagination stands in for reason: "The measurement of a space is at the same time a description of it, and thus an objective movement in the act of imagination and a progress" (97). This very same substitution of imagination in order for reason to grasp not space, but "the manifold in the unity," Kant goes on to assert in a statement that could only have encouraged Hannah Arendt, "annihilates the condition of time […] and makes *coexistence* intuitable" (97–8). In order for us to achieve an estimation of the empathy Fuller came to have in relation to the fellow humans for whom it was too late by the time the U.S. Army's 1st Infantry Division liberated the Flossenbürg camp, in order for us to begin to fathom the empathy Centelles had to have in relation to his fellow humiliated brothers for most of whom it was not quite yet too late, we spectators—distanced as we are by space and "distanced" by time—must nevertheless, despite all,[10] be able to imagine ourselves *now* in that space *then*. To put it a different way: There is far too much comfort, warmth, and promise of nurturing that we associate with the idea of *place* for *spaces* like Flössenberg or Bram or Dachau or to be elevated to that category. They were, at most, *spaces* even if they were spaces in or spaces at places with place names.

What, specifically, is involved when Georges Didi-Huberman takes stock, when he conducts one of his *état des lieux*? What does he describe, in other

---

[10] *Malgré tout* (after all) is one of the most abiding adverbs in Georges Didi-Huberman's vocabulary.

words, as having taken place *there* (and then) and what does he attempt to achieve *here and now*, in our reading, in our coming to terms with these états des lieux? The full title of the first major essay in *Remontages du temps subi* is "Opening the Camps, Closing (One's) Eyes: Image, History, Readability." There are three increasingly ethical stages in the project expressed in these terms. For the first of these tasks—opening the camps—Didi-Huberman draws explicit inspiration from Primo Levi's very first published testimony. In the part he contributed to *Report on Auschwitz (1945–1946)*, and anticipating the tenor and tone of much of *If This Be a Man* (1947), Primo Levi furnished us with what Didi-Huberman qualifies as "an implacable, objective, concise, documentary *état des lieux*" (2010: 28). Striving to walk in his footsteps in approaching Samuel Fuller's documentary footage made into *Falkenau*, the film by George Stevens and E. R. Kellogg, Didi-Huberman begins by describing as objectively and concisely as possible how the soldiers in the 1st Infantry Division, under their commanding officer, opened the Flössenberg concentration camp in Falkenau. Yet, however "implacable" his description in words, the pathos born in us from our foreknowledge of the nature of the events that took place in that place already orient the initial move of Didi-Huberman's stock-taking toward an ethical horizon. Then, starting with the gesture of closing eye(lids) (*"fermer les yeux"*), thus lending flesh to the promise in the second clause of his title, Didi-Huberman describes—as implacably as possible—the various acts the soldiers engaged or had the townspeople engage *in*, in order to restore a modicum of dignity to the dead who lay everywhere. And at this second of the three operations of Didi-Huberman's *état des lieux* of Falkenau, we might pause to recall for a moment various women with closed or open eyes with whom Marguerite Duras made it her duty to identify—with whom she identified out of a sense of duty, dignity, moral obligation—throughout her work, but with particular fervency in *Green Eyes*, or *Les Yeux verts*. Far from a serendipitously opportunist return to Duras (to whose work this chapter will return, in any case), opening our eyes wide and backing that requirement for vigilance with our minds at attention is the third moment in Didi-Huberman's *état des lieux*. Just as Stevens and Kellogg's film made from Fuller's footage was used to "bear witness" at Nüremberg and thus *open the eyes* of perpetrators upon their crime, so Didi-Huberman calls upon us, now (and here), to do the same. After commenting on Freud's famous dream upon the death of his father, whose core is the almost imperceptible but determinant slippage between *die Augen zudrücken* and *ein Auge zudrücken*, he writes that the historian and, by implication, we the readers, all of us, imaginatively, vicariously if necessary, must "in one and the same stroke, close the eyes of the dead (a particularly ethical gesture on opening a camp) and keep our eyes open upon their death (a particularly necessary act of knowledge and vigilance sixty years later)" (66). (I note, in passing, that it is Didi-Huberman who slips in the possessive *our* eyes.) "At one stroke"—"*dans le même geste*" is Didi-Huberman's expression—if not simultaneously, at least in a sequence with no pause whatsoever, even if the two parts of the gesture be separated by the sixty-odd years since the actual events.

Inviting us, once again, to read images and thereby bring a space of horror from the past into the present horizon of our place as potentially ethical actors is what Georges Didi-Huberman does in Appendix I of the same book. The photographic archive of life at the death-dealing limits of life made by Catalán artist Agustí Centelles (himself a prisoner) in Bram concentration camp provides a lens through which we may see what it is like when "one humiliated gazes at the humiliated." "*Quand l'humilié regarde l'humilié*" is the title of Appendix I. The subject that Didi-Huberman calls "*l'humilié*," and that I have translated as "one humiliated," is "not only man floored [*à terre*], it is man pinned to a ground that is no longer his but that imposed by another man's boot. Humiliation is forced immobility. It makes thought crazy and causes one to go mute. It cuts off all ties. It makes a mortal enemy of one's fellow man. It deals a mortal blow to time itself, since in the depths of humiliation perspectives and projects alike lay in ruins" (198). In sum (for these are all symptoms of the same phenomenon), one who is humiliated is as the subject in the first tetanizing moment of the experience of the sublime, as Kant described it in the "Analytic of the Sublime," except that the threat to life is not at the requisite safe distance, but right *here* in the form of the jackboot on the humiliated man's neck.

If being forced into a state of humiliation is altogether akin to the first phase of the sublime, it is nevertheless complicated by two elements: firstly, the humiliated one's not altogether reciprocal and, thus, somewhat skewed relationship with other humiliated ones who occupy the same space otherwise and, secondly (and perhaps not unrelatedly), the relationship of the archive that the humiliated one who remains, nonetheless, a photographer creates to the readers that we will have been of that archive. Regarding the first element of complexification, while it is true, as Didi-Huberman writes, "that someone humiliated [...] shares [*partage*] with another [...] humiliated one exactly the same experience, the same dereliction" (2010: 200), nevertheless, as Primo Levi reminded us emphatically when commenting on Vercors' *Silence de la mer*, "one is never situated in another's place" by which we must take Primo Levi to mean that we may never substitute ourselves for another no matter how identical to his experience ours may appear. This is the axiom that underpins Levi's relationship to those who died at Auschwitz. And Didi-Huberman also knows very well what the nature of this slight, but absolutely crucial, caveat to equivalence through vicariousness is: It lies in the term—enunciated twice: once as verb conjugated, then again as adjective—that I elided where the ellipses appear above. The term is *to look*, and it points emphatically at the second element of complexification. But before that, in order for us to see it on the page, here is the term restored to Didi-Huberman's sentence: "*L'humilié qui regarde partage avec l'humilié regardé la même expérience, la même dérélicition.*" This look, extended out to his brother in humiliation by the subject of the photographic gesture, makes the fellow into an object—not, of course, an object of the dereliction that they both endure, but of that gesture of objectification that looking and recording the look is however much empathy undergirds those gestures. So that while the humiliated one is, like his humiliated brother, in that state of terrorized awe that Kant said characterizes the first moment of the sublime, he is nevertheless, simultaneously, at that "proper distance"[11] that preludes and allows for the resolution of the crisis phase of the experience. The photographer-humiliated-one is simultaneously both himself and himself-in-the-other.

A conceptual node for understanding this logic of inclusive disjunction in such empathic situations resides in the powerfully bivalent term that we have already had occasion to introduce: *partage*. In general usage, "*partage*" may signify geopolitical partition, for example: the partition of India, of Palestine, of Poland. Yet "*partage*" also means the sharing of objects or the sharing of certain means of expression, of communication, of communion: photographs, memories, files on clouds, or voices. The objectifying-yet-empathic look that the photographer shares with his brother in humiliation to the extent that the latter *returns* the look is, in turn, fundamental for the long look we take. Our look at the archive, our look that joins the succession of looks constituting and preserving an ethical heritage extends the original sharing between torn and humiliated subjects, promising the community Kant envisioned on the basis of aesthetic judgment. The two-stage value that the Bram archive and *Falkenau* bring forth and bear consists of the image at its nascent moment, which is a distance-without-distance between an eyewitness who both is and is not a victim and the image at any subsequent

---

[11] Almost seeming to concatenate the action of the soldiers in the U.S. 1st Infantry with the action of deportee photographer Centelles, it is Didi-Huberman who invokes this "proper distance" when he writes, "When a camp is opened, the issue is how to stand to look and how to extend one's look [*savoir supporter et porter le regard*] [...]. Afterwards, it will be an issue of something altogether different: determining the point of view, finding the proper distance" (2010: 58). In "proper," here, we can read both *topographically appropriate* and *ethically adjusted*.

moment (i.e. the archive) where I read it and enter the ethically challenging economy of that distance-without-distance.

Seeing the site upon which an improved relationship with another as a function of proper distance is tantamount to saying that this is a function of proper proximity. Sounding, once again, much like Kant when he theorized for his "Analytic of the Sublime" what seasoned travelers to the Giza pyramids were prescribing for future visitors[12], Georges Didi-Huberman writes, "[t]oo far, one loses sight [...] too close, one loses sight [...]. In other words, an image is only readable when rendered dialectic [*qu'à être dialectisée*]" (2010, 38). Any dialectic hovers in the vicinity of a common ground. The one that according to Didi-Huberman brings the image to decipherability can be most readily understood if we imagine the binocular vision that enables our perception of depth: as close together as they are on our face, *each* of our two eyes *takes in* the world from an ever-so-slightly different point of view. Our brain then computes the very nearly—but never quite identical—visions to suggest a tri-dimensional image to the brain. The *proximate distance* by which, like two eyes on one face, multiple subjects in certain propitious spaces conspire while preserving their discrete subjectivities is at the core of what Walter Benjamin, in one of the richest and most quoted passages of *Das Passagen-Werk*, termed the 'critical point' of an image. Didi-Huberman's rule for the readability of the image is a restatement of this passage. Benjamin's first move regarding the image's critical point that I shall now isolate goes as follows: "[images] attain to legibility only at a particular time [...] a specific critical point in the movement at their interior." Although Benjamin's primary concern (over and against Heideggerian historicity) is the "historical index" of the image, i.e. its temporality, its *critical point* is here expressed in terms of the *spatial* function of a movement—an inner movement whose best concrete exemplification could very well be that cerebral calculus based upon the product of what each eye sees. Then, a few lines further, Benjamin describes the image itself, fully endowed with its spatial and temporal functions, while holding resolutely present the condition of possibility of our relationship to it—i.e. its visibility: the "image is that wherein what has been comes together in the flash with the now to form a constellation. In other words, image is dialectics at a standstill" (462–3).

With that arrest or suspension of dialectics we return, yet again, to the instant of shock and awe characterizing the onset of the experience of the sublime. It is at that instant, that "flash with the now," that the opportunity for empathy may occur. But while "[h]uman beings have a

---

[12] "[W]e must keep from going very near the Pyramids just as much as we keep from going too far from them, in order to get the full emotional effect from their size" (§26, 90).

unique capacity for insight into the minds and lives of other humans [and w]e can understand what it might be like to *be* them" (Zakaras, 504), proxy experience through empathetic proximity can just as easily cause integral loss of self-awareness and transform ethical remedy into poison. "Achieving proper empathy," like establishing the proper distance *vis-à-vis* the image or the sublime in nature, "is no small feat," another ethicist writes, thus the improper, pseudo-empathetic (and illusory) attempt to be in the place of another (the very definition of proxy), "raw [...] immersion [...] left unconstrained and regulated can be misdirected, even harmful" (Carse, 173, 191).

To untangle all this in a different, yet by now quite familiar way, we might return to explore examples from the work of Marguerite Duras. As we do, we might fruitfully maintain in the nether reaches of our mind the bivalence of *partage*—the cleave between us, the cleave uniting us. We share this space yet we are divided over this space. We share this space *and* we are divided over this space. Divided by the individuation of bodies and being, we nevertheless share, despite all, common ground. Let us consider *Hiroshima mon amour* from yet another possible vector of hermeneutic approach. From an antipodal cultural and existential distance, the Japanese man and the French woman in the film's story—He and She—tacitly recognize the same duty of memory: a duty that consists of never forgetting the premature death and unnatural trauma inflicted by that most aberrant form of power that we name *war*. In *Black Sun*, Julia Kristeva has not hesitated to identify this refusal to forget with what psychoanalysis names melancholia and warned of actual psychic damage that readers may incur from exposure to high doses of Duras's art.[13] Yet the lesson of the Hiroshima lovers also entails conscious, voluntary attenuation of that other trauma meted out by collectivities of all stripe on individuals in their difference. Of this somatic blow, Duras enjoins us through the *Hiroshima* scenario, as through the "Construction Sites" parable (and *pace* Kristeva), to recognize that in order for any survival at all to be possible, it is essential to allow the memory to fade.

Extending and reinforcing the trauma of witnessing the shooting of her German lover before her very eyes is the profoundly humiliating punishment of having her hair shorn by a jubilant lynch mob of "pure" citizens of Nevers. This brief scene, narrated in voice-over in Alain Resnais' film—and foreshadowed thematically by the images of radiated Hiroshima survivors with their hair falling out—is that of an especially ugly, but especially emblematic chastisement carried out pervasively as the Liberation

---

[13] Lisa Walsh puts it succinctly, "Kristeva reads Duras's morbid love affair with the beyond of the real as not only politically useless, but also psychically dangerous," after which Walsh cites *Black Sun*'s lapidary warning: "Duras's books should not be put in the hands of sensitive readers" (Walsh, 151; Kristeva, 227).

of France unfolded. It is a punishment that would also prove crucial in the development of Duras's politics. We know that among the victims of this misogynistic improvised justice, which with a certain temporal distance (a strangely mixed metaphor that we use all the time) has lost most of the legitimacy by which it once benefitted in general opinion, were prostitutes, housewives, rape victims, a few profiteers, some shop girls and others who were seduced by German men, enticed by them, attracted to them. What all these women had in common—a common ground in the meanest sense— was their unmarried status on the basis of which they were or were *perceived* to be freely deciding what to do with their sexed body. In this amalgam were women who, like the girl from Nevers, had actually fallen in love with some German or another. And for a woman to show any sign of being or wanting to be the master of her gendered being was an inexcusable affront to patriarchy, an infraction against an order agreed by both Nazis and Frenchmen under their boot: an infraction calling for retribution through abjection.

Perhaps because he shares, in 1959, the common ground of Hiroshima with the woman from Nevers, but certainly because he possesses that intuitive *intelligence-beyond-reason* that Duras conceptualized and strived to nurture in us through literary example, the man from Hiroshima easily fathoms the therapeutic possibilities of the affective chronological substitution that his French lover makes "under his care." This Hiroshima man, who was at as safe a distance from Hiroshima on August 6, 1945 as she was, steps into the role of psychoanalyst. He speculates, according to the algebra that the film works through before us, that if ever his "patient" is to fully engage and complete the mourning of her lover killed that summer, she needs his empathic support in order to face down her black sun. In terms that teeter on the verge of circular logic, she must remember sufficiently in order to begin to forget sufficiently. The temporal substitution (1945–59) must be supplemented and reinforced by a spatial one (Hiroshima 1959– Nevers 1945) that is predicated upon a third, medial substitution—that of speaking subjects: "When you're in the cellar, am I dead?" (*OC II*, 53). Standing in for the past lover, the lover of the present disgorges a river of words written for him by an author whose art, as one theatre critic put it in 1963, "has been defined as a glorification of silences."[14]

Marguerite Duras agrees: "I think my dialogues are silent. I mean that they take form in the silence surrounding them. They fall silent."[15] But, if so, then how might the gaping contradiction between logorrhea and

---

[14] Claude Damiens, "Marguerite Duras ou le silence au théâtre." *Paris-Théâtre* 198 (September 14, 1963): 38.

[15] Suzanne Lamy and André Roy, eds. *Marguerite Duras à Montréal* (Montréal: Spirale, 1981), 46.

Figure 7 *Femmes tondues* (shorn women), *"les poules à Boches"* ("kraut chicks"), Chatou, 1945. Public domain.

reserve—a dyad dominating "Construction Sites" in the endless ratiocination of the male narrator and the all but mute young woman—participate in the economy of trauma and empathy? Part of the enigma may dissipate if we think of the part that eroticism plays explicitly in *Hiroshima mon amour* and the allusive, implicit, muted manner that ecstasy is suggested in the 1954 story. Intertwined, sweaty bodies spill forth beyond the screen, just as the few breathless words—"*Tu me tues. Tu me fais du bien*" (*OC II*, 22; 25)—feed the vicarious inclination of our imagination. To this famous introit to *Hiroshima mon amour*, we may compare the potential for unbridled pleasure contained in "On leaving the field of reeds, he saw her standing on the other side of the creek, watching him approach her"—those final, almost flat words of the story that come after a lurid allegorical vignette of floral intercourse. Yet, what is simultaneously happening to the man (and, Duras hopes, to us) as he anticipates erotic climax is what also occurs in *Hiroshima mon amour* through the mediation of "tough love." Compare also the "floral harmony [that] caused a violent tide of presence and memory to rise up in every corner of the man's body" to the sharing—both psychic and somatic—of trauma and memory that occurs between the Hiroshima man and the Nevers woman. As in the scene with which "Construction Sites" closes, where the man finally "felt as though he were filled with knowledge," so does the Hiroshima man. As for the Nevers woman, her epistemological leap stemming from the conflation of past and present lovers is the key to her managing to break a melancholic vicious circle in which she had been trapped since 1945. Consider the "Note on the Images of Encounter"—one of those written sketches toward filmic images that Alain Resnais had Marguerite Duras write out before he shot certain scenes for *Hiroshima mon amour*. The encounter in question is that between the French girl and the German soldier near the end of the war. It is a description of ecstasy reminiscent of certain scenes, now fetishized, from premiere surrealist film *Un chien andalou* (1929): "I soon wanted to punish his hands. I bite his hands after making love" (*OC II*, 79; 84).[16] Although the woman from Nevers doesn't recount this information to her Hiroshima lover in 1959, she makes him understand it through their symbiotic psychic and somatic bonding: "His body had become mine: I could no longer distinguish them. I had become the living negation of reason" (*OC II*, 99; 106). Sharing the common ground of bodies may—fleetingly—prove therapeutic.

Since what we have just described will have also happened there, it is perhaps not so odd that we find the same uncertainty of memory, temporal disintegration, opaque characterization that would become the hallmarks of *Hiroshima mon amour* already lending contour and content to our obscure "Construction Sites." As the dialectic of logorrhea and silence, so the dialectic of amnesia and possible anamnesis. The endlessly competing forces persist and, in their immediate vicinity, thought must persevere even if hope of metaphysical resolution evaporates on the horizon. So too, Duras's work reels precariously between the taciturn and the loquacious. This too is a dialogical balancing act in the medium of style that ties memory to forgetting, rememoration to memorial distortion. The same inflections, the same play of influences upon the text of *Hiroshima mon amour* partake of the spoken and the unspeakable, between that which is obvious and that which is only probable, between what history can attest factually and that about which it can "merely" speculate. And if some pre-ethical praxis, some practice of the self that could lay the foundations for vivifying coexistence

[16] Duras's admiration for the work of Georges Bataille is surely one key to this dimension of the scenario and to the mood and themes of other writings in the immediate vicinity such as *Moderato cantabile* and *L'Homme assis dans le couloir*, in the latter of which the level of what some might judge to be abjection becomes quite explicit. The author of *Le Bleu du ciel* is part of the circle of friends that forms occasionally in Marguerite Duras's apartment at number 5, rue Saint-Benoît. In persuading Gallimard to release her exceptionally to publish *Moderato cantabile* at Éditions de Minuit, Duras not only joined—if temporarily—the group that we associate with the nebulous label of New Novel but also came much closer to the universe of Georges Bataille. It is from the little office in rue Bernard-Palissy that since 1950 Bataille directs the journal, *Critique*, which he had founded in 1946 and about which orbit Maurice Blanchot, Louis-René des Forêts, and other figures close to Duras.

can be derived from Duras's poetics, it is in the complex imbrication of silences between construction sites, between what occurred in 1945 Nevers and in 1945 Hiroshima.

In a 1975 interview of Hélène Cixous by Michel Foucault and organized by *Cahiers Renaud-Barrault*, the two idiosyncratically distinct thinkers observed the same dialectic of apocalyptic fiction and speculative moral thinking in the work of Marguerite Duras.[17] With that sudden brilliance in the midst of banalities conveyed in the manner of the dithyramb, Cixous had the following to say about *India Song*, which Foucault had not yet seen: "it's a sort of very black sun [*soleil très noir*], with this woman [Anne-Marie Stretter] at the center, the one who saps all the desires in all [Duras's] books. In text after text there's an engulfing [*ça s'engouffre*], a gulf, an abyss. It's the body of a woman that doesn't know itself, but that knows something there in the dark [*dans le noir*], that knows darkness [*qui sait le noir*], that knows death" (*DE I*, 1633–4; 160). Cixous had launched into this characterization of the Duras algebra, spurred on by Foucault's observation that that "memory purged of all recollection" that we repeatedly, insistently see operating in Duras's stories is a "space outside [*espace de dehors*]" (*DE I*, 1632) reverberating with that "thought of the outside [*pensée du dehors*]" he had observed in Maurice Blanchot's *Le Très-Haut* and discussed in a celebrated essay of 1966. The knowledge that Cixous thus evokes is the very knowledge that the man who communes with the woman over the construction site acquires under her tutelage: it is the knowledge acquired in the recovery of reason following trauma. Inspired by Cixous's meditation on the woman's body "that knows darkness," Foucault's interview with her becomes an exchange of equals, and the interviewer riffs on the absence of reciprocity in Duras—reciprocity having been systematically replaced by circulation (*DE I*, 1636; 162). Duras's plots—to the extent that there are any—function, according to Foucault, like the children's game known as *le furet*—whose closest equivalent in the English-speaking world would be "hide the key" or perhaps "huckle buckle beanstalk"—a game of the ferret, though, in which the object to be found moves of its own accord.[18] "Perpetual irony" reigns, Foucault says, and, taking up an image Cixous hands him, he compares actions in Duras's stories to the "shimmer like the sea" (*DE I*, 1636). Then, as often happens at the culmination of an improvised dialogue, Foucault finds the terms he wants for the fundamental dialectic motivating Duras's: "on the one

---

[17] M. Foucault, "À propos de Marguerite Duras" (*entretien avec* H. Cixous), *Cahiers Renaud-Barrault* 89 (October 1975): 8–22. The passages used here are translated by me from the reprint of the interview as it appeared in *DE I*, 1630–9.

[18] Suzanne Dow opted for circumlocution to translate *jeu de furet*: "a parlour game where you have to guess which hand the ball is in."

hand we never get inside either the characters or what's going on between them. And yet there's always another outside in relation to them [... a] *third outside* with their interference" (1638; 165; my emphasis)—a third outside *produced*, that is, *by* the interference *between* the two others. It is perhaps not coincidental that the "third outside"—*testis* or *terstis*—is the position and very definition of a witness.[19]

This "agreement" with the dynamic of extreme experience and responsibilities that attend survival is perhaps clearest when we realize how very much Michel Foucault's thought and writing are haunted—everywhere, but perhaps most especially at the stage his explorations had reached by the mid-1970s—by the same unspeakable horrors, the same world-historical traumas wrought in the mid-twentieth century that haunt Marguerite Duras's principal female characters. One needs only to recall his myriad descriptions in *Discipline and Punish* of how the delinquent is fabricated by an institutional machinery whose sole purpose it is to transform the misfit into a cog in a wheel that turns with predictability (177–8ff.).[20] Foucault is even more explicit in the preface he wrote to *Q.H.S.*, a sociological study of high security units within prisons by Roger Knobelspiess, published in 1980: "The H.S.U. system reveals, at the level of fact, the division [*partage*] longed for for so long between good and bad criminals, between those to be put right and those to be eliminated" (*DE II*, 827).[21] And, recalling *Discipline and Punish* once again, when Foucault dubs this process "normalization" (and, in doing so, alluding to the very institution—the École normale supérieure—where he received his post-baccalaureate education), he for all intents and purposes is asserting that he shares, albeit on the "privileged" side of the social spectrum, the experience of the delinquent (185–6). So that, while it would seem that, long before Giorgio Agamben's thesis in *Homo sacer*, Foucault might have agreed to go as far as to posit the camp—whether "camp" be meant a place for disciplining people into soldiers or a place for forcing labor out of prisoners—as the inevitable paradigm (Agamben would say "*nomos*") of post-Auschwitz society, in *cleaving to* the experience of those

---

[19] Cf. Jacques Derrida, who wrote that "the witness (*testis*) is someone who is present as a third person (*terstis*)," and Harvey, 2014, *inter alia*.

[20] We may note that actual encounters or common action between Marguerite Duras and Michel Foucault are very few. Didier Eribon mentions that Duras was among the lecturers that the French Embassy sent to Stockholm and that Foucault welcomed while he directed the Maison de France in Uppsala in 1955 (139). Duras and Foucault joined Jean-Paul Sartre and Simone de Beauvoir in calling for a demonstration to protest the extradition of Klaus Croissant to West Germany to face terrorism charges (Eribon, 411–12).

[21] Roger Knobelspiess, *Q.H.S.: quartier de haute sécurité*. Paris: Stock, 1980, 11–16. H.S.U. stands for high security unit.

to be "normalized," Foucault also, and more importantly and in solidarity with fellow inmates, held the camp to be the model-to-be-broken. The segregation stemming from inventions like "the delinquent" was a *selection* replicating the strategy of the nineteenth-century bourgeoisie to divide the underclass between the cooperative and the refractory and which very nearly triumphed in the Nazis' Final Solution with their division-without-division between *Häftlinge* and *kapos*. Foucault, as we shall see in the final chapters of this book, held out hope that the repetition of such efforts could be curtailed by generalized work on the self.

At this conjuncture in extreme moral tension, a return to Marguerite Duras's theoretically foundational text of 1954 via the sublime as Kant culminated the eighteenth century's thinking of it is in order.[22] No less steeped in eighteenth-century Europe's obsession with the theatre and the theatrical than more traveled Enlightenment figures, Immanuel Kant, in his narrative of the experience of the sublime, situates the phenomena of nature perceived by a consciousness at the center of a spectacle. Similarly, "Construction Sites" stages two such "spectacles," if we consider, in addition, how familiar the dramatic variation of the play-within-the-play was to the Enlightenment spectator, not to speak of the special values placed upon the "*en abyme*" structure. In the Duras story, there is, first, the spectacle of the construction site itself, which appears to attract the young woman inexorably as it simultaneously repulses her. This initial spectacle—which is as much an initiatory spectacle—stimulates, consequently, the curiosity of the man who wonders "what spectacle could possibly detain her." Further, there is the spectacle proper to the economy of desire that consists of the girl being stared at by the man: fixed, though not transfixed, by his gaze. The direct result of this borderline obsessive gazing is the pair's ultimate union. The scopophilia at the basis of this encounter (or union) is not, however, quite "perfect," in that we are never altogether sure that the young woman has ever noticed that the man was stalking her. The dovetailing or imbrication of these two spectacles, in any case, produces the pseudo-encounter that "for the man ceased being an event of his mind and tended to become an event of his life. He has ceased seeing it as an exigent spectator demanding perfection, as though such perfection could only be reached through art." And although at the moment where he finally reaches out to her, approaches her overtly by speaking to her while her gaze "still riveted" on [*encore agrandi par*] the vision that

---

[22] Kant's "Analytic of the Sublime" is the apotheosis of an entire century's fascination in England, Germany, and France with the concept of the sublime. Cf. Samuel Monk, *The Sublime*. According to Laure Adler, Dionys Mascolo supposedly reread Kant right after the Liberation. *Marguerite Duras* (1998), Gallimard (Folio), 352. He mentions Kant in passing in *Autour d'un effort de mémoir*, 61.

fascinates her shifts to the man, the *image* which perhaps can never be an event in *her* life, yet will persist in her mind, is *not* that of the man, but that of the construction site.

The ultimate sharing of this experience of trauma with another consciousness—thereby and hence engendering a healing process—must, again, be understood in terms of the Kantian sublime. Rereading the precise chronology of events presented in Duras's story, it is only when the man sees the young woman stupefied, dumbstruck, in a sublime stupor before the construction site—only on that day, emphatically, and not before that the man notices her at all. It is that emotion *in her* and legible *on her body* that causes him to notice her, to take an interest in her, and "little by little" to desire her. What emotion?—The tetanizing shock derived from the perception of a space with inextricable simultaneity for what it is and what it is not. Because *it both is and is not*, for the young woman, the site of a cemetery being expanded, the construction site causes her to experience a torn state: she is, as Brian Rotman has put it, elevating a commonplace to onto-ethical status, "beside herself."[23] As such she is able to reconnect with another, she is able to return to reason. In this respect, the construction site is simply a cemetery being expanded. But to the extent that the construction site remains, nevertheless, a space otherwise—hellish memory or awful prospect: a figment of the imagination, in either case—it shatters reason. To gain knowledge of this ground for ethics, the man wants to learn from the woman: "Every morning, every afternoon, several hours a day, he would go with a book and follow the progress of the construction, always hoping that she would return to the alley, toward her *frayeur*, her dismay." The effort that he imagines her making, the effort he guesses is operating within her, marvels him to such an extent that he himself "abandons himself [...] to the same ravishment, the same reassurance [*au même ravissement, au même rassurement*]."

What do the experiences of ravishment and reassurance share? And where do they depart? What differentiates them? A glib answer would be to say that the extent of their commonalities equals that of the man and the woman in the 1954 story. *Ravishment*—appearing here for the first time in Duras's work under such striking highlight—is an experience to which the author will go on, notably in *Le Ravissement de Lol V. Stein*, to attribute a privileged place. In "Construction Sites," Duras places ravishment and reassurance in such close juxtaposition—*il s'abandonnait un instant au même ravissement, au même rassurement*—not only for the part they play in a rhyme scheme augmented by parallel construction, separated only by a comma, sharing

---

[23] Cf. Rotman, 2008 and Harvey, 2010, 129-30.

the same simple adjective of equality (*'même'*), but because they seem to signify strikingly different—some might think "opposite"—experiences of the emotion. In ravishment and reassurance we have, before us, the two very *moments* or *movements* that together constitute the experience of the sublime according to Kant's "analytic." In Kant's terminology, those conjoined but separate instants are first, the momentary stoppage of vital forces, followed by a greater outflow thereof. Through the very same temporally dyadic experience, the man of Duras's story *feels* (even if he fails to *understand*) the "bliss of seeing something like the vision of an other."[24] Soon, imperceptibly, he will take partial leave himself in a partial integration with her. This is what "being beside oneself" means in its strongest sense; this is what the young woman already knows with that know-how or knack-beyond-reason that Duras so prizes. Yet, at the same time, through his experience of the sublime, as in every experience of the sublime, intrinsic to what the experience of the sublime means, the man at the construction site of desire will manage not to lose himself altogether—least of all *in* the other with whose experience he nevertheless communes. Almost identical on the page and so close when pronounced in French, *ravissement* and *rassurement* could be the most precise names in *any* language for the two antipodal moments in Kant's economy of the sublime: reason, ravished by awe, is ransomed by the imagination, thus regaining its composure and pride of place.

For certain ethicists in whose thinking morally-contoured empathy is the innate resource—albeit partial[25]—for caring and peaceful intersubjectivity, "Construction Sites" would be the literary illustration *par excellence* of such an economy of desire and understanding. When Alisa Carse cautions that "love can obscure accurate perception to be sure," then quickly adds that "it can also engage our focused and apt attention" (179), she is calling attention to the moral contours that must be lent to our naturally empathetic impulse in order for it to move human intercourse to qualitatively improved states. While unleashing my empathetic impulse, I must heed two competing temptations: that of self-absorption and the drive to vicariously possess the other, "each of which is a form of empathetic imagination gone bad" (181). Instead, I must ensure that I maintain reasonable partiality (even impartiality to the point of incuriosity is better than vicarious possession). I may then enter into a state of emotional resonance with another, even if the interdependence tends to be somewhat asymmetrical or skewed. The man

---

[24] I read this "something like" as altogether similar in function to that which Kant attributes to *als ob*: with its ability to suggest mental constructs that are "something like" what we would like to have presented to us in reality, the faculty that we call the imagination lends reason the wherewithal to work at bringing on better worlds.

[25] Cf. Bernard Williams, *Ethics and the Limits of Philosophy*.

in "Construction Sites" achieves this. In his communion with the young woman, he remains himself, the same, but altered, othered. Love, Duras's story illustrates, is an emotional locus—*a fortiori*, a space—where sharing and dissensus coexist naturally. Duras's man will even be said to have conserved his ability to see "those things that he was alone in seeing, that she didn't know he saw and that he saw better than she."

This shared economy of desire, this economy of the sublime in tandem culminates, climaxes, and comes to a conclusion, when the young woman forgets the construction site, forgoing it as if relegating the remanent memory of what had made it so irretrievably distressful to the man's mind to the dustbin of her unknown history. But just how does terror get mastered by sharing it with a fascinated partner who has not been witness to (because never a prisoner in) the camp? A vital question, since this ethical sharing is the condition of possibility for the infinitely banal sharing that we all expect from what is—despite all and after all—simply a love story. "Construction Sites" seems to imply that it is as much the empathic understanding reached by the man of the woman's experience that allays her trauma as it is her own "working through" of it. More importantly, however, and perhaps unique in Duras's parable leading to shared moral common ground is that the man must not understand his understanding. He must remain ignorant of whatever part he might have played in the remedy to her trauma. Once this oblivious translation is accomplished and achieved, she can see the "cure," the "*rassurement*" in his place—with him and for him. They will "see each other again," as the 1954 story demurely suggests.

In a paragraph of "Construction Sites" whose ostensible subject is the "increased desire" to see the young woman that the man experiences, he formulates the hypothesis that "if she hadn't overcome the distress [*trouble*] caused by the sight of things analogous to this construction site, she probably would not have been able to live to their meeting." Now, we have already seen how "Théodora," the early novel Duras left unfinished at her death in 1996, served as matrix from which emerged other works deemed successful enough to publish. "Construction Sites" is one of the earliest published offspring of "Théodora."[26] And, among the "sleepwalkers of despair" (*OC IV*, 1186) that populate "Théodora," the title character evolved more and more explicitly into a Jewish woman in Duras's vision of her. In light of these works that derive from the epic unfinished text, the supposition that the man makes about the young woman seized with horror before the most ordinary of sights might imply that, at least in his view, she is a camp

---

[26] For an in-depth review of the "genealogy" of "Théodora," see the "notice" by Sophie Bogaert, *OC IV*, 1525–9.

survivor, a survivor of the Nazi "concentrationary" universe,[27] and that her apparent terror before the otherwise anodyne construction site might thus be explained, be understood, might become comprehensible. If this were the case, the young woman of "Construction Sites" would be a fictional ancestor of Aurélia Steiner, the young Jewish girl with green eyes with whom an aging Duras identified. The known genealogical link of both "Construction Sites" and the Aurélia Steiner texts to "Théodora" certainly tends to corroborate this supposition.

The nature of the young woman's whole experience—both its origins in her past experience and its working-through, its *Durcharbeit*, under the watchful eye of the desirous man—is what "Construction Sites" refuses to enunciate. The story of the inconclusive evolution of "Théodora," however, authorizes one and only one hypothesis: Whatever the experience was, it was imagined by Duras as so real for a young woman and so enduring in her that it could be sensed and experienced empathetically, through morally modulated vicariousness, by a man who could otherwise have known nothing of that experience. It is thus that, in the literary universe Duras is creating for herself in 1954, a libidinal economy becomes an economy of the sublime. The construction site of the modern world, she so much as says, is also the construction site of desire, making both, somehow, "the least enunciated thing."

The power of empathy to draw subjects to common ground is acute when the subjects are not just thrown down, but held down. Abjected subjects are the object of Samuel Beckett's *Compagnie/Company*. Yet, as Beckett's title itself declares: even in abjection, there is solidarity. "Humiliation," Didi-Huberman contends, "is forced immobility" (2010: 198), yet even in the relationship between two humiliated individuals, a modulated distance respectful of self-sovereignty establishes itself. "When one humiliated considers a fellow humiliated one, *the work of humiliation itself* becomes visible." (It is useful for me to suppose that the author has in mind something closer to the working-*through* of humiliation.)

> The images that Centelles captured at Bram are all marked by a double distance: on the one hand, a sort of *empathy* devoid of pity, since he who looks never looks at the looked-at, who, sharing the same experience, is every bit as pitiable, from a superior position; on the other hand, an act of *observation* that is anything but clinical, since he who looks suffers from the same ill as the looked-at. (2010: 205–6)

---

[27] In 1946, survivor of Neuengamme and Buchenwald camps, David Rousset, published his essay, *L'Univers concentrationnaire*, translated as *A World Apart* in 1951.

In the context of Didi-Huberman's analysis of the dynamics in a community of humiliated ones, it is useful to remember that "he who looks" is a degraded "looking subject" in that, as with most of Samuel Beckett's characters, even "he who looks" has lost his status as subject to have become, rather (although the expression is admittedly awkward), a "looking abject." The gaze of one abject, one trained upon another is, necessarily, empathic.

The double distance Didi-Huberman sees operating when common ground becomes established is no arbitrarily measured gap: it is a double distance both greater and lesser than forms of empathy and observation when these movements of consciousness go bad. If the empathy that Didi-Huberman finds in Centelles' photographic record of Bram and in Samuel Fuller's documentary footage at Falkenau are exemplary to the point of emblematic, it is because these empathic impulses transformed into practices are manifestations of a fellow feeling that eludes the twin traps of self-absorption and possession by means of vicariousness. As for the acts of observation that the two artists perform, they are as far as can be imagined from the massively intrusive power move of the clinical eye. No work has yet shown more comprehension of that distance or better revealed the will of certain hegemonic practices to see it collapsed than that of Michel Foucault. Not only does power corrupt (even a Primo Levi ends up fearing such infection[28]), but—seduction being a function of power—it cruises shamelessly, unstoppably. As in *The Birth of the Clinic*, so in *The History of Sexuality*: "The power which [...] took charge of sexuality set about stroking bodies, caressing them with its eyes, intensifying certain areas, electrifying surfaces, dramatizing ambiguous moments. It wrapped the sexual body in its embrace" (*HS*, 44; tr. slightly modified). Not that gripping the body of another (especially while being gripped by her), seizing someone bodily with both hands (*prendre quelqu'un à bras-le-corps*) is necessarily intrusive or immoral—even handling a dead body can be one of the most moral things we do—but when the power *of* observation becomes power *as* observation, then the greatest, most immoral distance of all is in place: that between a subject and one abjected.

It was with the reduction to nearly naught of any such distance that a young Samuel Fuller and his fellow soldiers, under the orders of Captain Kimball Richmond, had the good townspeople of Falkenau perform immemorial burial rituals with the corpses of all those victims of Nazism. And the distance they were shortening as best they could—improvisationally, by performing and having performed what Fuller filmed—was not only that between the complicitous citizenry and the irretrievably abjected

---

[28] In *The Drowned and the Saved*.

Jews, ones who had been subjected to the ultimate objectification: this was also the distance that they themselves, as liberating soldiers, might also have been tempted hypocritically (another form of self-absorption) to establish between themselves and all those inanimate victims. Working with Fuller's own observations decades later in his 2002 memoirs where he describes, in a manner not unlike that of François Mitterrand speaking to Marguerite Duras in 1983 about Dachau, the soldiers' initially dumb-struck reaction at all the dead among whose remains they had to walk in order to get to the few yet hanging onto life, Marsha Orgeron writes perspicaciously:

> One suspects that despite attempts at dignifying the dead, the point is that the lives lost are ultimately just that. Patriotism and a sense of moral certainty aside, Fuller was not above being realistic about the notion of liberation: "We were liberating them. But there was no way of saving them. Very few would survive. They were only free to die."[29] The clothing, the observing, the burial all seek to restore dignity that is ultimately difficult, if not impossible, to confer. No amount of ceremony, the film seems to argue, can repair the irreparable. However, the film also suggests that this unusually careful ritual was a necessary drama for the survivors as well as for the liberators who intended, at minimum, to make motions towards civilized behavior and to force an apology, of sorts, from those who facilitated, either actively or passively, these conditions. (44–5)

And it is in commenting with reverence on these very scenes from *Falkenau* that Didi-Huberman finds himself using the very same idiomatic verb that Foucault employs when unleashing his scathing critique of the clinical gaze as quintessential power: "Fuller's film shows how men—hardened soldiers—went about opening a camp by opening, in horror, a space and a time for dignity: each corpse was dressed, each one covered with a shroud, each paid tribute to by a handful of earth tossed by the living into the common grave."

This ritual, coincidentally echoing the "Hades" episode of James Joyce's *Ulysses* to which I shall return in the next chapter, "demands that the living treat the dead according to ancient gestures of which the very term sepulture is one: gripping the body with both hands (*prendre le corps à bras-le-corps*)—the *pietà* gesture—clothe it, cover it, doff one's hat before it out of respect, bury it, mark its resting place" (2010, 54; my translation). Born of the same distance *vis-à-vis* a space I can only imagine—incongruously, yet necessarily,

---

[29] Samuel Fuller, *A Third Face: A Tale of Writing, Fighting, and Filmmaking*. New York: Alfred Knopf, 2002, 215.

infinite and infinitesimal at the same time—such rituals are empathic even when empathy comes too late.

But for the young woman at the construction site and the man who observes her, it is not yet too late. Although the story tells us that he managed to see what she might have seen, he does not and presumably will not ever have her experience. Seeing this much, however, with measured and dignified vicariousness, would qualify him as a caring partner for her. Should such empathy, then, be thrown to the reprehensible side of the divide between good and evil? Does it not behoove us to determine if his gaze is morally contoured and, thus, apt for empathy or if his gaze is, to the contrary, cynically clinical? "He all the same took great precautions so that she would not yet notice the surveillance to which he was subjecting her." To *subject* to *surveillance*: these indeed stand out as incriminating words. However, they are followed, in the same breath, by one of those Durassian observations that teeters on the brink of the absurd: "It pleased the man [to think] that she might have repelled the sight of the construction site [with] this [same] calm body that craved food with regularity." Is this expression of the man's distress—an obsession on the brink of madness—enough to inflect *surveillance* toward something more anodyne like "watchful eye" or even "caring vigil"?—quasi-synonyms that are tangential or even convergent with the way Fuller and his fellow soldiers must have taken in the sights at Falkenau. It is, after all, the man's vigilance (rather than a sort of supervision of some being considered inferior), his determined yet unobtrusive scrutiny of the woman's feelings and memories that her sighting of the construction site triggers within her that makes the man, in the end, aware of the process by which she managed, with the very fiber of her body, to master the horror that the cemetery-to-be-filled inspired in her. It is thus that he acquires an empathy that is neither self-absorbed nor identificatory. He learns, in Durassian terms, how to *be* in relationship to the construction site thanks to his "surveillance" and despite the tainted valence of that term today. No sooner has the man marveled, bizarrely, at how a same body that displays voracious hunger could conquer the terror of trauma's remanescence, he "abandons himself [...] to the same ravishment, the same reassurance."

This eye that one may be moved to keep on a fellow human rendered fragile or abjected, this proximity without immersion, proxy without identification, is, as I have strived to suggest, the vigilance that so interested Kant as he toiled to advance the question of aesthetics toward the enigma of ethics. Cleaving closely to another without encroachment or obtrusiveness, with utmost respect for her autonomy, encapsulates the dialectic nature of *partage* and would be the basis for peaceful and egalitarian society. Kant's

Empathy and the Kantian Sublime

Figure 8 Screenshot from Emil Weiss, dir. *Falkenau: The Impossible* (1988).

interest in the sublime was grounded in the sublime's contribution to "a mental disposition which is akin to the moral." The initial stage of that disposition—common to all humans—is an "astonishment that borders upon terror [...] dread and holy awe"—an acutely disruptive phase of the experience that subsides when the survivor's "imagination, regarded as an instrument of reason" helps her to regain "dominion over sensibility" (§29, 109). The imagination's rescue of reason may then lead to the establishment of sound new ethical parameters which are, in turn, ratified by *sensus communis*. But before the harnessing of terror, before the resolution in moral reasoning, Kant suggests that the initiatory experience may not be restricted to the vicissitudes of chance. To achieve "the magnitude of natural things, which is requisite for the idea of the sublime," he writes, as we have had occasion to show before, that in order "to obtain the full emotional effect" from astonishing sites, sites that defy all reason, one must both "keep from going very near [and] keep from going too far from them" (§26, 90).

An intuition of this distance-without-distance was present in the mind of Captain Richmond, 16th Infantry Regiment, U.S. 1st Army, when he improvised the semblance of a respectful inhumation of the Jews murdered at KZ Falkenau. That distance-without-distance was, however, neither that of his men in "I" Company, with a young Samuel Fuller filming, overseeing the ritual, nor that of the surviving prisoners arrayed to watch (and who arose in spontaneous unison the moment the first corpse was laid on a white sheet): Captain Richmond was propelled by moral urgency to teach the lesson of distance-without-distance to the dozen "good townspeople" whom he ordered to seize with over-determined care the bodies with both hands, dress them, prepare them for a "final rest." Suddenly, "right there in the same goddamned place," as Samuel Fuller put it in 1988, narrating the scenes he had filmed in 1945, right there (*à même*) where a mere fraction of the whole goddamned Final Solution had been carried out day in and day out, right under the noses of the good townspeople of Falkenau, those very same liars could finally feel, through the "disquiet of reason before the power of imagination,"[30] what it might have been like to have a boot holding one's neck to the ground (*à meme le sol*). In a trice, short of humanity, *Falkenau* presents *a lesson in humility through inhumation*.

Falkenau demonstrates and, also, *is* Kant's lesson. Commenting on Samuel Fuller's 1945 footage that only reached the public in 1988 through Emil Weiss's documentary, *Falkenau: The Impossible*, massively composed of that footage, augmented by Fuller's narration as he meanders, smoking his cigar, in a trench coat, through the ruins in 1988, Georges Didi-Huberman writes:

> [...] the film was left as is—mute, silent and, in a sense, blind. For over forty years it remained on the director's shelf. For all intents and purposes, unreadable.
>
> Unreadable because [it was] too close. And yet irrefutable as testimony. Of something that is too far off, one loses sight (as when one speaks of the camps in general or of the Shoah as pure paralyzing notion [*pure notion médusante*]). Of something that is too near, one loses sight altogether (the elaboration of a point of view, that is, an elaboration only possible by means of relationality, the work of montage, interpretation). (2010: 38)

All this returns us to the communicational position we have spoken about the least, but which is the most immediately important: the position of the spectator, of the reader, of the listener, of we who take in nature, events, works of art, and imagine other spaces in the here and now. All this returns us also to the prickly problem of identification through vicariousness. For

---

[30] This is how G. Didi-Huberman qualifies the attitudes of Plato and Descartes *vis-à-vis* madness in a section of *Atlas ou le gai savoir inquiet. L'œil de l'histoire 3* entitled "Folies et vérités de l'incommensurable" (2011a: 39).

if, as ethicists warn us, to be tempted by the illusion of absorption into another's being is to foreclose any possibility for life-giving intersubjectivity, what happens when the "other" is there, present, before the potentially moral subject not as a singularity, but as a plurality of individuals—a people? Isaiah Berlin, one of those unjustifiably obscured philosophical figures, contended, on the basis of his principle of value pluralism, that we can achieve a surprisingly high level of understanding of and respect for the values that animate distant cultures through inquiry that is motivated primarily by an empathetic imagination. The identification that I may achieve when imaginatively considering a distant community remains measured yet viable because I must take the plurality of others in, here, from that space over there. One analyst of Berlin's "cosmopolitan ethics"—a sort of ethics of spaces otherwise—has written that "[g]ood politics follow from proper self-understanding, which is itself bound up with the human capacities for empathy and imagination" (Zakaras, 496).

Berlin's thoughts on our capacity to vicariously imagine peoples otherwise and elsewhere help to better understand how Marguerite Duras might have got from vaguely imagining herself as a man who learns to share the historical trauma experienced by an individual woman whom he also desires to saying that she identified with a fictitious Jewish girl with green eyes. In memoirs devoted largely to reflecting on what Robert Antelme's survival taught him, Dionys Mascolo explains one of the most mysterious aspects of his own evolution—an evolutionary step that he shared with Marguerite Duras. Here is how, in oracular tones, the father of Duras's only child tells of how—through the medium of Robert Antelme, Duras's only husband—he and the author of so many construction sites *came to be* both communist and Jewish in their souls. This becoming, as we shall read, had nothing political about it: it was a becoming *elsewise* because *elsewhere*, yet a becoming that went to the being of their beings and a becoming predicated on their mutual love for a survivor who loved them.

> Reason has its own unreason. (Isn't "rationalism" already one of the names for this unreason?) / That's where those who historically contest the unique importance that the Nazi enterprise at its apogee, the Shoah, are wrong. The massacres, hecatombs, genocides that dot human history since Assyrian times are of another order. [...] They all lack Reason, where we are. Chthonic reason of the new modernity; chthonic modernity. / Starting there, from inside [Antelme's] circle, what response, remedy, antidote can be imagined? Imagine is the word—coupled with distrust of all received systems of ideas with their baleful indigence. Intuition alone of the species' unity leads the mind

naturally to the communist idea. And *this idea is not political.* / As we would later learn, the word "communist" belongs as much to Hölderlin as to Marx. It marks what all possible works of thought seek, what they all lack [...]. / It was in a movement analogous in nature—one parallel to the first, with no more voluntary reflection than with the first—that we would find ourselves Judaized. (Mascolo, 65–6)

Like the commitment to becoming Judaized in order to counter negation, the communist idea is not political, where "political" is an adjective placing nouns in relation to *politics*. Both are, however, manifestations of the relentlessly obtuse and anti-authoritarian nature of *the political*. In a section entitled *"Visages en chantier"*—faces under construction or, perhaps better, *under-constructed* faces—a section of *Peoples Exposed, Peoples as Extras*, the fourth volume in his series "The Eye of History," Georges Didi-Huberman suggests that what absolutely differentiates the political from mere politics is the uncompromisingly adversarial thrust of the former. Another photographic body of work upon which the art critic meditates—that of Philippe Bazin—suggests to him "an effort taking place at every instant, a travail without end, a perpetual construction site [*chantier*] of what is human being confronted with the historical conditions of its existence" (2012: 84). This Sisyphean labor is the quintessence of "the political unconditional [*l'intraitable politique*] as resistance of the human aspect and, still more fundamentally, of the human aspect" (2012: 83). Human, all-too-human is the Sisyphean labor of resistance that becomes the exemplar for other existents to follow in order to become human. And we note, in passing, the obvious reference to Robert Antelme's sole, but magisterial, book. This is a resistance, Didi Huberman continues, "against Everything in [the human's] treatment by institutions [*au Tout de son 'traitement' institutionnel*]." Some of the fog hovering over this tortuous formulation may dissipate if we indicate, more simply, that in Jean-François Lyotard's thought and terminology the *intraitable* is to what Didi-Huberman calls *traitement institutionnel* ("bureaucracy" in the broadest sense for Lyotard) what the *inhuman* is to the *human*—a pair joined in a logical relationship that is, moreover, not so dissimilar from that operating between the postmodern and the modern. The *inhuman* is what we were before the acquisition of language, which is tantamount to becoming "human" in the humanist scheme of things, just as "the postmodern" is what the modern, perpetually, will have been. This is as succinctly as I can express these two seemingly intractable Lyotardian dyads.[31] With due justice, Didi-Huberman immediately credits Lyotard for

---

[31] Cf. "Answering the Question: What Is the Postmodern?," Lyotard's essay added to the

Empathy and the Kantian Sublime

naming and describing this fundamental dialectic and crediting Miguel Abensour for having identified it as "an important paradigm in [Lyotard's] critical philosophy" (2012: 83).[32]

This dialectic which may be yet altogether "human," this dialectic, in any case, of an order transcending the mere material, is the dialectic that Marguerite Duras envisioned, albeit confusedly, with the tentativeness of the yet immature writer, that is, in that foundational early story. It is a dialectic generative of an unconditional ethics beyond rules that Duras had learned in tandem with Dionys Mascolo, through their loving proximity to Robert Antelme. It is the only dialectic through which the subject unscathed by the grindstone of history can come to share the experience of survival with the scathed. Expanding on the hypothesis that "in order to be oneself, one must be other" (54), Mascolo tried to explain—in reverse chronology—the process of this dialectic uniting subjects in a passage predicated on sharing that precedes the one we cited earlier by a few pages:

> + + + With the help of a few markers and reminders, I now need to indicate—among those that allowed us to survive—those reasons that may be placed under the sign of shared experience. / (Despite the apparent grammatical equivocality, it must be noted that the "we" used in almost everything that has been said also includes Robert. He receives along with us, simultaneously with us, the message that he conveys, just as our joining his state helps him staunch the desire to leave it. Contagion, seduction is dual, double.) (63)

Describing how multiplicities of us may come together on a common ground imagined elsewhere than where each of us stands is one of the most difficult tasks we assign to language, while *coming together there* is one of the easiest, one of the most natural things of which we are capable.

On the other hand, compromises like befriending an archivist in cahoots with fascists or turning a blind eye to atrocity next door are distant but undeniable results of the incapacity to see any "there" in spaces otherwise. An Oakland, for example, both of reality and of the imagination should be as Delphi in this evocation penned by John Sallis in July 2003,

---

English edition of *The Postmodern Condition* and his "Introduction: About the Human" in *The Inhuman*.

[32] Didi-Huberman's note refers to "De l'intraitable" in Jean-François Lyotard. *L'exercice du différend*. PUF, 2001, 241-60. Following the symposium from which this publication derives, Miguel Abensour and I had a long conversation in 2000, at the Café des Artistes on Avenue Ledru-Rollin, about the importance of *l'intraitable* in Lyotard's œuvre as a whole. I pointed out to him how insistent this attitude is as an object of his research, which he acknowledges in note 1, 258.

as he thought about "ancient memories": "It shone quite apart, as if, being there, it belonged also apart. Finally evening had come, bringing relief from the blistering heat, almost unendurable amidst the fumes from the traffic and the thermal reflections from the surfaces of the streets and buildings" (101).

3

Of Spaces Otherwise

Pas plus que l'océan, pas plus que le désert, pas plus que les glaciers, les murs du cimetière n'assignent de limites à mon existence tout imaginaire.[1]

No more than the ocean, no more than the desert, no more than the glaciers do the cemetery walls assign limits to my altogether imaginary existence.

—Robert Desnos

In Oakland, there is a cemetery whose far end, at the top of the hill, abuts a blind street. Sixty years ago, on Lilac Street, just two doors from a six-foot-tall plank fence delimiting the back of the burial place, lived a boy who

Figure 9 Home of Peace Cemetery, Oakland. Author's personal photograph.

[1] Robert Desnos. "VI. Pamphlet contre la mort" in *La liberté ou l'amour* (1926). Gallimard, "L'imaginaire," 62.

couldn't wait to grow tall and agile enough to scale the barrier and explore what was on the other side. Once that happened, he would occasionally join other neighborhood kids sliding down the hill of sunburned weeds on cardboard in yet unused sections to the south, facing west and the bay. But most often he preferred wandering alone among the headstones and monuments, wondering about the people named Kohn, Jaffe, Markovits, Litven, Schperberg, Katzman, Krakow, Roth and Fass, Silber and Finkel, Glasser and Bookbinder, and about the little lambs with front legs folded in sculpted marble sitting watch here and there. As the boy grew older, this place of imagination and wonder situated right next door to his home led to a thought: How does it happen that others who are so very "other" are, yet, so terribly familiar? And what do we do, what might we do, indeed, what *should* we do with such a realization?

Years later, reading, study, and the vagaries of intellectual affinities led him to the work of Michel Foucault: first *Les Mots et les choses* (*The Order of Things*), then *Surveiller et punir* (*Discipline and Punish*), then there would be the even greater freshness of attending those lectures Foucault delivered with intensity and the occasional burst of laughter at Berkeley while the man who grew up in Oakland struggled through his doctoral studies and as Foucault was working his thought through the volumes of *Histoire de la sexualité* that would eventually, finally, follow *La Volonté de savoir* (*The Will to Knowledge*). A few years later still, four months after Foucault's death in 1984, the student was struck by the deceptively simple title—"Des espaces autres"—of a lecture that Foucault had written in Tunisia and had delivered before the Cercle d'études architecturales on March 14, 1967, but whose publication he had authorized only a month or two before the mortal part gave out.[2] In that posthumously famous lecture, cemeteries are held up as a paradigmatic example of *des espaces autres*. Like other *heterotopias*, cemeteries, Foucault had said to his 1967 audience of students in architecture, are spaces apart from where we customarily live and build our dwellings, but they are spaces that are especially and quite uniquely *otherwise*. For it is not just my being situated *apart* from a cemetery that makes it other: something about these particular *espaces autres*, in whatever historical moment they may be considered, inflects my way of being, thinking, and judging from the way I carry out these functions of life in the spaces where I eat, sleep, play, work, dwell. I am different, in sum, because of the presence, somewhere else, of a cemetery.

Among the various *espaces autres* in Foucault's eponymous lecture, cemeteries have suggested to us a precise English language refinement for

---

[2] See headnote to "Des espaces autres" in *Dits et écrits II*, 1571.

this lay term illustrating heterotopias. While the two extant translations of the lecture reproduce the normal English order of adjective followed by noun resulting simply in "other spaces," both translators seem to have forgotten (or ignored) the fact that *autre* belongs to that handful of French adjectives that may, in some cases, be placed before the noun modified. *Des espaces autres* is one occurrence of such unorthodox syntax. When conventional noun–adjective order is thus broken with these common adjectives, a substantially different meaning is produced. Being *un homme grand* which, at nearly two meters in height, Charles de Gaulle was, has absolutely no bearing on one's becoming *un grand homme*, which Napoléon Bonaparte also achieved despite his diminutive stature. Similarly, the post-positioning of *autres* with respect to *espaces* shifts the value of the adjective from its usual meaning as, simply, "other." The spaces that Foucault discussed in 1967, and which one would learn are early expressions of the institutions regarding power studied in *Discipline and Punish*, are not merely "other" or supplementary or miscellaneous spaces. They are different. *Espaces autres* are so much more than different as well: they are spaces oddly other in that they seem to possess an elusive power to act upon us. So that even if one might be tempted to find satisfaction in the translation "spaces apart," *des espaces autres* are apart in more than one sense of that adverb adopted from the French, *à part*, itself derived from *ad partem* in Latin. Foucault explains that they are spaces topographically separated from the spaces where normatively regulated or legally sanctioned life unfolds.[3] Individuals who dwell in the *espaces autres* that are marginally, precariously inhabitable are segregated from the measured privileges of freedom, much the way Blacks were cordoned off from White society in apartheid South Africa. Usually absent, however, from these aspects of apartness is any sense of or sensibility for the existence of those who eke out a living in spaces apart. Other spaces apart are spaces altogether unpropitious to habitation. As Foucault's example of cemeteries tends to show, *des espaces autres* are elsewhere than where you or I live, yet uncannily and insistently *here*. They are different, apart from us, yet inextricably, uncannily a part of us: part of us is *there*. In sum, they cause us to function everywhere otherwise, to think other circumstances, to come to respect other manners of being. In short, *des espaces autres* should be thought and spoken of as *spaces otherwise*.[4]

[3] In an interview only two years before his death, Foucault gave Paul Rabinow this somewhat vague definition of heterotopias: "those singular spaces to be found in some given social spaces whose functions are different or even opposite of others" (Rabinow, 20).
[4] Otherwise descends from the Old English, *ōthre wīsan*. Otherwise is how *autre* would be translated in such phrases as "*la difficulté est tout autre*" or "*je me sens autre*." One could put it bluntly in French thus: *Un espace autre n'est pas (seulement) un autre espace.*

The subtle differences between the adverbs "apart" and "otherwise" are crucial to refining an understanding of cemeteries as heterotopias into grounds shared in common. In all of its applications save one, "apart" is employed adverbially. The one usage where it acquires adjectival force is when it comes to mean "away from others in action or function; separately, independently, individually" (*OED*, 4a). In this case, "by ellipsis," "apart" is not just aside: it implies no less than the "being, [the] existing" of that which is not here. That which is apart is not here ontologically. This is far too forceful and definitive an apartness for what the construction sites that spaces otherwise are and have the potential to do. "Otherwise," on the other hand, adds to apartness some sense of belonging, some saving grace by which that which is apart is also a part of this, here. This is perhaps why Foucault tends to meld utopia into his definition of heterotopia when, for example, he writes in the 1967 essay with utter irony of Jesuit colonies in Paraguay or when—with no irony whatsoever—he holds up the example of the mirror. In designating the mirror as a "hybrid space" he tries, however, rather too quickly to have us believe that the hybridity of the universally familiar reflecting instrument consists only in its being part heterotopia and part utopia. With due recognition for the vastly complex literature on mirrors, can we not with a certain certainty assert that when we gaze at ourselves in the mirror we know very well that that space, however idealized because of what it includes, is simply *right here*? Right here in our hand and right here in our mind. Even when I consider my reflection in the mirror to be a mere figment of my imagination, am I not domesticating a certain utopia (or dystopia), which is the facial landscape of my self? Am I not, in other words, solipsistically claiming to claim ownership of this image? In reflecting on the reflection, am I not rearranging my mind's furniture, allowing the topia of my gray matter to be inflected by heterotopia, altering it and, thus, making this space *otherwise*?

Just how paradigmatic of spaces otherwise cemeteries are can be gauged by the fact that although Foucault spoke of them as examples to illustrate only the second of his six principles meant to guide "heterotopology," as he called all future thinking about heterotopias,[5] they conform *simultaneously* to all three stages in Foucault's philosophical history of space. While we might agree with him that the relationship of collective consciousness to space evolved (or at least shifted) from the medieval preoccupation with hierarchy that he calls *localization* to the opening (starting with Galileo) of space to its infinite *extensiveness*, then to our present relational thinking of space as

---

[5] 1° (*DE II*, 1575–6); 2° (*DE II*, 1576–7); 3° (*DE II*, 1577–8); 4° (*DE II*, 1578–9); 5° (*DE II*, 1579–80); 6° (*DE II*, 1580).

juxtaposed *sites*,[6] while we might agree with him, in other words, that these three spatial conceptions tend toward mutual exclusivity in their historical succession, they all three operate actively in our conscious relationship to cemeteries. Consequently, when we read through Foucault's "example [of] the curious heterotopia of the cemetery" and his colorfully descriptive list of the "important mutations" this space otherwise underwent in successive periods, we realize the extent to which, if we may assume that our imagination plays a role in our consciousness thereof, a burial ground today is *a synchronic concatenation of those layers*. That "other city" apart from the center meant exclusively for the living, "where each family possesses its dark resting place [*sa noire demeure*]," is, at bottom, still "the charnel house [*le charnier*] where cadavers lost even the last trace of individuality" (*DE II*, 1576–7; Miskowiec, 25).

So paradigmatic of spaces otherwise are cemeteries, in fact, that they also exceed the very theoretical limits that Foucault places around heterotopias in 1967. Foucault writes that "The cemetery is certainly a place unlike ordinary cultural spaces. It is a space that is however connected with all the sites of the citystate or society or village, etc., since each individual, each family has relatives in the cemetery" (*DE II*, 1576; Miskowiec, 25). I may dwell, eat, work, play, have sex *here*, yet part of my being—consciously or unconsciously—maintains an oddly disjunctive tie to that space *over there*, on the other side of a wall or a fence, or even outside the city where Parisians, for example, have been opening cemeteries ever since the Revolution. Gilles Deleuze identified Foucault's discovery of this unorthodox logic at work when he opened words and things up to the stratum of utterances and visibilities. If, as Deleuze puts it, both "the archive [and] the audiovisual [are] disjunctive" (71; 64) then there is also "a continual relinking which takes place over the irrational break or the crack" (72; 65). It is auspicious for our study that Deleuze invokes the relationship between sound and image in Marguerite Duras's film, *La Femme du Gange*, where "the only linking factor is a void that simultaneously acts as a hinge and a crack" (72; 65) to illustrate the odd but insistent operation of inclusive disjunction for which, moreover, *partage* is another name.[7] Similarly, those *spaces otherwise par excellence* that cemeteries are

[6] Foucault's terms are *localisation, étendue*, and *emplacement*, which Miskowiec translated, successively, as "emplacement," "extension," and "site" and Robert Hurley gave as "localization," "extension," and "emplacement." Miskowiec's "emplacement" for *localisation*, when *emplacement* is Foucault's third term, creates an obvious conundrum. His "site," however, for Foucault's *emplacement* is far superior to the use of the all too false-friendly "emplacement."

[7] Deleuze concludes this luminous paragraph by stating that "Foucault is uniquely akin to contemporary film" (72; 65). For a further discussion of inclusive disjunction

play a role in our lives that shatters the distinction between "internal space" and "external space" that Foucault vowed he would maintain in speaking about space today. Earlier still in the lecture, after paying homage to the "immense" work of Gaston Bachelard and some lip service to unnamed phenomenologists, Foucault declared that "these analyses, while fundamental for reflection in our time, primarily concern internal space. I should like to speak now of external space" (23). But is it not precisely because the cemetery—be that cemetery developed in a space of banishment that the banlieue is still to this day meant to be—operates incongruously like one of those inner spaces that Henri Michaux spent a lifetime exploring that it is also the model heterogeneous space as Michel Foucault defined it? Is it not because an uncannily inclusive disjunction ties us to the cemetery that the cemetery is a space that "draws us out of ourselves, [one] in which the erosion of our lives, our time and our history occurs, [a] space that claws and gnaws at us" (*DE I*, 1573–4)? In fact, it is because the effect of the cemetery on human collectivities is homologous to the effect of the mirror on individuals—that other space otherwise—that the private thinking about heterotopia in terms of the otherworldly limits of the city harbors such ethical potential for the whole population that dwells within. As with the mirror, so the cemetery: a reckoning with "me as other." In sum, the cemetery is a quintessential *space without* whose function as a *space within* keeps us beside ourselves.

Sometimes, when one is beside oneself, one manages to become other than oneself *for oneself*.[8] One takes a partial and salutary leave from the ego into a space imagined—a space that one nevertheless never before imagined anyone could ever occupy. Prior to becoming other than oneself for oneself, the space otherwise was beyond the pale of one's mind, foreclosed from consciousness. But when we reconcile ourselves with such spaces, it is because we have come to terms—however tenuous and perhaps even misunderstood, at first—with the gross wrong in those spaces having become the locus reserved for the misery or death of our fellow species members. We wouldn't tolerate it for ourselves: why should we tolerate it where others are concerned? This, for example, is how and when even cemeteries—those spaces "where we bury 'our' dead"—can become construction sites for ethics. If not, how otherwise could Dionys Mascolo's excruciatingly described meditation on the lesson delivered by Robert Antelme's survival be understood?

---

in the work and thought of Gilles Deleuze, see "Disjunctive Synthesis (or Inclusive Disjunction)" in Zourabichvili, 167–71.

[8] Paul Ricœur, *Soi-même comme un autre* and Brian Rotman, *Becoming Beside Oneself*. Cf. *Witnessness*.

Everything he says has a tendency to teach me how he came "to be compelled to be other for oneself" (to take up Maurice Blanchot's formulation in commenting on *The Human Race*). But, at the same time, losing oneself thus to oneself means—and herein lies the confusing revelation that in a sense opens upon a future more frightful than death itself—becoming a sacred thing to oneself. (54)

Notwithstanding the resolute indeterminacy of the story Mascolo's partner and Antelme's former wife published in 1954, what so profoundly disturbs Duras's female character is the sight of a cemetery being extended. To her, this construction site (*chantier*) conjures the image—no doubt a memory—of mass graves—*charniers* or, as Duras called them in "Les Chantiers de M. Arié," *chantiers de la mort*. If all stories effect transformations, then the one effected by "Construction Sites" is that of the status of cemeteries: by the end of the story, they are no longer spaces *of* death, but spaces *between* death and life.

To conceive a story woven of such intricate empathic transference as "Les Chantiers," it would seem, from Mascolo's memoir, that Duras (as he himself) had to have experienced something quite homologous through the mediation of their love for Antelme. Here is Mascolo recounting the hours leading up to, including, and going slightly beyond Antelme's return from Dachau to the apartment in Rue Saint-Benoît that he had been sharing with his wife before his arrest by the Gestapo:

I am still in the rear of the car with Robert. We're sharing the same room. He goes on speaking. I rang Paris to announce our arrival. We get there in the afternoon. The girlfriend who stood watch at the window came downstairs to meet us. She is standing at the second-floor landing when we turn our faces toward her. She sees us, covers her face with her hands, and flees back upstairs. I later find her burrowed in darkness, behind layers of clothes, [...] against the far wall of a recess doubling as wardrobe in the most out-of-the-way room. It will take her a long time to approach him. (59)

What dominates and drives this memory, serving as grounds for the political and moral transformations that will take place in its author and Duras in the coming weeks, is a striking homology among spaces. Occupying spaces otherwise stimulates the imagination to new ethical configurations between humans. In removing herself to a recess in the most remote corner of the apartment, "the girlfriend" (so called coyly because, one supposes, she shares the status with both men, one of whom is writing the text about the other)—"the girlfriend" intuits not only the room that Mascolo had just shared with the Dachau survivor and the back of the car where they huddled but also the barrack bunks that the humiliated ones shared with fellow humiliated ones and the lice. Although infinitely less intense than that experienced by Antelme, the trauma that thrust Duras temporarily into a domestic tomb-like recess would seem to have authorized her to intuit and write about the trauma of actual survivors of terror.

Linguistic inscriptions of experience afford communities of readers the opportunity to imagine two quintessential spaces otherwise in virtual simultaneity. Dachau, April 29, 1945. Berlin, April 29, 1945. A man. A woman. The man:

> Pale dawn. Little by little, the wreckage emerges from the darkness. Muffled steps in the aisle of the first guys off to the shitholes. No more roll call. Not to have to move. That's all we want. Those who don't get up won't get any slop. Too bad. Just to stay lying down, not moving. I stuck my nose outside a little while ago, when I went to piss. I was trembling. I climbed back up and won't move any more. The lice sucked at me for a long time last night, and then quieted down. The daylight lends a terrible color to faces. Slowly, legs become disentangled and the striped ones start moving. Life, exhausted as soon as it wakes up, tries to make an appearance, coming slowly forth, like a wave.
>
> [...]
>
> For the first time since Dachau came into existence, Nazi time has stopped. Some of the barracks are still full of men, and the barbed wire still surrounds them. Bodies, still surrounded by walls, are rotting without their masters. Ripe. Ripe for dying. Ripe for freedom. Ripe, he who's about to kick the bucket. Ripe, he who's going to make it. Ripe for the end.
>
> [...]
>
> We are still waiting. For hours on end. Then soup again, outside. I'm hungry, and I force myself to get down from the platform. New bodies in the gutter. The sky is low and gray. American planes wheel above the camp. Bursts of machine gun fire are approaching.
>
> [...]
>
> The Liberation has passed. (Antelme, 285–7; translation modified)

For the woman, writing out events as they occurred to her and around her in the middle of Berlin proves challenging in a different way. She legends her entry for Friday, April 27, 1945, "the day of the catastrophe, tidal wave, written Saturday morning" (79). By the time, on Saturday, that she gets to what happened on Friday in that space rendered altogether otherwise by relentless bombing, she is strategizing somatic and psychological survival in face of what suddenly appears inevitable: sexual assault. Her catastrophe on that Friday consisted of having been gang-raped by triumphant Russian soldiers. After Saturday, her next opportunity to write comes on May Day 1945, at 3 p.m., when she "look[s] back over Saturday, Sunday, Monday" (61ff.). By then she had found if not a remedy to her predicament, a succedaneum in the form of Anatol, a brutish officer who will "protect" her more or less from the other men by becoming, for a while, her exclusive rapist. Her recollection of Sunday, April 29, 1945 goes thus:

> Now there are holes in my memory. Once again I drank a great deal, can't recall the details. The next thing I remember is Monday morning, the gray light of dawn, a conversation with Anatol that led to a minor misunderstanding. I said to him, "You are a bear." (I know the word well—*medvede'*—which was also the name of a well-known Russian restaurant on Tauenzienstrasse.)
>
> Anatol, however, thought I was getting my words mixed up, so he corrected me, very patiently, the way you'd speak to a child: "No, that's wrong. A *m'edv'ed* is an animal. A brown animal, in the forest. It's big and roars. I am a *chelovek*, a human." (82)[9]

Unlike Robert Antelme, who emphatically reclaimed his status as man against those who would turn selected humans into figures (*Figuren*) and ashes (thus, in circumstances diametrically opposed to Anatol's concept of man)—unlike Antelme, again, who almost immediately had listeners (who are virtual readers) like Dionys Mascolo and Marguerite Duras who, in turn, would be transformed in their humanity by his tale of that space otherwise that was Dachau, the words of the anonymous woman from Berlin fell on deaf ears for an inordinate amount of time. When, finally in 1954, her diary was translated from German into English by James Stern and published by Harcourt, Brace & Company, with a preface by a pseudonymous Kurt W. ("C. W.") Ceram, she became known to only a handful of readers—readers far removed from the Europe still quite *otherwise* in which her "unimaginable" tale *actually* unfolded. Appearing in Great Britain in 1955, it found its way into Dutch, Finnish, and the Scandinavian languages. Then, finally,

---

[9] *Chelovek* was legitimately translated by Philip Boehm as "person," but I have given the equally possible "human," in order to preserve the parallel with Robert Antelme. James Stern, the first translator of *A Woman in Berlin*, translated "*Ich aber bin ein Tschellawek, ein Mensch*" (95) as "human being" (111). The French translator gave "*un homme*," just as *Si questo è un uomo* refers not just to male humans, but to humanity in general.

Figure 10 Berlin, May 1945. Public domain.

in 1959 *Eine Frau in Berlin* was published in Germany to almost univocal indignation and condemnation of the victim. It was translated into French in 2006.[10]

Those spaces otherwise where women are pervasively raped, where peoples are exterminated, where foundlings and stillborn are definitively forgotten are all "great cemeteries under the moon," as Georges Bernanos called the Spanish republic raped by Franco's fascists.[11] Out of sight, out of mind — again, like Spain to the rest of the world in the late 1930s. Pretending that the crimes don't implicate the entirety of the species, we conveniently make them *those* spaces otherwise, not *these* spaces otherwise. They are not *here* for our conscience, we deem them "unimaginable," in other words, as if our imagination weren't capable of grasping them. In categorizing such spaces under the rubric of the unimaginable, we reject or pretend not to

---

[10] Translated as *Une femme à Berlin. Journal 20 avril–22 juin 1945* from the German by Françoise Wuilmart. Paris: Gallimard, 2006. The original title is *Eine Frau in Berlin. Tagebuchaufzeichnungen vom 20. April bis 22. Juni 1945.*

[11] For the conservative Catholic author Georges Bernanos, who published *Les Grands Cimetières sous la lune* in 1938, Spain under the boot of Francisco Franco became a space otherwise that definitively altered his views on his own religion and the causes it supported.

understand Samuel Beckett's injunction: "imagination dead imagine."[12] Or, with some punctuation, a few more words, and ellipsis made explicit: "So, you think imagination has died? Well just imagine, damn it!" If, however, Beckett's stance *vis-à-vis* the imagination's power is still too telegraphic or allusive, perhaps the scorn that Robert Antelme anticipated he'd need with respect to certain readers will be helpful:

> *Unimaginable* is no word causing division or restriction. It's a most convenient word. Walking around with that word as your shield, the word of the void, your step steadies, becomes resolute, your conscience pulls itself together. (289–90)

No division among our good compatriots, as he says with biting sarcasm, no restriction on the free use of the word "unimaginable," in other words, because everyone across all differences—political, national, cultural—can agree on the comforting convenience in deeming certain truths definitively inconvenient: they're just too upsetting to allow one's good conscience to consider their possibility; better to relegate them to the oblivion of the "unimaginable." With the "unimaginable" as one's default position whenever the cemetery gets too close to home, one will never acquire the experience of being beside oneself: an experience wherein the imagination may form reason as a function of spaces otherwise, in order that one's conscience be equipped to love, nurture, and protect one's fellows *in this space right here.*

Just as Marta Hillers dared, long before it was even marginally acceptable to do so, to speak—albeit anonymously—of the horrors suffered by German women in 1945, so—as late as 1999—did W. G. Sebald manage to unsettle many a good conscience with the publication of *Luftkrieg und Literatur,* or *On the Natural History of Destruction.* However, unlike Raul Hilberg's scholarly landmark of 1961, *The Destruction of the European Jews,* the space otherwise in both Hillers and Sebald's books is restricted to Germany proper: in these meditative testimonials, it is not the mass death pits of Europe-wide Auschwitz archipelago but the burial ground that Berlin had become at the end of the disaster. By asserting that German cities were too the loci of disaster, Hillers and Sebald dare to extend the Shoah to non-Jews. In this, *Eine Frau in Berlin* and *Luftkrieg und Literatur* are akin to the lamentably least known installment in Roberto Rossellini's Second World War trilogy. Filmed on location in Berlin by Robert Juillard in August and September 1947, *Germania anno zero* (1948) endeavors to show us not only a story of tenuous survival but also, especially, to show us the German city

---

[12] This is the title of a short prose piece that Beckett originally published as *Imagination morte imaginez* in 1965. For one discussion of its import, cf. Harvey 2010, 118–19ff.

as space otherwise. Although by summer 1947 the rebuilding of portions of Berlin was well underway, vast swathes of it were still ravaged by the massive bombing two full years after the battle that flattened the city. For all of the outdoor shots that the final installment of his war trilogy contains, Rossellini directed Juillard to train his camera exclusively on those particular streets of the defeated capital in order to convey the vision of total destruction one would have had had one been there in, for example, April 1945. It is the film's images that evoke Berlin as a vast cemetery, not the most salient part of the title. Those two words, "*anno zero*," year zero, unabashedly echo *die Stunde Null*, or zero hour, May 8, 1945—the day the capitulation of Nazi high command came into effect and after which all was meant to be altogether other than it had been for the previous thirteen years. As we know and Rossellini no doubt suspected, the *Stunde Nulle* policy set out by Germany's post-war provisional government allowed for remnants of Nazism to prosper under the fiction that the clocks had all been erased. Be that as it may, in what does the product of "*Germania*" and "*anno zero*" result? —Although the title that Rossellini lent his film contains a temporal unit modified by the integer that stands for nullity, it is the substantial emptiness of a site in "Germania," the relegation of a center of civilization to the state of zone—the "zoned out" state from which it was to begin again—that Rossellini tries to convey visually. Taken together, the Ground Zero of Berlin at zero hour signifies the spontaneous amnesia not only about its nullifying consequences, but about the conditions that had led to the Nazi era under which most Germans had, by 1947, well into *Nachkriegszeit* (post-war era), consented to pretend to exist. *Stunde Null* was not only a fresh start but also a capacious opportunity to forget or try to forget—to pretend to forget until one believed that much of what had happened simply hadn't.

In this respect, another place that shares key temporal features of the *Stunde Null* phase of post-war Germany is Ground Zero in Manhattan and the long episode of consensual oblivion which the act of lending that name to an area of utter devastation in the capital of Capital memorializes. That name—Ground Zero—took semantic form spontaneously from the collective mind of an obviously wounded people in the hours immediately following the collapse of the Twin Towers at the World Trade Center. Far from a neologism, however, the expression had preexisted 9/11 but simply vanished for some sixty years from popular memory. We had forgotten that we had already heard this handy bit of war technocrat jargon before. In early August 1945, when atomic bombs obliterated Hiroshima and Nagasaki, newspaper and radio reports everywhere explained that Ground Zero was the name atomic engineers used to designate the epicenter above which the massive explosions took place. Thus, in September 2001, when we suddenly restored "Ground Zero" to the common usage to which we put it today, we were performing a spectacular linguistic exercise in associative memory whose ethical and political significance is yet, however, to be fathomed. We have not yet wrenched from repression the understanding—of which the naming of Ground Zero is the seed—that a crime of similarly immense proportions was indeed committed in late summer 1945 at the site of two Japanese cities with a weapon we wrought. Were that realization to some day occur, it would constitute a singular moment of redemptive justice—at least at the epistemological level. However, the moment of anamnesis with respect to this name, Ground Zero, still eludes the U.S. population. Ground Zero, in other words,—"our" Ground Zero—has yet to become a space otherwise in the best sense of the term. The commemorative display of awful U.S. loss that today, at the foot of the Freedom Tower, greets millions of visitors has yet to become a construction site for common ground among all humans inhabiting the earth.

All three of the Grounds Zero known to human history thus far—Hiroshima, Nagasaki, Manhattan—are loci of obliteration. But as the forensic mind imaginatively moves itself out in any direction from the zero point, parts of victims' bodies begin to be found. A few dozen further yards out, the bodies, however ravaged and every bit as lifeless, become more and more whole, more and more intact. Such images—however "unimaginable" we may hypocritically deem them—must nevertheless be sustained by the imagination: How otherwise might we some day rise above our barbarity? We have no technologically mediated images of the annihilative detail of Grounds Zero *at the moments* of their occurrence and *within* their death-dealing space: only photographs and films of the individual, yet unnamed, victims made in the aftermath, as the great cemeteries are constructed and fill up. In contrast, images of details in the Nazis' lamentably successful attempt to eliminate European Jews are perhaps so much more vivid to us because exemplars of them exist both during and after the carrying out of the "Final Solution." The Shoah has afforded us a glimpse at some aspects of our relationship to cemeteries that Grounds Zero either conveniently do not or inadvertently—because of their utterly instantaneous nature—cannot. We might begin to understand the consequence of this persistent exception by observing that what Grounds Zero and genocides have in common is the *kind* of cemetery they produce: mass graves or, as French so tellingly designates them, *des fosses communes*. But even the small potter's field at the foot of the Mur des Fédérés in the southeast corner of Père Lachaise Cemetery containing the bodies of 147 Parisians does nothing to remind today's citizens of the atrocities carried out by the bourgeoisie to put an end to La Commune. And whereas the conjoined gestures of naming, recognizing, and memorializing occasionally draw the potter's field of Lower Manhattan toward what we do and have done with the *fosse commune* of the Auschwitz archipelago, so far no one with the Twin Towers hecatomb in mind has joined the Japanese in that burial ritual with regard to Hiroshima.

The difference between the commemoration of lost lives of individuals placed by the force of circumstance in undifferentiated spaces and the tradition of placing stones at the head of individual grave pits in cemeteries brings to the fore the question of the cemetery's structure and function today—the subject of Foucault's demonstration under the second principle "of spaces otherwise." To approach this question, we might consider for a moment what would become the premiere heterotopia for Foucault in most of his work subsequent to the 1967 lecture: not the cemetery, but the prison. While conventional wisdom might juxtapose the cemetery and the prison as two spaces that operate as functions of freedom—where prisons are designed for denying it and cemeteries "set free"—, according to Foucault, cemeteries today deny something that the potter's fields of medieval times did not: the freedom to be forgotten. When Foucault amplifies his sarcasm, speaking of each individual having "a right to his own little box for his own little personal decay," he is mocking the will to be remembered by a marked grave in a memorial park (*DE II*, 1577; 25 trans. modified). But Foucault only considers the absurdity of this practice from the point of view of the about-to-be-dead. What of the living, what of the survivors? Certainly the will to be remembered—even though one should know that decomposition commences, sometimes, even before the ability to will vanishes—is the absurd message the cemetery telegraphs, but the impulse in the living to memorialize the dead and honor them by disposing of their remains in a dignified manner is the equally powerful (and rational) correlate. What are the possible drives for that impulse, our impulse to honor the dead? Certainly what we might call, without irony, "the life of a cemetery" consists in more than the mere selfish "last wish" to rot separately from others and have my name inscribed on the place of decomposition. And beyond honoring that wish do we, the survivors, maintain gravesites merely out of guilt for what we denied the dead while they were alive and the will to offer woefully ineffectual compensation? Should cemeteries not also ensure that generations of the living continue to let other living beings live in peace during their lifetime? Do they not, to some extent, reassure us that we have treated well those who lay there, that we cared for them as best we could while they lived? Extrapolating, might cemeteries not also be spaces otherwise that brandish our pledge against barbarism? Assuming that we sometimes strive toward a *heterochrony* when they need no longer function as mnemonic devices, could cemeteries be our best declaration available today that we are no longer the barbarians that we so recently were? One of the most daring and powerful thinkers of the relationship of the living to the dead, Samuel Beckett, illustrated in the finale of his 1964 film, *Film*, the drama of becoming beside oneself that our experience of the cemetery may bring on. But before we look at *Film*, let us continue to consider the function of cemeteries today by taking such an extreme example of a burial place that it can hardly be considered such, yet is.

As is well known (but worth repeating), in attempting to destroy European "Jewry" the Third Reich strove with equal vehemence to erase all memory of its victims. Yet two images of the few that exist will suffice to show that the impulse to make cemeteries and thereby memorialize individual deaths for the living persisted even within the Shoah. I write "within the Shoah" as if it were a space alone. Indeed, the Shoah was a space (the Auschwitz archipelago), but it was also an epoch (starting from any of various starting points in the late 1930s to April 1945 and, then, beyond, in its remanence). The Shoah is also (as it should be) a space and a time here and now, both pragmatically (with all of its heinous reprises) and prophylactically (in trust that critical thought on remembrance of horror can curtail its recrudescence). One of the two images we are about to read actually comes to us from *within* the space-time named Shoah; the other comes to us *within and without* and from two distinct times: the first being the image of the immediate aftermath of slaughter: the second as commentary on the first, decades later. This commentary demonstrates our continuing need for the cemetery as bulwark against barbarism and, thus, the perpetuity—for now— of that space otherwise named Auschwitz.

We have already had occasion to present the first image, which is cinematographic. *Falkenau* is a meta-documentary film made by Emil Weiss on the basis of the documentary footage that Samuel Fuller shot in 1945. That footage features "the leading VIPs" of the town treating the Shoah cadavers with a semblance of the rudiments of a kind of ritual respect that we associate with cemetery burial: dressing them in the clothing of "civilization," laying them out regularly on "white bedsheets and tablecloths," folding their arms, placing them carefully on transport vehicles, carting them off to their "final resting place."[13] Far from carrying out these ritualistic acts of their own volition, the "VIPs" do so at the behest of Fuller's commanding officer. What might be the most striking component of *Falkenau*'s presentation of the image is not the young soldier Fuller's amateur footage but old

---

[13] "The leading VIPs" and the "white sheets and tablecloths" are Samuel Fuller's expressions as he narrates the archival footage; the others are my scare-quotes.

Fuller's narration. It is, in other words, the crusty cigar-laced voice of the hard-scrabble Worcester-Massachusetts-born son of Jewish immigrants that delivers a telegraphic tale of war as "organized insanity" as he strolls through "the same goddamned place" where he and his fellow troops supervised the no doubt silent ritual carried out under the watchful eye of camp survivors positioned on a rise. Irresistibly compelling are old Fuller's simple words as in trench coat among the ruins he gestures, cigar in hand, "You see houses all around." Fuller brings us with him as he recalls "the stench of death" that they experienced—a qualifier that he quickly adjusts, amplifying the olfactory memory into "it was more than a stench: it was a *stink*"—an augmentation that impels us to join the outrage of the commanding officer who "blew his top when [the VIPs] said, 'I didn't smell anything'" while reminding us that an image can stimulate our sense of the smell of a place, of an event, of death-dealing forces. "Normally," Fuller continues, "we would have shot every sonovabitch responsible for it." Instead, in tense quasi-silence, they did something marginally more "human": they directed them to perform the rudimentary burial ritual already described, restoring a modicum of dignity to those they had killed out of pure indifference.[14]

As to the first image, the one that comes to us altogether from *within* the Shoah, it is not a filmic, but a photographic image made furtively, at the limit of possibility. It is the most famous among "four pieces of [photographic] film [*pellicule*] snatched from hell," as Georges Didi-Huberman entitled his first chapter of a 2003 book—*Images in Spite of All*—that considers at length their provenance, the techniques likely deployed to make them as well as, of course, their significance and impact. How and under what circumstances this picture (and its three far lesser known companion pieces) was probably taken may be deduced from Didi-Huberman's restoration of the original framing. In most of its reproductions—as, for instance, the one that appears in Filip Müller's recollections published in 1979[15]—the cliché is cropped in order to orient the viewer exclusively on the *Sonderkommando* activities seen clearly being carried out at a fair (and tenuously safe) distance from the photographer.

And indeed, the laborious flopping of an endless cargo of cadavers into the smoke-shrouded pit is meant to be our focus, as it was that of the anonymous photographer. But without restoring all of the visual information he captured

---

[14] Dressing the naked corpses lends a dignity that Giorgio Agamben views as nearly completely foreclosed in contemporary social and political life. Cf. *Homo sacer: Sovereign Power and Bare Life* and Chapter 6 of the present work.

[15] Filip Müller, *Eyewitness Auschwitz* (1979). Müller (1922–2013) was a Slovak Jew who had been assigned to the *Sonderkommando* and escaped five successive liquidations. He is a prominent witness in Claude Lanzmann's epic film *Shoah* (1985).

Of Spaces Otherwise

Figure 11 Cropped detail of Fig. 12. As reproduced in *Auschwitz: A History in Photographs*, 174.

at that instant, we have nothing with which to extrapolate the thoughts and feelings that he might have had about what he was capturing photographically nor even the fact that he too was a member of the *Sonderkommando* who had daringly stayed back a few extra seconds to surreptitiously snap his shot of the horror.

But before speculating about what the photographer tells us, allusively, about cemeteries and our will to memorialize, let us consider what Didi-Huberman deduces with excruciating detail about the moment that this complex photographic statement was made:

> [...] in order to remove the camera from the bucket [enabling it to be snuck inside the Shoah], adjust the viewfinder, bring it close to his face,

Figure 12 Anonymous (Member of the *Sonderkommando* of Auschwitz). Cremation of gassed bodies in the open-air incineration pits in front of the gas chamber of crematorium V, August 1944. Oswiecim, Auschwitz-Birkenau State Museum (negative no. 2780).

and take a first sequence of images [—actually just two: the second of which is the "famous" one—], the photographer had to hide in the gas chamber, itself barely emptied—perhaps incompletely—of victims. He steps back into the dark space. The slant and the darkness in which he stands protect him. Emboldened, he changes direction and advances: the second view is a little more frontal and slightly closer. So it is more hazardous. But also, paradoxically, it is more posed: it is sharper. It is as though fear had disappeared for an instant in the face of necessity,

> the business of snatching an image. And we see the everyday work of the other members of the squad [i.e. the *Sonderkommando*], which is that of *snatching the last human semblance from the cadavers*, still sprawled on the ground. The gestures of the living tell the weight of the bodies and the task of making immediate decisions. Pulling, dragging, throwing. The smoke, behind, comes from the incineration pits: bodies askew, 1.5 meters deep, the crackling of fat, *odors*, shriveling of human matter. [...] Behind is the birch-tree copse. (11–15; my emphasis)[16]

Restoring the frame of the gas chamber door restores not only an indicator of the tenuous safety of the photographer's position: it suggests what he is saying about the quality of the work he and his fellow *Sonderkommando* members are being forced to perform. This immensely brave witness and documentarian not only cowers so that he might sneak his document out of hell, the frame of the chamber door reminds us of what prevents him from doing what any human should—under conditions of freedom—in face of inhumanity, viz. guarantee some ultimate "human semblance" out of respect for the dead by inhuming the human with humanity, with some remnant of formality, and thereby conserving at least a name that dignifies membership in the species. Out of the drenching *stink* that the extermination camp is, the anonymous photographer at Auschwitz-Birkenau tells us that until such atrocities have altogether disappeared from the history we make, we still need the cemetery—not so that "everyone [have] a right to his own [...] little personal decay," but so that *we* can say that we let that individual die in peace.

Thus, we have two images—one cinematic, one photographic, both pointing toward the procedures that create cemeteries as bulwarks against barbarism. We *have* them and we also, more importantly still, must *receive* them. We should, that is, be spectators or, more emphatically, be the intended readers of these images. We are those meant to receive them and do something based on an interpretive reception of them. If cemeteries are particularly interesting among spaces otherwise, it is because they elicit and catalyze other wisdom. What I am here calling "other wisdom" is a product of intelligence not easily (or not at all) obtainable in the spaces where we conduct our daily lives. This intelligence, however, comes not when we are at the cemetery, conducting a burial, placing stones on headstones, but when we are elsewhere, thinking back on the space otherwise. This is the other intelligence that Marguerite Duras repeatedly strove to zero in on by producing a persistent parade of literary and filmic approximations of

---

[16] One cannot help being stupefied by the bucolic resonance of *Birkenau*, meaning a birch grove, with that name now inextricably coupled with—sharing space with—Auschwitz.

them. Only when we imagine, as part of an act of memory, that place where we memorialize the dead (that place where we too will be when we are no longer) do we experience ourselves as other.

Gilles Deleuze's illustration—via Samuel Beckett's 1965 *Film*—of the three basic types of movement-images may help elucidate how our interaction with extreme spaces otherwise enhance and promote shared experience among the living. For Deleuze, the three successive locations constituting the 18-minute work directed by Alan Schneider, supervised by Beckett, shot in summer 1964 in New York's old Peck Slip neighborhood are "the action-image, which groups the street and the staircase; the perception-image, for the room; finally the affection-image for the hidden room and the dozing of the character in the rocking chair" (227).[17] Deleuze goes on to provide what is perhaps the most instructive reading we have of Beckett's scenario and film. The end of the film, however, suggests to Deleuze "death, immobility, black." These are notes that deviate from the precise algebra that Beckett and Schneider set up for *Film* and draw to a quite different conclusion. As I have demonstrated in detail elsewhere,[18] Deleuze goes astray in failing to sufficiently recognize that *Film* is an allegory of perception and *not* a philosophical tale spun from an actual or even an imagined life. If after the final cut to black we see Keaton's eye opening and closing, opening and closing, in an extreme close-up as we had at the film's prologue, it is because what has just occurred at the end of the "story" is the *integration* of the subject perceived with the invasively perceiving subject, who turns out—literally—to be one in the same. The allegory of ontological reconciliation conveyed to the viewer by the dance of shot-reverse-shot and direct looks at the camera at the conclusion occurs on the periphery of the minimal existence acted by Buster Keaton. Just as that existence maintains in life at the end of film, so cemeteries are not merely boneyards bereft of life: they are liminal spaces where the living and the dead are contiguous, where the living think through life by remembering death that awaits us all. In this light, can it only be because, as Michel Foucault argued, that in modern times we have associated the dead with contagious disease, all the while desiring to preserve our individuality unto death, that we have relegated cemeteries to the periphery of our cities? Given the persistent draw cemeteries exercise on the living, are those peripheries where we situate cemeteries not, more precisely, *middle grounds* between the city and what the city's condescendingly cosmopolitan denizens consider the degraded form of existence of those who inhabit

---

[17] All references are to the English edition of Deleuze's *Cinema I*.
[18] "Droit de regard droit. *Film* de Samuel Beckett au regard de *Tu m'*." *Étant donné Marcel Duchamp* 4 (2003): 84–93.

spaces far beyond the city's limits? A glance at a map readily reveals that in the case of Paris, which we will examine in detail in the next chapter, though "extra-mural," the ever-larger cemeteries concomitant with the dawn of the industrial era were opened as close to the city's last fortified wall as possible. Today they all remain in that belt immediately outside the city that is still (as the image of a belt might suggest) sometimes referred to as *la Zone*. In the case of Paris, then, the sites reserved for cemeteries were not far enough out of sight as to be out of mind. Rather, they were (and perhaps still are) liminal spaces, interstitial zones between life and death, no-man's-lands that the population positively maintained in its imagination.

In his first novel, *Voyage au bout de la nuit* (*Journey to the End of the Night*), a couple of paragraphs before he gives one of the rare literary descriptions of that liminal space around Paris, Louis-Ferdinand Céline,[19] through the voice of his alter ego, Bardamu, observes the following about himself and his contemporaries through the image of a unending cortège of Maccabees carted off to Saint-Ouen Cemetery: "Endless waves of useless beings keep rising from deep down in the ages to die in front of our noses, and yet here we stay, hoping for something … We're not even capable of thinking death through" (*Romans I*, 332; [287]). Obviously we must read Céline today through the cautionary lens of his rabid racism that was only to be fully revealed once France was occupied by Nazi Germany. But obviously also Céline is already jaded by humanity when he writes this and, thus, Bardamu's reflection is one of hopelessness. Obviously, yet again, the rejects of the urban center who work their way out to the periphery only to die are already deemed "useless beings" whose brief and absurd existence makes a mockery of hope. Nevertheless, Céline delivers in telegraphically simple language a profound lesson about the practical philosophy of which the very spaces we create and maintain for the dead may be the catalyst. Section 278 of Nietzsche's *Gaya Scienza*, entitled (after Goethe) *Der Gedanke an den Tod*—or *penser la mort*, as his French paragons would translate it—has served as crucible for much of that which is worth preserving out of twentieth-century philosophy or thinking.[20] Thinking death is not only (and certainly not primarily) a reflection on my own horizon, but an ongoing ascesis on the interdictions, interpenetrations, and responsibilities involved in my relationship to the equally thinking beings that surround me everywhere. It is a practice of conscious life exercised at the extreme limit of my responsibility for the peace and safety of another. Not only that, but as

---

[19] Known the world over simply as Céline, the author was born Louis Ferdinand Destouches and it was by that family name that he served in the French army during the First World War (cf. *Carnet du Cuirassier Destouches*, 1913) and practiced medicine.

[20] Heidegger, Adorno, Foucault, Lyotard …

Céline through *Journey*'s main character Bardamu implies, if we are to have any chance at all of thinking death and affording hope a true grounding, this limit experience will occur in relation to a space at the limit.

The cemetery at the edge of which psychic and cognitive energies were kindled, then intensified in "Construction Sites" is just such a space at the limit: not a void, as it may have at first appeared to the man, but a space that is, as Deleuze wrote, "simultaneously [...] a hinge and a crack" (72; 65). Its locale in the world of Marguerite Duras's actuality was Saint-Jorioz, situated in France, right at the Swiss border beyond which, during the war that had just ended, anyone wishing to escape the Nazis passed into neutral territory. In the imaginary and still vivid memory of Duras's intended reader of 1954, the fictional town with the enigmatic construction site was, therefore, at the limit between heightened certainty of premature death under fascist rule and actual (though slim) possibilities for reprieve and longevity in a tiny haven. Not only is Saint-Jorioz both *here* and almost *there*, the cemetery under construction is situated beyond the town's limits, between lakeshore and forest's edge. The fact that by virtue of no one yet being buried there it is not yet an active burial ground only reinforces the argument in favor of the imaginary dimension of our relationship to the albeit real space we call a cemetery. No doubt Marguerite Duras's meditation on construction sites results from her transposition of Robert Antelme's haunting memory of Dachau onto the body and soul of a young woman. Optimistically, Duras has this young woman find a solace in symbiosis with a sensitive man sufficient to elude psychosis and suicide. There is no reason not to speculate that it was thus that Duras hoped she'd helped Antelme persevere in surviving: all work and product of the creative imagination. And, like Beckett's *Film*, we must read "Construction Sites" allegorically to reap the full benefits of its lesson. For all its virtuality, the cemetery of "Construction Sites" is an actual necropolis to the extent that the young woman's mind's eye sees it as such. For the man, to the extent that he comes to see it as such for her, it mediates *his* evolution from all-too-human to the constant becoming that openness to the other entails. As Robert Desnos, who, like Robert Antelme, was pushed to the extreme limit of what a human life can tolerate, but who, unlike Antelme, could endure it no more, wrote: "No more than the ocean, no more than the desert, no more than the glaciers do the cemetery walls assign limits to my altogether imaginary existence." Cemeteries are indeed powerful spaces otherwise.

Looking back, again, at the words with which "Construction Sites" was built—"Construction Sites" with its space otherwise that we assume cannot be other than a cemetery—we are struck by the uniform and pervasive imprecision of everything: not only is the cemetery unidentified as such, but the characters are anonymous and bereft of national or ethnic particularity. Gender is the only mark of difference. Generic in all aspects, "Construction Sites" has the value of a body of general rules in which the formlessness [*Formlösigkeit*] and purposiveness without purpose that Kant discovered at the basis of the sublime reign supreme. One of the curiosities of the "Analytic of the Sublime" is Kant's mention of laughter as a dynamic—one that anticipates Freud's views on the same expressive production that has fascinated philosophers at least since Aristotle. "Laughter," wrote Kant, "is an affection arising from the sudden transformation of a strained expectation into nothing" (§54, 177). In lieu of sufficient precision about the nature of the space that is making both of them otherwise, lots of nervous laughter is exchanged without ever the word "cemetery" being pronounced by either of the hotel guests in "Construction Sites." It is, however, precisely "cemetery" that presents itself almost immediately to the mind of the reader as the most natural candidate for dissipating the vagueness surrounding that "everyday thing" that the young woman is thinking about with "a certain uncertainty." All the more so in that we soon read that "[i]t was a construction site as such, but of a particular use, it is true. It served as a perfect illustration of man's predictive faculties [*vertu de prévoyance*]." To describe the construction site, Duras multiplies such circumlocutions which, under other circumstances, in other contexts, might prove tedious and even annoying. Here, however, they stand for the utterly indeterminate "thing" that only serves to increase the enigma of this "particular use," undermining our certainty that in the eyes of the young girl, interpreted by the man, the construction site is indeed that of a simple cemetery.

Guessing, however, whether or not it is a cemetery that the workers are expanding in the prairie on the periphery of the alpine town is less important than what the young woman thinks she perceives and, crucially for the Durassian project overall, what the man *imagines* she sees. This imaginary regress no doubt explains the odd plural of the title: the site is there for the woman in the present of her presence at the convalescent home, her sight of the site conjures up even more powerfully present images of homologous sites past, the site is within the man's current and actual experience, the site acquires some of the memorial value it has for the woman thanks to a certain vicarious investment on his part, etc. Be the plurality of the construction site as it may, the resistance to naming the very focus of the story's ocular economy opens the reader's imagination to a particularly non-realistic poetic register tending to inscribe death into hyperbolic, excessive, quasi-hallucinatory images. Over the course of her oeuvre, Marguerite Duras persistently develops this dynamic for political and ethical aims. The laughter-in-lieu-of-naming in "Construction Sites" serves as a legitimate bridge forward in the deployment of that oeuvre to *Hiroshima mon amour* in that the erotically-charged exchange of laughter between Eiji Ozawa ("He") and Emmanuel Riva ("She") breaking the spell of film's initial solemn recitative is the audible version of the laughter said to be exchanged by the nameless protagonists of "Construction Sites." Reciprocally, just as the finger twitch that She observes at the end of the arm of the sleeping body of her Japanese lover directs her thought (represented by one of the film's briefest flashbacks) to the death throes of her German lover on the bank of the Loire in Nevers, so the laughter in a hotel bed in Hiroshima transports us back to the laughter in the forest before a clearing meant for a cemetery. This trajectory can be expressed in terms of several of the spaces otherwise we have examined by name. To the lovers in the rebuilt city of Hiroshima 1959, the vast cemetery whose epicenter is memorialized to this day by the Genbaku (A-Bomb) Dome; to the still-traumatized French woman she is, Occupied France—whose approximate epicenter happens to be Nevers—is the space incongruously otherwise where love with a Wehrmacht soldier was nevertheless shared; to the still-traumatized woman of the 1954 story, the construction site right over there, where the dead will be remembered by name, conjures up the vast cemeteries grotesquely denied (foreclosed) across a network of annihilation whose epicenter was a town in Poland whose name is the synecdoche for the Shoah. Ground Zero—Nevers—Auschwitz.

Auschstaat is the name Marguerite Duras invented for the site of a Soviet camp where a Jewish protagonist in a later novel is to be brought for elimination. Written in the wake of the Prague uprising and repression of 1968, dedicated to Robert Antelme and Maurice Blanchot, *Abahn Sabana David* is a political allegory in which a lowly building worker named David is ordered by the local Communist Party boss to assassinate Abahn for having challenged Soviet authority over the treatment of Jews, in particular, in the labor camps. Work accomplished through conversation, of which the propensity of the novel is composed, brings David to a change of heart after which he abandons his mission and, more importantly, his identity intertwines with that of the Jew he was meant to eliminate. In nomadic exile beyond the pale of Staat, the unnamed Jews (played variously by Sami Frey and Dionys Mascolo in the film version, *Jaune le soleil*) will pursue the ideal of a communism of the soul beyond the confines of party structures. Tellingly, in anticipation of our later analysis of the figure of *partage* as it pervades the thought of Michel Foucault and in relation to the inclusive disjunction that reigns over spaces otherwise, one of the titles Duras contemplated lending what would ultimately be *Abahn Sabana David* was "La Division dans l'Unité" to which she had added the remark, "*l'unité dans la division*," thus completing the structure as a straightforward chiasmus.[21] Division in unity, division *yet* unity: the teetering of two individuals who are beside themselves and, thus, on the brink of each other is just how the lovers of "Construction Sites" and those of *Hiroshima mon amour* come to commune.

As is attested by the bit of archive material that we briefly discussed in the first chapter, "Les Chantiers de Monsieur Arié," striking signs appear here and there, well before *Abahn Sabana David*, that Duras envisioned as Jewish at least one member—a woman—of a future community of lovers. One of the variants of the scenario she was preparing in late 1958 for *Hiroshima mon amour* is quite remarkable in that it radically exposes her tendency to concatenate Auschwitz and Hiroshima as *cemeteries denied*. Speaking in "Outa's Notebook" as if she herself were the anonymous character that Emmanuelle Riva would play in Resnais's film, Duras noted: "My mother was Jewish and had left us and since [19]42[22] was living in a department in the South." Had the idea driving this statement ever actually made it into the film, it would not have been at all plausible for the quite secondary (but far from negligible) character of the young woman's mother, played by Stella Dassas, to appear in the film. Furthermore, and more intensively from an historical perspective, had this idea materialized, the compromised safety of a young Jewish woman left behind within Occupied France, albeit with her Gentile pharmacist father, would have overshadowed the love story with the German soldier—not to speak of the increased unlikelihood of that relationship. Yet hypothetical complexification of details persists quite late in the scenario's maturation: a scene in a preparatory typescript that she was still planning for inclusion in the scenario as late as the autumn of 1958 reads as follows:

> Sewing a yellow star on my raincoat was yet another way of thinking of him. Nothing forced me to except, already, love. Alone in my bedroom, at midnight, I couldn't sleep. I was Jewish and I was just discovering it. This additional prohibition lent further complication to the affair. But I didn't know that yet. Obediently, I sewed the star. Exorcism. The sea at Champ de Mars Square is still beating behind my shutters. He must have come by, once again, this evening. I didn't open my shutters. I sewed the star of damnation. Its shape leads to death.[23]

---

[21] This is a manuscript sheet now in the archive and reproduced by Sylvie Loignon, 188, *Les archives.* DRS 18757 – *Jaune le soleil.*
[22] Duras had lined out "43."
[23] Dossier DRS 18.6 in the Duras archive at IMEC (Institut Mémoire de l'Édition Contemporaine).

It is impossible to decide whether the last two curt sentences tying mortality to the mark of the hexagram are heart-stopping and worthy of a sublime moment. Still another version of the script proposes a scene in which the father pins the yellow star of David to his daughter's chest. And as susceptible to rebuke as the French girl's liaison with a Wehrmacht soldier was, the status that the author thought at one point of attributing to her character would have made her blamable on a whole other register. In a "Note for Nevers" in the same archival folder, Duras contemplated casting her character as whore: "She might also have been a prostitute, but that profession would have bored her." A Jew who slept with the enemy then becoming a jaded floozy must have struck Alain Resnais as a bit excessive: the film therefore settles for a form of treason limited to the patriotic register.

Every bit as much as the dialectic of memory and forgetting that drives the famous interpenetration of personal trauma (her story) and collective trauma (history) presented in *Hiroshima mon amour*, the tension galvanizing the character played by Emmanuel Riva resides in her distance from the epicenters of both of the immense wastelands exposed in 1945. The relationship to cemeteries—virtual and foreclosed, present and past, encountered and imagined—of the young woman in Duras's forgotten 1954 short story was a prototype for the French woman in post-war Japan. Duras thus joins and rivals some of the most arresting thinkers who used literary discourse to describe our relationship to cemeteries. Céline's *Journey to the End of the Night* has already been mentioned. When we explore "zones of indistinction" in the next chapter, we will have occasion to return at greater length to Céline and his *Mort à crédit*—the 1936 novel whose failed reception opened the floodgates of the author's rabid racism. André Malraux's engaged kaleidoscope of leftist and anarchist resistance in the Spanish Civil War, *L'Espoir* (1937), and Georges Bernanos' enraged and outraged indictment of fascism, *Les Grands Cimetières sous la lune* (1938) during that same conflict, are two other novels from the same period where the significance of cemeteries for the living is explored. For visiting graveyards conceived in the literary mode for ethical extrapolation, cemeteries, in other words, that open out to the entirety of humanity, dozens of writers come to mind.[24] In the context of our insistent return to Duras and the vision for shared compassion that her 1954 story offers, however, three antecedents that we shall now briefly explore suggest themselves: Herman Melville's "Bartleby the Scrivener" (1853), James Joyce's *Ulysses* (1922), and William Faulkner's *As I Lay Dying* (1930).

---

[24] Here, any number of works by Samuel Beckett come to mind, as well as Roberto Bolaño's epic *2666* (2004).

If a zombie is, as John Cleese once famously said of a Norwegian Blue parrot, an "ex-man," then Bartleby is a zombie who persists at existence—barely, tenuously. Bartleby remains for a time beyond reason on *this* side of death. Faced with this work companion who comports himself as if he were a dead man walking without even the walk, the narrator of Herman Melville's story frets endlessly, assuring anyone who will listen "that Bartleby was a perfectly honest man, and greatly to be compassionated." Yet this survivor is shot through with an afterthought exuding guilt: "to be compassionated, however unaccountably eccentric" (48). Because of that irredeemable flaw in normality, nevertheless, and even though the narrator finds flimsy comfort in the thought that he did his level best to protect the Scrivener from this eventuality, "the silent man" (50) is ultimately "removed to the Tombs" (47) so aptly named for this zombie. Solitary characters that manage minimal survival—or "living on"—in *Film* or in the confined spaces of Samuel Beckett's later work are the direct descendants of Bartleby in his penultimate state, "Strangely huddled at the base of the wall, his knees drawn up, and lying on his side, his head touching the cold stones […] nothing stirred […] his dim eyes were open; otherwise he seemed profoundly sleeping" (50). The same compassion that above all else he enjoined the Tombs turnkey to have for Bartleby now moves Melville's narrator to reach out and "touch him. I felt his hand, when a tingling shiver ran up my arm and down my spine to my feet" (50). When in such a moment of *empathic vicariousness* the living reach what Améry knew well was "the mind's limits," only the imagination, as Kant taught, can preserve life and restore reason. And so, with the survivors concluding that Bartleby is perhaps indeed "[w]ith kings and counsellors," Melville's character does precisely that: "[i]magination will readily supply the meagre recital of poor Bartleby's interment" (50).

The interment of another poor soul is told in an anything-but-terse recital in the "Hades" episode of James Joyce's *Ulysses*. In Chapter 6, Leopold Bloom accompanies the funeral procession of Paddy Dignam to Prospect Cemetery (Glasnevin) in Dublin, "a treacherous place." In accordance with Joyce's narrative procedure throughout the modernist monument that *Ulysses* is, Bloom's thoughts to himself serve as our beacon as we move ever so ploddingly along with the spare funeral procession from the city center to Dublin's peripheral zone. The occasion and the eventual sight of the burial grounds remind Bloom of Rudy, the son he lost only a few days after the baby's birth and whose memory has already been rekindled by the still tentative entry of Stephen into his life experience. The Irish Jew is reminded too of his father, Simon. He meditates vaguely of fathers and sons in general, and recalls a parade of others dearly departed from his life. When we all finally reach Prospect Cemetery, the same silliness of our bourgeois rituals that provoked Foucault's sarcasm about the "little individual boxes for little individual decomposition" inspires Bloom to dig clichés and doggerel up out of his memory of collective consciousness: "We are praying now for the repose of his soul. Hoping you're well and not in hell. Nice change of air. Out of the fryingpan of life into the fire of purgatory" (91). But unlike Foucault who persists in his sarcasm, Bloom is almost instantaneously beside himself with existential uncertainty: "Does he ever think of the hole waiting for himself? The way you do when you shiver in the sun" (91). If "he" is Paddy Dignam, the speculative question makes no sense, since Paddy can think no longer. "He" can only be Leopold himself, displaced slightly and disoriented by the proximity to *what* he will be, virtually cleaving to Paddy's remains, as if shivering in the sun the way Melville's narrator shivered as he touched a Bartleby barely alive in the Tombs. So that, as the stream of Bloom's consciousness continues in its flow, the ensuing thoughts are not so much observations about the inevitable, but cautionary notes against succumbing to absolute inhumanity. Conjuring an ancient proverb (whose French equivalent replaces sight by body and mind with heart) the shovelsful resounding fainter and fainter on the casket produce an effect opposite to the letter of utterance. As "the clay fell softer. Begin to be forgotten. Out of sight, out of mind" (91) actually commits to memory Paddy Dignam's existence, albeit now ended, and Bloom's empathic interface with it. Reflecting, with imagery that anticipates Beckett's late trilogy, on what happens to corpses in their boxes beneath the earth after the final shovelful is tossed—"Plant him and have done with him. Like down a coalshoot. Then lump them together to save time. All souls' day" (93)—one is hard pressed not to be wrenched with a mental shiver from this image of a potter's field to the photographic image of mass annihilation snatched, in spite of all, from the ultimate space otherwise.

The experience of the burial ritual is not only an exercise in respect (or regret) for a departed fellow whom we have (or should have) let live in peace: it reminds us of what we will have been one day, when all the possibilities for becoming who-we-will-have-been, as Nietzsche might have put it, are exhausted. Eyes wide open, attentive, we face eyes shut, purposeless. How did I treat him when those eyes of his were as full of life as mine? Perhaps Samuel Fuller's commanding officer at Falkenau knew that this can easily become the only question that courses through the mind of the mourner next to the gravepit. In *As I Lay Dying*, William Faulkner certainly did, albeit with some of the same dark humor with which Joyce laced Paddy Dignam's burial. At a funeral, as our mind approaches the space otherwise, so powerful is the compulsion to reckon with one's own life record, to adjust, amend or persevere, that between mourners, furtive glances that take stock of our natural duty to our fellow human are exchanged. Referring to Darl, Tull says to himself,

> He is looking at me. He dont say nothing; just looks at me with them queer eyes of hisn that makes folks talk. I always say it aint never been what he done so much or said or anything so much as how he looks at you. It's like he had got into the inside of you, someway. Like somehow you was looking at yourself and your doings outen his eyes. (1984 [1930]: 81)

Desiring nothing more (and nothing better) than to hold steady on his erstwhile selfish course, it's all Tull can do to resist Darl's insidious look. Tull violently resists being beside himself. The cleave of being with the dead to which Bloom readily gave himself is not for him. Tull's recoil is a magnified version of Melville's narrator's undeniable denial: "It was not I that brought you here, Bartleby" (48). Attempting desperately to distance himself from the act banishing one's fellow man to the Tombs ("it is not so sad a place as one might think"), he who holds forth in Melville's stead does everything in his power to distract he who prefers not to: "Look, there is the sky, and here is the grass." To no avail. Bartleby's unequivocal retort—"I know where I am"—will haunt him forever (48). And us as well. The story's final cry, "Ah Bartleby! Ah humanity!" (51), failure to inhume the human. By asserting the leap from the particular exception to the universal rule, Melville rubs the bankruptcy of humanity delimited by definition, closed to spaces otherwise, in our faces.

As Foucault observed, cemeteries have, since around the beginning of the nineteenth century, been relegated to spaces outside the pale of urban civilization. In Walter Benjamin's grand plan for *cities* that deserve that respected name, spaces otherwise would be reterritorialized as part of our mental and actual landscape. Here is one of the thousands of heteroclite thoughts that make up his *Passagen-Werk*, or *Arcades Project*:

> To construct the city topographically—tenfold and a hundredfold— from out of its arcades and its gateways, its cemeteries and bordellos, its railroad stations and its ..., just as formerly it was defined by its churches and its markets. And the more secret, more deeply embedded figures of the city: murders and rebellions, the bloody knots in the network of the streets, lairs of love, and conflagrations. (83)

What is common to railroad stations and gateways, whorehouses and cemeteries is their status and value as *thresholds*. The idea is that, just as bordellos deterritorialize the eroticized body, removing it from the confines of bourgeois convention, so cemeteries shift consciousness to the threshold of consciousness, testing its limits. And because graveyards are places meant to commemorate the dead, they may link mourners to the lives they still have to live out and, especially, to how that will be done. Cemeteries are imaginary waystations between our record of acts up to *this point in time* (or home) and what we will decide to do *from now on* (our possible destinations). This is why Benjamin includes, among the nodes of the city's network, among the city's spaces otherwise, the "bloody knots" where rebellions have come to head. As Foucault reminded us as he succinctly concluded his long Introduction to Kant's 1798 *Anthopology from the Pragmatic Point of View*, "In the field of philosophy, the trajectory from the question, *Was ist der Mensch* ? culminates in the response that recuses and disarms it: —*der Übermensch*" (79). For us to move *beyond* the human, as Nietzsche so boldly invited us to do before we could, we must reckon with all the humans we have been but whose humanity we have so far denied.

Before dust turns all too soon into dust, Georges Didi-Huberman seems to share Benjamin's concern that the living preserve, protect, and revere *something* (if not their name) of the nameless among us in a section entitled "*L'inavouable lieu du commun*"[25] of a 2012 book with an equally difficult-to-translate title, *Peuples exposés, peuples figurants*.[26] Over the course of four pages, Didi-Huberman offers his deferential meditation upon having contemplated the photograph attributed to André-Adolphe-Eugène Disdéri of unnamed insurgents killed during the Bloody Week (*la Semaine sanglante*) of May 1871, which put an abrupt and spectacularly gruesome end to the Paris Commune. The photograph depicts twelve rebels, each arranged in a coffin.

At this point, Didi-Huberman makes explicit the concern that "exposing peoples appears at first to be an impossible quest, for the place of the common [*lieu du commun*] all too often resembles a commonplace [*lieu commun*]" (98). By "common," here, is meant at least three things simultaneously: commonality—that which each of these men had in common, that which they had shared: a political, economic, and social community; the sense of mutual interest and solidarity that motivated their actions; and the fact that these were common people, plebians, proletarians. The

[25] Playing on *lieu commun*, or commonplace, but to which I can only lend the cumbersome translation of "The Unavowable Place of That Which Is Considered Common."
[26] Let us try, again abandoning concision in order to render meanings and inferences: "Peoples That Are Exposed, Peoples Considered As Supernumerary" or "[...] Considered as Extras," as in a film production, also works, but doesn't quite capture the allusion to "figures" or "*Figuren*" – the horrendously abject category to which the SS relegated all those of whom they deprived everything, including their names. Didi-Huberman, 2012, 97–101.

Figure 13 Attributed to Adolphe-Eugène Disdéri, "Communards in Their Coffins" from *A World History of Photography*, public domain.

instant that photography froze so that it might be meditated upon in all potential ulterior instants holds the impending disposal of dead bodies in suspense, challenging the expectation that the next step—with "people like that"—would normally have been relegation of the remains to a mass grave, a *fosse commune*. Yet they each have their "little box" which, though narrow and cheap, is nevertheless individual. Foucault would no doubt have lifted any sarcasm or irony before this image. Is any respect being shown by the living for these dead? The cadavers left naked have been nevertheless swaddled in shroud and placed with some measure of care in their caskets. Someone has taken time to recognize *some* humanity in those considered by the triumphant bourgeoisie as subhuman. And, true, we might, as Didi-Huberman hopes, be led by the sight of this photograph to reflect on the meaning of the struggle known in history as The Paris Commune as a whole. But something far more certain is inscribed here. We look again at those vacant and sunken eyes: the twelve communards are not yet interred. At this point, Didi-Huberman reminds us of "that which exposes while exposing itself," which is the definition that Maurice Blanchot lent to "the community of man in the space of history and politics" (100),[27] and he invokes Georges Bataille, who affirmed of culture what Blanchot affirms of politics: they are "mixtures of power and impotence, [they] demand for the unlimited together with the principle of finitude" (100). Shot as vertically as possible so as to show the bodies as frontally as possible, this photograph that we attribute to Disdéri captured the minimal respect for individuals massacred that triumphant survivors can muster, ensuring—against the compulsion to efface the commonality that makes humans all-too-human—that the cause for which they struggled and because of which they were slaughtered would live on. But it is the photograph that does this, not the arrangement or "dressing" and *numbering* of the bodies *before* the photographic moment. Didi-Huberman wagers and hopes that, as a result of the work performed using our "mental looking force" (*seelische Schaukraft*),[28] the picture of the twelve dead Communards will not remain a mere "hunting trophy," but will rather serve to perpetuate "the protest, the revolt, the desire that these dead bodies not remain dead letters or commonplaces for history" (101). I would simply add that it is *our thinking about* the arrangement of the bodies in caskets, the ritual preparation of these dead men for interment in a cemetery, that will serve as principal fuel for our *mental viewing power* as it applies itself to Disdéri's photograph. It is that *punctum* that provides us with that mental bridge to the space otherwise where *our* ethical work gets done.

Equally important in Walter Benjamin's thinking about cityscapes past, present, and future was the "experience of the limit phenomenon."[29] It is Georges Bataille, of course, who most immediately comes to mind on the subject of limit experience. But Bataille is not the only or the first twentieth-century thinker to be preoccupied with the notion. As he would argue concerning the aura of the artwork, so Walter Benjamin thought

[27] "Ce qui expose en s'exposant" is at p. 25 in M. Blanchot, *La Communauté inavouable*, 1983. Jean-Luc Nancy, *La Communauté désœuvrée* (1988), *La Communauté affrontée* (2001) also appeared as a preface to a new edition of Blanchot's work.
[28] Didi-Huberman used the term *Schaukraft*, without the adjective, as it appeared in Siegfried Kracauer's "Die Filmwochenschau," *Die Neue Rundschau*, Bd. II, 1931 in *Kino. Essays, Studien, Glossen zum Film*, Frankfurt-am-Main, Suhrkamp, 1974, translated as "Les actualités cinématographiques" in *Le voyage et la danse*, 126 (cf. Didi-Huberman 2012: 98). We can, however, find Walter Benjamin as early as 1928 crediting philosopher and graphologist Ludwig Klages (1872–1956) for the expression "*seelische Schaukraft*" or "mental looking force" in a review of Anja and Georg Mendelssohn, *Der Mensch in der Handschrift* (1928), in *Gesammelte Schriften*, Bd. 3, 136. Klages uses the expression "*seelische Schaukraft*" in his 1917 study, *Handschrift und Charakter. Gemeinverständlicher Abriß der graphologischen Technik*, 9.
[29] Martin Jay, "The Limits of Limit-Experience: Bataille and Foucault." *Constellations* 2 (2) (April 1995): 155–74.

Of Spaces Otherwise 133

deeply and broadly about two types of experience capable of pushing at the limits that define "humanity": whereas *Erlebnis*—an "immediate, passive, fragmented, isolated, and unintegrated inner experience" like that described pervasively in Bataille's work—continues to be readily available to us in the modern world, *Erfahrung*, a "cumulative, totalizing accretion of transmittable wisdom, of epic truth" is today impoverished or atrophied, according to Benjamin.[30] Nevertheless, not only do spaces otherwise, like arcades, cemeteries, and bordellos, need to be part of a territory made integral for both body and mind, so too the spaces *between* here and there. Benjamin was extremely attentive to what the classical archaeologist Ferdinand Noack (1865–1931) had to say about the function of certain limitropic monuments in ancient Rome. The Romans, according to Noack, developed "a conception of the sacred as boundary or threshold" that was made manifest in the construction of structures, like Scipio's Arch, in eccentric or even isolated spaces.[31] For the committed thinker of the heteroclite that Benjamin was, it was not so much the use of these structures for "special occasions" that arrested his attention as "their isolation": the one as much as the other, he observed, contributed to their "cultic significance." Translated into the topographical vocabulary of nineteenth-century Paris, which for Benjamin was the paragon of the modern city, this isolated space, this hiatus between lived space and space otherwise would have been not the arcade, but *la Zone*. Although *la Zone* and its avatars are the subject of the next chapter, it is useful to begin to think about this interstitial area that urban historian Jean-Louis Cohen has called the "annulary threshold" of Paris, for the expansive Parisian cemeteries for the less-than-famous all cleave to the outer edge of the no-man's-land ringing the city that was once known as *la Zone*.[32] Before interment, before coming to the final resting place that Foucault mocks, there is the casket above ground. Before being committed to the earth, that little box sometimes remains open for a few minutes in order for the survivors to have a last look at the dead, however abject their status was in life. A final reckoning. What happens when that final reckoning is rendered perennial with a photographic cliché? —It's all cliché, or place in common, for cliché, or commonplace.

---

[30] I continue to quote Martin Jay, as referenced in Thomas Elsaesser's "Between *Erlebnis* and *Erfahrung*: Cinema Experience with Benjamin." *Paragraph* (November 2009): 292–312.
[31] Ferdinand Noack, *Triumph und Triumphbogen*, Warburg Library Lectures, vol. 5 (Leipzig, 1928), 162, 169 (*Arcades Project*, 97).
[32] Jean-Louis Cohen, "Les seuils de Paris, des fortifications au périphérique." Lecture at L'Université de tous les savoirs on October 28, 2003.

That fleeting last look is to the experience of temporality what *la Zone* was in the dimension of space for the modern inhabitant of the city of Paris. Both of these intermedialities play forcefully on the imagination, creating conditions propitious to ethical development. Before pausing at that space otherwise, however, let us look just beyond *la Zone*, but continguous with it, to the suburban landscape immediately outside Benjamin's "capital of the nineteenth century" where, as Foucault points out, the dead began being relegated at an ever-accelerating rate after the French Revolution. Cemeteries officially designated as "Parisian cemeteries" are, despite that moniker, segregated territorially into two quite distinct groups: those situated within the communal limits of the city and those situated in suburbs that hug the city limits, in what Parisians call "*la petite couronne.*" Appealing, as French officialdom is wont to do, to Latin, the first are *intramuros*, the second *extramuros*. The invisible wall on either side of which these two spaces extend follows the path of the last fortifications built around the entirety of Paris starting in 1840–1.[33] Whether on *this* side of the wall (or "wall"), inside Paris, that is, or on *that* side, in some suburb or another, all of these cemeteries are "Parisian cemeteries" because, in principle, only the dead who had died *in* Paris are buried *there*.

"Already by the 1860s, the City of Paris, the prefecture of the Seine and the police prefecture agree, with some trepidation, that the thirteen *intramuros* Parisian cemeteries have reached saturation" (Fourcaut, 105). Those cemeteries—big and small, famous and not—are Père-Lachaise, Montmartre, Montparnasse, Passy, les Catacombes, Grenelle, Vaugirard, Auteuil, Batignolles, Saint-Vincent, le Cimetière du Calvaire, Bercy, le Cimetière Sud de Saint-Mandé, le Cimetière de la Villette, Belleville, and Charonne. By the 1880s, when virtually no one was buried in any of these cemeteries any more, they were all located within the city limits as we see them today. In earlier times, however, even some of these Parisian burial grounds had been outside the capital: the village of Montmartre, for example, had only been incorporated into the urban area in 1860, as was Auteuil. Before the crisis of space for accommodating the Parisian dead came to a head in the last quarter of the nineteenth century, only three cemeteries reserved for inhabitants of the capital had been opened. On only five acres, the Cimetière de la Chapelle in Saint-Denis was quickly at its capacity of 16,000. The graveyards in Saint-Ouen and in Ivry opened a decade later but were not expanded to their current size of sixty-five to seventy acres until the beginning of the Third Republic. Even before the

---

[33] Construction began on orders of Thiers in 1840 but not authorized until an April 1841 law of Louis-Philippe.

Paris Commune—thousands of whose victims never made it to a cemetery at all—these auxiliary graveyards were proving woefully small. Soon after exiting any of the two dozen or so doors and postern gates, crossing the few hundred yards of no-man's-land, on which the next chapter is centered, there were towns in settings if not always bucolic, at least tending to the rural, into which cemetery expansion projects could easily be contemplated.

Easy in principle, however not so easy in practice. Among the mayors of the Paris banlieues, some wielded sufficient power to resist the will of the Goliath at the center. That's exactly what the ancient city of Saint-Denis did just following the Paris Commune when no less a power than Adophe Thiers who had brutally put down the insurrection pushed for an expansion of le Cimetière de la Chapelle and failed. So, as Fourcaut writes (pedantically using the adjective for Saint-Denis for tongue-in-cheek effect), "short of the dionysian site, the prefecture of the Seine managed, over the course of the 1880s to get the Parisian cemeteries of Clichy-Les Batignolles, Ivry, and Saint-Ouen expanded" (105). Pressure due to the surplus of cadavers to inter was further relieved over the course of the next decades by the creation of three brand new cemeteries, all far surpassing Père-Lachaise (108 acres) in area, thus lending new vigor to the significance of the term "necropolis." The Parisian cemeteries of Bagneux (150 acres) and Pantin (265 acres) would both be opened in 1886, while that of Thiais (255 acres) broke ground, as it were, in 1929.[34]

In "delocalizing" its dead to the suburbs, Paris succeeded, over the course of the nineteenth century, to find room for the mortal remains whose numbers were increasing with the demographic explosion and each of whom (or which) were taking up more space due, as Michel Foucault notes, to the bourgeoisification of burial custom even among the proletariat.[35] However, with the suburban cemetery construction sites finished and burials occurring apace, political and social relations between these outlying communities and the Parisian behemoth in the center are far from calm and settled. Insistently and persistently throughout the final two decades of the nineteenth century and well into the twentieth, "municipal assemblies [...] protest against these cities of the dead" for two specific reasons: cemeteries "restrict the development of industry [...] and risk infecting the air of their

---

[34] For comparison, Calvary Cemetery in Queens, New York, where about three million are buried, covers 365 acres. The largest cemetery in the world is Wadi-us-Salaam in Najaf, Iraq: five million bodies in 1,485 acres.

[35] Not only do bourgeois caskets become more expansive in proportion to the assumptions and presumptions of that class, but aspirational impulses among some in the working class cause a generalization of individual burial in individual coffins—however humble they be.

cities" (Fourcaut, 105). The dead of Paris may well "be able to rest far from their home in the seven extramuros cemeteries of Saint-Denis, Clichy, Saint-Ouen, Ivry, Pantin-Bobigny, Bagneux et Thiais, spread out over more than 320 hectares," that stench that the good citizens of Falkenau incredulously could not detect right under their hypocritical noses is ever-present (or imagined present) to the nostrils of Parisian suburbanites as well. Ironic would indeed be a paltry qualifier for the fact that the same Parisian imagination, just a few short decades later, could not (or would not) conjure up the future stench of annihilation that was detectable to any compassionate being on the thousands of Jewish bodies rounded up in Paris and corraled at Drancy—just six short kilometers from Saint-Denis—before shipment of the cargo to Auschwitz. Be that as it may, suburban repugnance at the new cemeteries was simultaneously associated with two other practices occurring on their territory and that continue to occur in cities across the world today: the evacuation of sewage and the transfer of people deemed odious to city life.

Massive expansions of spaces apart, where the city's refuse is deposited, must be imagined in order for these spaces away to begin to function as spaces otherwise. How to dispose of undesirable categories of people was and remains today of prime concern to the managers of order. And the estrangement of worthless people was and remains today—consciously or unconsciously—associated with the disposal of refuse and sewage. In this, nineteenth-century Paris was no exception. The massive transfer of beggars held in custody at Saint-Denis to a vastly expanded workhouse [*dépôt*] created between 1875 and 1883, where delinquent women, the indigent elderly, and the mad were already mixed might serve as an example among dozens of Paris's panicked relegations of human refuse to the periphery.

> The 1868 plan to transfer to Nanterre the workhouse founded in 1769 in Saint-Denis caused an uproar. Hostility from the city elders is intense. All express fear for "the country's ruin." The capital thus confirmed its secular tendency to expulse its sick, its beggars, its vagabonds, and its deviants beyond its borders. (109)

Summarizing, in summer 1897, the capital's evacuation program, prefect of police Louis Lépine's skill at metonymy revealed that the entirety of Nanterre had become a human dumping ground: "In sum, a holding center for beggars, a workhouse, a temporary refuge, an asylum, a hospital: that's Nanterre" (speech of June 17, 1897, quoted in Fourcaut, 111).

Dépôt or *dépôt de mendicité* is the term that I have translated as "workhouse" from the original French above, but just as spectacular exceptional punishment becomes generalized discipline in Michel Foucault's famous analysis of society policing itself, so *dépôts de mendicité* are subject to transformations—both practical and discursive—meant to "humanize" the institutions. Reforms in 1777, instigated by Turgot, nominally and, to a certain extent, actually turned *dépôts* into *ateliers de charité* (charity workshops) in which inmates produced textiles. But as Foucault demonstrated in the *History of Madness*, backsliding notwithstanding, the policy known as the General Hospital confined the poor and all other undesirables to a "dump"—the deeuphemized meaning of *dépôt*. As if by natural association with the dead in their cemeteries, the dying in their hospitals, the useless in their workhouses and asylums, the refuse and sewage that Paris disgorged for treatment in the outlying communes became indistinguishable from the rejects of humanity. "Throughout the nineteenth century," writes Fourcaut, "Paris expels cemeteries, hospitals, polluting factories, sludge and garbage dumps." But the volume of all these undesirable by-products of civilization increases to an extent that the stench returns to indispose the producers:

> Every summer, starting in the 1880, the issue of Paris' odors—its stench, that is—comes to the forefront among debates. The Ministry of Agriculture empanels an "odor commission" to study the problem. The report of inspectors of licensed treatment services concludes that the most noxious odors come from the phosphate fertilizer factories in Aubervilliers. (115)

For every licensed (and, one assumes, regulated) garbage and sewage treatment center, there were dozens of altogether improvised solutions. What Parisian raw sewage that *was* diverted from direct dumping in the Seine was piped out to suburban landscapes for manuring. The indisposition that suburban neighbors experienced in proximity of these manure farms would return to haunt Parisians too, especially in summer and depending on prevailing winds. Peripheral municipalities sometimes took action: the mayor of Nanterre, Aschille Hennape, "after a long trial, succeeded in forcing the closure of the pestilential Compagnie parisienne de vidanges et des engrais, whose stench had so riled the neighboring populations" (Fourcaut, 109). Little by little, even the suburbanites of "the capital of the nineteenth century" succeeded in quelling or repelling the worst of what Paris expels from its vital space. If there were no longer neighboring properties onto which garbage could be dumped or sewage pumped, then either treatment processes got improved or spaces altogether otherwise are found.

Once the stench of rot and shit dissipates from the air breathed, the dead in the neighboring cemetery are forgotten. Or are they? What about all the subhumans still alive? Where are the Parisians and respectable banlieue populations to put them? Perhaps not directly into a cemetery, but somehow on top. As outlandish as it sounds, this is one of the many solutions the Nazis came up with. Like cathedrals in Mexico upon Maya and Aztec pyramids, Kraków-Płaszów concentration camp, where the especially macabre SS-Hauptsturmführer Amon Göth oversaw operations, was constructed on the very site of old Jewish cemeteries. After the New Cemetery became full, new burials in the 1930s were directed to two plots: one on Abrahama Street, the other in Jerozolimska Street. These two Jewish cemeteries, however, were leveled in 1942 to make way for what would become the infamous slave-labor camp. Eventually, following the Nazi defeat, the camp too (which was depicted in Steven Spielberg's 1993 film *Schindler's List*) was bulldozed. What, putting ourselves in her place by force of imagination, would a survivor of Płaszów think at the sight of a construction site? To give rise to such thinking is perhaps the goal of those who each year assemble at *le Mur des Fédérés*—the Communards' Wall—in Père Lachaise Cemetery to commemorate the thousands massacred and dumped anywhere that could quickly become a "nowhere."

In his 1967 lecture launching the idea of heterotopias, Michel Foucault expressed surprise at how long it had taken for space to emerge as an historico-political problem. Given the enduring necessity for us to think the human species through cultural structures as important as cemeteries, we should be equally surprised at how long it has taken for space otherwise to emerge as ground propitious to making headway with respect to the riddle of whether it is possible or not to establish an ethics with anything like "universal" relevance. And, whereas space had faded into the background of Foucault's research by the time it reached the stage where ethics had taken center stage, we all know—because we all sense it innately—that no care of the self can go without care of *the other that I might be*. That common ground that I am calling a construction site for ethics is not so much a heterotopia as it is a shared meditation on the ground of spaces otherwise. Construction sites for ethics are simultaneously *apart from* us and, by dint of imagination, *a part of* us. Common ground becomes established when the psychic and emotional relationship to spaces otherwise is shared by two or more subjects—humans who share across a divide.

Underpinning, as condition, the notion that cemeteries are spaces arranged *apart* from the city is that there is space *between* the city and that space otherwise. For well over a century and until relatively recent times a space even more otherworldly than a cemetery existed with its own distinct and heteroclite life between the city of Paris and the neighboring cities, towns, and factories. Today, spaces just like it have become the norm for the majority of humans dwelling within the orbit of urban centers the world over. For much of the nineteenth century and well into the twentieth, denying the French capital and its neighbors the immediacy of adjacency, the *other space otherwise* was no reassuring "buffer zone" either, for it became inhabited, "overrun" by tens of thousands of souls living in limbo *vis-à-vis* established law. That space was called, simply, ominously, *la Zone*.

4

Zones of Indistinction

When Giorgio Agamben coined the phrase "zones of indistinction" to situate descriptively the "bare life" eked out by or meted out to a whole range of human beings from concentration camp prisoners, through refugees and migration detainees, to the deeply comatose, he made it explicit that he had Foucault's notion of heterotopia—or *places otherwise*—in mind. Notwithstanding *Homo sacer's* sweeping major claim that the camp is nothing less than the *nomos* of our world today, the last few pages of that book are—unexpectedly—not altogether dark: Agamben seems to imply that there may yet be a way to recognize and commune with the indistinct—those species fellows whom we consider "neither us nor them." Yet again, Agamben cautions against going as far as to imagine some "different economy of bodies and pleasures," as Foucault put it, "as a possible horizon for a different politics" (Agamben's words) as if reclaimed and triumphant "difference" were, by virtue of alternative politics, better and somehow more viable (187). A fuller citation of the conclusion to *The Will To Knowledge* (volume 1 of his *History of Sexuality*) than the one Agamben gives in *Homo sacer* would reveal, for one thing, that Foucault did not assert so clearly all that Agamben attributes to him. Nor was Foucault uncritically triumphalist in anticipation of a future for difference unchained and shifting to the center. That, however, is a point that we will need to place in reserve at this stage in the deployment of grounds for possible communing. More pressing at present, in order to test (as I will attempt to do in the final two chapters) Agamben's compelling and challenging thesis that the camp is our *nomos* against Foucault's complex, yet undeveloped and incomplete, thinking of *partage*, it is necessary to explore the *indistinction* that Agamben says characterizes a certain category of *space otherwise* known as a *zone*. This is because *inclusive* disjunction, which may appear as mere disjunction, reins over *partage*. Indeed, in order to grasp what indistinction means, it behooves us to investigate an almost forgotten, yet altogether concrete example of a zone that predates Nazi camps by a century. With the help of philosophers, writers of literature, filmmakers, photographers, and an Auschwitz survivor, this chapter will explore a particular zone known by just that name—*la*

Zone—and examine the existence of *la Zone*'s inhabitants, variously named *zoniers* or *zonards*.

As preview of those *beings distinct in their indistinction* that zone dwellers are, let us consider an example from the annals of irony: Some one hundred and fifty years before Jonathan Swift's infamously ironic "Modest Proposal," Michel de Montaigne considered, through the voice of a man-eating savage who refrains from "accepting common opinions" and, instead, "judges them by the ways of reason, not by popular vote [*la voix commune*]" (*OC*, 200; 228) and in ostensible seriousness, not so much what to do with cadavers—so long as their former selves had been left to live unmolested and with reasonable satisfaction of need—but whether it is worse to deprive fellow humans of peace and prosperity or to kill a few for food once in a while.[1]

> I think there is more barbarity in eating a man alive than in eating him dead; more barbarity in lacerating by rack and torture a body still fully able to feel things, in roasting him little by little and having him bruised and bitten by pigs and dogs [...] than in roasting him and eating him after his death. (*OC*, 207–8; 235–6)

Montaigne's wise cannibal came to this conclusion after having closely observed the manners in which Europeans treat their fellow humans. To see photographic or the still rarer filmic images of *la Zone*, or to read narratives by those who witnessed its existence or even by some of those who imagined it, is to realize that *la Zone* was a vast anarchic wasteland where Paris's barely living accumulated. Today, these indistinct individuals scrape together a living elsewhere, scattered here and there, littering streets far and wide. "Living on the edge," of course, references not only precariousness but spatial relativity. But for a century, they barely lived in a slum belt ringing the City of Lights and separating it from its established bourgeois and petty bourgeois *faubourgs*.

Today, we tend to think of a zone as an area that is emphatically, "necessarily" apart, an area of exception from the rule of norm, but an area that nevertheless possesses strict integrality—one that "has a solid shape," as mathematicians would put it—, an area that itself alone and separate harbors only alien life or that which is alien to life. From the Greek ζώγη (*zónē*)—a girdle or belt—a no-man's-land inhabited by tens of thousands

---

[1] Montaigne placed "*Des cannibales*" (Of Cannibals) as number xxxi in his first tome of *Essais*. It is thought to have been composed in 1579 or 1580. "*Je pense qu'il y a plus de barbarie à manger un homme vivant qu'à le manger mort, à deschirer par tourmens et par geénes un corps encore plein de sentiment, le faire rostir par le menu, le faire mordre et meurtrir aux chiens et aux pourceaux [...], que de la rostir et manger après qu'il est trespassé.*"

fully encircled Paris from the mid-nineteenth to the mid-twentieth century. By the mid-1930s, when he was writing *Mort à crédit* (*Death on the Installment Plan*) (1936), Céline could report that "there's hardly anything left of the walls or the Bastion. Big black cracked stonework, now debris, ripped like rotten teeth out of the soft embankment. Everything will go, the city is gulping its old gums" (21).[2] *La Zone*, along the city's disgusting "old gums," had already long been doomed to the excruciatingly slow obliteration that was only to be integral in the 1960s with the construction of the *périphérique*—the roadway that rings Paris today. But before *le périph'* and even before *la Zone*, there were *les fortifs'*, the fortifications. As a note in the Pléiade edition clarifying Céline's reference to "bastion" explains, in part: "Razing the rampart around Paris, equipped with its ninety-four bastions, began in 1920." The editor continues, demetaphorizing Céline's brilliant evocation of urban peritonitis, "The commune of Paris expanded in certain spots, following these demolitions." Explained more specifically elsewhere in the volume that presents both *Voyage au bout de la nuit* (*Journey to the End of the Night*) and *Mort à credit*, the reference to *la Zone* in this particular note speaks volumes about the indistinction that is partially the consequence of *la Zone*'s geographic and, by extension, demographic interstitiality. Its location can be figured by the way the word is used in referring to land annexed by Paris in 1930: "the zone between Clichy's edge, the old fortifications, and Batignolles cemetery" and again, only approximately, by a final remark concerning the evolving legal status of this inhabited no-man's-land that will lead to its eventual evacuation and eradication: "Previously delimited by the boulevards named after the [military] marshals, the city of Paris would now extend to the Route de la Révolte" (*OC I*, 1420). While the land annexed by Paris in 1930 was indeed part of *la Zone*, the "zone" referred to above is, more simply, a circumscribed area and not the vast shantytown that girded the city for over one hundred years. And while depicting a swath of territory between the boulevards ringing Paris named after Napoléon's military elite and Louis XV's escape route between Saint-Denis and Versailles to the west of the city is picturesque, this characterization of *la Zone* is woefully approximate and incomplete.

In attestable actuality, *la Zone* was a very precise space that nevertheless came to contain the most imprecise, barely human contents. The place name in French—*la Zone*—is an ellipsis for an official governmental term—"*la zone militaire* non aedificandi"—attributed to "a vast elliptical band, 250

---

[2] Throughout, I take liberties altering Ralph Manheim's valiant translation of *Mort à crédit*. Here, the original is "[…] *il reste presque rien de la muraille et du Bastion. Des gros débris noirs crevassés, on les arrache du remblai mou, comme des chicots. Tout y passera, la ville bouffe ses vieilles gencives*" (*OC I*, 517).

meters wide, measuring from the crest of the *glacis*, with a circumference of 34 kilometers; a surface area of some 800 hectares of diverse landscape consisting of plains, hills, streams, all under military authority" (Le Hallé, 249). That this band around Paris was meant to remain strictly uninhabited went hand in hand with one of the biggest white elephants in nineteenth-century French history: "Thiers's wall," so named because it was the pet urban design project of Adolphe Thiers, who was infamous (among other things) for having led the bloody repression of the Paris Commune in May 1871. While defensive walls might still have been thought to be appropriate and perhaps even efficacious for staving off an attack as late as the 1814–15 invasion of Paris by the armies of the Holy Alliance, by the 1840s the perfection of artillery had rendered such construction anachronistic and irrelevant. But Thiers—a confirmed megalomaniac—held sufficient power to forgo waiting for a royal decree and ordered work on a rampart around the city to begin in 1840. That eventual decree, opening the national treasury to cover the immensely wasteful expenditure the project incurred, was not promulgated by Louis-Philippe until April 5, 1841.

Lines of sight from the rampart and its bastions were meant to remain unobstructed so that military personnel could survey the Paris horizon from any vantage point for barbaric incursions. "It was therefore strictly forbidden to park or build anything whatsoever" in what was designated officially as the *non aedificandi* zone (Le Hallé, 249). Along with fortifications came the rest of the militarized topography: gates, guard-houses, and city tolls built into the wall, a 34-kilometer ditch over which bridges had to be flung, *glacis* and their backfill to serve as first defense against waves of invading enemy soldiers who never came. The elaboration and erection of this massive structure was perceived similarly to the way post-9/11 security measures have been received by much of the U.S. population, as attested by a letter from Michel Chevalier to the Comte of Molé published in 1841: "It has been said of the Paris fortifications that they are neither out of fear nor out of threat; indeed, they are not the result of either one alone, but of both together, along with war" (quoted in Fourcaut, 70). Like the rhetoric of Homeland Security and surveillance society today, Thiers's discursive campaign to instill terror in his bourgeois audience was relentless. If by the time this gargantuan project was completed in the 1860s the ruling classes could feel marginally safer *vis-à-vis* whatever type of incursion they were prognosticating at the moment, it had already become abundantly clear to the indigent populace in and around Paris (the very people who would have been the first conscripted in case of *actual* war) that the belt of land from which habitation was banned was nevertheless quite good land— land not subject to the rules governing civilian private ownership and land conveniently close to whatever work might be had or improvised in tenuous symbiosis with the metropolis. The "*zone militaire* non aedificandi" almost immediately became, in an ever-accelerating anarchic land grab, *la Zone*: a vast shantytown belt surrounding Paris. The barbaric invasion so feared from *outside* the nation was soon to be perceived as taking place from *within*.

Such was the observable location and population located in the actual space designated as *la Zone*. I have taken Céline as a first keen observer of that space otherwise. As his representations suggest, *la Zone* as quintessential zone of indistinction garnered special attention from creators with words. *La Zone* generated great interest from creators with pictorial images as well. In preparation for exploring the latter, who come closer and closer to imagining how *la Zone* could possibly serve as paradigm for sharing common ground with others, I shall invite the reader to touch upon a selection of literary evocations of zones, starting with two radical examples. Over the course of a hundred years beginning in the last third of the nineteenth and continuing over two-thirds of the twentieth century, the precarious and varied hordes that would park their caravans, pitch their tents, and erect their shanties at the gates of Paris would "invade" in a way far more subtle than the ever-threatening barbarians from foreign nations: their existence relentlessly pushed back at the limits set by bourgeois society to define existence itself. A modern poet as tuned to the inner experience in order to bring evolution to outer experience as Henri Michaux would anticipate critiques of late modern society such as those by philosopher Jean-François Lyotard. If there is a space outside one's own mind that Michaux thought should stimulate new perceptions and conceptions of reality from within, that space would have all the characteristics of a zone. Michaux abidingly plumbed the depths of this intuition by the use of the organic hallucinogenic drugs cannabis and mescaline. In 1961, with the construction of the *périphérique* well under way and the razing of shanties still a vivid memory for any Parisian in his sixties, as Michaux was then, he wrote:

> The prop you rested on your senses, the prop your senses rested on the world, the prop you rested on your general impression of being. They give way. A vast redistribution of sense perception occurs, which makes everything strange, a complex, continual redistribution of sense perception. *You feel less here, and more there.* Where "here"? Where "there"? In dozens of "heres," in dozens of "theres," which you were not aware of, which you do not recognize. Zones which were dark have become bright, heavy zones have become light. You have lost touch with yourself, and reality, even objects, lose their mass and their

rigidity, cease oppose much resistance to the omnipresent transforming mobility. (3)³

In and through such interrogative depths alone, knowledge is had. *Connaissance par les gouffres* is the title Michaux lent this text—literally, "knowledge through gulfs" or "out of gulfs, knowledge." Gulfs render knowledge unto the mind willing or daring to explore them. "Light though darkness," as Haakon Chevalier cleverly translated Michaux's title. Concatenating Michaux's mescaline-induced revelation with my experience of that space otherwise known as *la Zone*, it seems I can say that although a gulf has no doubt up until now separated my life from that of the *zoniers*, I can nevertheless come to lend "transforming mobility" to my cognitive powers by bridging that abyss.

La Zone ringing Paris may have finally been razed in the 1960s and its *zoniers* dispersed into H.L.M.s⁴ or elsewhere, but shantytowns reappear to surround and stare back at Capital and its capitals everywhere. Whether their names be *favela*, township, *gecekondu bölgesi*, *bidonville* or *villa miseria*, they are all variations of a category into which *la Zone* once also belonged. As jaded by Capital's development as Jean-François Lyotard had become by the 1980s, he nevertheless musters the will to pledge allegiance to the remnants of what zones may tell us of the task remaining to thought (i.e., philosophy) before the disappearance of the species. Although the Lyotard of *The Postmodern Condition* had drifted from militant Marxism to find alliances with Wittgenstein's linguistic pragmatism and the Kant of the *Third Critique*, he remained Marxian enough to seek solutions for our broken world on the fringes of "humanity" and "humanism." This is what he came close to accomplishing with *The Differend*, which sets the groundwork for just judgment in face of denial and negationism. While narcissism and consumerism render even the experience of the sublime to the mindlessness of superlatives, Lyotard would turn our attention to "[t]he immense zone [that] rustles with

---

[3] "*L'appui que vous preniez sur vos sens, l'appui que vos sens prenaient sur le monde, l'appui que vous preniez sur votre impression générale d'être. Ils cèdent. Une vaste redistribution de la sensibilité se fait, qui rend tout bizarre, une complexe, une continuelle redistribution de la sensibilité. Vous sentez moins ici, et davantage là. Où 'ici'? Où 'là'? Dans des dizaines d'*'ici', *Dans des dizaines de '*là'*, que vous ne connaissez pas. Zones obscures qui étaient claires. Zones légères qui étaient lourdes. Ce n'est plus à vous que vous aboutissez, et la réalité, les objets même, perdent leur masse et leur raideur, cessent d'opposer une résistance sérieuse à l'omniprésente mobilité transformatrice*" (OC III, 3). I have restored the word "zone" where H. Chevalier had placed "area" and the italics are mine.

[4] H.B.M. is the abbreviation for Habitations à Bon Marché, which were put into planning with the Siegfried Law of November 30, 1894. H.B.M.s were replaced by H.L.M.s (Habitations à Loyer Modéré) in 1949. There is eloquent early footage of them in Chris Marker's *Le Joli Mai* (1962).

billions of muted messages [where] despair is taken as disorder to be put right, never as the sign of an irremediable lack" (31).[5] Lyotard's "*correction*" ("disorder to be put right") seen here being applied to any and every expression of desperation is his version of the orthopedics Foucault saw imposed on subjects by institutionalized culture. The "irremediable lack" is the absence of effective solidarity with those who emit the "muted messages." But while this may sound like yet another late twentieth-century thinker on the brink of misanthropy, still believing as he did in his earliest work that the Cynics had it just about right, the late Lyotard thinks that we have the wherewithal to turn our mind into a soundproof room where voices from spaces otherwise may be heard, thereby saving philosophy from its own misery. *Soundproof Room* is the title of an exquisite and terse essay in which Lyotard gave voice to the almost mystical belief that he shared with André Malraux in art's capacity to protect a space in which innovative politics and ethics might still be thought and invented.

Literary discourse, from which the figural nature of Lyotard's style often made his philosophical writings indistinguishable, has been even more effective than philosophy at bringing *la Zone* to us rather than eliding it as an incomprehensible and rebarbative no-man's-land. And, provided that we have the patience to *look with a thinking gaze*, the far less discursive arts of photography and film promise to complete that process.

> From the Gay 90s to the end of the 1930s, the *Zone* gave rise to an abundant picturesque literature. "*Apaches*," prostitutes, ragpickers, *zoniers*, children in rags scurry around in a décor consisting of cabins, caravans, and improvised construction. The baton is passed to film, first with Georges Lacombe's documentary, then Eli Lotar and Jacques Prévert's *Aubervilliers* (1946). This gloomy repertoire intertwines the black belt [of anarchy] with the [communist] red banlieue in a classic amalgam of working class and dangerous class. (Fourcaut, 200)

While these broad strokes hardly do justice to the nigh ineffable subtleties we will soon be picking out from ancient and mesmerizing photographs of *la Zone* or even from Georges Lacombe's eponymous documentary of 1927, they do circumscribe the heyday of both pulp and highbrow literary repertoires that either alluded to *la Zone* or went as far as to take the annular shantytown as setting and its people as protagonists. Those writings, those photographs and films all began lending credence to the intuition that

---

[5] I have altered ever so slightly Georges Van Den Abbeele's fine translation of "*L'immense zone bruisse de milliards de messages feutrés.* [...] *Les désespoirs sont pris comme désordres à corriger, jamais comme les signes d'un manque irrémédiable*" (36).

Herman Melville expressed with uncanny prescience in the synecdochal "Ah Bartleby! Ah humanity!" In this minute twin exclamation we have Melville's sense that although humanity will have run its course, there is perhaps a future for the species if we can only learn to share the space that Bartleby occupied in passing. That intuition is the tenuous hope against all odds that Jean-François Lyotard stubbornly held even as he wrote his final set of essays, *Misère de la philosophie*.[6]

The point of departure for Lyotard's lines of last-ditch hope that the figural impulse in us might still save us from stultifying discourse was not Marx's response to Proudhon, but Guillaume Apollinaire's most famous poem, "Zone." Indeed, that "postmodern fable" reprises Apollinaire's title, "Zone" (Lyotard 1997: 17–32). As the lead piece to Apollinaire's 1913 collection, *Alcools*, "Zone" takes inspiration from Rimbaud's celebrated "Bateau ivre" to lead us on a mad stroll through spaces otherwise within and on the edges of Paris. An encomium to modernity, its enigmatic envoi of "*Soleil cou coupé*"[7] leaves the reader with the distinct feeling that all is not well with the human project in those months before the first modern world war. As our exploration of how photography and film captured *la Zone* will further adumbrate, the slum belt of Paris and its denizens preoccupied one of the twentieth century's least classifiable philosophers three decades before Lyotard. Along with those suspensions of space-time inscribed into the fabric of the city that were its covered passageways, the no-man's-land teeming with ragpickers, whose place on the map of Baudelaire's consciousness kept the great poet from becoming a social conservative. Hence, *la Zone* captivated Walter Benjamin and took pride of place along with passageways in the *Arcades Project*. At the top of the section, entitled "Ancient Paris, Catacombs, Demolitions, Decline of Paris," the thinker at the periphery of the Frankfurt School epigrammatically placed this line from Apollinaire's *Alcools*: "Even the automobiles have an air of antiquity here" (82). Walter Benjamin will be essential to our analysis of photography's unique faculty to penetrate the enigma of *la Zone* and coax its ethical use-value out of the dark.

---

[6] *Misère de la philosophie* was Karl Marx's 1847 biting riposte, written in French in Brussels where he sought refuge after having been exiled from Paris, to Joseph-Pierre Proudhon's *Système des contradictions économiques ou Philosophie de la misère*, published the year before. The title reverses the terms of Proudhon's subtitle, "philosophy of poverty," to peg Proudhon as a miserable philosopher. Primarily about economics, however, Marx doesn't have any more respect for Proudhon as an economist either.

[7] "Decapitated sun" (William Meredith), "The sun a severed neck" (Roger Shattuck), "Sun corseless head" (Samuel Beckett), "Sun slit throat" (Anne Hyde Greet), "Sun neck cut" (Charlotte Mandell). In severing "cutthroat" in two, Ron Padgett's "Sun cut throat" eerily suggests a quite severe sun.

Figure 14 Charles-Henri Hirsch, *Le Tigre et Coquelicot*. Photocopy of dust cover on author's personal copy.

Among the most prolific and popular writers of the first third of France's twentieth century, Charles-Henry Hirsch was the author of over fifty novels, several plays, and even some poems. This contemporary of André Gide, close friend of Paul Fort, and militant nudist was in charge of the literary and art columns at *Le Mercure de France* from the turn of the century to the middle of the First World War. Charles-Henry Hirsch is completely forgotten today.[8] In a belated recognition of the aesthetic he had had a large part in creating, he counted among the elder signatories of a *Manifeste du roman populiste* that was published at Lemonnier's instigation in January 1930.[9] In 1905, his novel entitled *Le Tigre et Coquelicot* had appeared. Hirsch tells of the bloody rivalry among la Teigne (the Louse), Facchi the Corsican, and the titular he-man, le Tigre, for the favors of the irresistible Coquelicot (Poppy). Based loosely on

---

[8] The last article of substance written about him and that JSTOR lists is "The Populist School in the French Novel" by William Leonard Schwartz, *The French Review* 4 (6) (May 1931): 473–9.

[9] Besides Lemonnier, other prominent names who appeared in and on the manifesto were Thérive, Louis Chaffurin, Louis Guilloux, Céline Lhotte, Jean-Louis Finot, and, among the older generation along with Hirsh, Lucien Descaves, Rosny, and Duhamel (Schwartz, 475).

the story of Amélie Élie (1878–1933), better known as Casque d'Or, immortalized by Simone Signoret in Jacques Becker's film of 1952, the lurid novel opens in winter with an epic slug-out, beneath the disaffected ramparts, over Coquelicot "between two superb males with knotty shoulders." On victory, Tiger ravishes an ecstatic Coquelicot whose mouth, at climax, he rubs with snow "like raspberry sorbet" stained with the Louse's blood... through most of the remainder of the novel, this over-determined sanguinary theme plays out almost exclusively in Coquelicot's imagination. This measure of relief for the reader notwithstanding, the establishing sequence of the pulp novel takes place in the vividly described *Zone*.

Figure 15 Demolition of fortifications, near Porte de Clignancourt, Paris, May 3, 1919, Agence Rol, public domain.

The pointlessness of the Thiers wall having long been obvious, the authorities began the long labor of demolishing them fourteen years after the publication of *Le Tigre et Coquelicot*. As the ramparts were dismantled, the thirty-four-kilometer ditch surrounding the metropolis was back-filled with rubble. With the exception of the excruciatingly slow disappearance of the *fortifs*' ("the city is gulping its old gums," as Céline put it) and the consequential creation of flatter land on which one could actually grow a few leeks or heads of lettuce or erect a hovel, nothing in *la Zone* changed except that it became increasingly populous and, in several areas, actually overcrowded.

While the slang spoken in Paris's slums and shanty belt had proliferated in cheaper popular novels for decades, *Journey to the End of the Night* brought the language of the underclasses to mainstream literature in 1932, a year before Casque d'Or's death. Céline, who had just beat out Raymond Queneau's effort to introduce contemporary *argot* with *Le Chiendent* (*The Bark Tree*),[10] deployed what was immediately recognized as a unique mixture of ellipsis and verbosity—an air of perpetual apocalypse:

> Around the metro entrance, near the bastions, you catch the endemic, stagnant smell of drawn-out wars, the stench of half-burned, badly baked villages, of aborted revolutions, bankrupt businesses. For years the ragpickers of the zone have been burning the same damp little piles of rubbish in ditches sheltered from the wind. Half-assed barbarians, undone by rock gut and fatigue. When they're not pushing streetcars off the embankment or pissing to their heart's content in the tollhouses, they go coughing out their lungs at the local dispensary. No blood left in their veins. No trouble. When the next war comes, they'll again make their fortune selling rat skins, cocaine, and corrugated steel masks. (206)[11]

With the literary correlates of Van Gogh's brushstrokes, in just over a hundred words, Céline gives us *la Zone*, parts of its topography, how those parts relate to the anachronistic military geography, the *zoniers*, their most prominent social and economic activities, and even a political cautionary tale.[12]

Among literary creators, Céline was uniquely qualified and situated to analyze *la Zone* because of what he did to get by financially most of his life. From modest petty bourgeois origins and growing up in Passage Choiseul, he managed, following years of medical study specially attuned to the needs of war veterans, to become a licensed physician in 1924.[13] In November 1927,

---

[10] *The Bark Tree* is Barbara Wright's astute translation of *Le Chiendent*, which literally means "crab grass." For a discussion about why "Dogtooth" might also work, see R. Harvey, "Queneau/Dog/Man/Body: Coup de Dédé ou jeu de Descartes?" *Gradiva* 6 (2) (1996): 18–32.

[11] "*Autour du métro, près des bastions croustille, endémique, l'odeur des guerres qui traînent, des relents de villages mi-brûlés, mal cuits, des révolutions qui avortent, des commerces en faillite. Les chiffonniers de la zone brûlent depuis des saisons les mêmes petits tas humides dans les fossés à contre-vent. C'est des barbares à la manque ces biffins pleins de litrons et de fatigue. Ils vont tousser au Dispensaire d'à côté, au lieu de balancer les tramways dans les glacis et d'aller pisser dans l'octroi un bon coup. Plus de sang. Pas d'histoires. Quand la guerre elle reviendra, la prochaine, ils feront encore une fois fortune à vendre des peaux de rats, de la cocaïne et des masques en tôle ondulée*" (OC I, 240).

[12] As little as political parties on the Left would like to hear it, Céline has the experience to know why revolutions, as conceived since the Enlightenment, fail.

[13] Louis-Ferdinand Destouches was among the first to see combat in the First World War. Seriously wounded on a mission, Destouches, who had attained the rank of *maréchal des logis*, was awarded the Croix de guerre. The details of Destouches/Céline's life are varied, complex, intriguing, but far too numerous to elaborate further on here. One of the best biographies is Henri Godard's *Céline*.

after having moved in together at 36, rue d'Alsace in Clichy with American dancer Elizabeth Craig, Céline opened a clinic in this same building, situated some 500 meters from the outer edge of the Cimetière des Batignolles to the east and west of which extended squalid swaths of shanties erected pell-mell in *la Zone*. Bardamu, Céline's surrogate in *Journey to the End of the Night*, recounts:

> I wasn't going to see [Robinson] quite so often now, because about that time I was put in charge of a small neighborhood dispensary for tuberculosis. I may as well call a spade a spade: it brought in eight hundred francs a month. My patients were mostly people from the zone, that village of sorts [*espèce de village*], which never quite pulls itself up out of the mud, sludge, and garbage, bordered by paths along whose fences all-too-precocious snotnosed little girls cut school to pick up a franc, a fistful of fries, and a dose of gonorrhea from some satyr. (*Romans I*, 333; 287–8)

Throughout this "*espèce de village*"—in fact, more like what Perec would qualify as an "*espèce d'espace*"—roam teenagers not unlike the outcasts of normative sexuality that Foucault would describe in *The Will to Knowledge*,[14] adults barely out of childhood who comport themselves oblivious of the moral straightjacket that the nearby city and suburb alike would have otherwise imposed on them. Noteworthy, however, is that whereas Foucault passes no moral judgment whatsoever on outcasts (in fact, sometimes, the opposite is the case), for Céline, the *zoniers* are absolutely hopeless. Giving us a glimpse of how the visual arts were receiving and mediating *la Zone*, Céline continues by painting a tableau of absolute futility in which he, nevertheless, seems to revel rather sadistically:

> A setting for avant-garde films where the laundry poisoned trees and all the lettuce drips with urine on Saturday night. In those few months of specialized practice, I performed no miracles. Miracles were sorely needed. But my patients weren't at all eager for me to perform miracles, they were banking on their tuberculosis to move them from the state of absolute misery in which they've been moldering ever since they could remember to the state of relative misery conferred by microscopic government pensions. Their more or less seropositive sputum had been getting them periodically rejected for military service ever since the war. They got thinner and thinner, thanks to fever maintained by eating little,

---

[14] Notable among Foucault's examples is Jouy, whose incongruous name coincides so well with his wanton expenditure of libidinal energies.

vomiting a lot, drinking vast quantities of wine, and working in spite of all, one day out of three, to tell the truth. (*Romans I*, 333; 288)

But for all the precious detail about mores of *la Zone*, delivered here with inimitably scintillating imagery, Céline keeps his distance. The more Céline will aspire to a literary career as sole source of income, the less he will care about *la Zone* and its inhabitants as patients to care *for* or to care *about* and the more they become ammunition for his lapidary and telegraphic prose aimed at everyone he hates. More precisely, the less immediate or unquestioned Céline's admittance into the Republic of Letters, the more explicit become his declarations of ontological difference from "*les Zizi*"—one of his pet derogatory terms for Jews. The queasy feeling that the *zoniers* are for Céline, simply, a less canny version of "*les Zizi*"—Jews as he construes them and about whom he will soon spew outright venom—is already virtually confirmed in his second novel, *Death on the Installment Plan*:

> I'm no Yid, metic, Freemason or graduate of Normale Sup'. I'm useless at promoting myself, I fuck around too much, I have a bad rep. For fifteen years they've watched me struggle out here in the Zone. Those dregs of the dregs have pulled every trick with me, show me every sign of contempt. Lucky they haven't fired me. Literature makes up for it all.
> (*Romans I*, 516; 20)

Yet, eyewitnesses of Céline's work as a practitioner of medicine—and, indeed, his own tone, at least in the first novel—contribute to a portrait of Dr. Destouches that evinces many signs of genuine commitment to helping improve the health of the lowest strata of society: the Paris lumpen *zoniers*. To read his abundant correspondence[15] and the most reliable narratives of that dimension of his life,[16] one might even be tempted to imagine a man who, under other historical circumstances, might have been tempted by reformist progressive socialism, instead of fascism. Personal circumstances of misanthropy and chronic paranoia would, however, have prevented him from ever entering any form of party politics. While Céline's impulse to help the down-and-out was not fueled by the self-abnegation of a Simone Weil, what he lacked altogether was any actual *empathy* with the dregs of humanity. Céline served civilization's health mission the way nineteenth-century medicine did. *Scientia sexualis*, Foucault explains,

> set itself up as the supreme authority in matters of hygienic necessity, taking up the old fears of venereal affliction and combining them with

---

[15] Céline, *Lettres*. Paris: Gallimard (Bibliothèque de la Pléiade, 558), 2009.
[16] For example, Henri Godard, *Céline: une biographie*, 2011.

the new themes of asepsis, and the great evolutionist myths with the recent institutions of public health; it claimed to ensure the physical vigor and the moral cleanliness of the social body; it promised to eliminate defective individuals, degenerate and bastardized populations. In the name of a biological and historical urgency, it justified the racisms of the state, which at the time were on the horizon. (HS, 54; VS, 73)

Similarly, Céline's cold dispensing of medical assistance and the floodgates of his racist venom that would soon swing wide open are far from incompatible.

After the publication of *Death on the Installment Plan* and its utter failure to match the success of *Journey to the End of the Night*, Céline's persecution complex *cum* racism would quickly spiral out of control with him now openly blaming it all on "the dregs of dregs," the Jews. Ever more convinced that he was an expert not only on the "real" reasons for his own failures, but on European and, indeed, world politics, there would soon be the diatribes in *Je suis partout* and the pamphlets that his vitriolic pen would excrete—the most famous of which was *Bagatelles pour un massacre* (1937). There would also be his attendance at fascist cultural events in Nazi-occupied Paris, such as the "Jews and France" exhibit at the Palais Berlitz in late 1941. Then still, short endless years later, there would be the fall of the Third Reich and Céline's flight through an apocalyptic Germany to exile first in Sigmaringen, then in Copenhagen. He would eventually recount these events and years in which he was misunderstood in a brilliantly insane trilogy of novels.[17] Insane because, as W. G. Sebald points out in "Air War and Literature," of the lead essay in what would be *his* final book, *On the Natural History of Destruction*, "Many who fled to the most remote parts of the Reich after the raids on Hamburg were in a demented state of mind" (Sebald e-book, 118). Brilliant because these three novels constitute a return to the very first reason why he became a writer. Sebald is once again helpful for situating the Céline of the late 1950s when he qualifies *Winterspelt* by Alfred Andersch as "literature as a means of straightening out one's own past life" (Sebald e-book, 179).

In thinking about literary evocations of *la Zone*, one naturally turns also to Céline's contemporary, Raymond Queneau. One recalls the sequence in *Zazie dans le métro* (1959) in the Saint-Ouen flea market, just outside Porte de Clignancourt, captured visually by Louis Malle in the film version of the novel (1960) on which Queneau served as consultant or those scenes in *Pierrot mon ami* (1942) featuring dirty old men ("*philosophes*") at l'Uni-Park, conceived after the real Luna-Park, which stood between Neuilly and the rampart remnants from 1909 to 1931.[18] While Céline's intercourse with

---

[17] *D'un château l'autre* (1957), *Nord* (1960), and the posthumous *Rigodon* (1969).
[18] *Pierrot mon ami* is referenced by Cohen, 215, n. 59; illustration 108. The moon-faced

la Zone and its inhabitants was from a banlieue-side perspective, barely separated from the squalid territory itself, Raymond Queneau peered into it and its denizens from slightly further out, where things were more placid. Starting in 1935, Queneau resided in the western city of Neuilly. Leafing through Queneau's hundreds of poems, one indeed encounters lines that seem to evoke *la Zone*'s landscape and the activities therein:

> A bike all sliced up
> a mugging about to happen
> thugs and louts
> [...]
> the whore hand on hip
> a hooked passerby leans in
> five francs for the darling[19]

But as the title of this little 1946 ditty indicates, "Saint-Ouen's Blues"[20] is obviously experienced in that town just *beyond* the shanty belt and, like the gap between the territories referenced in collections entitled *Courir les rues* and *Battre la campagne*, *la Zone* is a *space otherwise* whose principal virtue is as source for importing characteristics into Queneau's beloved banlieues. In one of his many aborted poems, probably written about the time of *Zazie dans le metro* (1959), he says that he walks along what is left of the ramparts beyond which he can see grass flying about.[21] But here, instead of just outside, this observation would no doubt require him to be situated at the *inside* edge of the swath of slums, which are curiously replaced by vacant lots. The title of this piece—"*Discorde mélodie des terrains d'épandage*" (*OC I*, 829-45) or "Discordant Melody of the Sewage Fields"—serves nevertheless as a reminder that, still well into the twentieth century, Paris considered the banlieue in its entirety as its dumping ground. As one of the foremost readers

---

Pierrot staring at the moon, which governs the minds of earth's lunatics; Luna-Park deformed for the purposes of fiction into *l'Uni-Park*—sounding a bit like "looney park" in English, which Queneau knew quite well.

[19] *Un vélo coupé en tranches*
  Un coup dur qui se déclenche
  Des voyous des malappris
  [...]
  La putain qui se déhanche
  Un passant séduit se penche
  C'est cent sous pour le chéri (*OC I*, 133; my translation)
[20] Published, as Claude Debon notes, in *La Rue* 6, July 12, 1946, 2 (*OC I*, 1211).
[21] *[...] mais moi qui*
  me promène aux fortifications j'hésite ainsi
  que je dise la mare des sintifs des saintifications
  et qu'au-delà s'envole l'herbe qui que quoi donc (*OC I*, 835)

Figure 16 View of Saint-Ouen and the Paris fortifications, postcard.

at Éditions Gallimard, located in the city's 6th arrondissement, Queneau necessarily traversed *la Zone* on his way to work and to reach his favorite outlying towns to the north and northwest of the capital.

Although in retrospect it would appear that Céline (with *Journey to the End of the Night* appearing in October 1932) and Queneau (with *Le Chiendent*, published in October 1933) were in direct competition to be the first to dramatically and massively introduce modern urban slang into mainstream literature, their manners of using the dialect—whose heart and soul was *la Zone*—could not have been more different. Queneau's interest in *argot* was that of a sort of linguistic entomologist; Céline's was not so much an interest as it was a visceral need. Queneau, while not exactly jovial all the time, was bent on making people laugh; the rare times Céline laughed at all, it was either jaundiced or downright dark and his effect on readers is more often unease than comic relief. Of the two writers, for better or for worse, Céline was better than Queneau at channeling the *zonier*'s linguistically mediated relationship to the society. But by "worse," in Céline's case, we must also mean mistrust and even hatred for the other, all others. In this sense, in the world according to Céline, where fiction cannot be differentiated from actual experience, *la Zone* functions quite like a "zone of indistinction" in Agamben's sense of the term; for Céline, *la Zone* is everywhere and putative genetic privilege over atavistic abjection—whose ironic name could be *Je suis partout*—is the guiding illusion. For Queneau, on the other hand, indistinction is within. Along with René Char, Raymond Queneau is one of the twentieth century's most abiding acolytes of Heraclitus. As such, he deploys countless examples of his supposed inability (or willful unwillingness) to know an individual's sex, to know an individual's identity, to know exactly what it is that an individual does for a living, to know her or his "true" personality.[22] In this sense, Queneau could purport to know the *zonier*'s indistinction from an ontological perspective. Ultimately, however, and for opposing reasons, neither of these masters of the *zonier*'s idiom could know the *zonier* empathically.

Rife with these ambiguities, the title character of Queneau's wartime novel, *Pierrot mon ami* (1942), translates the author's penchant for indistinction in order to exorcise his fear of mortality. For that author, *Pierrot mon ami* was no doubt an exercise in controlling his own morbid anxiety—common to so many—following defeat at the hands of the Nazis two years before. Two short years later, in his capacity as reader for Gallimard, while not glossing over the flaws in an inexperienced author, Queneau recommends the publication of Marguerite Duras's second novel, *La Vie tranquille*, by the prestigious publishing house.[23] Meanwhile, in 1946, a real-life Pierrot is killed: not "Pierrot mon ami," but "Pierrot le fou." Born in 1916, "Pierrot le fou" was the nickname lent to Pierre Loutrel who, as leader of the "Tractions Gang" (so called for the Citroën traction automobiles they drove while committing their crimes), became France's first "public enemy number one"—a status rounded out by his active collaboration with the Nazi occupier. Given the ambiguities that attend not a few of Marguerite Duras's own wartime activities and given her lifelong predilection for sordid news items, it is of little surprise that "Pierrot le fou" captivated her attention sufficiently to have a minor character in another neglected story mention him prominently.[24] Gaston, the jovial but "disillusioned" street-sweeper (*OC II*, 1063; 104) in charge of rue Saint-Eulalie, is the perfect foil for Madame

[22] This is a dimension of Queneau's thought that I believe Michel Foucault might have missed, but that no doubt would have interested him.
[23] On his reader's notecard, Queneau wrote: "Critique: One may suppose the author wanted to write in the manner of Camus, in *The Stranger*. It would be an exaggeration to say she succeeded. The first part isn't bad, thanks to the somewhat worn out trick of using the *passé défini*. The second part is boring. The whole is a tad botched. The author should rework her manuscript. That said, publishing this novel would be indicated." (*OC I*, 1428–9). Cf. also Raymond Queneau, "Un lecteur de Marguerite Duras." *Cahiers Renaud-Barrault* 52 (December 1965): 3–5.
[24] It is ironic, given Duras's oscillation between left-leaning resistance activities and collaboration, that Alphonse Boudard parodied the Communist Party's slogan when writing about Loutrel in *Les Grands Criminels* (Paris: Le Pré aux Clercs, 1989)—Chapter V is "Pierrot le Fou ou les Lendemains qui flinguent." Boudard himself, under his far better known pseudonym of San-Antonio, could be the subject of a study of *la Zone* and literary uses of twentieth-century Parisian slang.

Dodin, the acerbic concierge of the building where the narrator of the eponymous story lives. (Rue Saint-Eulalie is a thinly veiled version of rue Saint-Benoît, where Duras lived from 1942 until her death in 1996.)

> Gaston approaches Mlle Mimi and, as salutation, he says:
> "Pierrot's dead," (he's talking about Crazy Pierrot); "it's going to be more of a bloody bore around here now."

Or:

> "A nice crime, with a very difficult trial—that's the very best thing that can happen to a street-sweeper. There's no crime that hasn't got some piece of luck attached to it, no one suspects the sweeper of having witnessed it so no one interrogates him. That, for the sweeper, is the only possible distraction and the only chance he has to be taken seriously. I'll never have that kind of luck in this neighborhood, where crime is so rare. But if this opportunity were given to me and if the trial depended on my evidence, I'd make sure it dragged on for as long as possible." (*OC II*, 1066; 107–8; translation altered)

"Madame Dodin" had appeared in Sartre and Beauvoir's *Les Temps modernes* in 1952[25] and Duras included it, just before "Construction Sites," in her 1954 collection of short stories entitled *Des journées entières dans les arbres* (*Whole Days in the Trees*). In the lines just quoted, the street-sweeper voices the laconic announcement—"Pierrot is dead"—then his statement is interpreted by the narrator ("A nice crime [...] I'd make sure it dragged on for as long as possible."). The narrator is a woman who lives across the street from Mimi's boarding house, in the building where Madame Dodin reigns from the bottom of the socio-economic ladder as concierge and rails against the aberrant garbage disposal habits of the bourgeois inhabitants. At 5, rue Saint-Benoît, Duras was living right across from just such a *table d'hôte* and, of course, every building in 1940 Paris must have had a concierge like Madame Dodin. Delighting in terrorizing the hypersensitive Mademoiselle Mimi, while thrilling the irascible Madame Dodin, a product of what he says and what the narrator tells us he means, Gaston precisely mirrors the program that Marguerite Duras would deploy in her many reportages on sordid crimes and other *faits divers*.

That same Marguerite Duras, but one far more experienced and successful as a writer than when Raymond Queneau gave her her first break, had just plumbed the zone of indistinction that separates memory and forgetting in the scenario she had written for *Hiroshima mon amour* when she came

---

[25] *Les Temps modernes* 79 (May 1952): 1952–81.

across a human interest story in the popular daily press that would soon become transposed into her creative world. In our first chapter, we already retraced how Duras expanded and fictionalized the article she had come across in an October 1959 issue of *France-Soir*: a woman running a café in a working-class district thought she recognized her husband, long ago considered to have been lost in a concentration camp, in a hobo who drifted in asking for a glass of water. Duras took this news item as an opportunity to extend her work in *Hiroshima mon amour* on amnesia and the possibility of anamnesis by the free use of the imagination. The first step in the narrative adaptation of this anecdote was to shift the location of the woman's café from the 12th arrondissement in eastern working-class Paris to Puteaux, a modest manufacturing town west of the capital, on the left bank of the Seine as it loops back north after Boulogne-Billancourt, Nanterre, and Suresnes, not far from Mont-Valérien where, fifteen years before, the Nazis regularly executed resistance members. Just beyond Porte Maillot and a particularly densely populated stretch of *la Zone*, the banks of the river at Puteaux were not always as bucolic as the Impressionist paintings done seventy or eighty years earlier in the area would suggest. It is also noteworthy for this part of Duras's mental landscape, that exactly one year after Colpi's film, the murderous repression (under orders of police chief Maurice Papon) of a peaceful demonstration by Algerians on October 17, 1961 would be concentrated in these impoverished western reaches of greater Paris. Duras and Jarlot's translation of their story from Rue Daumesnil, east of Place de la Bastille, all the way to Place de la Vieille Église in Puteaux, west of Paris, was no one-step process made on a whim. As suggested by an interview that Duras granted the weekly *L'Express* in June 1960, the authors had originally thought to place the story in and around a café in Aubervilliers which is, again, just outside Paris, but this time to the north-east. Then, finally, so that the hobo's makeshift shelter could be situated on the banks of the Seine toward Boulogne-Billancourt and make credible the story's starting point on Bastille Day, with its traditional French air force fly-over along the axis of Avenue de la Grande Armée and the Champs-Élysées, Puteaux was the ideal location for the "Maison Langlois."

Among the most striking sequences of Colpi's film, as informed by the Duras–Jarlot scenario, are the meticulously subdued and empathetic scenes filmed at the hovel of the hobo (played by Georges Wilson) on the banks of the Seine. Through the usual process of identification with characters whose presence on the screen is sufficiently forceful, we follow Thérèse (played by Alida Valli) as she attempts to penetrate the mental landscape of this mysterious man living like a *zonier* in a shack engulfed in scraps of paper and the bare necessities that he acquires. Are the clippings of images and words from discarded magazines the hobo's extra-linguistic attempts to recover memory or does he accumulate them haphazardly, in an activity only marginally more reasonable than paper recycling? Thérèse will force the issue, banking on the former hypothesis. But her attempts to help the hobo complete the process of anamnesis fail miserably as the film draws to its conclusion. As stretched out and patient as the intimate shots of Thérèse in the bum's home are, the long sequence in which Colpi's camera follows Thérèse walking in high heels, lost in anguished thought, south along the Seine the several kilometers separating Puteaux from the hovel is sublimely lyrical. This pilgrimage—like the trek to the construction site in the 1954 story—culminating in a meticulous ritual of attempted, but failed, communing is vintage Duras—a judgment borne out by the archive.

That same empathetic reach is attempted without the aid of pathos in Agnès Varda's 1985 work, entitled *Vagabond* for English-speaking audiences, and *Sans toit ni loi* by the filmmaker herself. Literally "without roof or rule," idiomatically signifying "homeless," it is Varda's caring camera alone, instead of an intradiegetic character like Thérèse in *The Long Absence*, that does its best to follow Mona (Sandrine Bonnaire), to record in film "with dignity," as Didi-Huberman said of *Falkenau*, "those who have no name" (2012: 156). Mona, of course, is a name, but like a *Häftling* in Auschwitz tattooed on the forearm with a number, all human value that a name carries has left the individual who carries this one in Varda's film. Like the *Figuren* into which the Nazis turned Jews, Mona has acquired the status of film extra—*figurant* in French.[26] As photographic record of a *zonarde*, *Sans toit ni loi* is similar to *La Jetée* (1962), by Varda's fellow "Left Bank Group" comrade Chris Marker, in that it breaks with the restrictive rule of hegemonic film according to which a narrative must focus on a true protagonist—whether heroic or antiheroic. Like the unnamed guinea pig in *La Jetée*, Mona can be neither heroic nor antiheroic. However, the graininess of Varda's final cut of the final sequence is not so much the clichéd esthetic of the documentary as the admission that film—in contrast, as I will argue shortly, to photography—fails, no matter how close it can get, to sharing common ground with these stubbornly indistinct subjects off in their zone.

The visual arts, as their name suggests, have the obvious capacity to enable the spectator—that homologue of the book reader[27]—to rely far less

---

[26] This thought and the notions that carry it is inspired partially by the Didi-Huberman essay just cited, *Peuples exposés, peuples figurants*. On the page where he refers to "those who have no name," Didi-Huberman gives several examples of filmmakers whose works attempt such an empathic filming of nameless extras: Luis Buñuel, Joris Ivens, Glauber Rocha, Pier Paolo Pasolini, Aki Kaurismäki, Jean Rouch, Frederick Wisemen, Johan Van der Keuken, Michael Glawoffer, and Wang Bing, as well as documentarists Pawel Sala, Omer Fast, and Krassimir.

[27] And by "book reader," I do not mean what the *OED* gives as definition (b): "a hand-held

on the work of his imagination in order to visualize things. At the Studio des Ursulines in 1928, a "documentary" short feature by René Clair's assistant, Georges Lacombe, debuted. *La Zone: au pays des chiffonniers* is a twenty-eight-minute film that presents the workaday life of ragpickers as they shuttle between northern districts *within* Paris and their hovels in the zone just *outside* Porte de Clignancourt. At a time when "non-narrative documentary films about Paris were in vogue" (Smith in Aitken, 510), the raw material of *La Zone* is inflected with *narrative* qualities which, although avoiding anything like social realist propaganda, nevertheless add a certain element of pathos.[28] The film's subject is, as the subtitle suggests, a cohort or—more in keeping with what we are shown—a *clan* of ragpickers. The film's timeline runs from dawn until dusk on a single day.[29] In the long hours between those celestial events, the people of the urban base toil much, rest and restore themselves very little, socializing furtively while they do both. Lacombe is intent on showing the complexity of ragpicker labor and the diligence with which a multiplicity of skillful tasks are carried out. As one of the few critics who have written on *La Zone* remarks, "Lacombe depicted a harsh reality of urban society that many would prefer to ignore altogether. He did so with empathy: the chiffonniers do *useful* work" (Langlois in Aitken, 1035; my emphasis).

The first several minutes of *La Zone* are febrile and extremely powerful. Lacombe's sober but moving work opens, without preamble, within the city with the members of the ragpicking clan whom he will follow throughout the film quickly, yet meticulously, selecting recyclable materials out of *poubelles* before the city's carters make their rounds.[30] Variations of this triage by individual *chiffonniers* are shown in a series of vignettes, punctuated by fades to black and fade-ins. As we enter the third minute Lacombe has brought us to a *ligne de partage*—the edge of the city at Porte de Clignancourt where day workers walk or are bussed into the metropolis, where bourgeois in suits buy the morning paper, and where the ragpickers return to *la Zone* to continue their work processing recoverable refuse: more triage, further recycling

---

device on which electronic versions of books, or other text in digital form, can be read." I like original meanings.

[28] "*La Zone* positions itself at the phalanx of what is known as the 'third avant-garde' [combining] documentary film and sociological study" (Smith in Aitken, 510–11).

[29] "The narrative structure of *La Zone* [...] one day in the city [...] is also found in other films of the period, including *Rien que les heures* (Alberto Cavalcanti, 1926) and *Berlin: Die Sinfonie der Großstadt* (Walther Ruttman, 1927)" (Langlois in Aitken, 1034).

[30] Garbage cans had only been imposed on the capital's inhabitants—despite ragpickers' protests—forty-four years before Lacombe's film. Eugène-René Poubelle, préfet de la Seine. (Curiously, the street named after Poubelle in Paris' wealthy 16th arrondissement is one of the few streets so short that it carries only one numbered address.)

refinement, working directly on incredibly dangerous conveyor belts, hammering then stringing paper into bales, smashing metal objects in view of smelting, collecting dust for fertilizer... These activities that we witness in the first third of Lacombe's *La Zone* vindicate Benjamin's suspicion[31] that a famously enigmatic observation by Baudelaire about this figure from the Parisian underbelly had nothing to do with anything condemnable:

> The "jerky gait" of the ragpicker is not necessarily due to the effect of alcohol. Every few moments, he must stop to gather refuse, which he throws into his wicker basket. (*Arcades Project*, 364)
>
> The bearing of the modern hero, as modeled on the ragpicker: his "jerky gait," the necessary isolation in which he goes about his business, the interest he takes in the refuse and detritus of the great city. (*Arcades Project*, 368)

But, about half way through, after mocking a reporter shooting photos of an aging, bloated, and alcoholic La Goulue, Lacombe's documentary rarity gets distracted by the temptation of narrative which overtakes the film's objective thrust. The concluding sequence of the film conjoins it with the opening of Hirsch's novel of 1905. Showing *la Zone* in this bucolic light diminishes its power to fire the spectator's imagination. Although Lacombe's beautiful film "concerns itself with the act of living, concentrating itself on lives otherwise ignored" (Smith in Aitken, 511), it may mislead the viewer into imagining that these lives might somehow be integrated into life as defined by the bourgeoisie, that is, life as circumscribed by official discourse. For all of Georges Lacombe's documentary examination of a multiplicity of routines carried out in "their daily struggle for existence" (ibid.), his film doesn't quite succeed in revealing to us what Benjamin called the "critical point" of *zonier* existence: the ontological key to *being in a space otherwise*. Identifying, in a certain way, with the garbage they remove from the bourgeois city, recycling some and dumping the rest: by the detail of his labor, the *zonier* emphatically and definitively distances himself from bourgeois life, forecloses any possibility of integration, all the while asserting that there is a life *elsewhere*—in an elsewhere that is, nevertheless, *here*.

Perhaps because photography, more often than its technological offspring—film—stands back from narrative, foregrounding its reticence to *recount* in face of the scant wisdom in a saying like "every picture tells a story," or perhaps because subjects of the photographic apparatus can

---

[31] As *La Zone*'s inclusion in "Le Paris de Walter Benjamin," part of *Walter Benjamin Archives*, curated at the Musée d'art et d'histoire du judaïsme by Florent Perrier suggests, it is not impossible that the author of *Das Passagen-Werk* saw Lacombe's film during his time in Paris.

so much more often than in film *stare back* in such a way as to hold hasty claims to knowledge by the spectator in abeyance, the photograph seems far more apt to open onto an ontology of the inhabitant of a wasteland, a zone. "Garbage." —With this one-word sentence, Molly Nesbit begins a subsection of a chapter entitled "*Ombres portées*" or "Shadows Cast" within her capacious, exhaustive, magisterial presentation of *Atget's Seven Albums*. Although there were other photographers—Emmanuel Pottier (1864–1921), Henri Godefroy (1837–1913), Charles Lansiaux (1855–1922), and, of course, Charles Marville (1813–79)—who documented, albeit rarely, the sumptuous unseemliness of *la Zone*, the art of Eugène Atget (1857–1927) brought the people and the place into convergence in a way and to an extent that the others had not. Dozens of Atget's images of this space otherwise invite our look to linger at the same instant that we discover, in a shared yet distinct mesmerization, that the look of the *zonier* seems to linger on us. The generous unobtrusiveness of Eugène Atget's camera eye finds its match in Nesbit's acute analysis. Both artist and critic open possibilities for empathic communing with the other who, in the end, is me.

In reading Eugène Atget's album of photographs entitled *Zoniers*, Molly Nesbit would distill a space with a similar status—both topological and ethical: eternal. No less than the very *modernity* of the ragpickers who populated *la Zone* for over a century, Nesbit writes, "would survive demolitions and condemnations by boards of health. Their separation, their *écart*, would settle down elsewhere but it would not go away" (175). Their very being is a function of separateness, in other words, and the habitat of these beings is "[a] remove that was as much chosen as it had been encouraged" (175). Yet, through photography, as we shall see, they cleave to us spectators, beckoning us to activity.

"Garbage." The effect of Nesbit's full sentence composed of this single noun is explosive, impatient: it was indeed refuse that had moved to the center of Atget's vision when in 1912 he decided to pull the pictures of *la Zone* that he had included "in the *Paris Pittoresque* series and began to develop it further" (169) and shot many more images to create a distinct, topographically homogeneous "album he entitled *Zoniers*. *Vues et types de la zone militaire*" (170). From our initial perusal of these photographs we notice that, far more than a mere gallery of "specimens" or "types" living in the ring of squalor, Atget is intent on showing us "the *labor* of the ragpicker"—a toiling consisting in the treatment and extraction of value from the garbage provided by the waste of bourgeois life (170; my emphasis). But whereas, like Lacombe, "Atget was concerned to have all of the phases [of the *zonier*'s work] represented" (170), unlike Lacombe's filmic images, many of Atget's photographs in this special album reveal a distinct *erasure of differentiation* between garbage—the raw material of the ragpicker's labor—and the ragpicker's body. Becoming, in part (but an essential part), the garbage he treats, the *zonier* ensures something approaching his ontological distance from the bourgeois. This is the *critical point*—in the Benjaminian sense—of Atget's *zoniers* photographs to which we might have remained blind without Molly Nesbit's sympathetic, almost symbiotic, reading of this body of work.[32]

Looking at the *chiffonnier de la zone*, albeit across time severed from our present by oblivion and cut off in the very same place from space *formerly* otherwise and now "developed," Molly Nesbit sees what Eugène Atget had to have seen when he documented the ragpicker's *presence*, while leaving that man-*just-over-there* blissfully unexplained by narration (*logos*):

> The working ragpicker stopped work for the photograph. Work had to be deduced from the setting; the worker was slightly disengaged from it; the formality of the pose put him at some remove from his work and from the viewer, unable to see how the work was done. The pose acted as a screen. Atget would (or could) only describe the *métier* up to this point; after that a discretion or hesitation set in. An ellipse formed in the document. The ellipse reenacted the differences the ragpickers themselves had already established. One would never know precisely what rags meant to them. (171)

When photographed, the body performs, but in an almost entirely different way from the way it does when it is filmed: in Georges Lacombe's presentation, bodies move without interruption, incessantly, feverishly, furtively; in Eugène Atget's, bodies freeze—or, more often, *a* body does. If it moves at all, it is in the instant, in defiance of the rule that operators usually derive from the strictures of the apparatus: the rule of standing stock still. Either way—still or shifting in place—the ragpicker established "some remove" from the photographer and, consequentially, necessarily, a remove from all the readers of the image including us, today—a remove essential to the ragpicker's *being apart*, his indistinct, ineffable *Dasein*.

The ellipse that Atget's documenting gesture had to introduce is informed in part if not totally by the filmic support of the photographic inscription, which can produce only discrete, still images and not, as in cinema, the illusion of movement by dint of multiple images. But the ellipse is also a gap, a "discretion or hesitation" that Atget *caught*—no doubt by empathic contagion—from the objects of his attention, a hiatus not unlike the special

---

[32] Benjamin's concept of critical point bears some comparison to Roland Barthes' concept, as described and illustrated in *La Chambre claire* (*Camera Lucida*), of the *punctum*.

type of space that a zone is: a space apart and otherwise, that is *right here*. Although Nesbit provides a partial solution to this enigma in the next paragraph, when she writes that "it was precisely this garbage that was the ragpicker's prize" (171), a little further on, invoking Alexandre Privat d'Anglemont's encomium to the Cité Doré in *Paris anecdote* (1854),[33] stating further that "squalor and garbage [...] had moral and cultural value for the ragpicker, a concept that baffled outsiders" (171), she ends this first volley of brilliant observations about the ragpicker's use of garbage both as source of value for subsistence living and as badge of honor by underscoring the *zonier*'s policy of distinction with the invaluable insight that "the gulf between the *chiffonnier* and the rest of the city was carefully preserved by both *chiffonnier* and bourgeois alike, as if by mutual agreement. The ragpickers used their work to hold themselves apart from the rest of the city" (171). Nesbit nevertheless still needs the ragpicker's return of the look, back at Atget's camera, to get to the heart of what the *zonier* shares with us, yet withholds. With Nesbit's insistent repetition of the word "work" in the paragraph cited, we sense that she indeed knows "what rags meant to them." The existence of garbage and the being of men become indistinguishable. In *la Zone*, this ontological divide becomes indistinct. The *zoniers* are *garbagemen* and Molly Nesbit's critical work is meant to make these *beings apart* be part of, partake in *one* world.

In the second movement of Nesbit's scrutiny of Atget's photographs, she comes to dwell, as Baudelaire had done in *Paris Spleen*, on the eyes of the poor. Turning briefly, now, from the ragpickers' work to their existence as a mass (if not quite a collectivity), Nesbit will attempt to shift to their essence as imagined individuals. Atget's photographs uniquely enable this discovery with the profound ethical consequence of *life apart*. Nesbit thus first retraces the well-worn story of "the slow march to the *zone*" (175) from two opposite directions: the slum belt populated *centripetally* due to rural and foreign migration and *centrifugally* when lumpen elements of the capital were edged out under "pressure of real estate developers and health experts" (171). While this demographic history of the late nineteenth and early twentieth centuries highlights and reinforces the dependence of marginal populations on garbage for subsistence living—"The rags gave the ragpickers their independence from the modern industrial city, even though they could not exactly exist without it" (171)—the ethical value of this independence yet remains elusive. A political dimension of the *zonier*'s putative independence predicated on garbage might appear to be deducible from the "mores" of the

---

[33] The full title is *Paris anecdote. Les industries inconnues, la Childebert, les oiseaux de nuit, la villa des chiffonniers.*

Figure 17 Eugène Atget, Porte d'Italie, Zoniers, 1912 (13th arr.). Bibliothèque historique de la Ville de Paris.

ragpickers when Nesbit quotes extensively from Georges Mény's *Professions et métiers—IX. Le chiffonnier de Paris*[34] from whose analysis she concludes that "the ragpicker had pulled himself into a special corner of the proletariat, so special that his *indifference* to revolutionary politics was a constant source of astonishment" (172; my emphasis) and, finishing with a nominalized French adjective that Nesbit might well have plucked from Michel Foucault's notional quiver, "class difference here did not fall into the familiar Marxist categories; the ragpicker belonged to the *impensé*" (173). However, it is only when Nesbit returns to look with extreme care at individual clichés that Atget included in his *Zonier* album that she is able to correlate the chiffonnier's separateness from mainstream proletarian concerns with the deep space of his being.

Nesbit strives ever forth to plumb the *zonier*'s being with her empathic gaze. The negotiation between the photographer and the ragpicker to be

---

[34] About Mény's work, Nesbit writes: "appearing in a series sponsored by Catholic socialists, [it] analyzed the extent of the separation between the *chiffonniers* and the rest of the city. It was a disturbing gap, which grew more disturbing upon inspection. The differences were more than political here—they were incomprehensible" (172).

Figure 18 Eugène Atget, Chiffonniers, Porte d'Asnières, Cité Trébert, 1913 (17th arr.). Bibliothèque historique de la Ville de Paris.

photographed is only the starting point for this ethical reckoning: "When posed, aware of the process of representation, their attitude toward the photograph was rather different. Atget's photographs of the ragpickers, all of them posed, showed their diffidence very plainly." Putting herself in Atget's place at the very moment she imagines him having strived with all his being to put himself in the moment and place of the ragpicker, as in the example of the *garbagemen* half engulfed like the hobo in *The Long Absence* in refuse within their shanty near Porte d'Asnières, Nesbit can now, finally, fathom the tie between indifference to class struggle and esthetic indifference:

> Since the ragpickers had withdrawn themselves from bourgeois culture, it would follow that they would withdraw as well from something as bourgeois as a photograph. [...] The look gave them victory. For these

were by and large knowing looks, with a proper dose of suspicion, confidence, and sometimes a steady smile. Atget represented their symbolic control of themselves; he did not have his camera dominate, the way the know-it-all photographer did or a Jacob Riis would. For it was precisely this power of theirs that interested him most [...] / The steady looks and blurs gave the ragpickers their own remove. [...] the documents pushed both rag and ragpicker off into the deep of space. [...]. (173)[35]

Moving back slightly outside this glimpse afforded by the dialogical tandem of Atget and Nesbit of the *zonier in himself, at his ontological remove*, to the space-time of his habitat, and before moving on to other, similar spaces otherwise, it is worth our noting *untimeliness*[36] among traits of otherness characterizing *la Zone*. By untimeliness, I mean *la Zone*'s persistent endurance—its *perdurance* well beyond its planned eradication. In introducing Atget's zone album project carried out on the eve of the First World War, Molly Nesbit writes: "It had been known since 1898 that the fortified zone would disappear: the state was negotiating to sell the entire zone to the city for development of new housing and industry, which would raze and replace the long-outmoded fortifications of Louis-Philippe" (169). When urban historian Jean-Louis Cohen enumerates, describes, analyzes, and critiques the various failed plans for transforming the infamous and insalubrious annular shantytown into something really useful, he refers to the territory as some eternal "cemetery for urban plans."[37] By dint of its defiance of time, thus, *la Zone* lives on today, well beyond its razing, in imaginations fueled by literature, the arts, historiography. The imagination: the only function of consciousness where ruptures and cleavages can appear to be (and thus become) opportunities for suture and sharing. It matters little that few of Atget's photographs of ragpickers' dwellings-cum-workplaces actually depicted these proud workers eking out a living on the garbage of modern life: "the ellipses would not matter so much," writes Nesbit, "if it weren't for the looks, the blurs, and the pandemonium the ragpicker called home. All of these contributed to cut the passage of form to knowledge, all of them were hostile to the gaze" (175). Thwarted in our will to know by looking, we are taught by these photographs to see with our mind's eye: a deeper gaze.

Scanning the modern cityscape for kindred spirits among the altogether other, the critical eye of Charles Baudelaire came to an impasse, according

---

[35] Nesbit adds the aside, "The spaces were as carefully dug into the picture as Picasso's *trou ici*" (173).
[36] I am trying to guess at what Nietzsche must have meant by untimeliness when he titled his essays *Unzeitgemässe Betrachtungen* (1873–6).
[37] Jean-Louis Cohen, "Les seuils de Paris."

to Walter Benjamin, to which his close scrutiny of *zoniers* would provide a last-resort breakthrough.

> The "magic cobbles piled for barricades," in Baudelaire's draft of an epilogue [to *Les Fleurs du mal*],[38] define the limit which his poetry encounters in its immediate confrontation with social subjects. The poet says nothing of the hands which move these cobblestones. In "Le vin des chiffonniers," he was able to pass beyond this limit. (*Arcades Project*, 359)

Thus in the ragpicker, Baudelaire had, according to Benjamin's conceptual terminology, found the major *critical point* for going as far as he could in thinking ethically through the lens of modernity. The critical point is a function of the image and entails a movement. "Acceding to 'legibility' constitutes a specific critical point [*kritischer Punkt*] in the movement within the image," Benjamin wrote, crucially.[39] In the case of Baudelaire (or of Benjamin, or of Atget, or of Nesbit, or of any of us), the phenomenal *occasion* of movement is the look that passes between any one of these city dwellers and the *zonier*. The poet, the photographer, the critic or the philosopher looks out and the *zonier* looks back. From his ensconcement in no-man's-land—his embeddedness, there—he completes the creation of the critical point. Dialectical, thus, and perhaps the very kernel of all dialectics, the movement that mobilizes the image from *within* (*in ihrem Innern*), Benjamin explains, is *temporal* in nature, lending the image its historical gravity and its practical dimension. In the same celebrated section of his *Arcades Project*, Benjamin emphasizes that the "image is that wherein what has been comes together in the flash with the now to form a constellation" (462–3). And an example of that constellation—an instance exemplary of a general rule—comes into view, for example, when Molly Nesbit fathoms the "ragpickers' remove" created by their "steady looks" at Atget's lens (173).

Reading Eugène Atget's photographs of *zoniers*, Molly Nesbit would appear then, finally, to have succeeded in deepening the observation that Walter Benjamin made in reading Charles Baudelaire in preparation for his *Passagen-Werk*:

> The ragpicker is the most provocative figure of human misery. "Ragtag" [*Lumpenproletarier*] in a double sense: clothed in rags and occupied with

---

[38] "Projets d'un epilogue pour l'édition de 1861," according to the editors of the English translation (Harvard University Press).

[39] "Und zwar ist dieses »zur Lesbarkeit« ein bestimmter kritischer Punkt der Bewegung in ihrem Innern." I have taken the liberty of filling in the antecedent for "inner" or "within" and paraphrasing slightly this passage in a very dense paragraph that I will have occasion to quote again *in extenso* elsewhere.

rags. "Here we have a man whose job it is to pick up the day's rubbish in the capital. He collects and catalogues everything that the great city has cast off, everything it has lost, and discarded, and broken. He goes through the archives of debauchery, and the jumbled array of refuse. He makes a selection, an intelligent choice; like a miser hording treasure, he collects the garbage that will become objects of utility or pleasure when refurbished by Industrial magic" ("Du vin et du haschisch," *Œuvres*, vol. 1, 249–50). As may be gathered from this prose description of 1851, Baudelaire recognizes himself in the figure of the ragman. The poem presents a further affinity with the poet, immediately noted as such: "a ragpicker stumbles past, wagging his head / and bumping into walls with a poet's grace, / pouring out his heartfelt schemes to one / and all, including spies of the police." (*Arcades Project*, 349–50)[40]

Like Benjamin when he highlights the *rags both on and around* the ragman, Nesbit knows that the *garbageman*—regardless of whether he does so with ostensible pride or not—claims garbage as his essence. But whereas Benjamin will follow Baudelaire in identifying with the ragpicker as "archivist of debauchery"—something filmmaker Agnès Varda will also do in *Les Glaneurs et la Glaneuse* (*The Gleaners and I* [2000])—Nesbit knows that at the critical point where she meets the *zonier*'s look, there is also a critical *distance* to respect and which must never be breached: "Atget [...] did not have his camera dominate. [...] it was precisely this power of theirs that interested him most" (173).

Is reconciliation possible between the way Baudelaire sees himself working-as-poet-upon-seeing-the-ragman-working-as-ragman and the distance Nesbit deciphers, measures, and honors between her work and that of Atget's *zoniers*? Is this paradox of my own identity and the look at the other—which is, within the same *kritischer Punkt*, the look *of* the other—not akin to the Jew's glance *at* and, in virtual simultaneity, *away from* the so-called *Muselmann* in Auschwitz that so preoccupied Primo Levi?[41] Be that as it may (and these are questions we assign for attempted answers in the final chapter of this work), similarly to the way Emil Weiss in 1988 brought Samuel Fuller's film footage shot in 1945 at Falkenau to what

---

[40] Cf. Much can be said on behalf of the supposition that "Le vin des chiffonniers" was written around the time of Baudelaire's espousal of "beautiful utility." (The question cannot be settled with any certainty, because the poem first appeared in the book edition of *Les Fleurs du mal*. —"Le vin de l'assassin" was published for the first time in 1848—in *L'Écho des marchands de vin*!) The ragpicker poem strenuously disavows the reactionary pronouncements of its author. The criticism on Baudelaire has overlooked this poem (*Arcades Project*, 350).

[41] Cf. Harvey 2010, 7–8, 61–9 *inter alia*.

Benjamin seems to have meant by legibility (*Lesbarkeit*) by having Fuller narrate his memory of the place at the time of its use, while trudging through the ruins in the *present*,[42] favelas and cemeteries contribute to our vision and, hopefully, empathic knowledge of Auschwitz, *la Zone*, so many spaces elsewhere and otherwise.

Even secured beyond the pale of the city, *la Zone* nevertheless had to go. That lumpenproleteriat conglomeration that included the strangest of foreigners (*étrangers*), the poorest of the poor, crazed moonshiners, thieves, and ragpickers was just too heteroclite a group to tolerate anywhere within sight.[43] Pulling down the Thiers wall and razing the slums had been on the city's agenda since 1898 but demolition of the ramparts only began in earnest after the First World War. The final phase—clearing *la Zone* of its people and its hovels—would only be achieved (and not without variegated struggles) in the final years of the Algerian War (1954–61). Short of eradication, of which the Second World War had just provided the singularly most macabre example with the *Endlösung* (Final Solution), denizens of *la Zone* were dispersed or relocated to newly and cheaply built housing projects— glimpses of the process of which one finds memorialized in Chris Marker's 1963 work, *Le joli mai*. As much as documents like Atget's photographs and Lacombe's film have fixed for our eye the dynamic and necessary labor that brigades of *zoniers* carried out, the image that authority in power created, instilled in the normalized "good citizens," and maintained in the minds of those constituencies was that of an idle, degenerate, unclassifiable, dangerous horde committing the worst of crimes: unfettered, unregulated, unpaid occupation space on valuable land. That was, as it always is, the intolerable bottom line for ever-crass capitalism.

So much for economics. As for ideology, Céline's ultimate position that the slum belt epitomized an intrinsically "filthy zone" in the human landscape had long been tacitly espoused by the majority.[44] Between pictures of ragpickers, half-buried in their garbage staring back at the camera from haunting depths, and pictures by other photographers (Cohen 101, 119), where we see people lounging about in more vacant spots of *la Zone* landscape, picnicking, drinking, wiling away their time, the latter prevailed in the hegemonic imagination. *La Zone* was a place put to no particular

---

[42] See G. Didi-Huberman's remarks about this process (2010, 48) where I think he does an injustice to Freud by referring to Falkenau at the time of the Nazi atrocities as an "original scene."

[43] So heteroclite that this population was even beyond George Orwell's characterization of the "lumpen-proletarian fringe [...] composed partly of genuine artists and partly of genuine scoundrels" portrayed in Henry Miller's *Tropic of Cancer* (*Inside Whale*, 132).

[44] Cf. Didi-Huberman's discussion of the "'filthy zone' of the human appearance" (2012: 35–40).

use, inhabited by equally useless beings. And uselessness, no matter how innocuous, is not only unacceptable: it must not endure lest it become example. But just who were these people deemed altogether idle, doing nothing, engaged in no work? Other than the children of *la Zone* playing on the old absurd walls, these were, in fact, not *zoniers*, but inhabitants of the capital who headed out just beyond the edge of the city on a day off to get some sunshine, some less putrid air, some cheap wine, perhaps picking up a young prostitute, after which they would head back to their homes in propertied buildings.

The drivers of cars and trucks racing around Paris along the *boulevard périphérique*, finally completed in 1973,[45] those offspring of the slumming city-dweller quickly forgot the very name "*la Zone*,"[46] not to speak of its history, the actual work carried out there, its people. Meanwhile, those unacceptably disparate beings known as *zoniers* or *zonards* had been dispersed, only to gather under new epithets in new spaces otherwise elsewhere—either *zones* not yet deemed exploitable by capital development or zones of the imagination. Yet a handful of thinkers—philosophers and poets—in the aftermath of paroxystic destruction have clung tenaciously to the possibility of survival for the species by means of a reformulation of our relationship to zones of indistinction. These thinkers of spaces otherwise appear determined to shift us from a world split between *us here* and *them there* (where "them" can all too easily be reduced to a set of mere "its") to a world sutured with disparate parties everywhere: a world with zones *sheared* from "civilization" to a world of *shared* zones.

First and foremost among the philosophers of shared zones is Michel Foucault whose many studies of the medial spaces occupied willingly or by constraint by the mad, outlaws, metics, the intersexed, outsiders of all stripes are fertile grounds for the work ahead of us. Giorgio Agamben extends certain vectors of Foucault's explorations while inflecting some, as we have been implying, with his own darker convictions. In Georges Didi-Huberman's noble attempt "to extract some basic lessons for an

---

[45] Begun as early as 1956, the ring road was inaugurated by Prime Minister Pierre Messmer on April 25, 1973.

[46] As mentioned earlier, the boulevards ringing Paris just inside the former path of Thiers's Wall are all named after Napoleonic marshals. However, Boulevard de la Zone, which actually belonged to the municipality of Ivry-sur-Seine, was renamed Boulevard Hippolyte-Marquès in 1945, after a prominent local member of the French Communist Party who had just died following imprisonment during the Occupation. But the Ivry authorities had forgotten (or willfully ignored the fact) that the boulevard had been annexed by Paris in 1929 and for decades in the late twentieth century a "battle of names" worthy of the Picrocholine War imagined by François Rabelais was waged between the capital and the resolutely communist suburb.

archeology of visual knowledge"—notably in what he writes about Francisco Goya's *Caprichos* (1797–8) and *Disparates* (1815–23) and what he dubs "man abandoned to the night" (2011a: 63-4)—works in the wake of Foucault. Jean-Luc Nancy's efforts to conceive of a community formed by shared voices also seems to hold out hope that the species has the wherewithal to come to terms with its self-destructiveness.[47] Pertinent both to this hope and to the powerful bivalence of sharing that will be examined in further detail in our last two chapters is Jacques Rancière's work in the wake of Benjamin (and perhaps even—though less avowedly—Lyotard), that attempts to reformulate political space as an aesthetic space where the have-nots (another word for a *zonier*) possess a viable portion of what the haves have.[48] I am thinking here of his *Politics of Aesthetics* with its core notion of *partage du sensible*, or "distribution of the sensible," which would be "the system of self-evident facts of sense perception that simultaneously discloses the existence of *something in common* and the delimitations that define the respective parts and positions within it" (12; 8; my emphasis).[49] Although Gabriel Rockhill translates the notoriously polyvalent word *partage* as "distribution"—altogether appropriately from a conceptual point of view in Rancière's case—, since the "distribution of the sensible" also "discloses the existence of something in common [*un commun*],"[50] it is not unrelated to the logic of inclusive disjunction we hear forcefully when we translate *partage* as "cleave."

It remains, nevertheless, to rare photographic projects like that of Eugène Atget to suggest to us the common ground that might come out of space otherwise with the aid of imagination's force. Otherwise than film,

---

[47] *Le Partage des voix.*
[48] Cf. Didi-Huberman, 2012, 106; Rancière, *Le Partage du sensible. Esthétique et politique*, 12, 14, 17.
[49] Rancière first discusses the concept in *Disagreement: Politics and Philosophy*, 57–60, 124–5. Gabriel Rockhill explains his decision to translate partage as "distribution" in the case of Jacques Rancière: "Occasionally translated as the 'partition of the sensible', *le partage du sensible* refers to the implicit law governing the sensible order that parcels out places and forms of participation in a common world by first establishing the modes of perception within which these are inscribed. The distribution of the sensible thus produces a system of self-evident facts of perception based on the set of horizons and modalities of what is visible and audible as well as what can be said, thought, made, or done. Strictly speaking, 'distribution' therefore refers both to forms of inclusion and to forms of exclusion. The 'sensible', of course, does not refer to what shows good sense or judgement but to what is *aistheton* or capable of being apprehended by the senses" (89).
[50] As Gabriel Rockhill explains, "*le commun* – alternately translated as 'something in common', 'something common', 'what is common', or 'what is common to the community' – is strictly speaking what makes or produces a community and not simply an attribute shared by all of its members. The adjectival form of the same word, *commun*, is translated as 'common', 'shared', or communal' depending on the context" (109).

which inevitably *recounts*, thereby surreptitiously imposing a discursive metanarrative, and beyond the hermeneutic capacities of most philosophy or even literature (with the exception of *some* poetry), the photographic image proposes a *remanence for the future* of *what has been*.[51] Perhaps the photographic image works similarly to the way Goya's aquatints and etchings of madness and nightmares (nocturnal and diurnal) function on the spectator: by marking, that is, not only the abyss that separates the viewer from the altogether other, but also by suggesting, as Didi-Huberman writes, first picking up a line from *The Order of Things*, "'the very site on which their propinquity would be possible [*le site lui-même où elles pourraient voisiner*],' that *common place* that must be called a tableau" (2011a: 67; my emphasis).[52] Those Atget photographs that Molly Nesbit picked out as particularly penetrating, in their singular capacity to convey to the viewer a sense of the *zonier*'s being, possess one characteristic that is nearly always absent from mainstream film: the direct look at the camera. Whereas those silver screen characters (mere actors, lest we forget) with whom we so uncritically identify are directed to never look directly at the camera, the subjects of photographic portraiture most often do look straight at us through the lens. And Atget's ragpickers do so with a potent mixture of bold defiance tempered by demure retreat. While the direct look at the apparatus is all but prohibited by cinematic convention, photography's origins in the memorializing gesture—from biographical to policing—make the direct look at the camera a virtual requirement of film's predecessor.

Photography's direct look at the camera notwithstanding, imagination's force is required for the archive to lead us into a space otherwise and to its meaning for us here and now. As with *la Zone*, which has long vanished from the Paris horizon, so, for example, with the Gaza "dead zone" or any other such wasteland: if we are not among those barely eking out a life there, or at the very least nearby, our experience of it—if we have any experience of it at all—is purely imaginary. So if the privileged medium for accessing *la Zone* and *le zonier*'s being—albeit at that significant *remove*—is the photographic medium, then the function of this access is homologous to what Christian Metz said of cinema in comparison to theatrical representation: that the spectator's imagination is taxed more in the economy of cinematic perception than at the theatre, because the action on the stage "is taken charge of by real persons moving in real space and time" (31). Metz's idea—one that Denis

---

[51] The definition the *OED* gives for the word's usage in physics and geology—"magnetism remaining after the inducing field is removed"—is reminiscent of the word's obsolete definition: "The remaining traces *of* something; a residue, a remainder."
[52] Didi-Huberman is citing Foucault, *MC*, 8; *OT*, xvi.

Diderot had expressed some two centuries prior in *Actor's Paradox*—is that even though these "real persons" are not "being" their "real selves" during the time of the representation, they are, nevertheless here and now, in spite of all. Film, photography, and the faraway favela, on the other hand, are situated altogether elsewhere—uncannily "here" only by virtue of the screen, the paper, or the remanescent image "in my head." As was briefly demonstrated in the previous chapter, the example of Ground Zero in Manhattan instructs us like no other that a space otherwise is indeed that "other scene" whose very signifier is imaginary.

Just how does the imagination *work* with that "other scene" when one has been there? Primo Levi and W. G. Sebald were both formed by the execution of the Nazi program. But they could hardly have been formed by it more differently: Sebald's first birthday came just as Levi and the few other survivors of Auschwitz were being delivered from the "*anus mundi*, ultimate drainage site of the German universe" (Levi 1989: 65). Sebald was born, in other words, a year almost to the day prior to *Stunde Null*, the zero hour after which Germans attempted to program the turning over a new leaf, to try, in other words, to forget. And much forgetting indeed occurred, apparently. *Stunde Null* notwithstanding, something in the landscape of Sebald's Bavarian childhood drew him to the spaces otherwise that, due to the arbitrariness of chronological contemporaneity and the fiction of race, he had never known—spaces that had been razed or were crumbling, getting overgrown with weeds, like Sam Fuller's Falkenau—except that Fuller had been there.

> In one of my narratives I have described how in 1952, when I moved with my parents and siblings from my birthplace of Wertach to Sonthofen, nineteen kilometers away, nothing seemed as fascinating as the presence of areas of waste land [*Ruinengrundstücken*] here and there among the rows of houses. (Sebald e-book, 100; *LL*, 86)

From this fascination, W. G. Sebald, like Primo Levi, would spend a lifetime writing reconstructions of memory. Whereas Levi remembered what he had experienced, Sebald remembered what he had not. Using the two terms in German for experience that we have already had occasion to invoke, Levi's work in writing tended to derive primarily from an *Erlebnis* that was nevertheless defragmented, whereas Sebald's work in writing necessarily had to depend more on a type of *Erfahrung* whose connection to the world of the living today would have heartened Benjamin who saw this type of experience as largely atrophied today. Regardless of the methodology, however, the writerly ascesis in memory that both Levi and Sebald carried out in a sort of relay, it turns out, led each of them to eschew Manichean judgment and explore, instead, an equivocal moral zone that is found so often to be shared as to set the groundwork for a new and realistic ethics.

"The Gray Zone," as Primo Levi called it in the second and perhaps most powerful chapter of *The Drowned and the Saved*, is indeed the name of this shared ethical kernel. At once space and phenomenon, Levi's "gray zone" is a valuable tool in advancing our understanding of how heterotopias join us. One can but agree with Levi when he writes of "that ill-defined sphere of ambiguity and compromise" (67) that we need to dare reach into it and that it can only be fathomed, it can only take position front and center before our consciousness, once denial has been exorcised and dissipated for good. A Unitedstatesian's sense, for example, of the vast wasteland that this nation's armed forces produced in an instant at Ground Zero Hiroshima is, as Robert Jay Lifton and Greg Mitchell declare with the subtitle of their 1995 book on the subject, the all too convenient result of reality's collective distortion.[53] Were the "gray zone" to be finally understood as our shared common ground, one could begin to hope that as the notions of "no-man's-land" applied to that space otherwise in Lower Manhattan and "homeland" eerily applied to the U.S. slowly converge through the imaginary and arise to the daylight of our reason, our willfully selective denial of wantonly laying Hiroshima to waste is perhaps closer to cure in the form of a reality check than even the German "guilt" that, according to Sebald, keeps the fire-bombing of German cities wrapped in silence. For it is this very same "gray zone" into which Sebald thrusts the German reader and which the spontaneous consecration of a Ground Zero in Manhattan puts at the tip of the Unitedstatesian's tongue.

As Primo Levi had done with *The Drowned and the Saved*, so W. G. Sebald, after several novels evoking the period of the Shoah with sublimely evocative, tangential art, cuts to the chase with *On the Natural History of Destruction*. In contemplating a description of colors produced in the skies by the fire-bombing of Hamburg— a description filling "dozens of pages" written to him by a certain Harald Hollenstein from Zürich, "who spent his childhood in Hamburg and has tales to tell of everyday life under National Socialism"—Sebald muses, with only slight irony, with these words: "one wonders why no one, in contrast to those who wrote of the Great Fire of London or the fire of Moscow, described the burning German cities" (Sebald e-book, 116). Less than slightly ironic is the fact that Sebald himself had provided his own answer to this enigma some ninety pages prior, when he wrote, with directness of purpose, that "a nation which had murdered and worked to death millions of people in its camps could hardly call on the

---

[53] Robert Jay Lifton and Greg Mitchell, *Hiroshima in America: A Half Century of Denial*. New York: G. P. Putnam's Sons, 1995.

victorious powers to explain the military and political logic that dictated the destruction of the German cities" (Sebald e-book, 26).

The space in which those millions were murdered and worked to death was, of course, the archipelago of *Lager* arrayed across the Nazi empire. When the Third Reich finally fell, the nation out of which it had radiated was laid to waste by other means, yet with the exact same results: myriad death. Echoing Albert Camus's "*ni bourreaux ni victimes*" thesis,[54] W. G. Sebald writes concerning Peter Weiss that "It becomes increasingly clear [...] that rulers and ruled, exploiters and exploited are in fact the same species" (231–2). As we have just seen, Primo Levi courageously named this disturbing phenomenon "the gray zone." Explored already in *The Brothers Karamazov*, "the gray zone," under Primo Levi's analysis, is one of the most important ethical principles that we have available at the present time. The expression, "gray zone," takes a spatial notion and transforms it into a metaphor for the purpose of describing behavior. The gray zone is best examined, Levi tells us, in the "excellent 'laboratory'" (42) of the "concentration camp system" (38) comprising over 40,000 facilities—zones of exception. While "gray zone" metaphorizes that space to explore intersubjectivity, *Läger*, Gulags, ghettos, etc. all constitute spaces of bodily experience, variations of the "concentrationary universe" not exclusive to Nazi Europe but, as Levi stresses, eminently replicable—realms whose common system suspends all rules regulating survival and death. "Shoah" is one of the words found to describe the consequence of this system. Variously translated as "catastrophe" or "destruction," *shoah* also may signify *wasteland*. Within that endless wasteland, Primo Levi contends, "that simple model which we atavistically carry within us—'we' inside and the enemy outside, separated by a sharply defined geographic frontier [...] los[es] its limits" (38). In place of the sharp distinction allowing us to say and believe in a "we" versus "they," a threshold becomes the subject's mode of being: no longer is the distinction between inside and outside operable, the legal and illegal become absurd notions, nature and culture become as indistinguishable as human and inhuman, as life and death. Yet, rather than disappear altogether, these dyadic values invented and still, stubbornly, backwardly used in an attempt to hold "civilization" above "barbarism" become shared values within individual surviving parties of the wasteland. Survivors like Primo Levi, Jean Améry, Charlotte Delbo, and Filip Müller all limn this phenomenon. In their wake, Theodor W. Adorno, Marguerite Duras, Michel Foucault, Jean-François Lyotard, W. G. Sebald, Giorgio Agamben, and a host of others consider

---

[54] "Ni bourreaux ni victimes" was the title Albert Camus lent to eight articles serialized in November 1946 in the postwar newspaper, *Combat*.

whether or not the phenomenon is closer than the tenets of humanism to the present and tenuous future of *homo sapiens*. Walter Benjamin and, if we are to believe Benjamin, Charles Baudelaire were perhaps the prophets of this possible new reality.

"The flâneur is still on the threshold of the city as of the bourgeois class," wrote Walter Benjamin of his secular rabbi, Charles Baudelaire.[55] Thresholds are spaces of division and reconciliation: zones *of* and *for* sharing. Among the myriad reasons Benjamin had to admire Baudelaire, the audacity with which he shunned the bourgeois while approaching the destitute ranked high. "Everything, in sum, would appear to be played out in the risky vicinity of a threshold as thin as a razor blade, a narrow zone of interference, a psychological no man's land that would constitute the domain of the sacred." The "army of metaphors" careening about in this observation too would seem also to join those voices previewing what Primo Levi would state in demetaphorized language in *The Drowned and the Saved*. If I have used Nietzsche's famous metaphor for metaphors that he placed prominently in his "Truth and Lying" essay, it is because this description of a psychological zone in common that forms social commonality comes from the pen of Georges Bataille (Le Collège, 66), one of Nietzsche's most prolific twentieth-century proponents. As one Bataille reader puts it, before pointing out to us that in advancing this thesis about the foundations for a new alliance Bataille was actually referring to a sector of Paris's zone, "the sort of bush or no man's land extending between the area of the fortifications and the Auteuil racetrack" (Le Collège, 66), "the *zone* of the individual is also that of the social."[56]

Those among us who have lived through banishment to and sequestration in a wasteland or a prison know, without needing recourse to the vicarious imagination, the psychological—indeed ontological—correlate of the experience. The "laboratory" of the camp proved to the chemist Primo Levi that the "gray zone" is *a fact* of our moral (thus social and political) being. I would note here that it has always struck me as disturbing that, while not disputing Primo Levi on this subject, when Giorgio Agamben moves from the moral ambiguity Levi found shedding a shred of light after Auschwitz back to the permanence of the camp itself, he borrows a term—*nomos*—from the lexicon of Nazi legal philosopher Carl Schmitt. Be that as

---

[55] "Baudelaire, or the Streets of Paris" is the fifth note in "Paris, Capital of the Nineteenth Century," a "précis submitted to the Institut für Sozialforschung," according to Peter Demetz (xxxviii), first published in 1955 by Suhrkamp verlag as *Paris, die Hauptstadt des XIX. Jahrhundert* in *Illuminationen*. It was translated by Peter Demetz for *Reflections*, 156.

[56] Marc Blanchard, "Auteuil, le sacré, le banal, la zone." *MLN* [*Modern Language Notes*] 105 (4) (September 1990): 707–26.

it may, we will return to Agamben shortly. Compared to the inexorable hell described in *If This Be a Man*, at the inception of Primo Levi's struggle to understand the form of life called *survival*, the project of *The Drowned and the Saved*, near the end of that struggle, sounds almost hopeful. "The time has come," Levi writes at the outset, "to explore *the space* which separates (and not only in Nazi *Läger*) the victims from the persecutors, and *to do so with a lighter hand*" (1986: 40; my emphasis) and indeed, he is so bent on impugning *a system rather than individuals*, he announces a hypothetical conclusion even before his analysis illustrated by examples of the "gray zone": "If it were up to me, if I were forced to judge, I would *lightheartedly absolve* all those whose concurrence in the guilt was minimal and for whom coercion was of the highest degree" (44; my emphasis). It is with these guilty parties that Primo Levi can still have commerce for he, admittedly, is one of them. With his characteristic clarity and determination, Levi explains by taking a firm position with regard to the crucial metaphor: "only a schematic rhetoric can claim that that space is empty: *it never is*" (40; my emphasis). It never is: not then, during the Shoah, nor ever today. We invest that space with our imagination. Levi then proceeds to sketch in the characteristics of the occupants of the interstitial moral space whom he feels he *could* absolve *if he were* compelled to judge, that "hybrid class of the prisoner-functionary constitutes [the] armature" (42) of the space within "the concentrationary reality" (41)—the "concentrationary universe" by David Rousset's vocabulary. He continues, again pellucidly: "It is a gray zone [...] where the two camps of masters and servants *both diverge and converge*" (42; my emphasis). The announcement of the titular concept of "gray zone" then leads to Levi's description and analysis, in order of succession, of kapos, members of the *Sonderkommando*, and Chaïm Rumkowski, the ultimate cautionary tale. Levi's point, in all this, is to show the impossibility of completely separating ourselves off from the executioners. In the "gray zone," in Levi's words, "masters and servants both diverge and converge." In their division, in my words, they share that space. And, precisely, because they share while still sheared from each other, we, like Levi, may find common ground with them.

Other Shoah survivors, like Jean Améry, on the other hand, could never quite extricate themselves enough from the injunction, "depriving them so completely of their rights and prerogatives," as Agamben puts it, "that no act committed against them could appear any longer as a crime" (Agamben 1998: 171; 1995: 191).[57] This permanent "placelessness" that infused Améry's being,

---

[57] Giorgio Agamben first published this in French, as "Qu'est-ce qu'un camp?" in *Moyens sans fin. Notes sur la politique* (Paris: Payot and Rivages, 1995), then in *Homo sacer I*. I have slightly altered the syntax to fit my sentence.

to use a term Edward S. Casey has amply adumbrated in his extensive work on space, is expressed by W. G. Sebald with that hypnotic directness, characteristic of all his writing, that appears merely suggestive: "[t]he territory he took most for granted had become a more impossible point of reference than the most outlandish of places" (203). Sebald was referring to that broken, destroyed sense of place as Améry evoked it in the posthumously published *Örtlichkeiten* (1980) and that perhaps explains to some extent his suicide two years before. Even more importantly than this, however, the marked contrast between Améry's ultimate "placelessness" and Levi's ultimate focus on the "gray zone" helps set up a fundamental issue that would seem to leave Levi and Agamben in disagreement: Is the camp a space between spaces, an interstitial space that the unexperienced may experience imaginatively? or Is the camp a space beyond anything that might help the potential future executioners that all the living are to learn to become otherwise? Levi's "gray zone" appears to lean toward the first rhetorical question; Agamben's "zones of indistinction" would seem to affirm the latter. Between them is perhaps, once again, Baudelaire, if we are to follow Benjamin's retracing of the poet's daring steps in the *Arcades Project*:

> In "Rêve parisien" the forces of production are seemingly brought to a standstill, put out of commission. The landscape of this dream is the dazzling mirage of the leaden and desolate terrain that in "De profundis clamavi" becomes the universe. "A frozen sun hangs overhead six months; / the other six, the earth is in its shroud—/ no trees, no water, not one creature here, / a wasteland naked as the polar north!" (355)

Beyond myth and romanticization, *la Zone* that once ringed Paris—even though free of barbed wire or electrical fencing—was a territory under surveillance, a virtual concentration camp. The people who under economic and racial duress appeared like mushrooms after a spring deluge to take myriad fragile root there were also, lest we forget, under the watch of the military personnel assigned to the fortifications. The voice that Giorgio Agamben isolates as quintessential among Nazi explanations for the eerily similar sudden outbreak of concentration camps across the Reich speaks with an abject blend of feigned astonishment and bad faith. "[I]nsofar as the camps were located in [...] a peculiar space of exception [*peculiare spazio di eccezione*]—[Rudolf] Diels, the head of the Gestapo, could declare, 'Neither an order nor an instruction exists for the origin of the camps: they were not instituted; one day they were there [*sie waren nicht gegründet, sie waren eines Tages da*]'" (Agamben 1998: 169; 1995: 189). In Part Three of *Homo sacer*, entitled "The Camp as Biopolitical Paradigm of the Modern," the early paragraphs of which appeared earlier in the same year in *Moyens sans fin: Notes sur la politique*,[58] Giorgio Agamben sets out to extend work that only untimely death, he asserts, prevented Michel Foucault from completing:

> In the last years of his life, while he was working on the history of sexuality and unmasking the deployments of power at work within it, Michel Foucault began to direct his inquiries with increasing insistence toward the study of what he defined as *biopolitics*, that is, the growing inclusion of man's natural life in the mechanisms and calculations of power. [...] The inquiry that began with a reconstruction of the *grand renfermement* in hospitals and prisons did not end with an analysis of the concentration camp. (Agamben 1998: 119)

This, then, would be the last word of *Homo sacer*—an analysis meant to show that *distinction from zones of indistinction* is no longer possible, that the camp is no longer the exception but the pervasive rule, and appearing—despite himself?—to leave the last word to Nazi political and legal philosopher Carl Schmitt, "the camp, which is now securely lodged within the city's interior, is the new biopolitical *nomos* of the planet" (Agamben 1998: 176). The key term in Agamben's statement of purpose, above, is perhaps not *biopolitics*—which myopic grasps of Foucault's oeuvre have all too often rendered trite—but *inclusion*. In the debate today, at the heart of which Agamben hovers, the issue of whether or not we have all consciously—or, more frequently, unconsciously—been incarcerated in a seamlessly global zone of indistinction or if, on the contrary, we can still maintain critical distance even though something resembling *la Zone* may well be our fundamental political environment has yet to be resolved. As our last chapter will attempt to show, this quandary may yet not even have been resolved for Agamben, despite the dark conclusion of *Homo sacer*. For Walter Benjamin, who committed suicide rather than endure deportation, the camp, relegation to a zone where life ends, our "inclusion" even in a "new biopolitical *nomos* of the planet" would be a function of greater complexity: precisely an inclusion armed with the critical distance that the imagination affords. Baudelaire and all the poets in his wake, from Rimbaud to Apollinaire, taught Benjamin that although an aspect of our world, the zone—as long as we can place it into the stream of language, as long, that is, as we also entertain an imaginary relationship with it—cannot become the inextricable environment and ethical determinant of all human existence. We are cleft from the zone, yet we cleave to it.

---

[58] "Qu'est-ce qu'un camp?" In Giorgio Agamben, *Moyens sans fin: Notes sur la politique*. Éditions Payot & Rivages (Bibliothèque Rivages), 1995, 45–56.

Benjamin's commitment to the force of imagination notwithstanding—and it is a wager to which I shall return via Michel Foucault and René Char in the last chapter—it behooves us to examine the figuration of argument and discourse that brings Giorgio Agamben from his major premise that "the original political relation is the ban (the state of exception as a zone of indistinction between inside and outside, exclusion and inclusion)" to his conclusion that "today it is not the city but rather the camp that is the fundamental biopolitical paradigm of the West" (181). "The camp is merely the place in which the most absolute *conditio inhumana* that has ever existed on earth was realized: this is what counts in the last analysis, for the victims as for those who come after." In both style and content, this is a sentence that could have been extracted right out of Primo Levi's final great work, *The Drowned and the Saved*. In fact, these are Giorgio Agamben's words from the beginning of his essay, "The Camp as Biopolitical Paradigm of the Modern" in *Homo sacer* (166). Yet despite its obvious inspiration in Levi's "gray zone" and his meditation, begun already in 1947 with *If This Be a Man*, on the ethical import of the *Muselmann*, Agamben's presentation begs the question from the outset. As a result, already four pages *before* his altogether Leviesque statement on the *historical* significance of the camp—what it *was* and how we should think our *memory* of it today—Agamben is pushing his contention that the inhuman condition achieved by the Nazis definitively conditions our attitude toward life *today*: "[...] the concept 'death' [...] now oscillates from one pole to the other with the greatest indeterminacy, describing a vicious circle that is truly exemplary" (162). This putative *petitio principii* concerning the end of life renders us as utterly indifferent and callous with regard to others as to ourselves, making our ethical landscape into one seamless zone of indistinction from which no distinction is possible. And because this is already the case—definitively, apparently—Agamben can have his Leviesque statement followed by a rhetorical question that he immediately answers with a first sketch of his conclusion: "What is a camp, what is its juridico-political structure, that such events could take place there? This will lead us to regard the camp [...] as the hidden matrix and *nomos* of the political space in which we are still living" (166). Thus, very simply put, although "the camp *was* [...] the most absolute biopolitical space ever to *have been* realized," the camp *is* the model for relations among *homo sapiens* today (171; my emphasis).[59]

It would seem that Giorgio Agamben's precipitous leap to the conclusion that the *Lager* is the *nomos* of contemporary political sphere hinges on the

---

[59] For Unitedstatesians, there might be appreciable irony in the fact that some historians trace the origins of the concentration camp to those set up in Cuba by the Spanish in 1896—the same island on which the most famous concentration camp run by the U.S. is situated.

question that he claims is being forever begged concerning death. In order to demonstrate how we have come to be incapable of escaping that "vicious circle," Agamben offers up a series of salient precedents from the Nazi era and one disconcertingly unresolved debate in contemporary biopolitics. The conceptual language Agamben deploys in discussing two of the former stands out and is closely intertwined, I believe, with his success at drawing us morally into today's right to life controversies. The first example concerns the *Versuchspersonen*, or human guinea pigs, utilized by the Nazis with characteristic wantonness. Thus writes Agamben:

> Precisely because they were lacking almost all the rights and expectations that we customarily attribute to human existence, and yet were still biologically alive, they came to be situated in a limit zone [*essi venivano a situarsi in una zona-limite fra la vita e la morte*] between life and death, inside and outside, in which they were no longer anything but bare life. [...] in the biopolitical horizon that characterizes modernity, the physician and the scientist move in the no-man's-land [*terra di nessuno*] into which at one point the sovereign alone could penetrate. (1998: 159; 1995: 177).

The explicit language and function of *la Zone*, the characteristics of its denizens, and the eloquent synonym for the space otherwise—*terra di nessuno*—are all in prominent evidence. The possibility for subsequent generations to share that space for a marginally less immoral future is implicit in the very presence of Agamben's observation on the page for us to read. Agamben's second example is that of "[t]he Führer's body [which] is [...] situated at the point of coincidence between *zoé* and *bios*, biological body and political body. In his person, *zoé* and *bios* incessantly pass over into each other [*essi transitano incessantemente l'uno nell'altro*]" (1998: 184; 1995: 206). By violently wrenching us from an indistinction inscribed on the body of the victim to one illustrated on the body of the ultimate perpetrator, Agamben demonstrates the pervasiveness of the worst consequences of indistinction in a radical state of exception like the Third Reich. The third and final example comes in the form of a question that Agamben leaves unanswered but that is the consequence of a disquisition concerning the increasingly frequent occurrence of individuals barely living on in a seemingly endless comatose space he calls "a no-man's-land between coma and death" (1998: 161). Faced with that question—"What was the zone of life beyond coma?" (161)—we may readily recall dozens of high profile examples ranging from Terri Schiavo to Ariel Sharon, which may or may not suggest answers to us.

The political consequences of indistinction becoming pervasive and generalized could not be darker:

> If [...] the essence of the camp consists in the materialization of the state of exception and in the subsequent creation of a space in which bare life and the juridical rule enter into a threshold of indistinction, then we must admit that we find ourselves virtually in the presence of a camp every time such a structure is created, independent of the kinds of crime that are committed there and whatever its denomination and specific topography. (174)

Yet for all this pessimism (which, *pace* Agamben, truly anyone who follows the world beyond the bourgeois *oikos* can easily find justifiable), there might ultimately appear to be one type of indistinction—even in bleak *Homo sacer*—from which an entirely other set of principles for social interaction could arise. For there is a figure that haunts Agamben's discourse.[60] It is a figure whose logic is comprised of contradictory operations. We find this figure, for example, in this earlier description of the components that, in becoming indistinguishable, constitute the generalized *Lager* or zone in which Agamben sees us eking out a living today: "When life and politics—originally *divided and linked together* by means of the no man's land of the state of exception that is inhabited by bare life—began to become one, all life becomes sacred and all politics becomes the exception" (1998: 148; 1995: 165; my emphasis). To follow this particular iteration of the argument, before it became one, as a result of the logical operator whose name is "indistinction," there was a life and politics *divisi in origine e articolati fra loro attraverso la terra di nessuno*, "*divided and linked together* by means of the no man's land." Beyond the virtual recollection of *la Zone*, the slum belt ringing Paris, this formulation appears to express regret over the disappearance of a political complexity that *unites while* intrinsically *respecting the division* involved in particularities—"minorities" one might have said in the era of Foucault, Lyotard, and Deleuze. The formulation is wry and perhaps even a bit ironical. Could it be, however, that this tone is the sign that some positive *partage* persists in the universe of Agamben's thinking? It would be folly to maintain that a "constitutive nexus [*nesso costitutivo*] between the state of exception and the concentration camp" is a linkage leading to prosperous and healthy lives for all (1998: 168; 1995: 188). Yet it is in the *cleft* between such formations that thought maintains the critical tension and edge allowing it to envision other formations where subjects might *cleave*. In the next two chapters of this work, certain aspects of Michel Foucault's thought and style and what underpins both will be read and interpreted in such a way as to

---

[60] Just to be sure that what I, myself, am doing rhetorically, here, is obvious to all my readers: I am consciously introducing Jean-François Lyotard's early magisterial critical apparatus of discourse/figure (Lyotard 1971).

shed a slightly different angle of light, hopefully, on the final ellipsis of *Homo sacer*. As Agamben wrote in the early stages of "The Camp as Biopolitical Paradigm of the Modern," "It would be more honest and, above all, more useful to investigate carefully the juridical procedures and deployments of power [*dispositivi politici*] by which human beings could be so completely deprived of their rights and prerogatives that no act committed against them could appear any longer as a crime" (1998: 171; 1995: 191). If we, whose honest critical reflection is being called to order by this injunction, if we, who are *on the verge* of this zone, could get our thinking selves *into* this zone, beyond the threshold, then the nexus-threshold-no-man's-land-etc. which is all-encompassing, where right and wrong are distinguishable in action only with great difficulty, against the greatest odds, is the space where the imagination can come to the aid of reason.

The challenge I put before myself for the remainder of this book should now be somewhat clear and, in any case, ineluctable: Is dignity of distinction from integral and irretrievable indistinction conceivable? If so, what are the givens of consciousness that underpin such hope in the last instance? A first reduction is presently possible. A distillation of elements should presently enable us to hone in on a remainder of conceptual zones to explore. A two-by-two matrix may now be envisioned to organize what has been covered. Looking back, in what is now a largely recapitulative gesture, to what we have gleaned from the oeuvre of Marguerite Duras, we find, on the one hand, *a plurality of places* [*lieux*] in which narratives unfold; on the other hand Duras (but often in conjunction with her preferred narrative locales) often (almost always) foregrounds *a single place*, a *site*, one that is undifferentiated and indistinct, although it goes by different names: Occupied France, the construction site, the camp. This Durassian place (with emphasis on the singular) may be one that a character (and, thus, a reader) inhabits, but its hermeneutic and ethical power is unleashed when it is altogether elsewhere, otherwise than here. Looking still primarily forward, to aspects of the oeuvre of Michel Foucault that we are now about to mine deeply, we have, on the one hand, *space*, both in its singularity and in its plurality. Foucaldian *space* in its multiplicity includes the asylum, the clinic, the General Hospital, the prison, the École Normale, etc. and forms that geneaology of *spaces otherwise* that Foucault's retooling of archeology was meant to critique in a manner vastly more radical than historiography could ever achieve. On the other hand, as with Duras in regard to places, we find in Foucault's work—from one end to the other—a *singularity of space* as well. Its name has appeared here already, but voiced or written by others; the final two chapters of *Sharing Common Ground* will explore directly and indirectly Foucault's complex and variegated employment of *partage* as word and idea. It may be that this quasi-undecidable betweenness is for Foucault another term, for example, for the body (or sex). We will draw back systematically from such conclusions, as they would distract from a necessary focus on *partage* itself, independent of all concretizations or embodiments.

places (Duras) coast, river mouth, vision of the sea, Indochina, the forest, edges	*spaces* (Foucault) ship of fools, the General Hospital, asylum, clinic, prison
place (Duras) construction sites, Hiroshima/Nevers, the camp	*space* (Foucault) the body ... *partage*

As is possible (and even tempting) with all two-by-two matrices, this one may suggest chiasmatic relationships. Thus, the first branch of the x that one might trace diagonally would suggest an exploration of commonalities between Durassian *places* and Foucaldian *space*; similarly, the second branch, completing the x, would tend to draw Foucaldian *spaces* and Durassian *place* into comparison one with the other. Somewhere along this second branch cemeteries would no doubt be situated. But since what I am terming "Foucaldian space" is thus far the least adumbrated of the elements contained in this matricial array, it needs to become the principal focus of the remainder of this book. We must, however and throughout, never lose sight of the imaginary intersection of the two diagonals composing the *chi* [χ] of the chiasmus. For if in the process of putting this matrix to work we are to diminish the otherness of Durassian narrative places as well as diminish the otherworldliness of Foucaldian spaces otherwise, then we need to arrest our attention as often as possible on what might be identified, using a key Benjaminian notion, as the critical point (*kritischer Punkt*) at the center of our schema. Like an Atget photograph with its ragpicker staring out eternally at us, drawing us back in and elsewhere, the "image is dialectics at a standstill"—not the end of dialectics (after all, the dialectic is endless as long as *homo sapiens* has not yet met with extinction), but an occasion—like a Barthesian *punctum*—in the seemingly perpetual movement of dialectics in which reflection with ethical import can occur.

It is, once again, Marguerite Duras who appears uncannily, yet credibly, able to offer us an inkling of what that occasion may be when she strives to formulate a radically new understanding of what the activity of consciousness may entail. This struggle begins in "Construction Sites" when the impression comes to the reader and grows in her that the key to the enigma of the construction site eludes even the young woman.

The obsessively frequent occurrence of the word "thing" on the body of the text borders on the absurd and the specificity of nearly everything in the story remains at degree zero. Not just any noun, "thing" can stand for *all* things while signifying none, specifically. It is the generic term for designating all that exists, all that is conceivable. Everything or anything. "Whatchamacallit," "whosawhatsit," and a host of others in all languages are deployed to substitute for the words the speaker cannot recall to memory in order to formulate the statement that lies between mind and vibratory disappearance. Yet this young girl—a prototype for many later Durassian characters, including the Frenchwoman at Hiroshima—intuits that this thing is, nevertheless, something:

> The girl seemed to be trying to remember something. He understood that she was forgetting the construction site. She was trying to remember him [or it] with precision, just as he remembered her. The man looked at her and smiled. She too smiled and started to look at him, to look and to look at the man who remembered.

Duras's struggle to discover and reveal fleeting examples of "dialectics at a standstill" takes a great leap forward with *Hiroshima mon amour*, where she settles on a term for ethical thought's occasion. The term is intelligence— "decisive intelligence," she writes in the scenario's synopsis. It is a term, then, that would appear to have nothing special about it, except when we consider how Duras has her anonymous character inflect, deconstruct the term in the film's dialogue. "*C'est comme l'intelligence, la folie, tu sais*" (*OC II*, 35), she explains to her lover, and, with hardly contained political passion, near the end of the film, when the lovers are about to part, "*À mes enfants, j'enseignerai la méchanceté et l'indifférence, l'intelligence et l'amour de la patrie des autres jusqu'à la mort*" (*OC II*, 67). Duras insists, therefore, that an intelligence of a quite different order exists, but has no name. An "*intelligence à part*," one could think of it as something like what Michel Foucault meant when he expounded on "*des espaces autres*": not just another intelligence, but an *intelligence other*. Particularly well developed in women, Duras saw this savvy as highly moral and, to a large extent, in contradistinction to, bending, twisting, queering the habitual definitions of what is "human." Further, this intelligence other would operate in the vicinity of madness.

This is Duras oscillating between the constellation of places for experimentation through narrative and the zone or site *over there* where ethics can be constructed. Foucault, sometimes despite himself, will oscillate between the multiplicity of spaces in his geneaology of heterotopias and a heretical space for our body freed from humanism. The "new cartographer," as Gilles

Deleuze dubbed Foucault à propos of *Discipline and Punish*, relentlessly sought that same "twisting line of the outside [...] without beginning, without end, an oceanic line that passes through all points of resistance pitches diagrams against one other, and operates always as the most recent" (1983: 44). Or, as Edward S. Casey has it, "Foucault is the first to formulate fully the genealogical thesis: space and place are historical entities, subject to the vagaries of time" (1997: 298).

Rather than conclude, an open closure—as much part of the rest of this book as of the present chapter meant to be held in the reader's memory as she reads on—will now be formed by two invocations. One is the full citation of a passage of *Das Passagen-Werk* with which this chapter has worked; the other is a piece of almost pure speculation concerning an experience a young Paul-Michel Foucault might have had in Poitiers two decades before his emergence as one of the world's most influential thinkers of the last century—an experience that might well have been the kernel of that thought.

Let us read—without interruption this time—the language that Walter Benjamin brings to bear to convey a sense of how a single, isolatable phenomenon may enable an attentive imagination to move forth critically as it apprehends an artefact:

> What distinguishes images from the "essences" of phenomenology is their historical index. [...] These images are to be thought of entirely apart from the categories of the "human sciences," from so-called habitus, from style, and the like. For the historical index of the images not only says that they belong to a particular time; it says, above all, that they attain to legibility only at a particular time. And, indeed, this acceding "to legibility" constitutes a specific critical point in the movement at their interior. Every present day is determined by the images that are synchronic with it: each "now" is the now of a particular recognizability. In it, truth is charged to the bursting point with time. (This point of explosion, and nothing else, is the death of the *intentio*, which thus coincides with the birth of authentic historical time, the time of truth.) It is not that what is past casts its light on what is present, or what is present its light on what is past; rather, image is that wherein what has been comes together in the flash with the now to form a constellation. In other words: image is dialectics at a standstill. For while the relation of the present to the past is purely temporal, the relation of what-has-been to the now is dialectical: not temporal in nature but figural [*bildlich*]. Only dialectical images are genuinely historical—that is, not archaic—images. The image that is read—which is to say, the image in the now of its recognizability—bears to the highest

degree the imprint of the perilous critical moment on which all reading is founded.[61]

I offer three telegraphic observations in the wake of this dense, difficult, yet important statement whose value is that of a manifesto:

- we note the necessary *separateness* of such images from "the 'human sciences,' from so-called habitus, from style, and the like";
- *yet* (notwithstanding this first point), we note further the assertion that it is a movement *interior* to the image that enables the legibility of the critical point;
- finally, we receive the affirmation which, coming from a dyed-in-the-wool dialectician, is nothing less than astounding that the image, in its critical point, "is dialectics at a standstill."

Couple this with some speculation plausible for all its pureness. In the spring of 1930, when the eldest son of a surgeon's daughter and a well-heeled Poitiers physician, Paul-Michel, was three-and-a-half years old,[62] André Gide, one of France's best-known writers, published *La Séquestrée de Poitiers*, a sort of "true crime" story about a woman, Mélanie Bastian, who was imprisoned by her mother in her room for twenty-four years. Gide's story was based on the events in the life of Blanche Monnier, who was discovered in her home at 21, rue de la Visitation in Poitiers on May 23, 1901, incrusted in excrement, crazed by a quarter century of sequestration. Straightlaced town notable Dr. Paul Foucault, his wife, the former Anne Malapart, and their children lived at 10, rue Arthur Ranc, formerly known as rue de la Visitation. Concerning the Blanche Monnier scandal, David Macey rightly writes, "That the Foucault family did not know the story is inconceivable; that they did not talk about it is perfectly conceivable" (12).

The power of the horrific, of the outrageously extraordinary—especially when it occurs so close to home, so disruptively, so out of whack with the familiar, especially on the imagination of the young and impressionable—must never be underestimated. Although Michel Foucault would never write about Blanche Monnier, no doubt because she did not leave articulated traces as Pierre Rivière and Herculine Barbin had, is she not the epitome of the historian's notion of "parallel lives"? Did Michel Foucault not make it a repeated gesture and perhaps even the very point of his thinking life to bring himself into parallel with the most disparate brothers and sisters imaginable? Is it not striving to share all with she from whom one is the most sheared that Foucault held as his moral horizon? If not, then why his insistence on

---

[61] Walter Benjamin, *The Arcades Project*, 462–3.
[62] Michel Foucault was born on October 15, 1926.

the fundamental importance of Sade or of Artaud or of Klossowski for finally getting beyond the merely human? As repulsive as the notion appears at first superficial glance, Agamben intuits the quality of certain bodies to form a nexus for thinking our relationship to the oddness of our existence when he writes of Hitler's that it came to be the "point of coincidence between *zoé* and *bios*, biological body and political body." What if the *kritischer Urpunkt* for Poitier's young Paul-Michel, the zone of indistinction that impelled him forth to become the Michel Foucault that we know, were his fascinated imagination's construction site for the body of Blanche Monnier? After all, is it not at a very tender age that we learn traumatically that we must share the designation "I" with speakers who are so altogether other than us?

5

Foucault's Transgression

Words, mine was never more than that, than this pell-mell babel of silence and words, my viewless form described as ended, or to come, or still in progress, depending on the words, the moments, long may it last in that singular way. Apparitions, keepers, what childishness, and ghouls, to think I said ghouls, do I as much as know what they are, of course I don't, and how the intervals are filled, as if I didn't know, as if there were two things, some other thing besides this thing, what is it, this unnamable thing that I name and name and never wear out, and I call that words. It's because I haven't hit on the right ones, the killers, haven't yet heaved them up from that heart-burning glut of words, with what words shall I name my unnamable words? And yet I have high hopes [...]
Samuel Beckett, *Texts for Nothing*, VI.[1]

I come now to the ineffable center of my talk; it is here that a writer's hopelessness begins. [...] the central problem—the enumeration, even the partial enumeration, of infinity—is irresolvable. In that unbounded moment, I saw millions of delightful and horrible acts; none amazed me so much as the fact that all occupied the same point, without superimposition and without transparency. What my eyes saw was simultaneous; what I shall write is successive, because language is successive. Something of it, though, I will capture.
Jorge Luís Borges, *The Aleph*[2]

"The Hebrew language contains a letter that no one can pronounce," Daniel Heller-Roazen explains (19), the "silent letter *aleph* (א) [...] marks the forgetting from which all language emerges. *Aleph* guards the place of oblivion at the inception of every alphabet" (25). Daneri, the poet in Borges's eponymous story, tells us that "an Aleph is one of the points in space that contain all points" (280). The Hebrew language coexists with all other languages in the actual world, like the many spaces otherwise where we commune, and that idea of an unpronounceable letter comes to emblematize

---

[1] 125.
[2] 283.

the impossible point where language would coincide with the chimeric truth that Nietzsche so brilliantly mocked.

The experience of being drawn, when we are about one year old, toward the irresistible entry into language is no doubt as sublime (in the Kantian sense) as witnessing, at a remove, the Aleph of the Borges parable. Surviving that initiatory drama involves stepping over a threshold beyond which I must, among other exigencies, share the grammatical first person singular with every other speaking being in my linguistic sphere. Still enraged at age sixteen by this compulsion, Arthur Rimbaud defiantly proclaimed, "I is another." But even poetry couldn't heal the wound, so Rimbaud soon slammed the door opening upon the quest for the Aleph and left the realm of poetry for Africa, the cradle of humanity that Europe was still discovering, for spaces otherwise. To preserve a semblance of discrete existence, once I'm with and within discourse for good, I'm forced to forfeit the linguistic support of that individuality. Being itself is a space otherwise with respect to language. Since language penalizes me for having wished to remain singular and unique, I shall use language poetically, imaginatively, bending it to my will, and hurl transgression at the trauma of having brushed with the Aleph. That is what Michel Foucault did on the basis of the least poetic raw materials imaginable: historical fact, archival residue. Here is a letter that Michel Foucault wrote to Marguerite Duras probably some time in 1970.[3]

> Dear Marguerite Duras,
>
> I beg your pardon for having taken so long to answer you—to respond to *Abahn Sabana David*. It's just that reading it moved me so much that it left me, leaves me speechless. You know that since *Destroy, She Said*, I've fallen into your work, find myself caught in it, and I move about within it in every direction, my head in a fog, feeling my way, full of disquiet and yet, despite all, hope, as if it seemed to me that if I keep moving back and forth, haphazardly, some inevitable figure would finally appear to me. I reread *Abahn* several times and I'm probably not through. You are the writer I need. I would have liked to tell you something other than this ridiculously subjective sentence. Perhaps some day I will.
>
> With all my thanks,
> M. Foucault[4]

[3] Bernard Alazet, co-editor of the work referenced in the next note explained in a private e-mail: "we indicated 'between 1968 and 1970' by pure deduction, since hardly any of those intellectuals of the time ever date their correspondence. This letter from Foucault is probably from 1970, since *Destroy, She Said* is from 1969 and *Abahn* from 1970. But I can't date it precisely for you."

[4] Bernard Alazet and Christiane Blot-Labarrère, *Marguerite Duras*. Paris: Les Cahiers de L'Herne, 2005, 55.

This declaration of affinity with Marguerite Duras establishes a tone for our exploration of Michel Foucault's transgressive treatment of his own scientific lexicon.

Transgression is a culturally specific operation of consciousness that was elaborated to the point of becoming a master concept notably in the promiscuously variegated work of Georges Bataille. In close agreement with much of Bataille's experimental thought, Michel Foucault adopted variations on transgression both as objects of research and as intellectual practice. Whether deemed mad, delinquent, deviant or perverse, all of the subjects or categories of subjects upon whom Foucault trained his analytic sights are individuals who transgress or are judged to be transgressive with respect to societal norms. Whether sequestered and confined, disciplined (when not punished) or under orders to possess and display a "true sex," the subjects Foucault preferred to study evolved within orders of discourse singularly apt at revealing the transgressive moments of history. Whether from the realm of literature or that of philosophy or indeed from netherworlds where they cannot easily be distinguished as individuals, transgressive thinkers were those whom Foucault held in the highest esteem even to the point of emulating them in writing style and in mood: Sade, Lautréamont, Artaud, Cervantes, Genet, Bataille, but also Raymond Roussel, René Char, Borges, Roger Laporte, Samuel Beckett, Diderot, Nietzsche, Gaston Bachelard, and also, as we shall soon have opportunity to amply see, Blaise Pascal.

Nominally (at the outset) if not first and foremost (always) an historian at the cusp of philosophy, Michel Foucault's raw material was, of necessity, *temporal* in all aspects of temporality, its features, and its characteristics. The phenomena of duration, periodicity, inexorability, interruption, vagary and the like are of prime importance. Yet in order to inoculate any putatively unassailable historiography against the prejudice of the *present* and from the blindness of *proximity*, in order to compel the discipline to maximal objectivity, simply put, Foucault knew also from the outset that he needed to transgress long-established ground rules which, as each of his works show, explicitly or implicitly, were determined arbitrarily. As archaeology, then genealogy, supplanted classically conceived history as model for his explorations, not least among the considerations leading to his realignment of the field was Foucault's overwhelming realization that the Einsteinian revolution applies also to our knowledge of ourselves and that *time is a function of space*. Indeed, spatial metaphors, as excavators of factual phenomena know all too well, dominate the linguistic expression of our conception of time. In transgressing the strictures of the history of thought to establish an *archaeology of knowledge*, Foucault was modeling his trajectory on and taking his cue from a phenomenon in the observable behavior of knowledge-formation itself, to whit: a new episteme— essentially a new "world"—comes into being when an exhausted or irrelevant episteme is exhausted or transgressed.

We move on. Ways of thinking, which are essentially no different from ways of speaking, of making discourse, reach a point of no return at which they might nevertheless tarry for "moments" of surprisingly varied duration. But although ways of seeing, speaking, and thinking may ultimately cross that threshold, marks and memories of the territory left behind remain, even though once the opposite shore is reached, there is no turning back except for the archaeologist himself. For this retention of memory in transgression that the archaeologist he would become can sometimes succeed in reading, Foucault would occasionally use the exquisite word *rémanence*, which had captivated him at an early age while reading the poetry of René Char.[5] Notwithstanding his exhaustive descriptive analysis of specific knowledge formations or epistemes such as Antiquity, the classical age, the Enlightenment, and the Victorian era, the conjoined nature of their interrelationship, notwithstanding their separation by what first appear to be points of no return, was his great discovery. This discovery is the temporal correlate of our sharing of common ground by means of our relationship to spaces otherwise. Though in comparison to epochs such zones appear as points or instants, these transactional and transformative *areas in time* possess duration and even, sometimes, persistence or insistence. Given this quasi-contradiction and the fact that pivotal moments are pregnant moments far more complex and contradictory than eras named by historians, Foucault's challenge to himself was to go beyond available terminology and imagery in referencing them. The historian too reaches the point of no return and the archaeologist begins to supplant him, in order to stand vigil over language for the appearance, as Beckett put it, of "the right one, the killer, the unnamable word" for when a zone of knowledge becomes a construction site.[6] In reinventing language, the new space-time precipitates the invention of new rules for how we are to decide, for how we are to be with one another, for politics, ultimately. As we have noted before, this is the trajectory that Hannah Arendt derived from the unfinished project beyond Kant's *Critique of Judgement*.

Any straightforward, no-nonsense approach to the new purpose for archaeology that Michel Foucault developed will characterize his view

---

[5] René Char renders his sense of remanence in a prose poem under that title found in a collection of poems written between 1964 and 1970 entitled *Le Nu perdu* (Caws/Kline, 438–9).

[6] "I haven't hit on the right ones, the killers, haven't yet heaved them up from that heartburning glut of words, with what words shall I name my unnamable words? And yet I have high hopes [...]" Samuel Beckett, *Texts for Nothing* VI, 125. Cf. Robert Harvey, *Witnessness*, 36, 132.

of history as comprising a series of epistemes or cultures of knowledge punctuated by breaks. This approach would also inform us that he hewed this structure by emulating, adopting, and fusing Gaston Bachelard's notion of the "epistemological cut" (*la coupure épistémologique*) with Georges Canguilhem's theory of our "knowledge of life" (*connaissance de la vie*)—neither of which category was meant for the pursuit of historical research. As might be expected, however, when a thinker deploys a core principle across the expanse of any critical project, Foucault's writings present several names for the hiatus, pause or suspension between what historians before him tended to call eras or epochs: *coupure, rupture, division*... To the cut or the break which are metaphors too irrevocable to be anything but rhetorical exaggerations and too beholden to what had become conventional historiography for someone developing a new form of archaeology, Foucault would come to prefer somewhat attenuated terms—terms that we translate into English as "displacement(s)," "redistribution(s)," "discontinuit(ies)" in order to designate epistemes themselves and "*décalages successifs*" for mutations within epistemes.[7]

One of the nouns that Foucault hit upon as verbal approximation for these discontinuities between (or among) epistemes, however, is an acutely unstable lexical item and, thus, *productively transgressive*. We encounter it as early as *The History of Madness* in no less than the title of a key chapter of the book's third movement: "*Le nouveau partage*." From that critical point onward, by the sheer frequency of its use under Foucault's pen, by dint of its appearance at nearly every one of those celebrated crescendos culminating his demonstrations, abidingly and with enticing inconsistency from one end to the other of his work, the properties with which Foucault entrusts *partage* reveal themselves to be crucially suggestive among synonyms for *coupure*, yet so nearly illegible for the English-only reader that its translation(s) beg(s) correction, salutary adjustment. Its appearance in various Foucault texts has been just as variously translated into English as either "division" or "sharing" or, yet again, "share." But in actuality, since it conveys both sharing *and* division, *partage* is one of those "undecidable" words of which Jacques Derrida was so fond. As in texts ranging from André Malraux's *La Condition humaine* to Jean-Luc Nancy's *Le Partage des voix*, a Foucaldian *partage* becomes a division that *includes* sharing, which "division" fails in translation to convey (except, perhaps, sometimes in his earliest texts) and for which "sharing" only works if we understand it also as disjunctive. "Distribution," which Gabriel Rockhill

---

[7] Foucault discusses all this with singular clarity in response to questions put to him in Spring 1968 by readers of the journal *Esprit*. Cf. "Réponse à une question [sic]" *Esprit* 371 (May 1968): 850–74; reprinted in *Dits et écrits* I, 701–23. Quote is at 705.

wisely selected to convey Jacques Rancière's use of *partage*, would work far better than "division" in the case of Foucault. Whereas Rancière employs the term while working through the fraught problem to which Benjamin first gave voice of the interface between politics and aesthetics (and although this is not altogether separate from Rancière's concern), Foucault works in the realm of knowledge formation and ethics. Among all terms in the Foucaldian vocabulary for historical transgression, at the heart of the Foucaldian archaeology *partage* operates in such a way as to endlessly challenge the function that it names. In short, this synonym for shifts with overlappings in historical strata that Foucault introduced in contexts that we will now examine reigns over a truth-functional operation of inclusive disjunction.[8] And as previewed much earlier, the noun "cleave"—suggested to us by Gerard Manley Hopkins's concept of the "'cleave' of being"—most adequately carries through into English the complexity of *partage*.

By introducing a polysemic word like *partage* into the terminological constellation he deployed for naming the interstitial moment between worlds of cultural knowledge, Foucault was merely practicing what he found so absolutely compelling in the œuvre of Raymond Roussel. A month after completing the manuscript for *The Birth of the Clinic*, Foucault threw himself into the writing of *Raymond Roussel*. These two books would be published one straight upon the other in successive months in the spring of 1963. In an article published in the summer of 1962, he had written that "The enigma in Roussel is that each element of his language is caught [*pris*] in an incalculable series of possible configurations [*dans une série non dénombrable de configurations éventuelles*]." Foucault experienced such an urgency to delve long and deeply into the language of this particular (and particularly obsure) literary figure that he would take time out from his burgeoning intellectual project to devote an entire book to it. This is because he had already decided to adopt Roussel's credo that, in Foucault's words, "allowing for incompatible yet entirely possible systems for reading, several constructions may circulate in the same text: [in sum,] a rigorous and uncontrolable polyvalence of forms."[9] When he resumed his main task of discursive archaeology leading next to *The Order of Things* in 1966, in other words, an emphatically literary practice would explicitly guide Foucault's use of "the Great Foreigner"[10]

---

[8] Merriam-Webster, "a complex sentence in logic that is true when either or both of its constituent propositions are true."

[9] "[…] *plusieurs constructions peuvent articuler le même texte, autorisent des systèmes de lectures incompatibles, mais tous possibles : une polyvalence rigoureuse et incontrôlable des formes.*" "Dire et voir chez Raymond Roussel." *Lettre ouverte* 4 (Summer 1962). In *Dits et écrits* I, 211.

[10] Foucault called literature, in fact, "la Grande Étrangère" in a 1975 interview. We know, however, that in essential agreement with Nietzsche on the issue, the strangeness or the

that language is. And while the explicitness of this inspiration would soon dissipate into an implicitness so subtle that many readers would assume it had vanished altogether, literature—and particularly poetic language—would drive Foucault's thought up to the moment it fell silent.

We know that the ironies exposed by Foucaldian archaeology trump, supplement, and surpass by surprise what we routinely call the ironies of history and that this triumph of a superior order of irony is perhaps Foucault's single most important gift to critical thinking. What we know less is how Michel Foucault put the beautifully bivalent word, *partage*—*partage* as noun, but also *partage* in its avatars as verb, as adverbial component, as participle—to work in order to convey those ironies and ambiguities linguistically, revealing their internal transgressions. In his 1963 tribute to Georges Bataille entitled "Preface to Transgression," we see Foucault lending a yet rare amplification of its fusional valence to the notion of *partage*. As if previewing what would be the final object of his archaeological or genealogical project, and lending free reign to his poetic proclivities, he asserts that "[s]exuality [...] traces that line of foam [*la ligne d'écume*] showing just how far speech may advance upon the sands of silence." Then, a few lines later, he speculates as follows: "Perhaps we could say that it has become the only division possible [*le seul partage qui soit encore possible*] in a world now emptied of objects, beings, and spaces to desecrate" (261; 69–70).

Another example comes in that same year of 1963. Though maddeningly difficult to parse, no better evidence of Foucault's focus on the transgressive potential of the word *partage* can be found than the discursive spaces where he grappled with literature's most intractable exemplars. When Roger Laporte published his first novel, *La Veille*, in 1963, Foucault jumped at the occasion to review it extensively. *La Veille* is firmly situated in a modern French hermetic tradition extending from Mallarmé to Blanchot where the most uncanny experiences of consciousness are mined for their narrative value. Here is a telltale sentence from Foucault's review essay on *La Veille*:[11]

> And in this night, or rather (because the night is thick, closed, opaque; the night partakes of two days [*la nuit partage deux journées*], draws limits, lends drama to the sun that it restores, prepares the light that it restrains for a moment) in this "not yet" of morning, which is gray rather than black and as though diaphanous to its own transparency, the neutral word *vigil* gently glistens.[12]

---

foreignness of language is indistinguishable from that of its manifestation in literature. Cf. *DE I*, 1602.

[11] Roger Laporte, *La Veille*. Paris: Gallimard, 1963.
[12] "*Et dans cette nuit, ou plutôt (car la nuit est épaisse, close, opaque; la nuit partage deux*

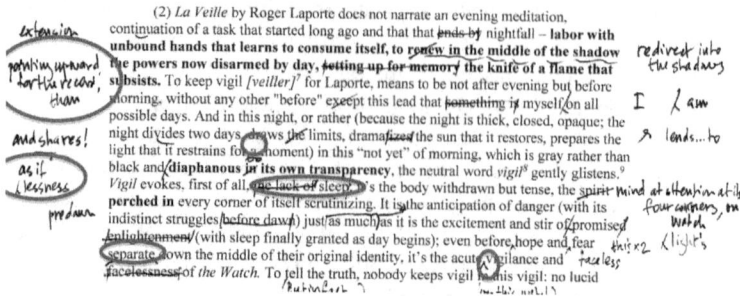

Figure 19 Author's screenshot of working draft of translation referenced in note 12.

Had the translators (Woodard and Harvey) followed the pattern set by all of Foucault's translators to date, they would have stayed with "divides" for *partage*. But since they know that the whole premise of Laporte's novel is the bivalence, the acute semantic undecidability of *la veille* (the day before; watchfulness; the vigil or wake), they know that Foucault also means to say that the night is at the cusp of two days, that there is a moment when I don't know if I'm still in "today" or already in "tomorrow," a moment, in other words, when, as the title of Foucault's review article has it, I am "standing vigil for the day to come." They thus opt for the verb "to partake of": "the night partakes of two days." Partaking of or sharing in two spaces separated by a divide is a solution that needs to be held present to mind and, when called for, held out as a possibility each time Michel Foucault uses *partager* or *le partage* to imply the inclusive disjunction that is a cleave.

Foucault's use of *partage* begins to proliferate in *The Birth of the Clinic*, then flourishes in *The Order of Things*. Virtually supplanting all other names for revolutions in what can be known by a world, Foucault's engagement with *partage* is no doubt in large part responsible for his gradual abandonment of the epistemic model, first supplanted by the archaeological, then by the genealogical model. Allowing *partage* to complexify how we view the establishment of truths is at the very least symptomatic of this shift in his own thought about shifts in thought systems. While we know that Foucault borrowed "*coupure*" and "*rupture*"

journées, dessine des limites, dramatise le soleil qu'elle restitue, dispose la lumière qu'elle retient un moment) dans ce 'pas encore' du matin qui est gris plutôt que noir, et comme diaphane à sa propre transparence, le mot neutre de veille scintille doucement." "Guetter le jour qui vient." *La Nouvelle Revue française* 130 (October 1963): 709–16. In *Dits et écrits* I, 289–96. Translated as "Standing Vigil for the Day to Come" by Elise Woodard and Robert Harvey. *Foucault Studies* 19 (2015): 217–33.

from Bachelard, less clear is what inspired *partage*. The 1963 article on *La Veille* is only one of many interventions on or inspired by literary works that Foucault published in that heady decade. As the allusions and examples coloring his books attest, his literary proclivities went to the Marquis de Sade, Friedrich Hölderlin, Stéphane Mallarmé, Georges Bataille, Antonin Artaud, Pierre Klossowski, and, of course, Raymond Roussel, on whose work he had devoted an entire monograph published that same year.[13] All of these facts are well known and attested in the black and white of extant bibliography. What has also become a "fact," however, is that Michel Foucault "abandoned literature" somewhere in the years immediately following May 1968. Once explicit references to literary sources disappeared, Foucault's putative surpassing of the literary became axiomatic, a cliché. In every step taken over the course of the remaining fifteen years that the archaeologist of thought would have to produce his oeuvre, literature or what I am calling "the literary"—that force, that language, the ethical opening that literature may be—would be, according to *doxa*, supplanted by purely scientific foundations.

That the deployment of the remainder of Foucault's project had soon outgrown the need for literary moorings might for some commentators be emblematized by the disappearance, beginning with the second edition of *History of Madness* in 1972, of a preface culminating with a quote without attribution. That preface had been the transcription of the speech Foucault pronounced as preamble to the defense of his dissertation, entitled *Folie et déraison*, in May 1961. Foucault's solemn introduction of his own doctoral work ended with this unreferenced quotation:

> *Compagnons pathétiques qui murmurez à peine, allez la lampe éteinte et rendez les bijoux. Un mystère nouveau chante dans vos os. Développez votre étrangeté légitime.*[14]
> Pathetic companions scarcely murmuring, go on with your lamp extinguished and give back the jewels. A new mystery sings in your bones. Develop your legitimate strangeness.

An exortation to rise up, a rallying cry: these words exude eleventh-hour hope. That Foucault cited them at this particular discursive occasion without bothering to name the source attests to their supreme place in the order of his thought and his conviction that they are too well known as to require bibliographic framing. These words were written by René Char around

---

[13] Michel Foucault, *Raymond Roussel*. Paris: Gallimard, 1963.
[14] "Préface" in *Folie et déraison. Histoire de la folie à l'âge classique*. Paris: Plon, 1961, i-xi; in *DE I*, 187–95, 195. The editors of *DE* note that "*Cette préface ne figure dans son intégralité que dans l'édition originale. À partir de 1972, elle disparaît des trois rééditions*" (187).

1940.[15] They come from a suite of prose poems in *Seuls demeurent* (1945) called *Partage formel* and that Char wrote while resisting fascism during the Occupation but only published after the war. These were words that Michel Foucault had not only memorized as an adolescent, but would carry with him from youthful nuptials with literature to the abrupt end of his life—at which moment they were functioning every bit as abidingly as in the 1961 dissertation defense in their condensed form as *partage*, the concept. We can thus but agree with Timothy O'Leary when he asserts that René Char's "imperative could stand as an epigraph to Foucault's entire work, a series of books that in their effort to 'think otherwise' constantly explore whatever is foreign to our ways of thinking and acting."[16] In the subterranean and allusive relationship Foucault will come to entertain with poetic language and literature in general after the 1960s and never forgetting his viscerally devoted reading of Char's *Partage formel*, *partage* becomes that killer word, to paraphrase Beckett, which punctuates and colors the thinker's writing throughout.

Here and now, emulating the poet's placement of the word in the title, before all others, we must begin to attempt to deeply explore the task that René Char—and, thus, Foucault—assigned to *partage*. The division that René Char inscribes with this word is altogether akin to that which Albert Camus, one of his closest friends and allies, audaciously made explicit in "Neither Executioners Nor Victims," his series of articles published in 1946 in *Combat*, the newspaper he had established during the Resistance. The subject of Foucault's *partage* is not so much engaged in an active dividing and allotting as in the distributive function that Rancière studies also under the term of *partage* but, rather, finds himself in a situation of cleaving to epistemes or moral positions across clefts that *coupures* would be. *Partage formel* names the absolute divide between the poet and Nazism.[17] "No holds barred," "take no prisoners," "scorched earth" are all methods irrelevant to the struggle that the poet opposes to the way of fascism. Rather, silence in utter revolt—the silence that accompanied the writing of the aphorisms making up the collection that goes by that name, *Partage formel*: this is the violence of the poet's resistance and his response—a solution. About the decision to cleave himself from a humanity that can include Nazism, Char

---

[15] Mary Ann Caws explains: "The poems of 1938 to 1944 [were] grouped under the title, *Seuls demeurent (There Remain Only...)* (Caws 1977: 24). Similarly to our rectification of "Of Other Spaces" in "Of Spaces Otherwise," the subtle rectitude of Caws's translation lies in the precisely correct placement of the adverb.

[16] Timothy O'Leary, "Foucault, Experience, Literature." *Foucault Studies* 5 (January 2008): 7. O'Leary gets the term *"penser autrement"* from Foucault in volume 2 of his *History of Sexuality* (*VP*, 15; *HS*, 9).

[17] Cf. Paul Veyne, 185–6.

wrote elsewhere in *Feuillets d'Hypnos*, that "The implanting of political concepts will proceed contradictorily with the convulsive stealth of a hypocrisy certain of its rights" (no. 7; 135). Yet simultaneously and in tandem with this resolute separation or distinction from evil, *partage formel* names the visceral *sharing* of existence that unites the poet to the poem, the sharing that cleaves, more generally, the subject to language, and that weds the resistance fighter to his comrades. All this, again, is fundamental in Foucault as well. This is another straightforwardly valuable and inspirational lesson Foucault learned in memorizing this particular collection by Char. The beings of these two things—poet and poem, *infans* and language—are incompatible, cannot be fused, resist fusion or confusion, and yet they must proceed hand in hand, in solidarity. Mary Ann Caws had it just right in the first major introduction of René Char to anglophone audiences: "Char's conception of poetry itself. *A place* committed and *yet apart*, where *action and concealment depend on one another* [...] This is a privileged example of the *exterior and interior geography*" (1977: 25). The terms I have underscored in this observation about inner and outer spaces attests, first of all, to Caws's profound understanding of the dynamics at work in Char's use of *partage*. They indicate too that she could very well have had in mind the other massive poetico-philosophical influence on Foucault: Gaston Bachelard's *The Poetics of Space* (1957).

Three years before *The Poetics of Space* appeared, in the detailed and visionary introduction to Jacqueline Verdeaux's translation of Ludwig Binswanger's *Traum und Existenz*, Michel Foucault had already made quite clear his debt to Bachelard and his knowledge of the preoccupations that the philosopher would soon put on display.[18] In this text that he would later repudiate for reasons that had nothing to do with Bachelard, he had gushed:

> Bachelard is right a thousand times over when he shows the imagination at work in the intimacy of perception and the hidden work that transforms the object one perceives into an object one contemplates [...]. Better than anyone else, Bachelard has grasped the dynamic labor of the imagination and the ever vectorial nature of its movement. (142)

But, then, as though already anticipating his major thesis in *The Order of Things* about the preeminence of the being of language over the being of man, he adds: "But must we follow him when he shows [this] movement culminating in the image and the thrust of the image inscribing itself into the imagination's dynamism?" (142). Nevertheless, while thus proudly tempering the gratitude he owes the lessons learned from his reading

[18] *Dits et écrits I*, 9–128.

of Bachelard, Foucault's introduction to Binswanger nevertheless quotes copiously from René Char's *Partage formel*, including one prominently positioned on the book's back cover.[19]

In this exquisite essay of 1957, Gaston Bachelard reviews a number of rather comforting and increasingly confined spaces—the house, the drawer, the corner—to culminate in reflections on their "intimate immensity" and the "dialectic of outside and inside" in which they participate. Freely and copiously appealing to examples from contemporary poetry—including that of René Char and Henri Michaux—*The Poetics of Space* sets the stage for Foucault's reflections on spaces otherwise. Yet, as delightful and comforting as Bachelard's examples of spaces that feed our poetic proclivities are, his study proceeds under the shadow of unforgettable destruction. As he embarks on his demonstration of how one's house functions as microcosm of the universe, he places these lines of hope written by Paul Éluard during desperate days in 1941 and published clandestinely in his 1944 collection, *Dignes de vivre*:

> Quand les cimes de notre ciel se rejoindront
> Ma maison aura un toit.
> When the peaks of our sky come together
> My house will have a roof.[20]

Bachelard's allusion—through Éluard's sly irony on the socialist theme of a "radiant future"—to a future Europe out from under the boot of Nazism was undoubtedly not lost on Michel Foucault. This desirable, viable, and actually functioning quasi-contradiction attracted Foucault's attention as a plausible schematic for getting him (and us) beyond the dialectic: one that could bring a truly new politics — perhaps one bolstered by an ethics. And this is why we suggest that René Char's *Partage formel* henceforth be translated as *Formal Cleave*.

---

[19] In a note in his quirky hagiography, *Foucault, sa pensée, sa personne* (2008), Paul Veyne, who was a close friend of *both* René Char and of Michel Foucault, identifies several unattributed quotes by Foucault of the poet: "'*comme une épave heureuse*' ['happy to be shipwrecked' (sic) in the extant translation] from *Allégeance* in *L'Ordre du discours*, p. 9; '*Jadis l'herbe était bonne au fou et hostile au bourreau*' in *Histoire de la folie*, p. 320; other citations appear in *DE I*, 164, 167 (at the top and the bottom of the page) and 197; the extremely rare verb *allégir*, in *Histoire de la folie*, 95, 320, 549 [...]. See also the epigraph in *DE I*, p. 65 and the citation from Char on the back cover of *Histoire de la sexualité* [*I*]. Also, his use of *allégresse* (cf. Char at the end of *Parole en archipel*). As we have noted above, the word *intransitif*, which he turns into a technical term is borrowed from *Formal Cleft*" (223–4, note 2; I have adjusted the translation, 184).

[20] The poem is entitled "*De Notre Temps*" in *Dignes de Vivre* (Monaco et Paris: Éditions littéraires de Monaco et Julliard, série Sequana, 1944). The translation is from Maria Jolas's translation of the Bachelard essay.

Claims that Michel Foucault somehow "outgrew" literature or, at least, moved beyond it as if it were some inferior medium for thinking are all the more misguided for the fact that throughout his oeuvre, Foucault's writing is deeply imagistic while maintaining its rigor and precision. Semantically rich and carefully crafted, Foucault's writing is at once poetic and philosophical. Claims that he overcame a literary youth are woefully superficial in that, as a general rule, the deeper a written thought is impregnated by the literary, the less its scribe needs to declare so by name-dropping and quotes. If proof, however, is required that literature yet remained vibrant in Foucault's analyses, one need only glance at the last page he ever published: the back cover of *Le Souci de soi* (*The Care of the Self*) which bears, without frill, a final tribute in the form of a quote from René Char—the only poet for whom Martin Heidegger would write poetry. And when in 1976, *The Will to Knowledge* elevated sexes endowed with the faculty of speech—under the guise of Diderot's "indiscrete jewels"—to the status of fulcrum for the entire argument in that first volume of his *History of Sexuality*, our indignation should be triggered at the claim that Foucault ever ceased appealing to literary examples after the upheavals of 1968 and, specifically, to René Char's call for "scarcely murmuring companions" to "give back the jewels."

Even a reader as attuned to Foucault's stylistic care and control as Jean-François Favreau considers Foucault's "fling" with literature spent by 1970 and dismisses these essential moorings on the grounds that Foucault prefers allusion to explicit naming or mundane quoting or just because Foucault puts the enterprises of dozens of figures from the world of literature to practice rather than engage in sterile theorizing about them. Here, for example, is what Foucault supposedly missed in Artaud and Michaux:

> In Foucault, it is never a question of experiences such as the writing out of dreams practiced by the surrealists or of writing that strives to bear witness to states of delirium (a fundamental dimension of Artaud that Foucault does not consider), nor again of experiences like that of Henri Michaux which we might define according to one of his titles as "knowledge from the depths" and in which writing is the depository of an experience that comes from without. (37)

While it is true that with regard to the figure of Artaud himself, Foucault only makes a case for the martyr, what are we to say about the unbridled passion for the literary use of language and the impassioned delirium that drives his book on Roussel? And what do we make of his proclivity for drug-induced hallucinatory experiences, as described by Mathieu Lindon, and which are part of the poet's experience since Coleridge, Baudelaire, René

Daumal, and hundreds of other moderns?[21] What about his adamant and abiding support for Pierre Guyotat, author of some of the wildest texts literature has known? As for what he putatively failed to take from Michaux, is not Michel Foucault's fundamental goal precisely to do what Favreau rightly says the Belgian poet did, that is, to make of "writing [...] the depository of an experience that comes from without"?[22] Is that not, precisely again, what Foucault saw in Maurice Blanchot and strove to put to practice in the form of a *"pensée du dehors"*?[23]

Explicit or implicit, Foucault's indebtedness to literature—indeed, the embedment of his thought literature's crown jewel, poetry—abides throughout his career. As an omnibus review of texts will show, Foucault's myriad and variegated use of *partage* and its grammatical and rhetorical relatives is the crucible of that indebtedness to the poetic. In *partage*, we have Foucault's most complex (and no doubt complete) expression of his fundamental contribution to a revolution in historiography. And in *partage*, within *partage*, every time *partage* occurs discursively (and thus put to work), Foucault is reminding us that if there was one position from which he never wavered, it was the one he declared with solemnity at his dissertation defense in May 1961:

> As far as a rule or a method is concerned, I've only maintained one: the one contained in a text by Char which, in addition, contains a definition of truth that is both most pressing and most restrained: "I retracted from things the illusion they produce in order to protect themselves from us and left them with the share [*la part*] they grant us." (*Folie et déraison*, x; *DE* I, 194–5)[24]

That credo is intact and its bearer every bit as resolute eight years later, when he delivers to the reading public his major theoretical manifesto, *Archaeology of Knowledge*:

> I cannot be satisfied until I have cut myself off from [*tant que je ne me serai départagé de*] "the history of ideas," until I have shown in what way

---

[21] Mathieu Lindon, *Ce qu'aimer veut dire*. Paris: P.O.L., 2011.
[22] Cf. his interview on the "Lectures pour tous" with Pierre Dumayet on June 15, 1966.
[23] Cf. 249, 387. In his reverence for Blanchot (consequential of his reverence for Bataille), Foucault differed little from other post-structuralist contemporaries. In light of recent revelations concerning Blanchot's fascistic and anti-Semitic proclivities (cf. Jean-Luc Nancy, David Uhrig, Michel Surya), a valuable project would be a serious comparison between Foucault's political engagements and those of Blanchot in the post-war period.
[24] *"De règle et de méthode, je n'en ai retenu qu'une, celle qui est contenue dans un texte de Char, où peut se lire aussi une définition de la vérité la plus pressante et la plus retenue… 'Je retirai aux choses l'illusion qu'elles produisent pour se préserver de nous et leur laissai la part qu'elles nous concèdent'."* The text quoted is from *Furor and Mystery* and is entitled "*Suzerain*" or "Liege Lord."

archaeological analysis differs from the descriptions of "the history of ideas." (*AK*, 104–5)[25]

Yet as unyielding and unwavering as this position is, are we not also compelled to recognize and accept that things are inevitably contaminated by us once they have granted any portion [*une part*] of themselves to us? And must the archaeological approach not recognize and accept that, just as a new episteme conserves something of the old, Foucault's approach will have continued *to partake of* descriptions and "the history of ideas"? Is it not precisely such *cleaving at the cleft* that enables evolution? Is the deepest, most radical transgression not that which operates as *inclusive disjunction*? When, as Foucault pointed out in his Introduction to Kant's *Anthropology*, Nietzsche came up with his answer to Kant's question, *Was ist der Mensch?*, was he not thinking of a subject both *cleft asunder from* and yet *ever cleaving to* what he'd just forsaken? By providing the following definition, Foucault hoped to further clarify the aim of breaking with "the history of ideas":

> The word archaeology is not supposed to carry any suggestion of anticipation; it simply indicates a possible line of attack for the analysis of verbal performances […]. It is also related to scientific forms of analysis, but is distinguished from them either in level, domain, or methods, and juxtaposed to them by characteristic lines of division […] (*AK*, 159)[26]

Did not Nietzsche—ever the Wisenheimer—find his answer, *Das Übermensch!*, precisely along the continuum of that "'cleave' in being," as Gerard Manley Hopkins put it?

Before we continue tracing the transgressive value that Foucault entrusted *partage* to convey in other works, let us remain, for a moment longer, with that first preface to his first major work, which is essentially the text he read when he defended *Folie et déraison* in its form as dissertation. That text is a veritable symphony in variations of *partage*. Organized in movements, he declares in the prelude that his quest will consist of an "attempt to get back through history to that degree zero of madness where it is an undifferentiated experience, the not-yet-shared experience of the sharing itself [*expérience non encore partagée du partage lui-même*]" (*DE I*, 187). At the

---

[25] "Je n'aurai pas le droit d'être tranquille tant que je ne me serai départagé de 'l'histoire des idées,' tant que je n'aurai pas montré en quoi l'analyse archéologique se distingue de ses descriptions" (179). The repetition of "the history of ideas" in the translation is a bit cumbersome, but ultimately necessary to ensure that Foucault's point is made.

[26] "Le mot d'archéologie n'a point valeur d'anticipation ; il désigne seulement une des lignes d'attaque pour l'analyse des performances verbales […]. Elle a rapport aussi à des formes scientifiques d'analyse dont elle se distingue soit par le niveau, soit par le domaine, soit pas les méthodes et qu'elle jouxte selon des lignes de partage caractéristiques […]." (*AS*, 269).

end of the second movement, Foucault states that the manner or context in which, or the banner *under* which this and the studies to follow will "confront the dialectics of history with the immobile structures of the tragic" will be "beneath the sun of the great Nietzschean quest" (*DE I*, 190; *HM*, xxx). Both the second and, to some extent, the third movements of the prelude are built on the leitmotif of *partage*—*partage originaire, ligne de partage, le partage absolu du rêve, le partage tragique du monde heureux du désir*, etc. The term has been uniformly and, one must recognize, *simply* translated as "division." While this is a perfectly legitimate choice in the case of the decision to sever madness from reason—*le partage de la folie* (191)—in other iterations, the operation and features attributed to *partage* prelude its rich ambiguities in Foucault's review article on Roger Laporte's *La Veille*. For example, in riffing on the motionless of the tragic, Foucault refers to "the simple *partage* into daylight and obscurity" (*DE I*, 193; *HM*, xxxiv). Just as midnight both partakes of the day passing, while "standing vigil for the day to come," so in "the decision that both bound and separated reason and madness, [that] perpetual exchange" through which it is clear that "the murmur of dark insects" is still audible, at least by Michel Foucault (*DE I*, 192; *HM*, xxxiii). Here, in the final paragraph of the third movement, where Foucault gives voice to his aspirations, to the hopes he has for what his "history of madness" might actually manage to accomplish for today's world, we see *partage* already champing at the bit to burst forth with all its productive ambiguity. Finally, if I have used musical metaphors to evoke Foucault's earliest treatments with *partage*, it is because Jean Barraqué (1928–73)[27] is, in fact, behind quite a lot of what goes on in the 1961 preface, just as he is behind aspects of the second movement of another key programmatic text: his inaugural lesson before the Collège de France in December 1970, *The Order of Discourse*. If in a text on Pierre Boulez published in 1982 Jean Barraqué is, as Didier Eribon has maintained, present "on every line," Barraqué's tacit presence is more poignant still in the famous prelude with which *The Order of Discourse* begins.[28] Right after quoting (without attribution) Beckett's celebrated conclusion to *The Unnamable*, Foucault imagines a statement by an allegorized desire-not-to-begin to which an equally allegorized institution responds with suspiciously sweet reassurance. The desire's use of the

---

[27] After studying "harmony and counterpoint with Jean Langlais, [he] joined Messiaen's analysis course. He came into contact with a group of brilliant young musicians and together they developed the logic of serial thought to an unprecedented degree" (G. M. Hopkins, 952).

[28] Eribon writes, more fully, that Foucault "speaks of Barraqué on every line even if his presence remains in the shadows since he's not named" (115). Paul Veyne agrees with and reinforces this reading. Eribon's full discussion of the relationship between Foucault and Barraqué is on 112–18. See also his *Réflexions sur la question gay*, 351–9.

phrase "*comme une épave heureuse*," or ""like a happy derelict" (with *neither* attribution *nor* quotes), borrowed straight from René Char points just as directly, as we shall see in our last chapter, to Jean Barraqué. This ultimate elegy to the unnamed love of his life[29] immediately precedes the lesson's first movement which, like the preface to *Folie et déraison*, proceeds on the leitmotif of *partage*. Foucault's passionate friendship with the composer not only taught him much about modern music and its interpenetrations with philosophy, but these were no doubt catalysts for Foucault's deep and vast readings of Nietzsche in the early 1950s. And these lessons shared with Jean Barraqué, whom he had met in 1952, are surely crucial to his having been cured, as he put it in May 1961 of the "dialectics of history."

Moving on to 1966 and *The Order of Things*, the crucial relationship between "the cogito" and what Foucault terms "the unthought" (*l'impensé*) and as he describes it towards the conclusion of that vast proto-archaeology is a fair example of *cleaving at the cleft*, a *partage* in which two elements or forces partake of each other despite what parts them. Man would be impossible, Foucault's conclusion insists, without his doubles or "doublets": this is the sense and, indeed, the title of the treatise's penultimate chapter. Like reason and unreason in the *History of Madness*, the inextricable intertwining of unthought with thought (where "thought" stands metonymically for the Cartesian legacy) is another avatar of the quintessential cleave whose two parts share in one another. Rather than the "locus of [the] empirico-transcendental doublet" (*MC*, 333; *OT*, 321)—that ineluctable rift promising illusions of truth and that was consecrated by Descartes—the species that is called man and that man is still called cleaves at the core of a matrix uniting thought and unthought. But what is "unthought"? One synonym used by "man" would be the Unconscious. More generally and more accurately, perhaps, that which is unthought is language insofar as "language [is] the web of innumerable possibilities" (*MC*, 334; *OT*, 323). The late nineteenth-century realization (in the West) that language is other than me erodes the facile link leading from "I think" to "I am." The certainty of my existence as founded on mere assertion is undermined by the *nachträglich* memory that the medium I employ to share thought—language—doesn't belong exclusively to me ("I") or does, but only as a sort of loan that I take out from the

---

[29] The only explicit public mention of Barraqué by Foucault that I have found is in answer to a question posed by P. Caruso in a September 1967 interview for *La fiera letteraria*, where he explains that "*je dois la première grande secousse culturelle à des musiciens sériels et dodécaphonistes français—comme Boulez et Barraqué—auxquels j'étais lié par des rapports d'amitié. Ils ont représenté pour moi le premier 'accroc' à cet univers dialectique dans lequel j'avais vécu.*" "Che cosè Lei Professor Foucault?," *La fiera letteraria* 62 (39) (September 28, 1967): 11–15; in *DE I*, 641.

bank of culture. The new certainty is based, as Foucault puts it in 1966, on the "necessity [*la loi*] of *thinking the unthought*" (*MC*, 338; *OT*, 327). From now on, we realize, "whatever [language] touches it immediately causes to move" (*MC*, 338; *OT*, 327). It moves and, as it moves, it is moved. By what? By its utterance, whose most powerful type is poetic. We are resolutely *after* Kant in that we *are* "that labour whose laws and demands are imposed upon us as if by some alien system" (*MC*, 334; *OT*, 323). From the moment this previously unrecognized doubt about words worms its way in, as Beckett might have put it, thought can no longer go on *without what it is not*. Foucault concludes the section with the familiar prediction that "modern thought is advancing towards that region where man's Other must become the same as himself" (*MC*, 339; *OT*, 328) or as he put it more lyrically in the last lines of the previous section, "We are bound to the back of a tiger" (*MC*, 333; *OT*, 322).

A thorough examination of *partage* at work in *The Will to Knowledge* as *simultaneous shearing and sharing* should reinforce considerably our contention that Foucault never broke with the inspiration he derived from René Char, specifically, nor from literature, in general. But first, two more examples from early in his meteoric career will be instructive. Foucault concludes the first chapter of his second book, *The Birth of the Clinic*, with this sentence so sumptuously crafted that its original commands space in the upper body of this manuscript: "[T]he space in which disease materializes, is isolated, and culminates is an absolutely open space, without either division or a privileged, fixed figure [*sans partage ni figure privilégiée ou fixe*], reduced solely to the plane of visible manifestations" (*NC*, 18; *BC*, 19).[30] We are now before *partage* conscripted to idiomatic use as principal component of a compound adverb meaning whole, complete, integral, bereft of cleave or cleft. But let us leave this usage for a moment and return to the object of Foucault's beautiful sentence which is "the space in which disease is fulfilled, isolated, and runs its course." This is the space in which activities engaged by experts are carried out under the aegis of a program, or *dispositif*, that he names spatialization. The object of Foucault's attention in this first chapter is spatialization, by which he means the logical core of the operation applied to disease within the space known as the hospital—a space that will become one of the quintessential spaces otherwise. Foucault demarcates the beginning of the history (not yet an archaeology) that *The Birth of the Clinic* will trace by the moment when disease is spatialized in that institution where both division and convergence take place: the hospital. He explains at length:

---

[30] As my translation may indicate, *The Birth of the Clinic* is sorely in need of a new English translation.

> The sick man is no doubt incapable of working, but if he is placed in a hospital he becomes a double burden for society: the assistance that he is given relates only to himself, and his family is, in turn, left exposed to poverty and disease. The hospital, which creates disease by means of the enclosed, pestilential domain that it constitutes, creates further disease in the social space in which it is placed. *This separation, intended to protect*, communicates disease and multiplies it to infinity. (18–19; my emphasis)[31]

That cleft of the ill *from* "society" nevertheless cleaves the diseased subject *to* all the other bodies through infection. And this "nevertheless" will prove incontrovertibly vital for the remainder of Foucault's work—an oeuvre which, starting with the *History of Madness*, would ever expansively be *on*, *with*, and *for* society's outcasts with whom he strove to share common ground.

The second example from *Birth of the Clinic* showcases Foucault's rhetorical and literary verve at work conjuring up the critical point where the cleavage, or division, that *partage* entails meets its cleaving property, its drive to sharing. As the analysis of the clinic approaches its conclusion, in which the invisible space within the body has been rendered visible, Foucault lends the spectacular title, "Open Up a Few Corpses," to the eighth chapter. The renewal of anatomical pathology, which led to this sea change, took place during the French Revolution. "Open Up a Few Corpses" appears without indication that the words are, in fact, not Michel Foucault's, but those of Marie François Xavier Bichat (1771–1802), the daring and ingenious "father" of modern histology. With what will soon become recognized as his hallmark ability to produce discursive drama, Foucault concludes the chapter by finally citing the words with which Bichat ended the foreword to his *General Anatomy* of 1801: "Open up a few corpses: you will dissipate at once the darkness that observation alone could not dissipate." To Bichat's will and testament to future physicians, Foucault comments succinctly, in a chiasmus whose audacious image not only strives to one-up Bichat, but probably owes much to the reading of Roger Laporte's *La Veille*, which had just appeared: "The living night is dissipated in the brightness of death" (*NC*, 149; *BC*, 146). Of all rhetorical devices, the chiasmus is one whose structure figures a two-by-two matrix at the center of which is the product of the four elements: the idea as kernel.[32] By conjoining light, darkness, life, and

---

[31] "*Ce partage, destiné à protéger, communique la maladie et la multiple à l'infini*" (*NC*, 18).
[32] Chiasmus is one of Foucault's favorite rhetorical devices. Ends of chapters are where they are frequently found. He ends "The Visible Invisible," the ninth chapter of *The Birth of the Clinic*, with a chiasmic variation: "Death left its old tragic heaven and became the

death in this exquisitely simple formula, Foucault puts discourse and figure simultaneously to work to inevitable inseparability of these fundamental phenomena.

In explaining how resistance functions, Foucault intricately plays the French cognate for cleavage (irrevocable splitting and separation) off its near synonym, *partage* (shearing *and* sharing), thus showing that while *clivage* is no more polyvalent in French than it is in English, once the shattering that he describes has occurred, the atomic agitation of individuals in their particularities is prone to form new couplings, new alliances:

> The distribution of forms of resistance is irregular: points, nodes, hotbeds of resistance are spread with variable density over time and space, sometimes decisively mobilizing groups or individuals, stimulating certain points of the body, certain moments in life, certain types of behavior. What of great radical ruptures, massive binary cleaves [*partages*]? There are a few, occasionally. But, most often, what appear are mobile and transitory points of resistance, producing societal cleavages [*clivages*] that shift about, fracturing units and fostering new assemblages, crisscrossing individuals themselves, cutting them up and reforming them, plotting out irreducible regions in them, in their bodies and minds. (*HS*, 96)[33]

Yet an example of the failure of cleavage (*clivage*) to achieve the productive temporal transgression of cleave (*partage*) or shared common ground would be Céline as he is represented in his construction of Bardamu partially out of pure fiction and partially out of his own experiences as a physician caring for the indigent people of *la Zone*.[34] This ultimately unethical example notwithstanding, were the hopeful alliances of which Foucault spoke in *The Will to Knowledge* not also possibilities—however dim—afforded by the

---

lyrical core of man: his invisible truth, his visible secret [*son invisible vérité, son visible secret*]" (*NC*, 176; *BC*, 172).

[33] I have substantially modified (and, I believe, improved) the translation of this passage: "[*Les résistances*] *sont donc* [...] *distribués de façon irrégulière : les points, les nœuds, les foyers de résistance sont disséminés avec plus ou moins de densité dans le temps et l'espace, dressant parfois des groupes ou des individus de manière définitive, allumant certains points du corps, certains moments de la vie, certains types de comportement. Des grandes ruptures radicales, des partages binaires et massifs ? Parfois. Mais on a affaire le plus souvent à des points de résistance mobiles et transitoires, introduisant dans une société des clivages qui se déplacent, brisant des unités et suscitant des regroupements, sillonnant les individus eux-mêmes, les découpant et les remodelant, traçant en eux, dans leur corps et dans leur âme, des régions irréductibles*" (*VS*, 127).

[34] In making this supposition upon reading Henri Godard's observations in part of his "notice" to *Voyage au bout de la nuit*, one is tempted to surmise that this weakness led to some of the failings of *Mort à crédit*. *Romans I*, 1208ff.

invention of the paddy wagon's precursor, as he described it in *Discipline and Punish*?

> [...] what, in June 1837, was adopted to replace the chain-gang was not the simple covered cart, which had been suggested at one time, but a machine that had been very meticulously designed: a carriage conceived as a moving prison, a mobile equivalent of the Panopticon. A central corridor divided it [*(qui) la partage*] along its entire length: on either side were six cells in which the two rows of convicts sat facing one another. (*DP*, 263)[35]

In any case, Foucault further elucidates what he means by the nodes or *foyers* produced by clefts (which I translated as "hotbeds" in the context of his discussion of resistance), under the heading of "the rule of immanence" a little later in *The Will to Knowledge*: "We will start [...] from what might be called 'local centers' of power-knowledge: for example, the relations that obtain between penitents and confessors, or the faithful and their directors of conscience" (*HS*, 98; *VS*, 130). He might as well have been speaking as he did in his 1970 letter to Marguerite Duras of the dynamics of "feeling [his] way, full of disquiet and yet, despite all, hope" that he experienced in reading "back and forth, haphazardly" the work of "the writer [he] need[ed]."

As governed subjects, so discourse. Thus, in the section concerning the "Rule of Tactical Polyvalence of Discourses" in this initial volume of the *History of Sexuality*, Foucault writes:

> [W]e must not imagine a world of discourse divided [*partagé*] between accepted discourse and excluded discourse, or between the dominant discourse and the dominated one; but as a multiplicity of discursive elements that can come into play in various strategies. (*HS*, 100; *VS*, 133)

Discourse, as Foucault sees it, is structured similarly to the way Ferdinand de Saussure envisioned the structure of the signs of which discourse is composed: the signifier is inseparable from the signified, while ontologically radically distinct.

Though not the structuralist that commentators of the time and historians, since, have tried (and persist in trying) to make him out to be, Foucault knew that the process of becoming a subject does not necessarily

---

[35] *Or ce qui, en juin 1837, fut adopté pour remplacer la chaîne, ce ne fut pas la simple charrette couverte dont on avait parlé un moment, mais une machine qui avait été fort soigneusement élaborée. Une voiture conçue comme une prison roulante. Un équivalent mobile du Panoptique. Un couloir central la partage sur toute sa longueur: de part et d'autre, six cellules où les détenus sont assis de face* (*SP*, 267).

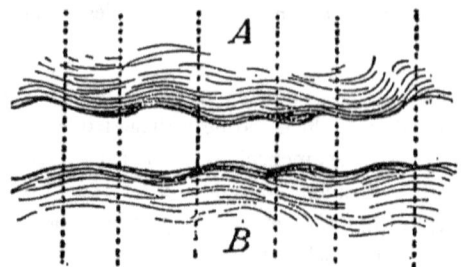

Figure 20 Ferdinand de Saussure, "the linguistic fact" illustrated, *Cours de linguistique generale* (1916).

entail absolute subjection to structures, that "structures" of the subject in other words are neither ontological nor transcendental. As a consequence, the subjects that we become necessarily transgress strict division and seek simultaneous fusion. Shearing is always, necessarily, sharing.

And when the sharing properties of a cleave intensify, it may achieve a productively transgressive capacity with respect to the powers meant to keep it in check. Reversing the order in which Foucault presents these sentences, but not the logic that connects them, why do "parents, families, educators, doctors, and eventually psychologists [...] have to take charge, in a continuous way, of [the] precious and perilous, dangerous and endangered sexual potential" of children? —Because "children were [and are!] defined as 'preliminary' sexual beings, on this side of sex, yet within it, astride a dangerous dividing line" [*en deça du sexe et déjà en lui, sur une dangereuse ligne de partage*] (*HS*, 104; *VS*, 138). The danger inherent to this cleft is not that it divides too much, but that it does not divide enough. After all, the cleft, which is biopowerfully natural to the children, is only dangerous to the adult power entities bent on forming them, having them conform to predefined standards for normality. The line, by itself, does not do what it is supposed to do. Under no circumstance may a child be allowed to remain astride the cleft. That is the worst transgression imaginable. Intervention from authority is called for. This is where "Pedagogization of the Child's Sex" intervenes.

Nevertheless, Foucault's use of the expression *"ligne de partage"* in *The Will to Knowledge* does not always lean so clearly toward implying opportunities for resistance or transgression. Rather, it is designed to conjure up the image of a rampart, a defensive structure of the psycho-social order improvised—much like Thiers' Wall—to protect the bourgeoisie from the deviancy that it hallucinated beyond the pale of the space it made for its class: "a dividing line that would set apart and protect its body." Foucault immediately explains the difference between this division and the cleft that so preoccupies the pedagogues:

> This line was not the same as the one which founded sexuality, but rather a bar running through that sexuality; this was the taboo that constituted the difference, or at least the manner in which the taboo was applied and the rigor with which it was imposed. (*HS*, 127–8; *VS*, 169)

In other words, because this *ligne de partage* is a dividing line established, promulgated as law, and enforced on the very principles of artifice or fiction, its secret is that it convinces anyone that it is natural, like the one in children that is so threatening. Just like the inventions of man and god, this mystification still enjoys long life.

As the conclusion to *The Will to Knowledge* approaches, so grows the explicitness of Foucault's emergent concept of biopower which functions, as we know, as much as *self*-policing as it does policing of selves by extrinsic power: far more efficacious than law enforcement at maintaining normality is a well-trained tyrant within. "[W]hen the life of the species is wagered on its own political strategies," then society has reached what Foucault calls "the threshold of biological modernity" (*HS*, 143; *VS*, 188).[36] Yet here, once again, instead of a leap out of one epistemological configuration into an entirely different one, the new man is built on the foundations of the old: "For millennia, man remained what he was for Aristotle: a living animal with the additional capacity for a political existence; modern man is an animal whose politics places his existence as a living being in question" (ibid.). Not only does this being tarry at the threshold between a political existence predicated on biopower and the threat to life itself under the reign of biopower's extension into biopolitics, fundamental aspects of both epistemes collude to suggest a third possibility superceding a commingling of the first with the second. This collusion is the less overt dimension of the dynamics of *partage* that we are attempting to coax back out of obscurity.

Of course, it is also at this point that Foucault presents the reader with the most famous—and no doubt the most important—early statement regarding the consequences of the hegemony of biopolitics: "*On pourrait dire qu'au vieux droit de* faire *mourir ou de* laisser *vivre s'est substitué un pouvoir de faire* vivre *ou de* rejeter *dans la mort*" (*VS*, 181)—a quasi-chiasmus whose slightly adjusted translation would be: "One might say that the ancient right to *take* life or *let* live was replaced by a power to *foster* life or *relegate* unto death" (*HS*, 138). Looking as objectively as possible at the world today (I write this in Paris in January 2015), one would be hard-pressed not to

---

[36] For some reason, the translator omitted the key adjective, "biological."

recognize that, in fact, the "ancient right" of the tyrannical and modern biopolitics do indeed coexist, sharing and trading opportunities to regulate, define, normalize, make decisions regarding life's limit: death. Biopolitics has not, for all that, "replaced" the ancient right. Nor does biopolitics preclude biopowerful coalitions from superceding it. Reading Foucault with care, we must understand one thing: that between forms of power, there is no absolute division without remainder, no *partage sans partage*, no cleft without cleaving, clinging, collusion. Heteroclite forms of power conspire to eradicate heretics of all stripes. Indeed, it is the heterogeneous nature of such conspiracies that renders power so intractable, so that when we go back to Foucault's first proposal concerning the analysis he is about to conduct in the *History of Sexuality*, we already see the two valences of *partage* at work:

> Power is not something that is acquired, seized, or shared [*s'acquiert, s'arrache ou se partage*], something that one holds on to or allows to slip away; power is exercised from innumerable points, in the interplay of nonegalitarian and mobile relations [*dans le jeu de relations inégalitaires et mobiles*]. (HS, 94; VS, 123)

The first sharing is one that would weaken an attribute that is meant to be anything but weak—*power*; the second is accumulative, fortifying and implied in "the interplay of nonegalitarian and mobile relations." And it is in this second sharing of forces that we also might see Foucault's late explorations of coalition building among heretical elements of society as indicative of the radical continuity of his mission fueled by literature: "Pathetic companions [...] Develop your legitimate strangeness."

Our conclusion will return to the heretical and its relationship to shearing shared, but let us at present run up a subtotal of the conceptual transgression that Foucault achieved in hitting upon *partage* for expressing the spatio-temporal nexus driving his "critical history of thought."[37] Just as spaces otherwise are both spaces *apart* and spaces that are *part of* "this" or "our" world, so the seemingly interstitial periods between epistemes or discursive formations of knowledge are anything but neat and clean breaks: one episteme partakes of another in the manner of the "'cleave' of being" that Gerard Manley Hopkins envisioned uniting us in our differences. Hence the impurity of "the times"[38] breeds the transgressive behavior

---

[37] "L'année de sa mort, il définissait ses livres comme 'une histoire critique de la pensée'; histoire parce qu'elle ne procède pas modo philosophico ; 'une recherché empirique, un mince travail d'histoire' (AS, 265) se donnera 'le droit de contester la dimension transcendantale'" (DE IV, 632); Veyne 2008, 64.

[38] I'm thinking of how "one" says "in these times" or, better yet, how Karl Kraus said "*in dieses großes Zeiten*" and what he meant ironically by it.

of subjects unbeholden in their singularity to either of the two epochs in contention. Although Foucault's exploration of the ways in which knowledges are formed is both vast and altogether devoid of the prescriptive impulse (and in this respect readers who want nothing better than *to be led* were right: he had no "philosophy"), the transgressive opportunities afforded by discursive spaces in which two eras cleave (in which epistemes intermingle) are fertile ground for the work in common engaged by the militant. Paraphrasing, then finally resorting to simply quoting from "Of Spaces Otherwise,"[39] Georges Didi-Huberman highlights the transgressive temporality inherent in heterotopias. They are "spaces of crisis and deviance, concrete assemblages of incompatible spaces and heterogeneous temporalities, socially isolated but easily 'penetrable' *dispositifs*, concrete machines for the imagination that 'create a space of illusion that exposes every real space, all the sites in which human life is partitioned, as yet more illusory'" (Didi-Huberman 2011a: 70).[40] *Partage*, or the cleave, in other words, opens upon the horizon of transgression, while division, cut, and rupture foreclose it.

Frequently inspired by Foucault—whether explicitly or implicitly—Georges Didi-Huberman tirelessly argues for (while providing endless examples of) an ethical valence of *partage* that can be put to immediate practical use and that mirrors and undergirds its conceptual power. Next to his explorations of the disparate (e.g. Goya, Hokusai) and the heteroclite (e.g. Warburg) in search of possible pictural "common grounds,"[41] we could profitably juxtapose his discoveries in the founding of dignity from the rubble of inhumanity through elementary projects in common. Thus,

> sharing [*partager*] the very same barracks 62/D at the Bram concentration camp [with Salvador Pujol] is as much as to say that friendship, in such situations, constitutes the very purport of the work to be accomplished, the minimal community in which any ethical and political gesture is founded. The photographs made by Agustí Centelles at Bram are thus—beyond all issues of authorship—the work of *two* friends toiling together at the same enterprise of dignity. (Didi-Huberman 2010: 201; my emphasis)

---

[39] "Of Spaces Otherwise" is a "*texte magnifique*" writes Didi-Huberman.
[40] I have slightly modified the Miskowiec translation of "*créent un espace d'illusion qui dénonce comme plus illusoire encore tout l'espace réel, tous les emplacements à l'intérieur desquels la vie humaine est cloisonnée.*"
[41] Cf. Didi-Huberman 2011a, 67. The unnamed translator(s) translate(s) "*l'espace commun des rencontres*" lengthily as "the common ground on which such meetings are possible." Incidentally, Foucault's brilliant pun on "*palais de leur coexistence*" at the end of the previous paragraph is completely missed by the flat "feasible lodging."

And moved by Primo Levi's account of shearing transformed by minimal hope into sharing, Didi-Huberman lends a face to his interest in Jacques Rancière's politicization of Jean-Luc Nancy's elevation of *partage* to axiomatic status expressed as "the part of those who have no part" [*la part des sans-parts*].[42] Thus, Didi-Huberman pauses at Primo Levi's contemplation of "the empty watchtowers" of Auschwitz in January 1945, then goes on to remark, in his own words, "that day Primo Levi observed how the hope born of the vision of empty watchtowers stimulated among several prisoners a first gesture of sharing food [*partage de la nourriture*]," adding that the consequence was something Michel Foucault would probably never have thought to put down in black and white, "the concrete sign," that is, "that humanity could take back its rights."[43] Given the types of activism in which Michel Foucault did engage, on the other hand, it would be tempting to surmise that for him, today's Syrians, Afghani, Somali migrants, Roma, and various other itinerants would be among the "pathetic companions" whose "strangeness" from humanity he would have been eager to help cultivate.

The transgression to which the cleave lends structure and force harbors dangers. The "mad philosopher" (*DE I*, 1162)[44] is one who shares sufficient experience with madness to enter their fold, to show readers and other interlocutors the way into that fold, at the risk of never returning from that fold unscathed, with their reason intact. This is the madness towards which nevertheless, with fearless steadfastness, Michel Foucault ever strove. This is why the particular figures of Sade, Hölderlin, Nietzsche, Freud, Artaud, Bataille, and Klossowski—some of whom succumbed to the fold—haunt Foucault's work from the outset, from the first pages, that is, of the *History of Madness*. The risk is always madness, "which is not nothing." The thrill as well as the duty of the mad philosopher, however, is going outside oneself, being beside oneself, and surviving in order to share the experience of sharing. This is why Foucault expressed delight at having "fall[en] into" the acutely borderline work of Marguerite Duras, why despite "finding [him]self caught in it, [his] head in a fog, feeling [his] way, full of disquiet," at reading *Abahn, Sabana, David*, Foucault nevertheless experienced the extremely rare impulse of hope "that if [he kept] moving back and forth, haphazardly, some inevitable figure would finally appear to [him]."

---

[42] Cf. Didi-Huberman, 2012, 106 and Rancière 2000, 12, 14, 17ff. As he kindly reported to me, this is how Gabriel Rockhill translated Rancière's phrase. Risking a neologism, I would have liked to make it "the share belonging to the shareless."

[43] Didi-Huberman, 2010, 29.

[44] To my knowledge, Foucault only enunciates the figure in these terms once, in his famous "Réponse à Derrida" of 1972, but the "mad philosopher" limns his work from its inception with *The History of Madness*. He names many of them in his "Preface to Transgression."

Similarly, what mesmerized Foucault about Roger Laporte's novel was its uncanny temporality situated "before hope and fear separate [*se départagent*] down the middle of their original identity" (218). That fear, whose incarnation is an unnamed woman, and that hope, carried by an unnamed man, are what end up cleaving at the culmination of Marguerite Duras's 1954 parable, "Construction Sites." Recovering or discovering shared common ground for such heteroclite pairs as hope and fear was the challenge Foucault put before himself in order to vanquish the disquiet inherent to Borges' Chinese encyclopedia (which had initially—and for a long time—made him simply laugh) once it dawned on him how its disorder would be received by *doxa*.[45] As he does so frequently, with so many of his stories, Borges thrusts before our eyes the futility and flight from reason consisting of some incongruity wherein impossibilities (utopias) console while realities (heterotopias) only disturb.[46] He boldly demonstrates how "heterotopias [...] desiccate speech [and] sterilize the lyricism of our sentences" (xviii), whereas in Roger Laporte, who "experiences neither return nor eternity, but rather something still more archaic, [who] lends voice to the repetition of what has not yet taken place, like the oscillation of a time not yet inaugurated" (221), we can make out a dawn—however distant—of reconciliation. Foucault goes on describing how Laporte's writing restores a certain blank lyricism to the heteroclite: "writing appears at a distance without reference point, where, absolutely remote, it is like a lost proximity" (a bit earlier he refers to "gray bands of absence or retreat between the white zones of proximity") finishing the sentence by further elucidating what is meant by "proximity": "near since it makes itself known *between* words and *from within* each of them" (221; my emphasis). In the preface to *The Order of Things*, Borges' Chinese encyclopedia would suggest to him "the empty space, the interstitial blanks *separating* these beings one from another" (*MC*, 8; *OT*, xvi; Foucault's emphasis; translation modified). Literature alone can dramatize the conundrum. Therefore literature alone limns a future.

Let us reprise Foucault's transgression before turning to the *point d'hérésie*—an extension of *partage* grounded in Blaise Pascal and in René Char. On January 30, 1842, Jules Michelet took down the following thoughts in his journal—thoughts in the midst of which he inserted an injunction in the imperative mode:

---

[45] "Ce texte de Borges m'a fait rire longtemps, non sans un malaise certain et difficile à vaincre" (9).

[46] "Les utopies consolent: c'est que si elles n'ont pas de lieu réel, elles s'épanouissent pourtant dans un espace merveilleux et lisse [...]. Les hétérotopies inquiètent, sans doute parce qu'elles minent secrètement le langage, parce qu'elles empêchent de nommer ceci et cela [...]" (*MC*, 9).

> Words that have never been spoken, words that have remained deep in hearts must be heard. (Search your own heart. They're there.) History's silences—those terrifying pauses in which history has nothing more to say—must be lent speech, for they carry history's most tragic accents.[47]

Modernity's second century has, at the very least, shown even further proof than Michelet's century did that the historian was dead right about the necessity of lending voice to the moments muted by the species' botched project of man. Whether history is inexorably condemned to producing the tragic or not, I shall not balk at venturing to speculate. But in order to induce muteness to at least mumble, if not murmur, a plan for articulation has to be realized. In the work of Michel Foucault, that articulation carries the name *transgression* and the figure formed by *partage*—a division without rent, a shearing shared, a cleft for cleaving—informs the movement named transgression.

In that cleave lies dormant hope for inoculation against the infernal empirico-transcendental doublet which would, in turn, doom the concept of man to its disappearance. The being that passes as "human" is infinitely finite due to the incommensurability of our coming into being through the being of language. Yet a potential for transgression today cleaves to the watershed [*la ligne de partage des eaux*] between putative objecthood and putative subjecthood. The claim made in this reading through the lens of *partage* is that the transgressive cleave idiosyncratic to Foucaldian thought maintains two valences in history in its endless procession, recession, and repetition, justifying and informing Foucault's conviction that the eternal return is always an eternal beginning.[48] *Partage* incrementally *informs* Foucault's work, *transforming* it into a transgressive apparatus of thought. To the subtractive function of space and time that *partage* constitutes in that coursing and recoursing [*corso e ricorso*] of history, transgression stands as the positive, the exuberantly additive function. Unlike in Bataille, where transgression is often paroxystic, butting up against a limit beyond which there may only lie death, Foucault's transgression thinks beyond the normative to discover vivifying forces in domains thought to be beyond our reach. Whereas Bataille's transgression brings the subject to exclusive disjunction, Foucault's transgression, modeled after his use of *partage*, dares to face inclusiveness in separateness. It is in that inclusiveness that, despite all, a modicum of optimism can be heard to murmur even in the darkest of archaeological explorations. In Nietzschean terms, while

---

[47] "[…] *il faut entendre les mots qui ne furent dits jamais, qui restèrent au fond des cœurs (fouillez le vôtre, ils y sont) ; il faut faire parler les silences de l'histoire, ces terribles points d'orgue, où elle ne dit plus rien et qui sont justement ses accents les plus tragiques.*" Entry for January 30, 1842 in Jules Michelet, *Journal, I. 1828–1848*. Éd. P. Viallaneix. Paris: Gallimard, 1959, 377–8.

[48] Veyne on Foucault on Nietzsche.

Bataille thrashes about in the "lion" phase among Zarathustra's metamorphoses, Foucault is predisposed to the proto-hopeful affirmations of the "child" phase.[49] If cleaving at the cleft is of the nocturnal imagination, Foucault's transgression is indeed, as in Sade or in Bataille, an altogether diurnal operation, flooded in the light of empirical evidence. If the drama of the one has its place at the zero hour of midnight, the ecstasy of the other indeed occurs under the blue of noon. In sum, far from philosophical concepts, *partage* and transgression are functions that can claim roots in the realm of poetry.[50]

Partage figures division, but always sutured by the potential for future transgression. Its semantic tension is acute and without respite. Although the figure of *partage* intensifies the language of *The Order of Things*, it had already informed relationships fundamental to the tale of *The Birth of the Clinic* in, for example, that overdetermined gaze capable not only of seeing more deeply and far better than any other gaze, but in a *look* that can *listen* and *speak* as well[51] or when clinical practice very nearly achieved the coincidence between the final instant of a pathology and the first present moment that is no longer mine, since I am post-mortem.[52] When the faculty of sight cleaves so to the other senses and to the faculty of language in its hermeneutic mode, then death is shown to hew seamlessly to life, becoming the new truth of its limit and definitional criterion.

> *Fureur et mystère tour à tour le séduisirent et le consumèrent. Puis vint l'année qui acheva son agonie de saxifrage.*
> Furor and mystery, by turns, seduced him, consumed him. Then came the year that put an end to his saxifrage agony.

These are among the most famous lines penned by René Char. Michel Foucault not only knew such lines by heart but took them as mental experiments to extend thought beyond the confines of reason. We know that central to Michel Foucault's concerns is the manner in which subjects are seduced, then consumed by language—language, which we nevertheless cherish. The challenge that the subject puts before herself is how to become other than what the community of discourse would force her to be. Like the saxifrage that takes seed in the tiniest infractuosity of a rock, fulfilling that challenge cracks the rock open, allowing for the plant to occupy space otherwise.

---

[49] Thanks to Elise Woodard for this observation.
[50] I asked René Char's foremost English translator, Mary Ann Caws, if she had ever or would have even translated *partager* (or *partage*) as (to) cleave. She graciously responded "Yes indeed, as in *partage de midi*, it is surely the boat cleaving the water."
[51] "*un regard qui écoute et un regard qui parle*" (116).
[52] "[...] *faire coïncider, ou presque, le dernier moment du temps pathologique et le premier temps cadavérique*" (143).

Let us again and for one final round consider, in light of Kant and Foucault's abiding affinity with the anthropological thrust of his work, a few more of those passages in which he makes the cleft at which cleaving occurs work toward a novel theory of transgression that he will elaborate—still under the sway of René Char—in the last decade of his work. Like poetic invention, which Foucault took to heart, the stamp of Kant — with whom, by whom, for whom, more than any other philosopher, he began his explorations—is legible on nearly everything he wrote. Foucaldian history or archaeology or genealogy is nothing if not, first and foremost, an exploration of the archive and a reckoning in the most thorough and dispassionate form of the conditions of possibility for such or such apparatus of knowledge. What was a man at the time he was invented? What was considered to be the truth of a man then? What about now? For Kant too, a *partage* informs the human condition. No better example of such a "'cleave' in being" at the heart of Kant's unapologetically anthropological view of man is the sublime and how it rends the fabric of good form that is beauty. After a youthful, somewhat frivolous exploration of that veritable leitmotif of eighteenth-century European philosophy[53] and, especially, after the French Revolution had sent shockwaves across the continent reaching as far as Königsberg and beyond, Kant reintroduces the sublime as the Second Book of his *Critique of Judgement* gets under way. Or, rather, beauty and our putatively immemorial judgment thereof are so embattled in Kant's view that the sublime—which he now elevates to the status of experience rather than that of a mere feeling or quality of phenomena—introduces *itself*, intrudes *in spite of all* on the aesthetic dimension of Kant's critical project. The role of the sublime in the *Third Critique* taken as a whole is that of an unexpected but ultimately welcome hitch, a tear in the otherwise smooth and seemingly seamless cloth of an aesthetics dominated by the beautiful. Conformity with preestablished and supposedly eternal criteria for an object to qualify for a judgment of "beautiful" has no bearing whatsoever on the sublime.

Kant begins "The Analytic of the Sublime" with an overview of similarities between the experience of the beautiful and the experience of the sublime. Then, quickly, their first main difference is introduced, the consequence of which—perhaps ironically, but so importantly—will be that "[... whereas] the beautiful seems to be regarded as the presentation of an indefinite concept of understanding, the sublime [...] that of a[n indefinite] concept of reason" (§23). The shock of the sublime, the advent of terror, requires that the imagination come to the rescue of reason lost. Once recovered,

---

[53] *Beobachtungen über das Gefühl des Schönen und Erhabenen [Observations on the Feeling of the Beautiful and Sublime]* (1764).

reason reckons the overall experience, draws conclusions, and resumes the production of discourse. Kant reckons that reason recovered following the experience of the sublime will produce new rules for judgment. And aesthetic judgment is only the beginning of judgment, for it forms the basis for ethical judgment, which in its turn forms the basis for political judgment.[54]

The experience of beauty and the experience of the sublime are delimited one from the other by the limitlessness inherent to the experience of the latter. A transgression that must come under some control of the subject through the combined action of imagination and reason is thus at the core of Kant's claim that

> there are also remarkable differences between the two. The beautiful in nature is connected with the form of the object, which consists in having boundaries. The sublime, on the other hand, is to be found in a *formless* object, [insofar as] *boundlessness* is represented.

It is Kant who underscored "boundlessness," or *Unbegrenztheit*; it is I who have highlighted "formless" or *formlosen*. Now, in René Char's *Formal Cleave*, form, coupled with a definite formlessness that is for all intents and purposes the poetic correlate of Kantian *Formlosigkeit*, oscillates by means of a transgressive dynamic that Foucault will emulate in his most forward-looking moments. Not uncoincidentally, it is in those moments, those passages of his writing, that we find some of his most lyrically sumptuous creations. That oscillation occurs at and across a dividing line [*ligne de partage*] as if form and formlessness were destined not so much to adhere to that asymptotic border, but programmed to never abandon it.[55]

No more prominently does Foucault put the productively bivalent power of *partage* on display than in his description—via *Don Quijote*—of the dawn of the modern episteme in *The Order of Things*. On the one hand, Foucault thrusts the figure of the cleft front and center with what can only be its decisive, incisive, segregative force:

> after the Kantian critique, and all that occurred in Western culture at the end of the eighteenth century, a new type of *division* [*partage*] was established: on the one hand mathesis was regrouped so as to constitute

---

[54] Hannah Arendt, *Lectures on Kant's Political Philosophy*.
[55] Cf. Neil Hertz, "The Notion of Blockage in the Literature of the Sublime" in *The End of the Line: Essays on Psychoanalysis and the Sublime* (New York: Columbia University Press, 1985) and Sara Helen Binney who, in an online article entitled "Oscillating Toward the Sublime," remarks that for both Kant and Hertz the "movement [of the sublime] is an oscillation from the self to something greater and back to a renewed understanding of self," http://www.metamodernism.com/2015/04/02/oscillating-towards-the-sublime-2/ (accessed December 25, 2016).

an apophantics and an ontology [...] on the other hand, history and semiology [...] united to form those interpretative disciplines whose power has extended from Schleiermacher to Nietzsche and Freud. (*MC*, 88–9; *OT*, 74; my emphasis)

Yet his consciously purposeful use of this side of the word's varied conceptual charge makes room for what stands antipodically to the trenchant function, to include that which is shared in common between entities, individualities, singularities: "To know is to speak correctly, and as the steady progress of the mind dictates; to speak is to know as far as one is able, and in accordance with the model imposed by those whose birth one *shares* [*dont on partage la naissance*]" (*MC*, 101; *OT*, 87; my emphasis). While the epistemological shift Foucault limns in the first quote, and which the translator rightly expresses as "division," is occurring, a new unified front between history and semiology emerges. Despite the "cleft," in other words, new interpretative disciplines, extending from Schleiermacher to Freud and beyond, recognize each other and exercise new discursive practices predicated on shared common ground. Despite the model imposed by the very knowledge-discourse nexus into which one is born, then, new vectors of biopower, like new rules for judgment in the Kantian vision that we derive from the *Third Critique*, can nevertheless take root.

It is in the twilight of representation that the human sciences emerge and that Foucaldian archaeology can most strategically and with fresh eyes dust off "man," which he insistently reminds us is an invention. As invention of reason, and although *homo sapiens* may very well survive "man," the designator and state that it names are anything but ontologically originary or certifiably eternal. The chapter of *The Order of Things* entitled "Man and His Doubles" is exemplary of this now infamous story. But as we have had occasion to discuss, Foucault already mobilizes from his army of metaphors a long and complex series of *partages*, "a series of more or less obscure divisions" that condition the possibility of critical thought, which is the apotheosis of the humanist invention.[56] A Kantian beginning, thus, for the modern episteme. But if we are to continue, as I am convinced we should, to understand the Nietzschean thrust of Foucaldian genealogy as aligned with—indeed haunted by—Kant's later work, it is most important to focus on the "ambiguity" (Foucault's word) inherent to the "discourse of truth"—the "discourse of truth," which is of a piece with "truth discourse" ("*discours vrai*") (331).[57] Here is Foucault: "it

---

[56] It would be unduly tedious here to enumerate them, but the reader may find them at pages 330–1 in the French and pages 319–20 in the English.

[57] "*Le discours vrai*" is yet another inversion of usual noun–adjective syntax in French whose consequential expansion of meaning the literature-infused Foucault is acutely aware.

is a question not so much of an alternative as of a fluctuation [*oscillation*] inherent in all analysis, which brings out the value of the empirical at the transcendental level" (*MC*, 320; *OT*, 331). This oscillation, I would contend, is the same phenomenon Kant observed in the experience of the sublime and that results in what Sara Helen Binney has called a "renewed understanding of self" leading, I would say, to new rules for building community.

The conundrum of the famous empirico-transcendental doublet, the conundrum that ensures that the irrepressible drive to seek "the truth" will always explore false paths, the conundrum that subtends the title of this chapter, "Man and His Doubles," is that reason tarries at the threshold of its goal. What should unconditionally rivet our attention is that it is in the very nature of this point of *partage* where man is invented that the invention is always already susceptible to transgression, vulnerable to its own supercession, open to that which is *other than itself*. And the transgression, here, carries the name "inherent oscillation." In that oscillation too lies the possibility of a beyond man, an *Übermensch*. The evidence proving that Foucault had realized by the time he wrote *The Order of Things* that he had found in *partage* the killer word for a cleft where cleaving is possible and protected, and that this word-concept depicts the transgression that *homo sapiens* must perform in order to achieve an unwritten destiny beyond man, resides in how Foucault brilliantly culminates this long paragraph with one of his signature stylistic flourishes modulated by the key term. *Homo sapiens* of *The Order of Things* is still arrested before the threshold, mesmerized by the oscillation, not quite ready to, as Char put it, "develop [his] legitimate strangeness." Despite Kant's critical revolution and its reverberations through Nietzsche, Bachelard, Benjamin, and so many others, "pre-critical naiveté," Foucault writes, still "holds undivided rule" (320). The unassailable, uncleavable sovereignty of that rule is a *"règne sans partage"* (331).

Yet even in that state of pre-critical naiveté and despite the three-century-old invention of critique, the impurities that man's positive activity endeavors to eliminate return with redoubled force within "that hiatus, minuscule and yet invincible, which resides in the 'and' of retreat and return, of thought and the unthought [*l'impensé*], of the empirical and the transcendental, of what belongs to the order of positivity and what belongs to the order of foundations" (*OT*, 340).[58] The vicious cycle of failure to reproduce the metaphysical promise of truth perpetuates itself in the permeability, in other words, of a

---

[58] Foucault's repetition of *"et,"* here, is reminiscent of the same gesture used by Deleuze to mimic the stuttering logic of the rhizome. *"écart, infime mais invincible, qui réside dans le* 'et' *du recul* et *du retour, de la pensée* et *de l'impensé, de l'empirique* et *du transcendantal, de ce qui est de l'ordre de la positivité* et *de ce qui est de l'ordre des fondements."* (*MC*, 351; my emphasis).

partage that invites a transgression that promises a *common presence*. It is fortuitous for our survey of shared common grounds that René Char lent the title, *Commune présence*, to a vast anthology that he assembled in 1964 for Éditions Gallimard.

We have now seen ample examples of how complex the deployment of the *partage*-transgression nexus is in *The Order of Things* and how acute is the necessity to review and, when appropriate, revise or adjust attempts to translate *partage* into English.[59] Elsewhere in his work, and other than the couple of unattributed citations that Paul Veyne identifies,[60] Foucault only invokes René Char in passing and only twice in the collected *Dits et écrits*. First, in his 1962 article for *Critique* on Jean Laplanche's book of 1961, *Hölderlin et la question du père*. In the penultimate paragraph of "Le 'non' du père," giving his own explanation for Hölderlin's so-called Jena depression at the realization of "man's finitude and the return of time," Foucault suddenly cites the beginning of "Seuil" from *Fureur et mystère* (255):

> *Quand s'ébranla le barrage de l'homme, aspiré par la faille géante de l'abandon du divin, des mots dans le lointain, des mots qui ne voulaient pas se perdre, tentèrent de résister à l'exorbitante poussée. Là, se décida la dynastie de leur sens.*
>
> When the dam named man started collapsing, sucked forth into the giant crack of divine abandonment, words from afar, words that had no intention of getting lost [in the disaster], attempted to resist. At that moment, the dynasty of their meaning was decided.

Here, among many other things, we have the fact or being of *homo sapiens* and the fact or being of language held fast in a cleave to the drama of their incommensurability under the regime of *mere man*. Foucault then extends the quote, appearing to pass over the Rimbaldian thrust of Char's next one-line paragraph where he states that the poet's action comes as a consequence of this catastrophe: *"J'ai couru jusqu'à l'issue de cette nuit diluvienne."* "I ran to the way out of that diluvian night" (261*). Here, in the figure of the exit, we are invited to accompany the poet upon the limit which, when transgressed, gives way to something beyond man, however strong might be resemblance to "the human," because the *Übermensch* would, of course, be embodied by the same species.

The last explicit invocation of the Provençal poet is proffered toward the end of Foucault's short life, in a text commissioned in 1982 for a tenth

---

[59] New English translations of many of Foucault's works are direly needed, but *The Order of Things* is one that is not in bad shape. *The Birth of the Clinic*, on the other hand, is riddled with errors.

[60] See note 16.

anniversary edition of the Fall Paris Music Festival, where Pierre Boulez presented a complete cycle of improvisations based on Mallarmé entitled *Pli selon pli*.[61] This tribute to the great composer whom he knew, but not intimately, is striking and moving, yet purposely strange in ways that illustrate the cleave at work. Rhetorically terse, Foucault situates Boulez within a modernist genealogy beginning with Mallarmé and coursing through Paul Klee, Henri Michaux, and René Char—even extending across the Atlantic to e.e. cummings: an artistic family, in sum, that shared the gesture of brandishing the formal in the face of formalism. The presence, here, of the nuclear catalyst of *partage formel* or the "formal cleave" is unmistakable. But the mention of Char appears, nevertheless, to be more or less in passing, no more than one name among several in an enumeration. We do know, of course, as Foucault did, that Boulez embraced Char to a degree unmatched by his interpenetrations with either Klee or cummings, for example. Crowning his early lyrical period was the profane cantata *Le Visage nuptial*, composed in 1946–7 but not performed until December 1956 by the choir and orchestra of Radio-Köln, inspired by and incorporating Char's poem of the same name. In June 1955, in Baden-Baden, Boulez had performed an interpretive transposition of three poems from Char's *Le Marteau sans maître*. So, as Foucault honors the request for a commemorative statement on a musician he admires and who is a contemporary, but with whom he enjoys no particularly personal acquaintance,[62] Char is embedded in this deep history of creativity that all of Boulez's admirers will know. But then, suddenly, compactly, in a fulgurant paragraph laced with similes and metaphors borrowed straight out of the beloved poet's quiver, Foucault gives us the structure and logic of the cleave conjoining Char and Boulez through their respective media. As if daring us to accuse him of anachronism if not illogism, Foucault offers forth a sentence that beautifully (if incongruously) appears to credit Boulez for work by Char (and not Mallarmé, who was alone the inspiration for *Pli sur pli* which was being performed at the anniversary edition of the festival for which Foucault wrote this piece) that the poet was composing when the musician was eight years old! Referring to *Le Marteau sans maître* Foucault writes: "*la musique élaborait le poème qui élaborait la musique*" (*DE II*, 1040)—"[the?] music elaborated the poem, which elaborated the music"—which is in a sense true, if we decide to understand the first instance of "*la musique*" as *music* and not *the* music.

For our exploration of the textual dimension of the Foucault-Char alliance to be thorough, we need also to invoke two lost opportunities, two occasions

---

[61] "Pierre Boulez, l'écran traversé," *DE II*, 1038–41.
[62] Cf. Eribon, 112–13.

on which they met, in a certain sense, textually, while never actually meeting in person. One was their common contribution to—and thus the encounter of their names on the front cover of—the June 1966 issue of *Critique* devoted to Maurice Blanchot. Sharing the cover of issue no. 229 with the poet and the philosopher are Georges Poulet, Jean Starobinski, Emmanuel Levinas, Paul de Man, Françoise Collin, Jean Pfeiffer, and Roger Laporte. Char's is the lead article; Foucault's comes after Levinas's and before de Man's.

The other "lost opportunity" was this quatrain that René Char wrote four days before what he could not conceivably have anticipated—Foucault's death:

> Demi-jour en Creuse
> Un couple de renards bouleversait la neige,
> Piétinant l'orée du terrier nuptial ;
> Au soir le dur amour relève à leurs parages
> La soif cuisante de miettes de sang.

> Half Day in the Creuse
> A pair of foxes, disrupting the snow,
> Were treading at the edge of the nuptial den;
> At dusk their hard love reveals to the surroundings
> Their burning thirst in crumbs of blood.

These lines, whose translation we have adapted from that of Nancy Naomi Carlson in the July 2012 issue of the *Cider Press Review*, were read at Foucault's interment. The surreal irony that sometimes cleaves literature and life or, in Char's poem, foxes cleaved in hard love, must not have been lost on the mourners of "Fuchs" on June 21, 1984.

> Ce qui est intéressant dans la théologie c'est toujours les points limites où l'hérésie pointe.
> What's always interesting in theology are the limit points where heresy shows up.
>   Gilles Deleuze, Cours à Vincennes, January 14, 1974

The words with which Michel Foucault opened his remarks leading to the defense of his dissertation on May 20, 1971 were not his own. Foucault began thus: "Men are so necessarily mad, that not being mad would be being mad through another trick that madness played" (*HM*, xxvii).[63] These words were written by Blaise Pascal sometime between 1656 and his death in 1662 and arranged among his posthumously published *Pensées* under the

---

[63] "*Les hommes sont si nécessairement fous, que ce serait être fou par un autre tour de folie, de n'être pas fou.*" *DE I*, 187. Pascal, *Œuvres complètes*, 1134. Pensée 184 [484].

rubric of "*Contrariétés*," a few "thoughts" before the section that no doubt a copyist entitled "*Folie de la science humaine et de la philosophie*."[64] Pascal, it turns out, is not as odd a fellow traveler for Michel Foucault as one might surmise if we recall that Port Royal and its Grammar would be pivotal in *The Order of Things*. The other trace of Pascal in *The Order of Things* is the four-fold occurrence of the rare expression "*point d'hérésie*." It would appear that Foucault's call, channelling Char, for "pathetic companions" to develop their "legitimate strangeness" as well as the entire overture with which this injunction culminated was deemed premature by Foucault, for he had not yet pursued his archaeological explorations far enough for his understanding to cleave to their "scarce murmuring." It was therefore yet presumptuous to pretend to any status of spokesperson for the mad, the delinquent, the perverse, the queer. Assuming this hypothesis based on the suppression of the first preface to what would become *The History of Madness* is correct, then we must resume and conclude our examination of the formulation, "*point d'hérésie*," as an aspect of *partage* through which Foucault deepened his transgressive exploration of transgression and its practitioners.

A "*point d'hérésie*" is not quite yet heresy, but a heretical intensity approximated by a linguistic invention of Pascal's that Foucault picks up, grammatically alters, and retools for his own use. The cleave that is neither division nor espousal is inscribed in the act of heresy at the threshold of its occurrence: this is the situation that Foucault calls "*le point d'hérésie*." In *The Will to Knowledge*, Foucault sees heresy at work on both sides of the dyad consisting of power and singular subjectivities. On the side of power, it appears before the biopolitical era in, for example, the function of the

> three major explicit codes which, up to the end of the eighteenth century, apart from the customary regularities and constraints of opinion, governed sexual practices: canonical law, the Christian pastoral, and civil law.

Such were the legal strata overarching the subject. But as for their effect on sexuality, "these different codes did not make a clear distinction between violations of the rules of marriage and deviations with respect to genitality" (HS, 37–8; VS, 52). By the time biopolitics is well under way as the new hegemonic power relation, its classificatory obsession could be summed up as a compulsion to point out deviancy in the form of heresy. Already in *The Order of Things*, Foucault had thoroughly rehearsed how the biological

---

[64] I am grateful to the eminent Pascal scholar Philippe Sellier for confirming my suspicion that the bundles of Pascal's thoughts were given titles by those who transcribed them after his early demise.

sciences were meant to harness and tame the entirety of nature by naming every manifestation thereof and pigeon-holing each into classes, orders, families, genera, and species. "So too," he writes in *The Will to Knowledge*,

> were all those little perverts whom nineteenth-century psychiatrists entomologized by giving them strange baptismal names [...]. These fine names for heresies [*Ces beaux noms d'hérésies*] referred to a nature that was overlooked by the law, but not so neglectful of itself that it did not go on producing more species, even in the absence of order [*même là où il n'y a plus d'ordre*]. (HS, 43; VS, 60; translation altered)

By "order," here, Foucault means both new classificatory appellations that would replenish the entomologist's stockpile and an intractable disorder that the law knows very well inheres to the insects being named. The will to know, the book's titular subject, proves to operate according to a logic of *partage* that is the quintessence of perversion ("*compagnons pathétiques*"). The example of *Les Bijoux indiscrets* heightens Foucault's polemical tone as he ironically adapts one of the parables of Jesus:

> Is sex really hidden? Concealed by a new sense of decency, kept under a basket by the grim necessities of bourgeois society? On the contrary, it shines forth; it is incandescent. Several centuries ago, it was placed at the center of a formidable *demand to know*. A double demand, in that we are compelled to know how things are with it, while it is suspected of knowing how things are with us. (HS, 77–8; VS, 102)[65]

But while power busies itself endlessly differentiating by means of names and thereby producing species, the little perverts busy themselves by refusing to reproduce the species while infinitely, instead, producing difference.

What exactly is an act of heresy if not a transgressive decision that wrankles orthodoxy precisely for its refusal to leave the confines of what it transgresses? The transgression from *within* an ideology that heresy is, then, a transgression that will not leave *doxa* unscathed because it infects *doxa* through its categorical refusal to *trespass the very space it transgresses*? To Edward S. Casey's invocation of Pascal's admission of the impossibility of "fix[ing] the finite between the two infinites" filtered through Hannah Arendt's lament regarding what Casey calls the "lack of public place," Foucault's retort might well have been that *that place* is precisely the "*point d'hérésie*."[66] Foucault's discursive and theoretical grappling with the *threshold*

---

[65] The parable appears in each of the gospels. Mt. 5.15 reads as follows: "No one lights a lamp to put it under a tub; they put it on a lampstand where it shines for everyone."

[66] "The modern subject finds himself caught between the extremes of universe and self—which is to say, between the infinite exteriority of the spatial universe and the

of *heresy* is far less frequently in evidence textually than his experiements with *partage*. But the two theoretical tools are intimately related, for heresy is one of the more obscure and rare notions that serve Foucault to think divisions that somehow, contradictorily, hold together. As Étienne Balibar recently pointed out, already, as early as *The Order of Things*, one finds Foucault using the expression "*point d'hérésie*."[67] Foucault uses the expression in the nominal form. This grammatical form for the already rare expression is highly unusual if not entirely unique in the French language. Foucault conjures up the expression when describing the epic choice that general grammar had to make in the eighteenth century:

> [A] new and more complicated patterning presents general grammar with a necessary choice: either to pursue its analysis at a lower level than nominal unity [...] or to reduce that nominal unity by means of a regressive process [...]. These possibilities are presented [...] as soon as the theory of languages takes as its object discourse and the analysis of representative values. They define the point of heresy [*le point d'hérésie*] that splits all eighteenth-century grammar. (*MC*, 115; *OT*, 100)

This new coinage comes to Foucault from an already existing expression of commonplace wisdom. Here is what the *Grand Vocabulaire François* of 1770 explains about phrase: "It is said, proverbially, of someone of limited intelligence ['who possesses no genius' is the antiphrasis used] *qu'il ne fera point d'hérésie*—that one need not fear heresy from him"—or, if we want to secularize it, we need not fear sedition from such an individual. The point is that it is not a question of some nodal point of heresy but, rather, a question of *no* heresy whatsoever—*point d'hérésie* being an emphatic negative.[68]

The text of *The Order of Things* is inscribed precisely four times with the formulation "point of heresy": twice, first, in occurrences separated by a mere page in the "Articulation" section of Chapter IV, "Speaking," and twice once again in Chapter VI, "Exchanging"—first in the section on "The

---

infinitesimal interiority of the Cartesian cogito. 'Nothing,' says Pascal, 'can fix the finite between the two infinites which enclose it and which escape its grasp' (n° 72). In between is a vacuum, one of whose main expressions is a lack of the 'public realm,' to use Arendt's term for the primary privation of modernity. I would prefer to call this dearth of the public realm a lack of public place—an absence of concrete, perceptible locales that allow for bodily ingression as well as for shared historicity." (Casey 2009: 363).

[67] Étienne Balibar recently made a wide-ranging case for the influence of Pascal on *Les Mots et les Choses* based on Foucault's use "four or five times, perhaps" of the expression "*point d'hérésie*" in the 1966 masterpiece. Balibar's classical erudition is invaluable, but he never examines Foucault's use of "*point d'hérésie*" as a very occasional, but very well thought-through alternative for *coupure*, *partage*, and so forth.

[68] The variant of the explanation that one finds in the *Littré* goes thus: "*Il ne fera point d'hérésie. Se dit d'un homme sans esprit.*"

Pledge and the Price," then in "The Creation of Value." Then, disseminated across the surface of this vast "archaeology of the human sciences," is an array of what Étienne Balibar calls "quasi-literal equivalents such as 'point of choice', 'fork of a choice', 'real choice of opinions', 'alternatives', [that] express exactly the same idea" (2015: [6]). I cannot but agree with Balibar when he asserts that the "category," as he names it, of "the 'point of heresy' [...] plays a strategic role in the book's formal construction [...] implicitly direct[ing] its argument" ([2]).[69] As in our experience in grasping the significance of a lexical item heretofore foreign to us, each of the argumentational contexts in which Foucault names a point of heresy serves to lend it definition and consolidate its meaning. It is therefore worthwhile to examine each of those contexts.

By the eighteenth century the analysis of representation and signs, whose model since the middle of the century before had been the Port-Royal Grammar, had disengaged the sentence enough from the seemingly inexorable exigency of representation and (just as medicine was beginning to do with the nascent clinic) begun training its eyes on minutiae beneath the surface of immediate signification. Clearly, emphatically, thanks to the force of the expression, "point of heresy," what Foucault insists upon is that despite the necessity—indeed the exigency—that a choice be made between these two paths, the analysis of language will remain heretical, thus rendering possible the modes of discursive and linguistic analysis familiar to us today. At the cleft, on the verge of cleavage where opposing analytical forces tear at it, trying to force it to make a decision—αἵρεσις in Greek—the will to knowledge regarding language cleaves to the opposing methods, wagering that the truth about language will only be discovered if a plurality of approaches be considered. This is the logic of Pascal turned to a secular problem. On the threshold of one of his famously counterintuitive arguments to distinguish true heresy from its false friend, the Jansenist polymath wrote of Christian faith that it "embraces many truths which seem to contradict each other."[70] This is simply a summary—albeit in philosophical language—of biblical wonders such as the ecclesiastical embrace of both "a time for laughter, [and] a time for tears" (3:4), the dual nature (god and man) of Christ, and, as Pascal himself puts it so succinctly, combining

---

[69] As an aside, Balibar adds that the point of heresy category had "until now remained relatively marginal in the interpretation of *The Order of Things*" (ibid.).

[70] "*La foi embrasse plusieurs vérités qui semblent se contredire*," OC, 1329. Pensée 788 [275 in the Brunschvicq arrangement] actually begins thus : "*L'église a toujours été combattue par des erreurs contraires, mais peut-être jamais en même temps, comme à présent*" (The church has always been attacked by opposite errors, but perhaps never at the same time, as now), but the quote used above is quite close to the beginning of the rather long "thought."

antithesis and chiasmus—two of Foucault's favorite rhetorical devices—"the two natures that are in the righteous [...] righteous, yet sinners; dead, yet living; living, yet dead; elect, yet outcast."[71]

It turns out that for at least twenty-five years, starting with a lecture before the Société française de Philosophie meeting at the Sorbonne on February 22, 1992, Étienne Balibar has been examining occurrences of the "point of heresy" (*le point d'hérésie*) either tacit, as in Descartes' second *Meditation on First Philosopy*, for example,[72] or literal, as in Pascal, where the expression helps the author of the *Pensées* explain the duality (or duplicity) intrinsic to Christianity, or again in *The Order of Things* where Foucault switches the valence of the expression from negative adverb to affirmative nominal in order to articulate a crucial nuance in the meaning of *episteme*. Balibar is thus the first thinker, to my knowledge, to have excavated the history of this heretofore neglected notion[73]—a rhetorical tool which is nonetheless fundamental to understanding ambiguities in one of the pillars of Foucaldian historiography. "The category of the *episteme*," Balibar has recently written, "cannot be understood [...] if we do not take into account its intrinsic correlation with the 'point of heresy.'" A preview of the promise of Balibar's latest essay on the subject is revealed when he adds to this declaration of intention that the point of heresy "signals the conflictual dimension of discursive knowledge" (2015: 5). Plumbing the function of the point of heresy helps dissipate the enigma of how it happens that, at the moment of epistemological rupture, there arises "a choice between antithetical opinions (i.e. *doxai*, judgments, positions) a choice [...] whose result is arbitrary but derives from a necessary antithesis within the shared premises" (2015: 6). This leads Balibar to observe in terms of transgression what we have been asserting throughout this chapter about the transgressive function Foucault assigned to *partage* in the realm of epistemology: "there are *limits* for any *episteme*, whose paradoxical 'experience' signals a possibility of transgression" (2015:

---

[71] "*Et enfin les deux hommes qui sont dans les justes. Car ils sont les deux mondes, et un membre et image de Jésus-Christ. Et ainsi tous les noms leur conviennent, de justes pécheurs, mort vivant, vivant mort, élu réprouvé.*"

[72] In this lecture, Balibar detects a point of heresy in Descartes's elimination of *cogitare* from the formula, "*ego sum, ego existo*," which affirms human existence without either divine intervention or the necessity—as one finds it in *Discours de la méthode*—to think it through.

[73] In reference to *The Order of Things*, Balibar's student Diogo Sardinha compares Pascal's use of "*point d'hérésie*" as "schema of coherence" with Kant's "play of the faculties" in *Ordre et temps dans la Philosophie de Foucault* (prefaced by Balibar), 200–4ff. Like Balibar, Sardinha glosses over Foucault's transformation of Pascal's use of the negative adverb ("*il n'y a point d'hérésie*") into the altogether affirmative nominal "*un/le point d'hérésie.*" This grammatical shift is also, tellingly, an elevation.

6). "Foucault's articulation of knowledge (*episteme*) and choice (*heresy*)[74] in archaeological discourse," he adds, "is obliquely commanded by a reference to the Pascalian reflection on this subject"—a reflection in which "the idea that the unity of opposites is precisely what forms the paradoxical condition of a theological utterance of truth" (2015: 7).

To examine the implications of what Balibar means, here, let us further pursue our reading of Pascal's thought on the unity of opposites. After the series of chiasmatic formulations cited earlier to describe the dual nature of the righteous, Pascal concludes that "There are a great number of truths, both of faith and of morality, which seem contradictory, and which all hold good together in a wonderful system." This is straightforward, almost a truism. But then, playing rhetorically, logically, and almost maddeningly on both sides of the threshold of heresy in a manner that would necessarily intrigue Foucault, Pascal writes that "The source of all heresies is the exclusion of some of these truths; and the source of all the objections which the heretics make against us is the ignorance of some of our truths." Not exactly "damned if you do and damned if you don't" or "it takes one to know one," but the heretics accuse "us" of heresy and they're right, yet irony of ironies: they don't know why: "exclusion is the cause of their heresy," Pascal continues, "and ignorance that we hold the other truth causes their objections." Pascal is manifestly speaking absolute sense from the "side" of what Foucault would later name "the unthought," *l'impensé*.

As Balibar's analysis emphasizes, we are exposed, throughout *The Order of Things*, to "the idea that 'authors' or 'schools' may subjectively believe that they are separated by radical antagonisms, whereas in fact they are only displaying the equivocity of the same principles" (2015: 9). In Pascal's thought and logic, this would be analogous to the heresy (or not) of Luther:

> The heresy of to-day, not conceiving that this Sacrament contains at the same time both the presence of Jesus Christ and a type of Him [*et sa figure*], and that it is a sacrifice and a commemoration of a sacrifice, believes that neither of these truths can be admitted without excluding the other for this reason.

It is at this point that Pascal pronounces the phrase that Foucault picked up, modified grammatically into a nominal phrase, and injected into *The Order of Things* as an agent complexifying the notion of episteme:

> They adhere to this point alone, that this Sacrament is typical [*figuratif*]; and in this they are not heretics [*et en cela ils ne sont point hérétiques*].

---

[74] Balibar explains that like Pascal, Foucault is of course "using 'heresy' in its etymological sense of 'choice' or 'decision' between alternative possibilities" (7). Cf. *hairesis* in Greek.

They think that we exclude this truth; hence it comes that they raise so many objections to us out of the passages of the Fathers which assert it. Finally, they deny the presence; and in this they are heretics [*en cela ils sont hérétiques*].

The "empirico-transcendental doublet," Foucault's famous and rather intractable term for the human's intrinsic duplicity, "names an ubiquitous being or entity which should feature *at the same time on both sides* of the divide" (2015: 19; Balibar's emphasis). These features of the "'cleave' of being" or the point of heresy are immediately apparent in the very first passage of *The Order of Things* where Foucault has the expression appear explicitly and that Balibar quotes *in extenso* (11–12):

> The sentence is now populated with syntactical elements—patterns far more intricate than the broad figures of the proposition. This new patterning confronts general grammar with a choice: either to pursue its analysis at a level below nominal unity and to bring into prominence, before signification, the insignificant elements of which it is constructed, or else to reduce that nominal unity by means of a regressive process, to recognize its existence within more restricted units, and to discover its efficacity as representation below the level of whole words, in particles, in syllables, and even in single letters themselves. These possibilities are presented—indeed, they are prescribed—as soon as the theory of languages takes as its object discourse and the analysis of its representative values. They define the *point of heresy* that splits [*le point d'hérésie qui partage*] all eighteenth-century grammar. (*MC*, 115; *OT*, 99–100; translation modified)

In what I read as barely contained enthusiasm, Balibar comments that in this "dynamic pattern of thinking where the possibility arises of 'walking on two roads' [...] something like a dialogical adventure within rationality, whose details are retrospectively understandable, but never formed a simple repetition of the initial *partage* [...] a double inscription for the extremes" (2015: 12). He thus recognizes—though without extension—the intrinsic link between the cleave that Foucault names *partage* and the point of heresy in Foucault's conceptualization of the *episteme*.

With his use of the point of heresy, "[w]hat Foucault seems to be adding [...] is the idea that *the transition never ends* [... that]—in Pascalian terms—a possibility must be faced that *epistemes* are not simply divided internally by some local points of heresy [...] but [are] permanently antithetic" (18; Balibar's emphasis). The influence of Pascal on Foucault's transgressive nuancing of historical upheaval is all but explicit when *The Order of Things* ties the transformations in the analysis of language to those in the analysis of wealth:

> [W]hereas grammar had two separate and reciprocally adjusted theoretical segments at its disposal: one forming an analysis of the proposition (or of judgment), another an analysis of designation (of the gesture or the root), economics knows only a single theoretical segment, but one that is simultaneously open to two readings made in contrary directions: one that analyses value in terms of the exchange of objects of need—of *useful objects*—, the other in terms of the formation and origin of objects whose exchange will later define their value, in terms, that is, of nature's prolixity. Between these two possible readings we recognize a point of heresy that is by now familiar [...]. There are no differences between these two modes of analysis other than the point of origin and the direction chosen to traverse a network of necessity that remains identical in both. (*MC* 204; *OT* 191, translation modified)

In holding the point of heresy up as Foucault's "'transgressive' figure of epistemological reflection" (18), Balibar thus vindicates my assertion made earlier that Foucault's transgression functions as an inclusive disjunction modeled after *partage*. No better proof of this can be found than when Balibar affirms[75] that one must suppose that "there are not 'two epistemes,' but a single one for Foucault, albeit one with two 'faces', or two antithetic regimes of visibility" (28). Following this analysis, with which I fully agree, it is tempting to speculate whether Foucault hesitated in writing that first sentence where the point of heresy appears, wavering between "*qui*" and "*que*." Had he chosen the latter of these relative pronouns, the sentence in English would have gone thus: "These possibilities [...] define the point of heresy that all eighteenth-century grammar shares"—the point of heresy which cleaves the eighteenth century and *to which* the Enlightenment cleaves. But even if we leave it as "*qui*," we are nevertheless clearly meant to understand that if it *is* a split, as the extant English translation has it, it is a separation that is *articulated across a divide*.

When Balibar rephrases the empirico-transcendental doublet as "an ubiquitous being or entity which should feature *at the same time on both sides* of the divide," he is essentially describing that bivalence of the cleave as *both* division and commingling, as cut with continuity, as simultaneous shearing and sharing. In order to become *episteme*, Bachelard's

---

[75] To be precise, Balibar makes this affirmation in reference to an argument made by Lucien Vinciguerra in *La Représentation excessive: Descartes, Leibniz, Locke, Pascal* (Villeneuve d'Ascq: Presses Universitaires du Septentrion, 2013).

epistemological break must eschew the clearness of the cut to become a discontinuity that maintains some shred of continuity: actors of conscience and makers of discourse, Foucault boldly asserts of the end of the age of history, both see and work across "this breach in the expanse of continuities [*cette ouverture profonde dans la nappe des continuités*]" (*OT*, 217; *MC*, 229). Yet general grammar maintains in linguistics, natural history maintains in biology, the analysis of wealth maintains in economics, and the age of order maintains in the age of history. In sum, in the situation of *partage*, or the cleave, an altogether negative can maintain in an altogether affirmative: this is precisely what Foucault extrapolates from Pascal's *point d'hérésie*. For what has seemingly gone unnoticed is the grammatical elevation or promotion that Foucault wittingly applied to the phrase: in transforming the emphatically negative adverb (*ne ... point*) as in, for example, "there is (*absolutely*) no heresy" or "they are not (*at all*) heretics" into the nominal "*here* is a point of heresy" (*voici un point d'hérésie*), Foucault potentializes heresy, renders it immanent, virtually present.

The opposing epistemological valences of which history is comprised are only so in appearance. When Pascal asserts that there is no heresy in holding contradictory beliefs, he is accrediting, validating, and endorsing what mere rigid *doxa* would label heresy. When Foucault asserts that grammar or money or life, during the Englightenment, reached a point of heresy, he is affirming that while a *choice* was indeed made to *break* with doxological analyses of this or that object (language, life, labor), the path abandoned and the path adopted intertwine, despite all. The science of general grammar grew, of course, out of Port-Royal, the center of Jansenist thought. But Pascal, as his *Lettres provinciales* show here and there, was in no way reticent to mitigate the austere precepts of the Jansenist position with regard to Jesuits, for example.

Striking on the mother lode of the point of heresy, Foucault advanced his program to nuance the logic of epistemic history, thus priming himself for its extension in genealogical archaeology. He honored his discovery by grammatically promoting the expression borrowed from Pascal from negative adverb to affirmative nominal. Given the logical homology—epistemological or otherwise—between heresy with the cleave, we need henceforth in our reading and study of Foucault's legacy to be more circumspect before always, in all cases, translating *partage* as division or divide. Just as Pascal's transgression consisted of reclaiming the heresy of a duplicitous being ready to espouse the unity of opposites at the risk of dying for the cause, Foucault's transgression was to conceive of history and discourse (and of the strange species that make them) as ever breaching their confines: departing from man, taking leave of what he was, daring to commune with others via spaces otherwise, the overman nevertheless *partakes of* man.

Other than in *The Order of Things*, Foucault hardly mentions Pascal. But when he does, it is in framing a particular situation of *partage* that is precisely a *point d'hérésie* in Foucault's sense of the term. After a long disquisition by Noam Chomsky during their famous debate of November 1971 in Eindhoven where the American linguist exposes his reasons for praising (ironically) Descartes's postulate of a second substance, Foucault, not without a certain superciliousness, contents himself by adding "one or two historical points," one of which goes thus:

> I think you will find both in Pascal and in Leibniz something closer to what you're looking for: in Pascal, in other words, and in the whole Augustinian current in Christian thought, you will find the idea of a deep spirit, of a spirit folded upon the intimacy of the self, affected by a sort of unconscious, and which can develop its potential through a deepening of the self. This is why the Port-Royal Grammar, to which you refer, is, in my view, more Augustinian than it is Cartesian. (*DE I*, 1347)

Incredibly premonitory of his later work on "the care of the self," this reference to Pascal also shows how closely Foucault associated his Augustinian bent with the ethical potential in the "'cleave' of being" that heresy makes manifest. He mentions Pascal just one more time, that I know of, in answer to a question in the ranging April 1983 interview with Hubert Dreyfus and Paul Rabinow about his work in progress at that moment, much later, on the "geneaology of ethics." The questioner asked him, "In your own writing, you always show a big break between the Renaissance and the classical age. Was there an equally significant change in the way self-mastery was related to other social practices?," to which Foucault responds, "Let us start by saying that the relationship between Montaigne, Pascal, and Descartes could be rethought in terms of this question. First, Pascal was still in a tradition in which practices of the self, the practice of asceticism, were tied up to the knowledge of the world."[76] Soon, but so late, he would publish *The Use of Pleasure* and *The Care of the Self*, both of which extend this abiding interest in Pascal's asceticism.

The logic of the threshold or point of heresy thus insists and persists to the end of the Foucauldian project. We find it operating in the "sexual mosaic [*le disparate sexuel*]" as it struggles mightily against the will to truth deployed by modern society and science under the guise of the repressed sexuality:

---

[76] Dreyfus and Rabinow, 251, tr. R. Harvey; cf. *DE II*, 1229.

this power had neither the form of the law, nor the effects of the taboo. On the contrary, it acted by multiplication of singular sexualities. It did not set boundaries for sexuality; it extended the various forms of sexuality, pursuing them according to lines of indefinite penetration. [...] It produced and determined the sexual mosaic. Modern society is perverse, not in spite of its puritanism or as if from a backlash provoked by its hypocrisy; it is in actual fact, and directly, perverse. (*HS*, 47)

A bit further on, he will tellingly name the practices that this "mosaic" deploys differentially as "unorthodox sexualities" (*HS*, 49)—"*sexualités hérétiques*" (*VS*, 67). Elsewhere in that first volume of his *History of Sexuality*, toward the middle, just before the transition of Part IV and the example of Diderot's *Indiscrete Jewels*, Foucault's rhetoric tightens as he introduces "the point of weakness where evil portents reach through to us." This point, which is also point of heresy, is where "we demand that sex speak the truth"—no, worse than that, "we demand that it tell us *our* truth" (*HS*, 69). Foucault has kneaded logic in order to break our expectations, for, as he writes:

We tell it its truth by deciphering what it tells us about that truth; it tells us our own by delivering up that part of it that escaped us. From this interplay there has evolved, over several centuries, a knowledge of the subject; a knowledge not so much of his form, but of that which divides him, determines him perhaps, but above all causes him to be ignorant of himself. (*HS*, 69–70; *VS*, 93)

So that by reciprocal logic—the logic of the cleave—what would allow the subject to know himself would be the shearing thought that I share my difference elsewhere, where you are: our common ground. Nothing much had really changed since *The History of Madness*: in explaining that magisterial work nearly twenty years before *The History of Sexuality*, he had characterized the heresy that weds reason to unreason as a "decision simultaneously joining and disjoining reason and madness [in a] perpetual exchange" (*DE I*, 192). The project he therefore put before himself was "to attempt to get back through history to that degree zero of madness where it is an undifferentiated experience, the not-yet-shared experience of the sharing itself [*expérience non encore partagée du partage lui-même*]" (*DE I*, 187).

We have returned full circle to where René Char's *Partage formel* came to Foucault's lips for that final exhortation in 1961 when he defended his thesis, "Folie et déraison." It was as if the *docteur ès lettres* in the making were channeling the Provençal poet in order to already—at this ever-so-early moment—call upon his mad and queer sisters and brothers to rise up in transgression against the *division* separating them from the human, all-too-human:

> *Compagnons pathétiques qui murmurez à peine, allez la lampe éteinte et rendez les bijoux. Un mystère nouveau chante dans vos os. Développez votre étrangeté légitime.*

As for Char himself, who with his empathically virile verse and terse aphoristic oracles unwittingly contributed to clarifying the most crucial of Foucaldian concepts, heresy runs rampant in his work, and riding astride the formal cleave is the sole reason for our existence. From Sade to Bataille and from Rimbaud to Artaud, heretics abound. René Char's evocative monikers for these fiercely independent and wilful comrades abound as well: a far-from-exhaustive list of these rigorously crafted names would include "*grands astreignants*" (great binders), "*bref[s] compagnon[s]*" (brief companions),[77] "*vie[s] insécable[s]*" (indivisible lives),[78] "*hermétiques ouvriers*" (hermetic workers), "*compagnons de vindicte*" (comrades in vindication), "*les transparents*" (the transparent ones), "*enfants sans clarté*" (children without light), and, of course, "*compagnons pathétiques.*" Martyred en masse four hundred years before, in the valley south of the Luberon range, a few kilometers to the east of which his native Isle-sur-la-Sorgue is situated, one particular group of heretics was recovered from the obscurity of historical fancy by René Char and held up as quintessential forebears of Resistance fighters during the Nazi occupation of France. These were René Char's antecedents, for as soon as France capitulated to Hitler's army and thenceforth abidingly, Char proved among the most active of anti-fascist soldiers. Having survived where so many millions had not, René Char, in his post-1945 poetry, paid relentless tribute to his Resistance comrades and their "*alliés essentiels*" among the ordinary population of Provence.

Springtime in Mérindol is idyllic. But for the Vaudois of that area in 1545, Mérindol was where a fanatically Catholic France—altogether homologous to Vichy France—cleft them violently from their right to live.[79] If we know, before reading, that the poem commemorates the annihilation of an entire village's population, then its first words are already ominous: *Couchés en terre de douleur, / Mordus des grillons.* Yet the referent that is "grounded"

---

[77] *Feuillet d'Hypnos*, 141.
[78] *Feuillet d'Hypnos*, 143.
[79] On the Mérindol massacre, Pierre Miquel, *Les Guerres de religion*, 1980; Audisio, *Les Vaudois du Luberon*, Mérindol: Association des Études vaudoises du Luberon, 1984.

Foucault's Transgression

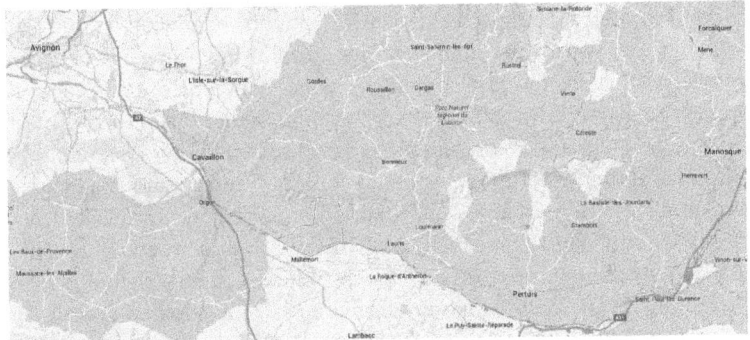

Figure 21 Luberon region. Google maps screenshot.

and "bitten by crickets" turns out to be the "sweet fruit of Brémonde" where Char spent some of his childhood. Char moves us on through this tour of the region to Buoux, a "mistreated boat." Just as the Rimbaldian reference reminds us, death lurks everywhere as the poet "endures the stone-by-stone demolition of his abode" (*De mon logis, pierre après pierre, / J'endure la démolition*). It is not incidental, in this context, that Sade's family estate at Lacoste too is located in this very same Luberon region—Sade who valiantly, violently cautioned about the hidden flaws of hyper-rationality. We read on. Suddenly, the mild Provençal winter (*L'hiver se plaisait en / Provence*) mutates into a springtime punctuated by flash floods typical for the southern ramparts of the Luberon—floods caused, however, not by the effect of the sun, but by the pyres built for burning heretics: *Sous le regard gris des Vaudois; / Le bûcher a fondu la neige, / L'eau glissa bouillante au torrent*.

While it is quite clear that Michel Foucault developed his special use for the point of heresy from the Pascalian toolbox, he just as clearly lent his ear to René Char, who with *Sept parcelles de Luberon*[80] amplified with peremptory vigor the faint murmur of those pathetic others they shared as mutual companions, rendering possible the development of their *legitimate* strangeness and transforming Mérindol from a place of historical amnesia into not only a place for remembrance, but most urgently into a place to cleave (*lieu de partage*) that is our essence as

---

[80] Wallace Fowley translated the title as "Seven Fragments of Luberon" (*Poetry Magazine*, 1964). Although the fragment or the aphorism is one of Char's favored forms, I am convinced that with "*parcelle*," Char was referring primarily to the parcels of inhabited land that ring the Luberon range.

social and ethical beings. Yet challenges abound to my contention that Foucault saw positive contamination—free-flowing osmosis—between *epistemes*, that he foresaw common ground between "our" space and spaces otherwise. Edward S. Casey, for example, writes that during the last fifteen years of his life, Foucault's "concerted search for *des espaces autres* punctuating the historical and political order of things (and challenging that order itself) could not depart more dramatically or drastically from Bachelard's involuted topoanalysis of the places of a receptive reverie" (1997: 299–300). Indeed, if no cleaving obtains at the cleft, then no "receptive reverie" can surge up when we cast our terrified gaze upon construction sites. For Giorgio Agamben—widely considered one of the most profound inheritors of the Foucaldian project—there is no thought *outside* those sites, for "[t]he camp [...] is the new biopolitical *nomos* of the planet" (1998: 176). This thesis, that Agamben drives home in *Homo sacer*, is founded on premisses that seriously contradict the schema of the point of heresy and the trangressive nature of *partage*, as I see it. Agamben explains: "the sovereignty of the living man over his own life has its immediate conterpart in the determination of a threshold [*la fissazione di una soglia*] beyond which life ceases to have any juridical value." A little further on, as if from outside the *nomos* (but whoever among the living, according to Agamben's definition, can ever heretoforth stand outside it?), he refers, however, to "a new decision concerning the threshold (*une nuova decizione sulla soglia*) beyond which life ceases to be politically relevant and can, therefore, be killed without the commission of a homicide" (1998: 139; 1995: 154). Notwithstanding our impression of some fundamental contradiction at work in this latter example, these are serious challenges to my position. For if "the community," as Jean-Luc Nancy writes, "remains to be thought along the line of shared *logos* [*le partage du logos*]" (1982: 90), a decision must continue to find ways of persevering, in taking place without division. Looking at the other across the cleft is the fundamental gesture of ethics itself or else ethics has no part of what we will be. Georges Didi-Huberman adds this to Nancy's injunction about the pursuit of thought: "a shared *aïsthèsis* appears just as necessary for thinking the community within the conjoined issues of the human species and humanness" [*le questionnement conjoint de l'espèce humaine et de l'aspect humain*] (2012: 101).[81] For such an *aïsthèsis* leading to ethical interrelations to exist, however, a transgressive concept and a transgressive practice are necessary. Poetically infused, Michel Foucault hit upon that concept and that practice in the term "*partage*" and its Pascal-inspired correlate,

---

[81] This is found in the section entitled "*L'exposition mise en partage*."

"*le point d'hérésie.*" This is Foucault's transgression. When entities on either side of a caesura commingle, the division is, in reality—in practice, that is—a mere "'cleave' in being," which is no division at all. The embrace of the cut entails the conviction that fusion between sides is still, despite all, possible.

6

The Cleave Informs: René Char and the Hope of Heresy

Sur les pistes transparentes, aux neiges, aux terres et à l'orage,
je livre mon double visage.
Je fais courir les faisans
– ils sont déjà froids et raides –
les faisans des forêts des jeunes années,
qui ne sont pas encore.

René Daumal, "*Le Partage*"[1]

How does one avoid betraying the fragment, while striving for the passage?

Mary Ann Caws[2]

The voice with which Michel Foucault analyzed biopolitics in action was as engagingly affectless as the inexorable process he had placed under the scrutiny of his critique. Spreading with cold relentlessness, the consequences of the sovereign political application of power over life on populations of the ever-evolving species are indeed grim. Such practices and such facts— the facts of social and political life in today's world—perhaps contribute more than anything else to today's readers' nearly exclusive focus on *biopolitics* as though that were Foucault's sole preoccupation during the last ten years of his work. This focus all too often excludes, denies or ignores Foucault's yet more foundational analysis of *biopower*—a phenomenon from which biopolitics derives or, we might say, of which biopolitics is an aberration— and which Foucault considered a vivifying force. While it is true that in some of the Collège de France lectures Foucault would sometimes conflate biopower and biopolitics as if the terms were interchangeable, in *The Will to Knowledge* he wrote that biopower "multiplies life" (138) and, in "*Omnes et*

---

[1] René Daumal, *Poésie noire, poésie blanche* (§ Poésie, 1924–31), Paris, Gallimard, 1954, 177. "On transparent paths, to the snow, to the earth, to storms, / I divulge my dual countenance. / I run the pheasants / - they're already cold and stiff - / the pheasants of the forests of younger years, / which are not yet." (my translation)

[2] Caws 1981, 11.

> # LA
> # MONARCHIE
> ## ARISTODEMO-
> ### CRATIQVE,
> #### ou
> ## LE GOVVERNEMENT COMPOSE'
> ### ET MESLE' DES TROIS FORMES
> #### de legitimes Republiques.
> ### AVX ESTATS GENERAVX DES
> #### Prouinces Confederees des Pays-bas.
> #### Par Loys de MAYERNE TVRQVET L.

Figure 22 *La Monarchie aristodémocratique* by Louis Turquet de Mayerne, 1st edition, title page, screenshot.

Singulatim" (although we have to be circumspect regarding the textual object of this strange Foucauldian commentary[3]) that biopower in its primitive pre-biopolitical form may even tend to favor enhanced or "extra life" (319).

Foucault writing on biopower and on biopolitics was certainly Foucault at his most writerly, if we might recall for a moment the distinction that Roland Barthes made so sharply between intransitive and transitive practitioners of language. Yet just as Foucault modulated and complexified the sharpness of Barthes's "death of the author" into an "author function" that operates with variability and oft contradictory multiplicity while the voice produces discourse out of language coursing pell-mell through the subject about to speak, so the subject named Michel Foucault also eschewed intransitivity in those "biopower years," working with equal fervor—and in an altogether other voice that was heard only starting in the week he died—on the care of the self. In face of the bleakness that biopolitics metes out across the cleft dividing man from himself, the ever Janus-faced thinker at the "'cleave' of being," the philosopher nicknamed "Fuchs" was equally capable and altogether willing to cleave to murmurs of hope from biopower indicating that through the persistence of thought some renewal of youth could be yet to come. "Fuchs" did so in the wake of René Char.

"*Ne t'attarde pas à l'ornière des résultats*" wrote René Char in 1943: "Do not linger in the rut of results." Written in Europe's darkest hour and elaborated

---

[3] The text that Foucault interprets is Louis Turquet de Mayerne's 1611 utopian treatise written for the Dutch States General, *Aristo-Democratic Monarchy*.

further at the very moment when the shroud over the Shoah was just being lifted for all to take stock and begin, slowly, and all too often reluctantly, to hear the murmurs, Char's *Furor and Mystery*—of which *Formal Cleave* is the crux—is shot through with hope. René Char, whose writings Michel Foucault cherished, had chosen to confront a world transformed by totalitarianism and its minions into a pervasive *Lager* and death machine by engaging full force in Resistance and struggling for a new dawn. "*Résistance n'est qu'espérance*" ["Resistance is but hopefulness"] (*FH*, 168). Turning against his youthful dalliance with Surrealism, René Char would have willingly agreed with Ernst Bloch's contention—in *Das Prinzip Hoffnung*—that the concept of the Unconscious, unduly laden with and thus turned toward the past as it is, can and should be replaced by *das Noch-Nicht-Bewußte*, the Not-Yet-Conscious.[4] Thus, hope incongruously lingered among the ruins of a Europe at its most abject: no more than Malraux in his 1937 novel, *L'Espoir*, did Bloch repudiate his *Principle of Hope* in face of the hopelessness. It wouldn't even take Theodor Adorno long to revise his initial contention that poetry could no longer be written after Auschwitz.

On the other hand, Giorgio Agamben, determined to locate an unassailable ontological solution to the present and foreseeable future condition of the species, has famously declared that the concentration camp is the *nomos* of all contemporary social and political existence. He has done so as if authorized to speak in Foucault's name. The left Heideggerian's popularity among today's young intellectuals has no doubt further contributed to the almost exclusive focus, which we have identified as a problem stemming from skewed vision, on Foucault's critique of biopolitics. As well-intentioned as it may be, Agamben's obsession with biopolitics causes him to underplay—to the point of oblivion—biopower's vivifying and life-preserving valence. He declares Foucault's important and subtle distinction of it from sovereign power to be "perfectly trivial" (87), then stretches and generalizes biopolitics in order that he may affirm the inevitability and universality of bare life—a shell of existence from which there is no escape (the absence of any line of flight being the very essence of the Schmittian notion of *nomos*), that affords no future for the species, no truly messianic[5] margin for play, no margin for error.[6] Notwithstanding such hopelessness stands the Foucaldian corpus in its integrality—a wholeness that attests textually, factually that is, to the persistence of *Partage formel* as formal framework for Foucault's overall project. Ever maturing in Foucault's mind, ever building in transitivity, the

---

[4] Ernst Bloch, *Das Prinzip Hoffnung* (1938–47), translated as *The Principle of Hope*.
[5] Dare we invoke the word in its Benjaminian valence?
[6] Cf. the section entitled "error's margin" in Harvey 2010, 27–9.

idea of *formal cleave* persists in its mutation from nominative to predicative, lending hope a rationale for renewed positivity beyond the segregationist event of the cleft. From scission, separation, and division the cleave insists on informing Foucault's thought even as he names and describes the function of biopower in its guise as biopolitics, affecting the subject from without, and biopower in the forms of *ars erotica* and the care of the self, *effected* in spite of all by the subject. Of what does cleave inform Foucault's thought? —It infuses Foucault's thought with the remanence[7] of his deep reading of René Char. The cleave maintains that all severing is, by the same stroke, a sharing: over construction sites, over zones of indistinction, over all places otherwise, subjects shattered, split asunder by crime, injustice, capital's perversions, by the exercise of biopolitics—all such subjects (all subjects, finally) nevertheless, despite all, still manage to find common ground and resist. Over and against those nefarious forces wrought by none other than ourselves, however "natural" they might appear, the artifice of critique will always prevail, if only for a time. No miraculous messianic solution, then: only stubbornly relentless *thought*—critique as resistance. This is the part of Foucault that Agamben, in his haste to say what the contemporary subject *is*, is wont to ignore.

Just as Michel Foucault regarded the differences between biopower and biopolitics as inseparable from their challenging interpenetrations, René Char was clear about what he meant—expansively—by "formal cleave" (*partage formel*). One of the few poems from the same era that René Char bothered to date is "*Le Loriot*"—"The Oriole":

> *Le loriot entra dans la capitale de l'aube.*
> *L'épée de son chant ferma le lit triste.*
> *Tout à jamais prit fin.*
> The oriole entered the capital of dawn.
> His song's blade closed the bed of sorrow.
> All ended forever.[8]

The date: September 3, 1939. Two days earlier, the Wehrmacht had invaded Poland. On the day Char wrote "*Le Loriot*," France and England declared war on Germany. Knowing, as literary history proves and the texts themselves inform us, that *Formal Cleave* was written in the midst of the fascist hecatomb sweeping over Europe, the poet declares by means of this title his utter separation and distancing from Hitlerism and its allies. But immediately and

---

[7] Still used in physics to refer to residual magnetism, *remanence* is, according to the *OED*, an obsolete term for "The remaining traces *of* something; a residue, a remainder" and ought, in my view, to be revived.

[8] Translated by Jackson Mathews in *Selected Poems of René Char*, 94.

also—at the same time, in the same place, that is, in apparent contradiction to the heroic stance of repudiation—*Formal Cleave* equally declares the poet's determination to *cleave towards* an escape, a life-affirming end to the hegemony of the death-dealing forces. "To each collapse [*effondrement*] of proofs the poet responds with a salvo of future," René Char declares in text XLIX.[9] In fact, the recurrent insistence with which Char affirms what the poet is and what the poem does stands, in and of itself, as the affirmation of the possibility that oppression can be overcome and construction arise from collapse. It was, after all, with the very word "collapse" that Foucault described the near muting of voices that the *History of Madness* was meant to recover. It is worth quoting the passage *in extenso*:

> the critical consciousness of madness was increasingly brought out into the light, while its more tragic components retreated ever further into the shadows, soon to almost vanish entirely. Only much later can a trace of the tragic element be again discerned, and a few pages in Sade and in the work of Goya bear witness to the fact that this disappearance was merely an eclipse [*que cette disparition n'est pas effondrement*]; the dark, tragic experience lived on in dreams and in the dark night of thoughts, and what happened in the sixteenth century was not a radical destruction *but a mere occultation*.[10]

The translator's occultation of "*n'est pas effondrement*" by the periphrasis "merely an eclipse," thus shifting from the realm of construction and destruction to that of light and darkness, should not lead us astray: it is all but certain that Michel Foucault had the poet's rally cry from *Formal Cleave* in mind in this singularly clear description of how unthought survived the onslaught of reason in order to go on sharing common ground with it. Foucault's point is not lost: sovereign power did not quite manage to instantiate generalized bare life. And in his later terminology, this attribute of the cleave, this conviction of the resistant, these flashes perceptible in Sade and Goya are tantamount to seizing biopower in order to turn it against the forces of biopolitics. So that perhaps, braced by the possibility and perspective of a transgressive practice of language — that *being* so utterly out of man's control — old Michelet's outlook on the silences and murmurings

---

[9] "À chaque *effondrement* des preuves le poète répond par une salve d'avenir."
[10] "[…] *la conscience critique de la folie s'est trouvée sans cesse mieux mise en lumière, cependant qu'entraient progressivement dans l'ombre ses figures tragiques. Celles-ci bientôt seront entièrement esquivées. On aurait du mal à en retrouver les traces avant longtemps ; seules, quelques pages de Sade et l'œuvre de Goya portent témoignage que cette disparition n'est pas effondrement ; mais qu'obscurément, cette expérience tragique subsiste dans les nuits de la pensée et des rêves, et qu'il s'est agi au XVIe siècle, non d'une destruction radicale, mais seulement d'une occultation*" (HF, 39).

of history as signifying tragedy and only tragedy[11] might be converted—by work or by *a* work—into renewed hope. As Michel Deguy once put it, commenting directly on "*Le Loriot*": "far from all having ended forever as in some final destruction, *all begins* with the work, the work receiving its finishing touches, that is, seizing a limit, entering culmination."[12]

A letter that René Char wrote to his friend Paul Veyne helps illuminate the poet's vision of the cleft that in fact cleaves, the circumstances under which the poem, or what Veyne calls this "message in a bottle," took shape and in what space otherwise the writing occurred:

> I wrote enraged during walks in the Luberon. I took bits of paper and a pencil with me. I thought poetry was going to disappear—perhaps for centuries: even if the Nazis didn't kill us all, we'd never be able to breath. So what poetry will have been before this stifling had to be said one last time and the word "poet" had to be hammered away at. It was a kind of will and testament to poetry, for perhaps these papers of mine would never be found or published. But a will doesn't need to be known in order to exist. (Veyne, 185)

René Char thus converted his rage at the paroxystic triumph of biopolitics—a situation that, as we said, Giorgio Agamben claims is today an *ineluctable* ontological fact—into a nearly solitary practice of biopower grounded in the intertwined justices of resistance and poetry:

> Certain epochs of man's condition undergo the frozen assault of an evil that is bolstered by the most dishonorable elements of its nature. At the center of this hurricane, the poet will, through self-abnegation, complete the meaning of his message, then join the side of those who, having removed from suffering its mask of legitimacy, ensure the eternal return of the headstrong porter, the ferryman of justice. (*PF*, LI*)

The epochal gash of fascism triumphant was a case of the cleft at its morbid extreme. Events being cyclical, however, the mortally wounded species inevitably receives suturing by just surgeons—surgeons of justice—patiently shuttling the needle of renewal back and forth. Thus Foucault, every bit as beholden to Nietzsche's cyclical philosophy of history as René Char, saw himself in the genealogy of such headstrong porters.

---

[11] Here, we recall these words from Michelet's journal, quoted in the previous chapter: "[…] *il faut entendre les mots qui ne furent dits jamais*, […] *qui sont justement ses accents les plus tragiques.*"

[12] "[…] *loin que tout ait jamais pris fin à la façon de la destruction finale*, c'est tout qui commence *avec l'œuvre, à savoir l'œuvre, recevant une finition, s'emparant d'une limite, entrant dans son achèvement.*" Deguy, "Accompagnement du loriot," *La Licorne*.

The Cleave Informs: René Char and the Hope of Heresy

As demonstrated repeatedly by the proliferation of definitions of the poet and of the poet's task that René Char offers in the sequence of aphorisms bringing *Seuls demeurent* to a close, there is a formal cleave too in the relationship between subject and predicate.[13] At each iteration, the language game of defining something, whose endlessness was demonstrated in Ludwig Wittgenstein's *Philosophical Investigations*, stages the play in which a noun is subjected (or subjects itself) to that which cleaves it, that is, to that which engenders it expansively.[14] In René Char's demonstrations of this rule determining language's formal cleave, the name is always either "the poet" or "the poem," so that their interdependence be demonstrated in the very struggle of their distinction. Examples proliferate in the collection; three, here, will illuminate these preliminary observations:

> At the threshold of gravity, the poet like the spider constructs his path in the sky. Partially hidden from himself, he appears to others, in the light beams of heretofore unknown, unheard-of, but mortally visible ruse. (*PF*, xxxix; 121*)

> In the poet are included two obvious facts: the first delivers straight off all its meaning under the variety of forms available to the exterior real; it is rarely deepening, is only pertinent; the second finds itself inserted in the poem, it tells the order and the exegesis of the powerful and whimsical gods who inhabit the poet, a hardened obviousness neither withers nor fades. Its hegemony is predictive. Declared, it takes up a considerable space. (*PF*, XLI; 121)

> Every breath proposes a reign: the duty of persecution, the decision to maintain, the spirit of setting free. The poet shares in innocence and in poverty [*Le poète partage dans l'innocence et dans la pauvreté*] the condition of some, condemns and rejects the arbitrariness of others.
> Every breath proposes a reign: until the fate of this monotype head weeping is settled, persevering, and breaking off to shatter in the infinite, boar's head [*hure*] of the imaginary. (*PF*, L; 125*)

Jean-Claude Mathieu, one of René Char's most insightful interpreters, admirably circumscribes the dialectic at work in the poet's poetics:

---

[13] Mathieu masterfully demonstrates this further meaning of the formal cleave in the section of his book entitled "La définition, partage formel du nom" (178ff.).

[14] "[…] *le mouvement même de la définition* […] *renvoie le nom à ce qui le partage, son engendrement, sa cause, le détour et le désir de l'autre qui fait appel dans le prédicat ou la relative*" (Mathieu, 180) ; "*double appartenance*" (Mathieu, 180).

The definition posits the name and deposits in the predicate, which alters it, thus achieving the "formal cleave" between the poem and the poet. The predicative binding of two terms into formal equivalence usually achieved by the assertion is fulfilled here by predicative signifiers that denote becoming, alterity, and contradiction. (179)

The poem is not the poet: it is the force within him that coaxes the poet outside himself into spaces that he shares, necessarily, with those he is not. All of these definitions (and the ones that will follow in this chapter) that René Char enshrined in prose poems that Michel Foucault committed to memory in his youth and carried with him to his last breath demonstrate that the coursing of language through us—even in limit cases like Raymond Roussel and Antonin Artaud—is a perpetual striving toward common ground.

Returning to the realm of the political—a realm which, for René Char, is always informed by the realm of the poetic—let us consider, once again, his injunction that we have quoted many times, but this time in the context of the full aphorism from which Michel Foucault excerpted it. "*Compagnons pathétiques qui murmurez à peine, [...] Développez votre étrangeté légitime*" follows directly upon this short reminiscence:

> Coming of age, I saw rising and growing taller on the wall between [*le mur mitoyen*] life and death an increasingly bare ladder, invested with a unique power of evulsion: the dream. Its rungs, beyond a certain height, no longer sustained the smooth sleep catchers [*épargnants du sommeil*]. Following the confused vacancy [*brouillonne vacance*] of injected depth, whose chaotic figures served as reserve for the inquisition by men quite gifted, yet incapable of sizing up the universality of the drama, darkness now draws aside and LIVING becomes, in the form of a harsh allegorical asceticism, the conquest of extraordinary powers we feel profusely traversing us, but which we express only incompletely, for want of loyalty, cruel discernment, and perseverance. (*PF*, XXII; 112-13*)

Out of context, and knowing that it surges from the pen of Resistance fighter René Char, the call to pathetic companions could appear as a call to arms of a quite specific type: an appeal to legitimate enemy combatants of the biopolitical force known as Nazism to rise up en masse in an effort to regain the right to live. *In* context, however, the immediate attraction of Michel Foucault writing his monumental and iconoclastic *History of Madness* to the injunction becomes all the more apparent: the contextual tale René Char tells before addressing his ragtag comrades is one in which he recounts their struggle to survive at the hands not of the Nazis, but at the hands of the medical experts self-assigned to police the psyche as well as at the hands of writers and artists who bought so wantonly into Freud's new science that they believed it should become the subjective component of worldwide revolution. The "ladder" is psychoanalysis; *partage* is at work in the adjective "*mitoyen*"; violently extractive, the rare medical term, "evulsion," would have to be Freud's *Traumdeutung*, the interpretation of dreams; and the "confused vacancy," automatic writing or some other similarly wacky surrealist experiment; finally, over and against the perverse biopower created from the collusion of science and the arts there arises, confusedly, the "extraordinary powers" of those who will be called upon in the second paragraph to amplify their voices beyond the millennial murmur. In aphorism XXII, in sum, René Char speaks transitively. He speaks *of*, he speaks *to*, and he speaks *with* the "abnormal" who also happen to be his most likely potential comrades in resistance. Succeeding uncannily to speak *both* in the name of these pathetic companions *and* among them, René Char achieves something Foucault would strive dispassionately and tirelessly to do throughout his work: to lend voice to heresy—transgression, that is, from within.

Picking up on the Nietzschean thrust of *Formal Cleave* LI, cited above, major translator-commentator of René Char in the English-speaking world, Mary Ann Caws, put it eloquently, conjuring up several of the images that fueled Foucault's archaeological project with its characteristic passion:

> The poet, who declares himself "ferryman" [*passeur*], takes on board only those with whom the present and presence may be shared [*partagé*]. The passage from one moment to the next is a passage shared in the two senses of the word. Cleaving the waters [*partage des flots*] that separate island-fragments into an archipelago will become manifest in the wake [*passage-trace*] one may or not follow. (Caws 1981: 12)[15]

The only project that we are tenuously capable of achieving, according to René Char's oeuvre, is that of a "common presence" between an I and a thou, between the poet and his reader, between two empathic beings who tacitly vow to resist oppression and assert what Foucault would name their biopower. The ethical means toward this goal—"loyalty, cruel discernment, and perseverence"[16]—are enumerated at the end of the paragraph just before the admonition addressed to "pathetic companions." As Caws explains in analyzing "*Faim rouge*" (Red Hunger), a René Char poem that discretely

---

[15] Caws' translation back into English of the first edition (?): *L'Œuvre filante de René Char*. Paris: Librairie A.-G. Nizet, 1981.

[16] These may be compared to Primo Levi's list of the survivors' means in *The Drowned and the Saved*. Cf. Harvey 2010, 21–6ff.

references the death—"in a green cleft [*vert partage*], under the cold sun"—of one beloved:

> [...] the green cleft bears, in this case, all the weight of both division and sharing: its color is that of hope and resurrection. It suggests the simultaneous division and sharing of the poem as agent of a common presence. The two readings converge like the memory of a green water tracing in one's heart the deepest valleys of its hidden and common destiny. (1981: 114)

As in the famous Rimbaud sonnet, "*Le dormeur du val*" (with the two red holes [*deux trous rouges*] of the last line echoing the peaceful green hollow [*trou de verdure*] of the first), contrary to the commonplace we pronounce when someone dies, death is not a passing, but a passage that conditions the possibility for the living to cleave loyally to their brethren. Yet as complex as the interplay of *partage* and *commune présence* can become in René Char's poetic world, the dialogical imagery of the cleft to which someone or something cleaves may very well have come to him from an altogether mundane source: the unusual geological situation of the poet's birthplace and lifelong hometown, L'Isle-sur-la-Sorgue. La Sorgue (*Sorgà*, in Provençal), the river flowing *both* through *and* around the town, springs forth some eight kilometers upstream at Fontaine-de-Vaucluse but soon splits at a watershed only to rejoin at a downstream confluence. The two branches of the river literally embrace the land—an island on the Sorgue—upon which the town—L'Isle-sur-la-Sorgue—has been since Roman times when it was a strategically situated *castrum*.

Van Kelly would thus appear to be spot on in pointing out that "Char's closing address to oppressed companions [...] dovetails with Foucault's critique of the origins of psychiatry and psychoanalysis" (121)—two manifestations of biopower turned biopolitics of particular concern for Foucault ever since his 1954 Introduction to Binswanger's *Traum und Existenz* through all three volumes of the *History of Sexuality*. Despite Foucault's skepticism about collective action,[17] the insistence of René Char's presence within the flesh of his writing[18] (in the form of sentences, phrases, certain

---

[17] As Kelly writes of the madmen whose history Foucault retraces, "Unlike Char's *maquisards*, these internees are powerless to resist" and "differences foster dissidence after the fact" (124) yet Foucault himself was not averse to collective militant endeavors, as his participation in the establishment in 1971 and action of the Groupe d'Information sur les Prisons (GIP) attests.

[18] Kelly writes with great sensitivity to what the gesture entails of Foucault's erasure of all references to Char, while continuing have his thought be infused by Char's poetry: "This liberation from authorial aura [...] does not really suppress Char so much as it pushes us to infer something from Foucault's own use of the poet's 'sentences'" (126).

key terms like "the intransitive" or verbs like *allégir*—echoing *allégeance*, a rare word that no doubt reminded Foucault of Jean Barraqué, transformed into concepts) tends to perpetuate the possibility that he would not have altogether rejected Char's "shared communion among the persecuted" (123) even if such communion must begin with the care of the self. After all, René Char too struggled mightily to "sense what has been minimized" by "rationalist maneuvers," as Kelly writes; like Foucault after him, Char too toiled to assist minds "torn between the oppositional modes of reason's utilitarianism and madness's extravagant expenditure" (125). That is precisely why Foucault added—without attribution, as he was wont to do—language premonitory of his future archeological digs from Char's poem, "*Suzerain*" ("Liege Lord"), to his skeptical observation in the preface to the first edition of the *History of Madness* that:

> The liberty of madness can only be heard from the heights of the fortress in which it is imprisoned. There, freedom "has only the morose registry of its prisons, and its wordless experience as a persecuted thing; all we have is its description as an escaped convict." (xxxii–xxxiii)[19]

By doing so, he was holding out hope not for some messianism predicated (as every messianism is) on blind faith, but on a hope grounded in the reality of the "'cleave' of being." A hint of that hope which Foucault began to roll out in *The Care of the Self* from the perspective of the subject in his singularity is legible in some of the more lyrical passages toward the conclusion of *The Will to Knowledge* concerning *ars erotica*:

> The effects of this masterful art, which are considerably more generous than the spareness of its prescriptions would lead one to imagine, are said to transfigure the one fortunate enough to receive its privileges: an absolute mastery of the body, a singular bliss, obliviousness to time and limits, the elixir of life, the exile of death and its threats. (*HS*, 57–8; *VS*, 77)

The body, cleft from consciousness at the dawn of classicism, here and now becomes like the lost and nearly forgotten language and its images whose depths the poet explores until they begin again to murmur. *Ars erotica*, the care of the self, the poet ever striving to commune with his "*grands astreignants*" are all cases of biopower trumping or at least tempering the vicissitudes of biopolitics.

---

[19] "*La liberté de la folie ne s'entend que du haut de la forteresse qui la tient prisonnière. Or, elle 'ne dispose là que du morose état civil de ses prisons, de son expérience muette de persécuté, et nous n'avons, nous, que son signalement d'évadée'*" (HF, vii). Foucault changed Char's imperfect tense ("*disposait*"; "*n'avions*") used in reference to his encounter with "*l'homme violet*," or Sade, to the present tense.

Figure 23 René Char and Martin Heidegger. Photograph by Roger Munier. By kind permission, Jacques Munier.

Giorgio Agamben's ontological bent contesting the figure of the cleave in René Char's wartime poetry which, in genealogical turn, informs the function of *partage* in Michel Foucault's thought, converges—differentially and, we might add, eerily—upon the figure of Martin Heidegger. Irony of false cognates between languages obliging, the German philosopher for whom care (*die Sorge*) summarizes our various manners of being-in-the-world made his only visits to France at the invitation of the poet from L'Isle-sur-Sorgue. The seven conversations that would be gathered to constitute the first of *Vier Seminare* took place in September 1966 in Le Thor, just west of L'Isle, and in various other locations in the immediate vicinity of René Char's hometown. Heidegger would return to Provence in 1968 and 1969 for a second and third of the four seminars.[20] Among the captive audience in 1966 was a twenty-four-year-old Giorgio Agamben who, still in 2014, had vivid recollections of the druid's visit (2015: 262–3). As René Char's guest, it was only fitting that Heidegger would center his inaugural seminar series primarily on Heraclitus. The pre-Socratic thinker had been as central to René Char's poetry as it was to Heidegger's ontological project— particularly as regards the possibility of healing after a cut, the regaining of

---

[20] The fourth and final seminar in this series took place in Zähringen, just outside Freiburg-im-Bresgau in 1973.

integrality after dispersal and atomization. "Heraclitus is that proud, stable and anxious genius," he wrote of him in 1948, in the *Grands astreignants* series, who "shares transcendence with others while taking leave of others" (OC, 721; my translation).

Heidegger returned to Le Thor in late summer 1968 for a second seminar principally on Hegel. On September 2, Giorgio Agamben and the other attendees took these notes down as Heidegger began to form a bridge from his commentary of Heraclitus to what he was about to say concerning Hegel:

> To be able to see the parts (as such) there must be a relation to the unity. If we consider that, since Heraclitus, this unity is called εν, and that, since this inception, the One is the other name for being, then we are referred back to the understanding of being spoken of in *Being and Time*.
>
> At this juncture, Heidegger recalls the criticisms that followed the publication of *Being and Time*. Heidegger was accused of having derived "being" from "is" and then of having developed his "philosophy" from this "abstraction." To these critiques, he answers still today that "being is not an abstraction drawn from the 'is'; rather, I can say 'is' only in the openness of Being."
>
> We return to tearing, understood on the basis of what is torn apart, of the rift [*Riß*]; the experience of which is only possible in a certain "return to" unity: this is so much the case that in Hegel it *must* be there. (Heidegger 2003: 19)

This was the first and only time among the *Four Seminars* that Heidegger references *der Riß* by name. Let us note that the translator has given, understandably enough, the English cognate, "rift." If it weren't for the decisively productive interference from the nearly synonymous *Kluft* that Heidegger's ear had picked up thirty years before, the translator might just as legitimately have translated *Riß* as cleft. As we shall see in a moment, a rift is only a rift in name: it is in fact a cleave! But somehow the name, rift, must be allowed to maintain. Now, the notion of *der Riß* is fundamental—paramount, actually—for grasping Heidegger's conviction that the Hegelian dialectic is a function neither of radical severing nor of fundamental continuity but of inclusive disjunction. No more momentous a dialectics can there be than the strife [*der Streit*] that arises between earth and world when, in Heidegger's words, "a world opens itself [and] the earth comes to rise up." No more thorough a description of the dynamics and consequences of Heidegger's concept of *der Riß* may be found than in his influential 1935 essay, "The Origin of the Work of Art" [*Der Ursprung des Kunstwerkes*]:

As the world opens itself, it submits to the decision [*zur Entschiedung*] of a historical humanity the question of victory and defeat, blessing and curse, mastery and slavery. The dawning world brings out [*zum Vorschein*] what is as yet undecided and measureless, and thus discloses the hidden necessity of measure and decisiveness [*von Maß und Entscheidenheit*].

But as a world opens itself the earth comes to rise up. It stands both as that which bears all, as that which is sheltered in its own law and always wrapped up in itself. World demands its decisiveness and its measure [*ihre Entscheidenheit und ihr Maß*] and lets beings attain to the Open of their paths [*in das Offene ihrer Bahnen*]. Earth, bearing and jutting, strives to keep itself closed and to entrust everything to its law. The conflict is not a rift as a mere cleft is ripped open [*Der Streit ist kein Riß als das Aufreißen einer bloßen Kluft*]; rather, it is the intimacy with which opponents belong to each other [*sonder der Streit ist die Innigkeit des Sichzugehörens der Streitenden*]. This rift carries [*Dieser Riß reißt*] the opponents into the source [*die Herkunft*] of their unity by virtue of their common ground [*aus dein einigen Grunde*]. It is a basic design [*Es ist Grundriß*], an outline sketch [*Auf-riß*], that draws the basic features of the rest of the lighting of beings. This rift does not let the opponents break apart [*Dieser Riß läßt die Gegenwendigen nicht auseinander- bersten*]; it brings the opposition of measure and boundary into their common outline [*er bringt das Gegenwendige von Maß und Grenze in den einegen Umriß*]. ("Origin," 63; *Ursprung* 50–1)[21]

Taking stock of the array of terms that Heidegger deployed in the original German and based or playing on *Riß*—*das Aufreißen* (cf. *das Aufriß*), *dieser Riß reißt*, *das Grundriß*, *das Umriß* ...—it becomes undeniably apparent that *Riß* is meant as linguistic denominator for describing the ontological dialectic of strife that the work of art stages. Yet it is also far too easy to become distracted by Heidegger's virtuoso performance in *Riß* and miss the key variation or modulation provided when *Kluft* intervenes in Heidegger's process of thinking through the construction site of the work of art. The importance of that variation—indeed the semantic pertinence of *Kluft*—is confirmed when Heidegger declines functions and consequences that we associate far more readily with a cleave than with a rift: the "opponents belong to each other," "the source of their unity," "their common ground," the "rift does not let the opponents break apart [but] brings the opposition into their common outline," etc. In fact, unless the lexicographical riff on *Riß* was somehow of more impor- tance than conceptual precision, one must wonder why Heidegger did not

---

[21] Quoted in Hillis Miller, 14.

simply let *Kluft* supplant *Riß* as the term for the crucial originary event. Had he done so, he might not have led such careful, linguistically and philosophically sophisticated commentators as J. Hillis Miller down the path of believing that the concept of the bridge—which Heidegger amply develops in "Building Dwelling Thinking" (*Bauen Wohnen Denken*)—was absolutely necessary in order to compensate for the violent disruption introduced by *Riß*.[22]

The topographical question could be put as simply as this: Does the rift that opens up due to the conflict between earth and world result in a bottomless abyss? If so, is that rift impassible for man without a bridge? Or does the rift thus opened form, instead, some valley traversable with or without the aid of a bridge, albeit via difficult paths? By introducing the body of the species into Heidegger's tale of the origins of the work of art (which is, after all, a work exclusively realized by *homo sapiens*) an equally careful, linguistically and philosophically sophisticated commentator provides a sensible way of interpreting Heidegger's conundrum. "Ironically," Edward S. Casey writes in a footnote to the following passage, "the 'rift' lends itself to a somatic interpretation never given by Heidegger." Fortuitously for our effort to link this strife to that between Foucault and Agamben, Casey provides us with just such an interpretation:

> In "The Origin of the Work of Art," Heidegger writes of the fateful "strife" (*Streit*) between earth and world. In this struggle, a particular building, e.g., a Greek temple, offers a "common outline" (*Umriß*) between the conflicting forces, something "fixed in place" for the enactment of the strife itself. Overlooked in Heidegger's forceful description, however, is the role of the human body in making the conflict between earth and world possible in the first place. The lived body is the concrete medium of this conflict, which is fought on *its* terms. My body brings me into place—whether it is "a place of conflict" (*Streitraum*) or a "place of openness" (*Spielraum*)—and maintains me there (Heidegger, 61). As itself a proto-place, the body constitutes my corporeal here. But precisely in its action of proto-placement, my body takes me up against counter-places, including conflictual places, at every moment. In this countering (and being encountered), the body constitutes the crossroads between architecture and landscape, the built and the given, the artificial and the

---

[22] "In 'The Origin of the Work of Art' the linear figure is the *Riß*, or cleft, [a] dividing fissure" (Hillis Miller, 12). But the necessity of a bridge, the definitive gulf that Hillis Miller reads into this figure, loses the inclusiveness that *Riß* also harbors: "to inscribe a cleft or a *Riß* is to be drawn along it, and ultimately perhaps drawn into a gulf or abyss" (Hillis Miller, 13). So that what he calls for on the very next page is not necessarily necessary for this cleft to operate inclusively as intended: "Insofar as the *Riß* is a fissure, a gorge, or gulf, man needs a bridge to cross it" (Hillis Miller, 15).

natural. Were it not for the body as a proto-place, existing in opposition to counter-places, the earth/world confrontation itself could not occur; there would be no "common ground" for this confrontation and no basis for the mediation effected by the work of art, e.g., the temple at Paestum taken as exemplary in Heidegger's essay of 1935. (2009: 131)

The irony in the body's absence from Heidegger's myth of origin lies in his insistence on *Riß* to the detriment of *Kluft*, even though he makes quite clear that by "*Riß*" he means "*Kluft*." Once that body—*our* body—is introduced onto the scene, the negotiation of the strife between earth and world opens up and a resolution in the form of the artwork becomes possible. "The human body," Casey continues:

> also establishes zonal places, areas of leeway in which free movements relatively unencumbered by the burdens of strife can be undertaken. *Leeway* is the English equivalent of *Spielraum*, place of openness (literally, "play-space") and is at work in Heidegger's notion that the task of the artist or architect is "to liberate the Open (*Offenen*) and to establish it in its structure." But where Heidegger locates such liberation in the action of *Streit* itself, I would situate it in the near sphere. Leeway is the full arc swept out in the near sphere by the bodily modulations of zonal places. (ibid.)

Translated into Foucaldian terminology, this is biopower being exercised absolutely free of the dark shadow of its nefarious extension in biopolitics.

A thinker's epistemological context, of course, is always of primary importance and must, therefore, be taken into account: Heidegger's object (at least in the "work of art" essay) is that of aesthetics and its fundamental moment, its founding moment; Foucault's object is subjectivity whether cultural or historical, but always historically embedded; Agamben's object is political, and ever driven by ontological aspirations. But who would deny Foucault's commitment to addressing the contexts and objects dear to both Heidegger and Agamben, and also, always, from the political standpoint, even if some of those contexts and objects periodically retreat into the background? Was Foucault any less political than he was in *Discipline and Punish*, say, when he returned—first in the 1981–2 Collège de France lectures on "the hermeneutics of the self," then again in *The Care of the Self*, the final volume of the *History of Sexuality*—to the study of *biopower as practiced by the subject upon himself*? Indeed, his final lecture of that 1981–2 academic year broached the subject of "bio-technique, testing of the self, and objectification of the world" with the following words: "challenges to Western philosophy."[23]

---

[23] The second hour of the lecture on March 24, 1982. See *The Hermeneutics of the Self*.

Through the eight volumes of which it is composed, Giorgio Agamben's *Homo sacer* project may be considered as built primarily on his formative studies of Martin Heidegger and Michel Foucault and as an elaborate extension thereof. As in the case of Michel Foucault honing in on, then working productively with *partage* (cleave) as a viable (if complexifying) adjustment to the radical notion of epistemic rupture, Martin Heidegger too found precision rather than absolute difference in his introduction of *Kluft* to modulate the radicality of *Riß* in the tale of the artwork's origin. Likewise is the relationship between biopower and biopolitics: for Foucault, that is; certainly not for Agamben. In *The Will to Knowledge*, where biopower makes its debut as what drives *ars erotica* to resist and perhaps even sometimes trump *scientia sexualis*, we learn that its social aim is not so much repression but the enhancement of the productivity of individuals in the species. In the intervening years, Foucault's speculative research focused—as the vast majority of young people reading him today know all too well—on biopolitical government of populations, only to turn attention to biopower in the form of the government (care, hermeneutics) of the self. Was the final thrust of Foucault's work in *The Care of the Self* a turning of his attention *back* to biopower? Was it, in short, a return? Absolutely not: for biopower was always there at the core of biopolitics and in the necessity of defending society. "To turn his attention to biopower" is merely a phrase of convenience for what was in actuality a second amplification (after the first one in *The Will to Knowledge*) of the *biopower valence* within the dialectical ecology that holds both biopower and biopolitics in its cleaving embrace. Through that final amplification, Foucault—as René Char had done in *Formal Cleave*— was affirming a certain power of the self over the power of repression by laying out some of the conditions for that possibility. In a trice, for Foucault, biopower and biopolitics are entangled according to the logic of *die Kluft*, whereas for Agamben biopower and biopolitics strictly obey the logic of *der Riß*.[24]

Agamben's adherence to what I am calling the logic of *der Riß* perhaps explains, in the end, the sheer oddity in the unexpected glimmer of hope that seems to shine forth from the last page of *Homo sacer I*: "It is on the basis of these uncertain and nameless terrains, these difficult zones of indistinction, that the ways and the forms of a new politics must be thought" (1998: 187; 1995: 209).[25] Yet we recall that the central and lapidary contention of this study of "sovereign power and bare life" is that "the camp, which is now

---

[24] Valuable studies of the interrelationship between biopower and biopolitics in Foucault include Genel 2004, Andrieu 2004, and Huffer 2009.
[25] "È a partire da questi terreni incerti e senza nome, da queste malagevoli zone di indifferenza che andranno pensate le vie et i modi di une nuova politica."

securely lodged within the city's interior, is the new biopolitical *nomos* of the planet" (176). How did we get from such a bleak reconstruction, a vision of irremissibly relentless totalitarian biopolitics to the possibility of a new politics? The key, Agamben waits until the eleventh hour to tell us, resides in our own "zones of indistinction"—zones in which, presumably and against all odds, the altogether nefarious rift of which *the decision to distinguish* consists—a decision of scission, a decision to separate, to segregate, to annihilate—is finally disarmed, neutralized, checkmated.

Now, in *Remnants of Auschwitz*—the third installment in the *Homo sacer* series—Giorgio Agamben identified the so-called *Muselmann* as a paradigmatic subject inhabiting the quintessential "zone of indistinction." "*Muselmann*" was the name—bound to be controversial for obvious reasons—that came to attach to the camp's "living dead" and first described by Primo Levi in *If This Be a Man*.[26] As when one reads Levi's first survivor narrative, so in reading *Homo sacer III* (*Remnants of Auschwitz*)—at least until the very end—Agamben leaves us with the distinct impression that no *Muselmann* remained alive in the aftermath of the Shoah. Indeed both Levi's and Agamben's arguments about the relationship of survivors to the dead are predicated on the assumption that all *Muselmänner* succumbed to the Nazi death machine. Yet by definition, no *Muselmänner*, first of all, were among the victims gassed on arrival at the death camp. Further, and although we can assume that the vast majority of them did indeed perish, some, in fact, survived, as the appendix of *Remnants of Auschwitz* attests by presenting, from the archive, words spoken and written by these surviving remains. To be fair, this appendix obviates the basic blunder of claiming that no *Muselmann* emerged from Auschwitz alive,[27] however, Agamben's fundamental definition of the "remnant of Auschwitz" as "neither the dead, nor the survivors, neither the drowned, nor the saved, but what remains between them" (2002: 164) tends to nullify the conditions of possibility for this remnant, as witness, to ever speak to us.[28] How is it, then, that out of the zone of indistinction where the remnant of Auschwitz dwells Agamben can make out "the ways and the forms of a new politics"? Certainly if as Foucault states in *The Care of the Self* that "politics is 'a life' and 'a practice' [*bios kai praxis*]" (87), asserting that "the *Muselmann*'s behavior […] might perhaps be a silent form of resistance [*une forza inaudita di resistenza*]" does little to convince one that there is enough force, resilience or even ruse, here, to counter the overwhelming repression of biopolitics. We truly need to juxtapose this

---

[26] Cf. Levi, 90 and Harvey 2010, *passim*.
[27] So does Primo Levi. In *The Drowned and the Saved*, he writes that "the term *Muselmann* [was] given to the irreversibly exhausted, worn out prisoner close to death" (98).
[28] I developed these points in *Witnessness*, 20, 40, 65–6 *passim*.

desperate glimmer of hopefulness with René Char's far more plausible and actionable efforts (and Foucault's obvious agreement with them) to amplify the murmur of the pathetic companions.

The problem, however, may not lie so much in Agamben's choice per se of the *Muselmann* as emblem and leader of a struggle for "silent forms of resistance" or "a new politics" as it lies in the notion of zones of indistinction. The indistinction characterizing those zones becomes the ontological fact of all its inhabitants to such an extent that *all* of them (all of us) are potential *Muselmänner*. Because it is predicated on "a fundamental division [*une scissione fondamentale*]," lost forever more, according to Agamben, is any hope for the constitution of a people.[29] Yet as Primo Levi showed in *The Drowned and the Saved*, the cleft between "we" and "they" is one that does not preclude cleaving. That is the very point of heresy at the crux of "the gray zone."

We will return to Levi's "gray zone" in a moment. Meanwhile, Agamben's reconstruction of the *Muselmann*'s behavior is a composite of information he gleaned from studying Primo Levi's *If This Be a Man* and Robert Antelme's *The Human Species*. That behavior mirrors the space otherwise in which the *Muselmann* still somehow manages, barely, to get around: within the zone of the camp, "he moves in an absolute indistinction of fact and law, of life and juridical rule, and of nature and politics" (185). Agamben reduces fact, life, and nature to the permanent and inalterable coldness that Antelme tells us the *Häftling* feels, while law, rule, and politics become reduced to the boundless SS cruelty meted out on that frigid body. "The camp inhabitant," Agamben feels, that Antelme authorizes him to conclude "was no longer capable of distinguishing between pangs of cold and the ferocity of the SS" (185). Survival, however, as the writings of Robert Antelme and Primo Levi serve as perennial reminders, is predicated on the reestablishment—at the very least—of some modicum of distinction or play between the inescapable habitus where indistinction reigns and the psycho-somatic experience of indistinction.[30] How then, under this condition, could the *Muselmann*'s behavior ever constitute any form of resistance whatsoever, albeit silent? Yet according to the incongruously messianic conclusion to *Homo sacer*, indistinction is so powerful in the zone of the camp that stupefying wonderment

---

[29] "'[P]eople' is a polar concept that indicates a double movement and a complex relation between two extremes. [...] the constitution of the human species in a political body passes through a fundamental division [*une scissione fondamentale*]" (Agamben 1998: 177; 1995: 199). Not even an Arthur Rimbaud could sustain the tension of the "polar." "The obsession with development is as effective as it is in our time because it coincides with the biopolitical project to produce an undivided people [*un popola senze frattura*]" (Agamben 1998: 179). These are two absolute extremes neither of which is true to the historical experience of the species.

[30] Cf. note 6.

or perplexity before biopolitics incarnate even reaches the SS: "Here a law that seeks to transform itself entirely into life finds itself confronted with a life that is absolutely indistinguishable from law, and [...] this indiscernability [...] threatens the *lex animata* of the camp" (185). Indistinction experienced by and incarnated in the *Muselmann* will, against all odds, have been, according to Agamben, transplanted into the SS officer in the form of indiscernability.

An SS officer disposed to come within range of something as subtle and productive as a point of heresy?—Diametrically opposed to hope, this is pure wishful thinking. With the opportunistic help of F. W. de Klerk and a few others, Nelson Mandela—no doubt the world's last great resistance figure to date—knew the point of heresy and knew they had to displace it, moving it just close enough to apartheid's myrmidons for "reconciliation" to dawn even in the conscience of such players. Through the eyes of Jorge Luís Borges' chilling character Otto Diedrich zur Linde, we can measure the precise limits of what the racist totalitarian is capable of seeing when faced with indiscernability: "Nazism is intrinsically a *moral* act, a stripping away of the old man, which is corrupt and depraved, in order to put on the new" (231). This self-proclaimed and proudly "abominable" (230) creature about "to be shot as a torturer and a murderer" (229) in Borges' parable, "Deutsches Requiem,"[31] knows too all about the utter withering of distinction: "Hitler thought he was fighting for *a* nation, but he was fighting for *all* nations, even for those he attacked and abominated" (233) and "There are many things that must be destroyed in order to build the new order; now we know that Germany was one of them" (234). In writing that "Certain epochs of the human condition undergo the frigid assault of an evil that is bolstered by the most dishonorable elements [*points*] of human nature" (*PF*, LI),[32] René Char was expressly reserving just enough distinction, just enough of a margin of error between the writer of these words—one member of a collective, if minoritary, "we"— and the object of his observation—they who perpetrated the cold-blooded atrocities—such that the dimmest point of heresy might yet be envisioned in the collective not-yet-conscious (Bloch's *Noch-Nicht-Bewußte*). This is the hope against all hope to which René Char gives voice in the sixth "leaf of Hypnos": "The poet's effort aims to transform old enemies into loyal

---

[31] "Deutsches Requiem," published a year before *If This Be a Man*, had done in three or four pages what it would take Jonathan Littell no less than 905 to accomplish in *Les Bienveillantes* in 2006. Borges' story first appeared in February 1946 in *Sur*. He subsequently included it in *El Aleph* in 1949.

[32] "Certaines époques de la condition de l'homme subissent l'assaut glacé d'un mal qui prend appui sur les points les plus déhonorés de la nature humaine."

The Cleave Informs: René Char and the Hope of Heresy

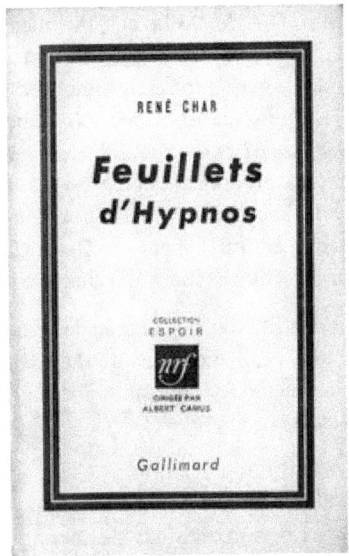

Figure 24 Cover of first edition of Char's *Feuillets d'Hypnos* in the *Espoir* (Hope) Collection at NRF–Gallimard. Screenshot.

adversaries, every fertile tomorrow hinging on the project's success."[33] But where there is naught but indistinction and indiscernibility, there is no room for this heresy and there can be no "legitimate strangeness." This impasse is the ultimate consequence of Agamben's concept of the zone of indistinction in which, according to him, we all heretofore dwell.

Primo Levi would no doubt have agreed—albeit with mighty trepidation—with René Char's hopeful wager. As we saw previously, even though Levi is barely referenced in *Homo sacer* (and, in any case, not on this subject), Agamben had to have developed his allegory of the zone of indistinction from "The Gray Zone," the second chapter of *The Drowned and the Saved*, where Primo Levi uses the term not to designate a space otherwise that permeates and, finally, defines being, as in Agamben, but as an ethical category that must be embraced in order to obviate such a definitive transfusion. In "The Gray Zone," Primo Levi exhaustively explores the ethical cleave where "the network of human relationships [...] could not be reduced to the two blocs of victims and persecutors" (37) and where "that simple model which we

---

[33] "*L'effort du poète vise à transformer* vieux ennemis *en* loyaux adversaires, *tout lendemain fertile étant function de la réussite de ce projet* [...]." *Les Loyaux adversaires* is the title of the thirteen poems between *Feuillets d'Hypnos* and *Le Poème pulvérisé*.

atavistically carry within us—'we' inside and the enemy outside, separated by a sharply defined geographic frontier" (38) in fact no longer abides. And because that model proves hopelessly simplistic without, for all that, collapsing into a zone of absolute indistinction, hope remains. For Levi's ultimate purpose in *I sommersi e i salvati*, as the title he lent this late volume suggests, is to determine a program whereby *those who did not drown* can go on resisting death-dealing forces or, in Foucaldian-Agambenian terminology, resisting the biopolitical behemoth. René Char's version of this program goes as follows in Michel Foucault's cherished *Formal Cleave*:

> Recognize two sorts of possibility: the *diurnal* possible and the *prohibited* possible. Make the first, perchance, equal to the second; place them on the royal way of the hypnotic impossible, the highest degree of the comprehensible. (*PF*, XLVII: 123*)[34]

Survival in Auschwitz, as Primo Levi informs us as well, was predicated on the cleft cleaving between these two possibilities. Like *The Drowned and the Saved*, *Homo sacer* too is rife with divisions, distinctions, breaks, separations, fractures, and splits. But to no avail. For despite Agamben's myriad references to actual thresholds and those textual interludes bearing that noun metaphorically as title to conclude each of the book's movements, neither subjects nor even agents of the law can ever stand outside the law or even approach its exit. The very fact of being born a citizen of a nation precludes one ever taking any critical stance whatsoever. The "fiction implicit" in the notion of "man as a free and conscious political subject" is "that *birth* immediately becomes *nation* such that there can be *no interval of separation* [*alcuno scarto*] between the two terms. Rights are attributed to man [...] solely to the extent that man is the immediately vanishing ground [...] of the citizen." (1998: 128; my emphasis). And, a bit further on, after analyzing distinctions now forgotten between active and passive rights in earlier forms of pseudo-democracy, Agamben emphatically declares that "[o]ne of the essential characteristics of modern biopolitics [...] is its constant need to redefine the threshold of life that distinguishes and separates what is inside from what is outside [*la soglia che articola e separa ciò che è dentre da ciò che è fuori*]." (1998: 131; 1995: 144–5). The threshold, in other words, is not only a frustratingly moving target and attaining it is mere cruel illusion. While Mandela cheated despair and managed to move the threshold just close enough, even the torment of Tantalus is too amusing for fascists. Standing in contradiction to the collapse of the cleft by which we might go on is Ernst Bloch's *Principle of Hope* where he wrote prescriptively, yet delightfully without a program, that "the broad

---

[34] Jean-Claude Mathieu comments on this passage, 171ff.

window full of nothing but outside world needs an outdoors full of attractive strangers, not full of Nazis [and] the glass door right down to the floor really requires sunshine to peer and break in, not the Gestapo" (v. 2, 734).

In an open letter entitled *Sortir du noir* (*Out of Darkness*) that he wrote in 2015 to László Nemes, director of *Son of Saul*, Georges Didi-Huberman laid down the following words reminiscent of the primal ethical scene according to Emmanuel Levinas: "An image that emerges from the darkness is an image that breaks out of the shadows or from indistinction and comes to our encounter" (21).[35] The locus of that encounter is precisely the gray zone that Primo Levi envisioned. At this conjuncture we must return to—by which I mean both to *turn again* and to *visit anew*—that chapter of *The Drowned and the Saved* in order to examine just what Giorgio Agamben, both learning and subtracting, took from it. It is necessary to understand just why he deemed it necessary to attempt to improve on such an already subtle, soberly argued, and eminently useful ethical category as the gray zone. We have learned through the examples presented here, throughout, that the space in which I meet and find communion with an image or a pathetic companion is—biopolitics notwithstanding—a space where distinction between "me" and "the other" must be reaffirmed in order for the tension of cleave driving ethical interrelationship to obtain. As Primo Levi proceeded to characterize his specific examples of inhabitants of the gray zone—*kapos*, members of the *Sonderkommando*, Chaïm Rumkowski—the reason why he took such a venerable figure as Vercors to task is that this eminent spokeman for the Resistance and founder of Éditions de Minuit had broken a fundamental rule: "one is never in another's place" (Levi 1986: 60). To claim to be in another's place would collapse the tensive energy necessary for respect to maintain. And yet it is tempting to see in the final words of "The Gray Zone"—all along whose thirty-three pages Primo Levi had sustained that tension between "we" and "they" without which the gray zone itself is not possible—a sudden capitulation, a collapse of the zone into one of indistinction. Those last lines read as follows:

> Like Rumkowski, we too are so dazzled by power and prestige as to forget our essential fragility. Willingly or not we come to terms with power, forgetting that we are all in the ghetto, that the ghetto is walled in, that outside the ghetto reign the lords of death, and that close by the train is waiting. (1989: 69)

---

[35] The letter was published as a small book. This is my translation of "*Une image qui sort du noir, c'est une image qui surgit de l'ombre ou de l'indistinction et qui vient à notre rencontre.*"

At first glance, this lugubrious assessment about "we hybrids molded of clay and spirit" (ibid.) indeed reads like a preview of Agamben's apocalyptic vision of our entrapment in today's *nomos*. Yet everything leading up to Primo Levi's last word in "The Gray Zone" enjoins his readers to engage once and for all and persevere in the most difficult ethical exercise imaginable: not only, as we saw previously, has the time come "to explore the space which separates [...] the victims from the persecutors," but we must—and starting first with Primo Levi himself—imperatively "do so with a lighter hand" (40). That space—that cleave—is the gray zone. The immense difficulty of ethical judgment both within and outside of the gray zone is that, as with all cleaves, distinction and indistinction coincide spacially and are synchronic. The "most disquieting feature" of the *Lager* is that "the two camps of masters and servants both diverge and converge" (42). We and they intermingle, indeed tending toward the indistinction that Agamben says is now immutable fact, yet as Primo Levi maintains, "[p]erhaps for reasons that go back to our origins as social animals, the need to divide the field into 'we' and 'they' is so strong that this pattern, this bipartition—friend/enemy—prevails over all others" (36-7). So strong, that is, that despite the fact that in what David Rousset dubbed the "concentrationary universe"[36] "the 'we' lost its limits [and] one could not discern a single frontier but rather many confused, perhaps innumberable frontiers, which stretched between each of us" (38), these "thousand[s of] sealed off monads"—those who by sheer luck survived the ramp—engaged immediately, "atavistically," in "a desperate covert and continuous struggle" (38) "consist[ing] in an unconscious attempt to consolidate the 'we' at the expense of the 'they'" (40). The motor of this struggle is, like it or not, nothing other than biopower at work in all its ambiguity. The various "prisoner-functionaries" [*die Funktionshäflinge*] that occupy the vast gray zone of the *Lager* are actually envigorated by the corruption necessary for their survival and, thereby, bizarrely, embody a chance to reconstitute a community for which we use the first person plural pronoun: "Rather than wearing one down, power corrupts; all the more intensely did their power corrupt, since it had a peculiar nature" (46). This is the case both for the most innocuous members of "the hybrid class of the prisoner-functionaries" (42)—the bed-smoothers, for example, "who exploited to their miniscule advantage the German fixation about bunks made up flat and square" (44)—to the most repellant: the kapos or the members of the *Sonderkommando*. Somehow, to an extent that is endlessly "disquieting" (42) to him, all of these denizens of the gray zone where "masters and servants both diverge and converge" (42) resemble Primo Levi in their will and striving to "lift

---

[36] Cf. David Rousset, *L'Univers concentrationnaire*. Minuit, 1965.

[themselves] above the norm" (41) and distinguish themselves from the "anonymous mass" (56). It is thus that Levi must admit that they become (again, to some extent, but an extent never negligible) his "companion[s]-in-misfortune" (39) and that he deems it his duty as a professional survivor to caution against "the imprudence of issuing hasty moral judgment on such human cases" (43-4). Ranging from the petty and the mean to the violently nefarious, the "components of the gray zone are bonded together by the wish to preserve and consolidate established privilege *vis-à-vis* those without privilege" (43; syntax altered). His generosity and honesty recovered after Auschwitz notwithstanding, Primo Levi recognized and readily admitted that because surviving necessarily entails, in addition to luck, the dubious attitudes of ruse and prevarication, he must, in the end, and however reluctantly, count himself among the components of the gray zone: "only a schematic rhetoric can claim that the space is empty: it never is, it is studded with obscene and pathetic figures" (40). Thankfully, our "pathetic companion," Primo Levi mustered the wherewithal to articulate above the murmur to which biopolitics had relegated him and his silent brothers and sisters.

On further consideration, the bleak lyricism of the chapter's last sentence is laden with cautionary value. It is a warning against ever forgetting, but of a sort quite different from the banality of remembering: within Primo Levi, from the very inception of his analysis of "the gray zone," there are two functions of the "we" subject at work. When he asks, in the chapter's first sentence, "Have we—we who have returned—been able to understand and make others understand our experience?" (36) he is already reluctantly—guiltily, but necessarily—speaking *for* the "complete witnesses" (83-4) and thus doing that very thing for which he reproached Vercors. In the same stroke, however—"we too are so dazzled by power and prestige as to forget [...]"—he is recognizing that there is some Rumkowski in him, as in all of us. These multiple "we"s meet not in some zone of indistinction where no decision is any longer possible, but in the gray zone where they must work out how to go on.

And, thus, each "I" somehow, in spite of all, goes on struggling to break out of the utter darkness and silence of the zone to which each will nonetheless return, striving for an aleph whose brightness could, were it attained, never be sustained. In caring for one's self, each self eyes another, reaching out a hand, pulling that other one toward some common ground. Each ferries the other from zone toward aleph. "Life," i.e. consciousness, is decision ever reaffirmed. "Ever," that is, as long as the body endures. *Micro*biopower, one might say, versus biopolitics. "*Je suis né comme le rocher*," René Char wrote somewhere between 1963 and 1965, "*avec mes* *blessures. Sans guérir de ma jeunesse superstitieuse, à bout de fermeté limpide, j'entrai dans l'âge cassant*" (*OC*, [765]). Of course, like the rock, like everyone, I was born with my wounds, my scars, but brittle like rock, I reached a point where—unlike rock—I had learned to conduct myself with brusqueness, abruptness, a certain brutality.[37] I reached my point of heresy when I entered my phase of acrid decisiveness, a definitive stage that I call "the age of curtness."

"*L'âge cassant*" is the title of the fifth and final part of a sweeping collection of prose poems and aphorisms that René Char published in 1971 under the title, *Recherche de la base au sommet*. "*Je suis né comme le rocher* [...]" is the incipit of this section's lead aphorism. Earlier in the collection, we are regaled with portrait after portrait of antecedent and contemporary figures whose "limpid firmness" in face of ambient darkness inspired René Char's own practice of the self, which forged on in the gray zone without, for all that, relegating the illness of "superstitious youth" to the junkyard of denial. Arthur Rimbaud is perhaps a prime antecedent example, for he "sprang forth in 1871 from a world in agony that chose to ignore that agony, turning mystical, obstinately adorning the sunset with tints of the dawn of some golden age" (*OC*, 726). In face of gross biopolitical mystification, of which the colonialist "civilizing mission" was one of the most egregious manifestations, Rimbaud walks all the way to Paris from his native Charleville, "sees [the Paris Commune], relates, then disappears," leaving "the horizons of poetry and sensibility riddled with bullet holes" in his wake (*OC*, 727). The context out of which the meteoric Rimbaud crashed through the fetid atmosphere epitomized by 1871 is riddled with victims of the struggle whom René Char adopts as "*grands astreignants*":

> Romanticism has nodded off and dreams aloud. Meanwhile Baudelaire, all of Baudelaire, has just died after having wailed, he, out of true pain. Nerval had killed himself. The name of Hölderlin is unheard of. Nietzsche is getting ready, but he's already returning each day a bit more torn apart from his sublime ascensions. [...] Suddenly the earth's screams, the sky's color, the line traced by steps are all modified. Meanwhile nations bloat paradoxically and oceans are traversed by those shark-men that Sade predicted and that Lautréamont is describing. (*OC*, 726–7; my translation)

---

[37] I follow Gustaf Sobin's fine translation of "The Brittle Age" except to introduce what the diachrony of written language renders impossible without explanatory footnote: the metaphorical sense of "*cassant*," i.e. brusque or curt in manner or in speech. Cf. René Char, *The Brittle Age* and *Returning Upland*. Denver: Counterpath Press, 2009.

In other times, Teresa of Àvila, Saint-Just,[38] Van Gogh, Artaud too: these are the figures that René Char convoked to populate his own, personal genealogy. This self-made ancestry is one great gallery of heretics, the great majority of whom were martyred by "civilization."

A programmatic crescendo for cleaving to hope through heretic action is achieved as we arrive at the middle forty-two aphorisms that make up "The Age of Curtness." Between

> Who would dare to say that what we have destroyed was worth a hundred times more than what we had dreamt and ceaselessly transfigured in murmuring to the ruins? (*OC*, 766; 41)

and

> What was, no longer is. What isn't must become. Two hands, full of fervor, from the labyrinth with its twin openings, spring out. For want of a spirit, what instigates the livid, the atrocious, or the blushing dispensator? (*OC*, 766; 47)

René Char inscribes the following categorical imperative as a consequence of deeds performed by the species (historical events) and the ways in which the species read them (the experience of historiography):

> The history of man is a long succession of synonyms for the same vocable. To contradict it is a duty. (*OC*, 766; 45)

That indirect object pronoun—"*Y*"—capitalized at the head of the sentence is a lexicographic sword of Damocles holding the poet, the resistant, and all his "pathetic companions" to their heretical duty. If, as Timothy O'Leary justifiably affirms, "Develop your legitimate strangeness" is an "imperative that could stand as an epigraph to Foucault's entire work, a series of books that in their effort to 'think otherwise' constantly explore whatever is foreign to our ways of thinking and acting" (2009: 77), then the demand to *contradict history* could be its rival or its counterpart. Or its bookend ...

In fact it is. As if recruiting René Char as elder valedictorian of his entire project about to be curtailed by death, Foucault placed this very aphorism from "The Age of Curtness" not just on one but on *both* of the last volumes of the *History of Sexuality*. Volume 2, *L'Usage des plaisirs*, appeared on May 14, 1984; Pierre Nora brings volume 3, *Le Souci de soi*, to a hospitalized Michel Foucault on June 20. He died on the 25th. As Jean-Claude Milner has written, "illness weakening him more and more, we know that Foucault

---

[38] "*Quelquefois mon refuge est le mutisme de Saint-Just à la séance de la Convention du 9 Thermidor*" (*Feuillets d'Hypnos*, 185).

put all his effort into completing these two books. It would be legitimate to suppose that everything was carefully weighed—in particular the back covers." Consequently, Milner adds, "Foucault wished to have something essential heard concerning the integrality of his oeuvre" (7). Taking a cue from Char's aphorism, eschewing deductive discourse, as Foucault and Char before him were both wont to do, we can and should say that the essential lesson and legacy is that the heretic incarnates contradiction and that the dialogical cleave is site of this contradiction teetering between the human and the inhuman.

This *sub rosa* compact that Michel Foucault concluded with René Char is once again forcefully illustrated in a curiosity found in the opening minutes of Foucault's inaugural address at the Collège de France. As approximation of his misgivings about embarking as speaking subject upon a discourse regarding "the order of discourse" and just before launching into a twelve-page virtuoso description (under the sign of an altogether negative, segregationist *partage*) of the "provisional theatre" in which he had thus far produced and planned to continue to carry out his work (10–23), Foucault had intoned the famous lines at the end of Samuel Beckett's *The Unnamable* ("I must go on."). This, of course, echoes what Foucault had already thought and written on several occasions about the disappearance of the "I" subject and the dissolution of the author function.[39] Having quoted Beckett, then, and while assuming the words sufficiently famous so as to dispense with attribution, Foucault goes on to remark on how common such a "*desire* to be freed from the obligation to begin" must be among speakers (*OD*, 8; *DL*, 51, my emphasis). He then performs a discursive twist far more characteristic of medieval rhetoric than of ours: imagining words spoken within him, he conveys to his audience at the Collège de France the speech of an allegorized desire. Foucault's voice thus channels desire's desires as the character, Desire:

> Desire says: "I should not like to have to enter this risky order of discourse; I should not like to be involved in its peremptoriness and decisiveness; I should like it to be all around me like a calm, deep transparence, infinitely open, where others would fit in with my expectations, and from which truths would emerge one by one; I should only have to let myself be carried, within it and by it, like a happy wreck." (51)

"[...] *comme une épave heureuse*" in the original language. Rimbaldian imagery through and through, if one thinks of René Char's adolescent

---

[39] *The Order of Things*, "What Is an Author?" Cf. Maurice Blanchot, "Où maintenant, qui maintenant," *NRF* (October 1953) ... *Le Livre à venir*.

"*astreignant*" embracing with giddy self-destructiveness the dangers of the unknown after having been "bloated by the stagnant fumes of acrid loving (*L'âcre amour m'a gonflé de torpeurs enivrantes*)"—"Ô que ma quille éclate ! Ô que j'aille à la mer ! May I split from stem to stern and founder, ah founder!"[40] Or, setting out on the Char pathway and given Foucault's deceptively simple title, we might suspect that Desire's words descend from "*L'ordre légitime est quelquefois inhumain*," a short poem found in *Les Loyaux adversaires* (*OC*, 238) whose title and text echo *Formal Cleave* as they telegraph Foucault's transgression into that which is beyond the human as well as what his work has in store beyond *The Order of Discourse*.[41] We would be very close to the unmarked reference, but not quite there.

"[…] *comme une épave heureuse*" are the last three words of a key sentence in the very last poem of *Furor and Mystery*—that sweeping compendium of everything René Char wrote during and enduring those terrible years between 1938 and 1944 and slightly beyond: 1947.[42] That text bears the title "*Allégeance*," eliciting the question as to whom allegiance is due or for whom it operates. In prose, the poet speaks of his love, purposely leaving undecided whether the word—*mon amour*—refers to an individual object of the sentiment or to the sentiment itself. *Amour* being a masculine noun, undecidability is exacerbated by the poet's insistent use of the concomitant pronoun, *il*: if indeed an individual and not the sentiment, then the poet's love could very well be a man and for a man. Love too might be like freedom: a blissful state never quite within reach but toward which my reach extends. Rather than refer metonymically to a body endowed with consciousness with which I experience the most sublime of feelings, the one feeling bereft of which melancholia may set in, my love may well be a configuration or an

---

[40] I have decided to use Samuel Beckett's perhaps idiosyncratic, but decidedly wonderful translation of these lines from Rimbaud's epic poem of 1871.
[41] *Ceux qui partagent leurs souvenirs,*
La solitude les reprend, aussitôt fait silence.
L'herbe qui les frôle éclôt de leur fidélité.

Que disais-tu ? Tu me parlais d'un amour si lointain
Qu'il rejoignait ton enfance.
Tant de stratagèmes s'emploient dans la mémoire !

Those who share their memories,
Solitude reclaims them, so silencing.
The grass caressing them grows from their fidelity.

What were you saying? You spoke to me of a love so distant
That it rejoined your childhood.
So many stratagems serve memory! (228–9; translation slightly altered)
[42] *Seuls demeurent* (1938–44), including *Partage formel*, *Feuillets d'Hypnos* (1943–4), *Les Loyaux adversaires* (s.d.), *Le Poème pulvérisé* (1945–7), and *La Fontaine narrative*, 1947.

eventness that I share with others, yet from which I am sheared. In short, my love might be yet another iteration of the formal cleave.

> My love has passed into the streets of the city. It doesn't matter where in these times torn apart. No longer mine, anyone can speak to my love. He no longer remembers. Who indeed loved him?
>
> Seeking to be mirrored in the vows of unknown eyes, moving through that space which is my fidelity, my love gives shape to hope and thoughtlessly casts it away. He is *preponderant without partaking*.
>
> I live within the depths of my love like a happy derelict. Unbeknownst to him, my solitude is his treasure. My liberty sounds him at the meridian on which his flight is inscribed.
>
> My love has passed into the streets of the city. It doesn't matter where in these times torn apart. No longer mine, anyone can speak to my love. He no longer remembers. Who indeed loved him and, from a remove, lights his way lest he fall? (313*; my emphasis)[43]

From personified passion (possibly) in the form of a masculine noun referenced in the first three sentences, in not remembering and, especially, in being susceptible to being loved, "*mon amour*" turns out most likely to be a person of the male sex around whom my passion gathers. So that while "like a happy shipwreck" is indeed a fair translation of the "épave heureuse" that Foucault's desire desires, so is "like a happy wreck" or, even more precisely, "like a happy derelict." The nearly untenable dialectic that Foucault sees this poem evoking is akin to the "realisation of the absurd" along a "suture [between] the real and the fantastic" that Didi-Huberman considers Goya as having been unique in achieving pictorially.[44] And before Goya, Dante who, in order to share in the gaze of Matelda, had to dare proceed from the

---

[43] "*Dans les rues de la ville il y a mon amour. Peu importe où il va dans le temps divisé. Il n'est plus mon amour, chacun peut lui parler. Il ne se souvient plus; qui au juste l'aima?*
   Il cherche son pareil dans le vœu des regards. L'espace qu'il parcourt est ma fidélité. Il dessine l'espoir et léger l'éconduit. Il est prépondérant sans qu'il y prenne part.
   Je vis au fond de lui comme une épave heureuse. À son insu, ma solitude est son trésor. Dans le grand méridien où s'inscrit son essor, ma liberté le creuse.
   Dans les rues de la ville il y a mon amour. Peu importe où il va dans le temps divisé. Il n'est plus mon amour, chacun peut lui parler. Il ne se souvient plus; qui au juste l'aima et l'éclaire de loin pour qu'il ne tombe pas?"

[44] "*Le grand mérite de Goya consiste à créer le monstrueux vraisemblable. Ses monstres sont nés viables, harmoniques. Nul n'a osé plus que lui dans le sens de l'absurde possible. Toutes ces contorsions, ces faces bestiales, ces grimaces diaboliques sont pénétrées d'humanité. Même au point de vue particulier de l'histoire naturelle, il serait difficile de les condamner, tant il y a analogie et harmonie dans toutes les parties de leur être; en un mot, la ligne de suture, le point de jonction entre le réel et le fantastique est impossible à saisir; c'est une frontière vague que l'analyste le plus subtil ne saurait pas tracer, tant l'art est à la fois transcendant et naturel.*"

water's edge to the depths of being's cleave. Dwelling contentedly at his love's core comforts the speaker-as-derelict that Michel Foucault ventriloquizes. Dwelling thus also situates the desire that envelopes this whole economy—*his* desire—on common ground with the "pathetic companions" that René Char enjoined him to join. We must remember that "*Les Épaves*" was also the title Charles Baudelaire lent in 1866 to that collection of six poetic scraps of jetsam excised from *Les Fleurs du mal* after the 1857 obscenity trial because they dealt with lesbians, prostitutes, jewels, and such heretics as Lola de Valence, Sappho, Eugène Delacroix, and Honoré Daumier.[45] Thus, beyond its value as the privately talismanic tribute to Jean Barraqué and loving intensity lost that we previewed in the last chapter, the fact that Michel Foucault embedded this image borrowed from René Char at the pivotal moment of an oeuvre whose last word would be from René Char as well authorizes me, I am convinced, to let René Char's words convey for Michel Foucault the hope for common ground out of heresy that these two thinkers shared.

Taking our cue from René Char, then, as Michel Foucault ever did, we might entitle that final phase of Michel Foucault's work, plucking a phrase from the very first *Formal Cleave*: "The Inextinguishable Uncreated Real." The real, like any other concept, is a construct of *homo sapiens*: the primate endowed with a vast array of complex languages with which he ever— "inextingishably," we might say—describes his experience of consciousness. Ever rife with possibility, then, the "uncreated real" that will supercede the past accumulated in the present would appear to posit the likelihood of evolution within the lifespan of the species. History, which is a segment of the real that we have also constructed using our linguistic and rhetorical faculties, has shown convincingly that we have already evolved in the 120,000 or so years since our emergence from *homo erectus*. To at least come to vague, very approximate, barely adequate, yet expressible terms with pain, suffering, and death, we managed to invent primitive superstition to assuage the sheer, stupid, thoroughly justified terror from which we suffered for tens of millennia. From superstition, we evolved again to myth-making and paganism, then on to successive monotheisms to construct false comfort in face of the anxiety over anticipated death that conscious existence entails. And beyond that? Reason. Reason with its systematically empirical bent leading to scientific knowledge ever supple and willing to reexamine its miscalculations and errors. Reason has been poised for a few hundred years, ready to supplant religion and all other remnants of belief in the unprovable. Yet, as Sade's oeuvre warned us, reason too can produce

[45] *OC*, 131–60.

monsters. Though doggedly persistent, given the totalitarian power that it enjoyed for millennia, religion, like superstition before it, has shown signs of being doomed to extinction in time for *homo sapiens* to benefit from its disappearance well before a new species of primates replaces ours as masters of the earth. If thinking were ever to altogether replace the embarrassingly childish practice of praying, then our innate fellow feeling would be able to humble science into an alliance for another phase—a last ditch effort among members of the species—to go beyond humanity.

Just as in past epochal shifts that entail incremental sophistications of our ability to explain the universe—including consciousness of our individual existence—and to come to terms with the terror and awe it causes us, schismatic or heretic behavior sometimes sets the order of the day. Heresy stands ready: first as the possibility, then as the means toward evolution within the lifespan of the species. A politics that would honor our most ineradicable hope would be built on an ethics built on judgment built on reason, all built on the ruins of religion, myth, and blind fear. René Char held out just such a hope. Piercing the steel sarcasm of one of his premier heretics, it is not incongruous that he heard such hope in Sade's injunction to the French to buck up and try harder if they really want to be republican. Had narcissism and selfishness become our prime ontological denominators, the species would never have survived as long as it has. As Nietzsche knew and even Heidegger reluctantly admitted, *Innerlichkeit* is not irremissibly or impermeably inner: we go forth. In doing so, we move toward each other. I approach you. And while we can never be entirely one with another (indeed, as Primo Levi emphatically reminded us, we *should* never be one with another), being of the same species, each of us is like the other. This commonality is the basis of sociality, society, community. French poets from René Char to Michel Deguy have been fascinated by what one is tempted to think of as the organic link—suggested by the form of the adjective "*commun*"—between being *like* one and being *as if* one. Brotherhood need not, therefore, be prescribed vacuously by mottoes: it transcends the founding of nations—political entities that separate us, no matter how much we pay lip service to unions across borders. Survival—the survival of individuals as well as of the species—sets and ever resets the groundwork for establishing borderless commonality, thus stirring and spurring hope. Going forth toward the other, becoming a guest in the house of his being, receiving his hospitality, I cleave not despite the cleft, but *respecting* the cleft. This is the foundation of the social, of society worthy of that name. Any politics not erected on this foundation is illusion, delusion, deception, and ultimately mortiferous. Survival, on the other hand, and the hope that it generates is biopower resisting biopolitics.

The Cleave Informs: René Char and the Hope of Heresy

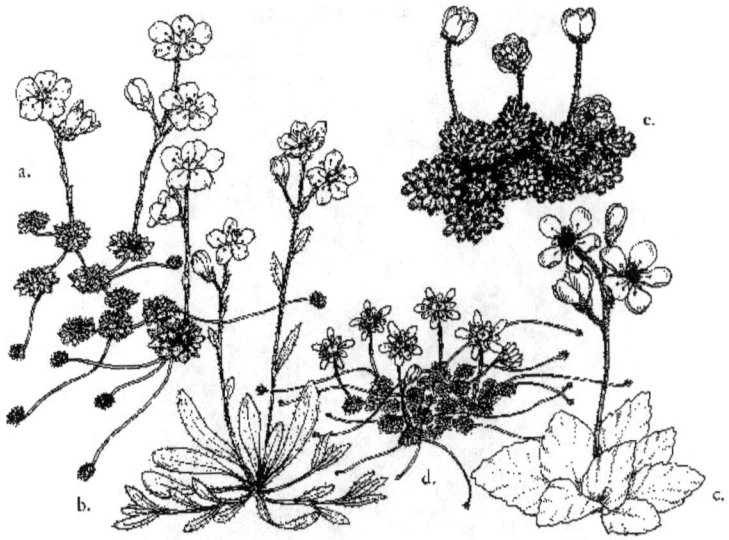

Figure 25 Five species of saxifrage (*Saxifraga*): a, *S. flagellaris*; b, *S. hirculus*; c, *S. melanocentra*; d, *S. neopropagulifera*; e, *S. punctulata*. Plant Encyclopedia, Alpine Garden Society.

To begin to draw this first mapping of common ground to closure—even if partially open on another horizon—let us survey the nexus of heresy, hope, the common, the cleave, and their relation to a certain ground that is neither *zone* nor *aleph*, but a ground in transformation. Let us, in other words, amble as Michel Foucault did freely through the poetic field that René Char staked out and seeded with the hope that can bloom from heresy, from the dynamics that a community of resistance may produce. Let us embrace that common ground.

René Char illustrates everywhere that heresy is a form of the positivity that Michel Foucault would come to call biopower. In going underground (*prendre le maquis*) as soon as the Nazis occupied France, René Char "made of himself the heir of those writers in the French language who," Isabelle Ville writes, "in every violent period of history took sides" (9). Poetry has no purpose if its practitioner is not prepared to risk his life to go against the grain of popular opinion—*doxa*, the ancient barrier of orthodoxy—in a supreme effort to save the name of the species. Ville reminds us that one of René Char's models for resistance was Étienne Dolet (1509–46) "who, convicted of heresy, was burned along with his books at the stake on Place

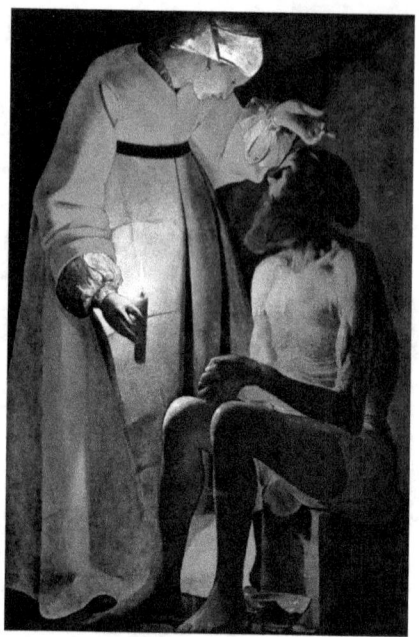

Figure 26 Georges de la Tour, *Job raillé par sa femme*, date unknown (1620–50).

Maubert" in Paris and whose name was also invoked by certain editors like José Corti working in clandestinity during the Occupation. The names of René Char's martyred mentors are many. Their heretical bravery—like that of Louis-Antoine de Saint-Just (1767–94)—may be the fruit of emulatable action taken in what we know of their life or it may—as in the case of Georges de la Tour (1593–1652)—extend from the value that their art took on for René Char personally as he sought strength to persevere in his resistance to totalitarianism. René Char's "gratitude" to the seventeenth-century painter is for having "mastered the Hitlerian shadows with a dialogue between two human beings."[46]

In a postcard reproduction of de la Tour's *Job Mocked by His Wife*, for example, the poet could remind himself at will of the intimate cleave—over and against a politics of rift—binding us in peaceful coexistence. The silent heresy suggested by the painting is altogether like the attitude struck by the otherwise prolix and eloquent young revolutionary Saint-Just before the void: "Sometimes my refuge is the muteness of Saint-Just at the Convention

---

[46] "[…] *Reconnaissance à Georges de La Tour qui maîtrisa les ténèbres hitlériennes avec un dialogue d'êtres humains*" (*Feuillets d'Hypnos*, 178; 195).

of 9 Thermidor. I understand, oh how well, the *practice* of that silence, crystal shutters closed forever on *communication*" (*FH*, 185; 195). What is striking in these otherwise antipodal examples is how the murmur of the pathetic pierces, extending through space and time, to us in the here and now. In reading *Pyrénées* (*OC*, 304), Lucienne Cantaloube-Ferrieu captures the stubbornly principled stance adopted by René Char and his "steadfast partisans" (*FH*, 60; 153): that "heretical passion of those great abused ones," as *Pyrénées* calls it, "is a magnificent and mortal fever which, on March 16, 1244, led to the stake at Montségur those Albigensians who preferred becoming 'cremated ones [*crémats*]' rather than renegades [*renégats*] of their religion."[47] Alive, still, in the company of all these "steadfast partisan[s]" the poet's duty (which, by implication, should be the duty of all survivors) is to rally their brethren timidly, silently resisting orthodoxy among us today: "Flood with sunlight the imagination of those who stammer instead of speaking, who blush in the instant of assertion."[48] In this iteration lies the promise of a renewed echo of the murmur from the "pathetic companions." What they share, what they hold in common is a longing toward community through a secular pagan communion inspired by Heraclitus and expressible by means of "heretofore unknown, unheard-of, but mortally visible ruse" (*PF*, xxxix; 121).

In face of heretic resistance, how utterly hopeless would be the future of the species if as Giorgio Agamben has it, "the *Muselmann*'s behavior [were] a silent form of resistance [*una forma inaudita di resistenza*]" (1998: 185; 1995: 207). However important to preventing future genocides the survival of a handful of them has been to the archive, it is painful to imagine the *Muselmann* as a preview of the species as its last exemplars expire. Are we there yet? Are we that yet? Is the species a populace of "living dead"? If so, Agamben is right. If not, Foucault after René Char. *Formal Cleave* and *Leaves of Hypnos* present hope in raw form, hope as incommensurable wager—a wager not founded in belief, but in the incredulity that impels heretic action. This choice and commitment to hope in face of the worst we have already seen. Yet their expressions are worth reexamining bundled together while remembering that Michel Foucault memorized these aphorisms and let them guide him to the end:

---

[47] Lucienne Cantaloube-Ferrieu. "Traversée des Pyrénées." In Jean-Pierre Vernant and François-Charles Gaudard, *L'Esprit et les lettres. Mélanges Georges Mailhos*, 82. My translation of the Char.

[48] "*Ensoleiller l'imagination de ceux qui bégaient au lieu de parler, qui rougissent à l'instant d'affirmer. Ce sont de fermes partisans*" (*Feuillets d'Hypnos*, 60; 153).

> For every collapse of proofs the poet responds with a salvo from the future. (*PF*, XLIX; 125*)[49]
>
> Resistance is but hope. Like the moon of Hypnos, full tonight in all its quarters, tomorrow vision over poems passing by. (*FH*, 168; 191*)[50]

Into every inscription of "poet" by René Char, Michel Foucault would read the "archaeologist" he would make himself into via literature, history, psychology, and philosophy. Inextinguishably uncreated, hope holds the promise not of unpredictable, yet mundane and eminently forgettable news, but of the yet-unheard-of, "the foreseeable but not yet formulated" (*PF*, X; 109).[51] This is the paradox of hope that poetry carries. Indeed, the title of one of the poems in *Seuls demeurent*, "*Ne s'entend pas*," applies to much of [René Char's] future work" (Caws 1977: 25). "*Ne s'entend pas*" can mean either "unheard" or "unheard of" and imply that which has never before been heard. Used transitively, as in "*Jean ne s'entend pas avec Paul*," it harkens to the formal cleave of comrades who, despite love and respect, nevertheless fail to always get along. The poet, like the anthro-archaeologist who will emulate him, determines his work to be an ethics in the making, where ethics at the verge of heresy is the basis for any politics. "No renunciation," continues Mary Ann Caws, quoting another of René Char's by-words (*FM*, 42), "[s]uch a tone chooses *to annihilate*, for the time it lasts, *the line* commonly thought to hold between text and life: this is not a literary statement, but rather, a moral declaration" (ibid.; my emphasis).

Potential for the "uncreated real," the first aphorism of *Formal Cleave* tells us, is surprisingly not altogether some projection onto the blank slate of futurity but, rather (and far more challengingly), here, in the present, in the form of "several incomplete persons" who may be transformed ("dismiss[ed] from reality") by the heretical empathy ("the magical and subversive posers of desire") of poetry ("imagination") into viable brethren ("return[ed] as a presence entirely satisfying").[52] Who are these recoverable, reformable specimens other than denizens of the gray zone who are never "lost causes"

---

[49] "*À chaque effondrement des preuves le poète répond par une salve d'avenir.*" Here, I have preferred Lawlor's translation to Caws's "To each collapse of proofs the poet responds by a salvo of the future." In 1977 Caws had translated it as "The poet answers each crumbling of proofs by a volley of future" and quite rightly reminded us of Char's unwavering stance "obstinate, concerned, standing against a time of mediocrity" (26).

[50] "*Résistance n'est qu'espérance. Telle la lune d'Hypnos, pleine cette nuit de tous ses quartiers, demain vision sur le passage des poèmes.*"

[51] "*Il convient que la poésie soit inséparable du prévisible, mais non encore formulé.*"

[52] "*L'imagination consiste à expulser de la réalité plusieurs personnes incomplètes pour, mettant à contribution les puissances magiques et subversives du désir, obtenir leur retour sous la forme d'une présence entièrement satisfaisante. C'est alors l'inextinguible réel incréé*" (*Partage formel*, I; 107*).

The Cleave Informs: René Char and the Hope of Heresy

because the species cannot endure without them? Like "the fire next time" that James Baldwin called forth, this future that René Char envisioned, "this branch of the first sun," "this inextinguishable absolute" that remains in our grasp will be "indecomposable" if only the fuel of communing with the fulgescent other can be achieved.[53] Ephemeral as it was, René Char caught a glimpse of this hope for a few months following the treaties putting an end to the Second World War: the catastrophe that had succeeded the delusional frivolity of surrealism.

> *Fureur et mystère tour à tour le séduisirent et le consumèrent. Puis vint l'année qui acheva son agonie de saxifrage.* (PF, XIII)
> Furor and mystery one then the other seduced and consumed him. After that, the year that ended his saxifrage agony. (111*)

Once unchained, the heretic Prometheus who stole fire for man is finally free to transplant himself. "Escorted by the unexpected," the poet "recogniz[able] in the traits of [a] subtle stake" will go forth striving toward "realized love of desire enduring as desire"—desire as indistinguishable fire.[54] Yet he will quickly learn that the soil far from the stony cleave is also far from eternally fertile.

In the deceptively simple language of a moralist, René Char, in a letter he wrote in 1963 to Henri Peyre, described in the following manner the flaws inherent to a nonetheless responsible use of poetic gifts: "An oeuvre that is integral in its principle, a work vast like a stone, like a tree, like a man, vast independently from its volume and its energy, its revolutionary fides is riddled with defects, foibles, blemishes. We all share this responsibility."[55] As Heraclitus taught, we are as ever subject to change as we are divided within and among ourselves. Yet we are bound by the responsibility of breaking with these traits and habits and reclaiming the dialectical ecology of the cleave in which heresy operates for the sake of hope. In the conclusion of his 1958 disquisition on "The Essay as Form," Theodor Adorno said as much just as he raised a note of caution at Nietzsche's unbridled affirmative spirit:

> [...] the essay [...] has no name but a negative one for the happiness that was sacred to Nietzsche. Even the highest manifestations of the spirit, which express this happiness, are always also guilty of obstructing

---

[53] "*Disposer en terrasses successives des valeurs poétiques tenables en rapport prémédités avec la pyramide du Chant à l'instant de se révéler, pour obtenir cet absolu inextinguible, ce rameau du premier soleil: le feu non vu, indécomposable*" (Partage formel, XII; 111*).
[54] "*De ta fenêtre ardente, reconnais dans les traits de ce bûcher subtil le poète, tombereau de roseaux qui brûlent et que l'inespéré escorte*" (Partage formel, XX; 113*; Caws has "funeral-pyre", but see "inquisition" in XXII); "*Le poème est l'amour réalisé du désir demeuré désir*" (Partage formel, XXX; 117*).
[55] "Mariage d'un esprit de vingt ans," *Dans l'atelier du poète*, 519.

happiness as long as they remain mere spirit. Hence the essay's innermost formal law is heresy. Through violations of the orthodoxy of thought, something in the object becomes visible which it is orthodoxy's secret and objective aim to keep invisible. (23)

Even a skeptic and heretic like Charles Baudelaire could perceive a glimmer of such light when reflecting on a Goya "*capricho*" whose darkness, despite "the horror of vagueness and the indefinite," nevertheless harbors beauty and, thus, hope:

> Goya's great merit consists in having created *a credible form of the monstrous*. His monsters are born viable, harmonious. No one has dared go further than he in making *the absurd* appear *possible*. All those distortions, those bestial faces, those diabolical grimaces of his are *impregnated with humanity*. Even from the special viewpoint of natural history it would be hard to condemn them, so great is the analogy and harmony between the parts of their being. In a word, the *line of suture*, the *point of junction* between the real and the fantastic is impossible to grasp; it is a *vague frontier* which not even the subtlest analyst could trace, such is the extent to which the transcendent and the natural concur in his art.[56]

In order to share in the gaze of Matelda situated in that space otherwise across the Lethe, one must be willing to allow oneself and, if needs be, compel oneself to proceed like Dante's character, Dante, to the depths in the "'cleave' of being," yet always remember the shore left.

It is just such a heretical attitude that rekindles hope even when the subject is crushed and confined by the arbitrariness of laws. Just as Foucault wrote in the last sentence of "Stakes" in *The Will to Knowledge*, "We must [...] conceive of sex without the law, and power without the king" (*HS*, 91; *VS*, 120), René Char advocated positioning oneself like a "backward sun [*un soleil arriéré*]" behind, over and against "the closed eye of [...] prefixed Laws" to come to an "understanding with the unexpected" (*PF*, VI; 108–9*).[57] Far from mere positioning, however, this is an unending struggle: "Our effort has to relearn the sweat required. And we go on, fighters grounded [*lutteurs à terre*] but never dying amidst exasperating witnesses and indifferent virtues" (*PF*, XXIV; 115*). This is a Promethean struggle, but the struggle of a pagan heretic in partnership with an equal, with common

---

[56] "Quelques caricaturistes étrangers, II" [1857] in *Curiosités esthétiques*, textes établis par Henri Lemaître. Paris, Éditions Garnier Frères, 1962, 298–9. My emphasis.

[57] "Derrière l'œil fermé d'une de ces Lois préfixes qui ont pour notre désir des obstacles sans solution, parfois se dissimule un soleil arriéré dont la sensibilité de fenouil à notre contact violemment s'épanche et nous embaume. L'obscurité de sa tendresse, son entente avec l'inespéré, noblesse lourde qui suffit au poète."

ground to be surveyed on the horizon, cleaving like so many of Beckett's pairs in a dialectic of two in one, in an "as-oneness" that preserves the cleave in the common.[58] "Escape into his one's equal, with immense perspectives of poetry, will someday perhaps be possible" (*PF*, LV; 127*). The poet, the archaeologist, the man daring to look beyond a humanism incapable of living up to its principles,[59] heretics all find their "transcendent presence" not in some chimeric paradise outside phony free zones like Vichy but presence in "an *actual* diamantine point" at the threshold of "pilgrim storms" and somewhere this side of the aleph (*PF*, XXXVI; 119*).[60] "[W]e, fervent killers of real beings in the successive person of our chimera" stand ready "to transform fabulous fact into historical fact" (*PF*, LV; 127*),[61] that is, to be transplanted not in space, but in time, for the temporal margin for action equips site with horizon. The "saxifrage agony" of Prometheus ends when, as with Primo Levi in Auschwitz, one can appeal to a modicum of ruse not yet destroyed by prefixed Laws:

[58] It is worth reproducing nearly *in extenso* Christopher Elson's meditation on the choices before the translator confronted with Michel Deguy's crucial and pervasive use of *comme, commun(e)*, and the related pun, *comme-un*: "One of the most important challenges for the translator of Deguy is to find ways to convey the density of his thought of comparison, a reflection that is both poetic and ontological in its implications. The French *comme* condenses the senses of English 'like' and 'as' or German *wie* and *als*. Deguy has worked on and with its ambivalent two-sidedness virtually since the beginning of his career. The cumulative richness of these years of poetic and philosophical reflection on *comme* is present in the translator's mind at each occasion of choice. [...] Deguy makes it clear that he privileges the like over the as but cannot escape from the undividedness of the comparative and the definitive, the proximity in *comme* of the open multivalence of *like* and the identitary risks of *as*. [...] A crucial decision must be made with respect to Deguy's tendency to substantify the adverb or conjunction '*comme*' in order to treat comparison theoretically: *le comme*, when it is used analytically as a conceptual operator, will be treated in English translation as a compound common noun, 'the like-or-as,' despite the possible awkwardness of that expansive choice—I think the reader needs this occasional reminder; this will not be the case in expressions like *l'ontologie du comme*, which is translated as 'the ontology of like,' suppressing the implicit definite article and condensing the two-sidedness of like-or-as for the sake of elegance. (Sometimes too it is a matter of rendering an impossible pun like '*le comme-un des mortels,'* which I tend to translate as 'as-oneness of mortals.')" C. Elson, "Translator's Notes." In Michel Deguy, *A Man of Little Faith*, Albany, SUNY Press, 2015, xii–xiii.

[59] It is true that when René Char became Captain Alexandre for a few years, it was in the name of a "humanism conscious of its duty."

[60] "*Le logement du poète est des plus vagues; le gouffre d'un feu triste soumissionne sa table de bois blanc. / La vitalité du poète n'est pas une vitalité de l'au-delà mais un point diamanté actuel de présences transcendantes et d'orages pèlerins.*"

[61] "*Sans doute appartient-il à cet homme, de fond en comble aux prises avec le Mal dont il connaît le visage vorace et médullaire, de transformer le fait fabuleux en fait historique. Notre conviction inquiète ne doit pas le dénigrer mais l'interroger, nous, fervents tueurs d'êtres réels dans la personne successive de notre chimère. Magie médiate, imposture, il fait encore nuit, j'ai mal, mais tout fonctionne à nouveau. / L'évasion dans son semblable, avec d'immenses perspectives de poésie, sera peut-être un jour possible.*"

Uproot him from his land of origin. Replant him in the presumably harmonious soil of the future, given the possibility of incomplete success. Have him smell progress. That is the secret of my *knack* [*habileté*]. (*FH*, 51; 149*; Char's emphasis)⁶²

And, once again, like Primo Levi who had the decency to aver that survival in face of Nazi biopolitics is predicated on dubious (heretical, that is) attitudes like prevarication, which do not generally receive high praise on the scales of morality, René Char will call for a certain specific type of evil that one should probably set off by scarequotes:

> The loss of truth, the oppression of this managed ignominy which calls itself *good* (evil—fantastic, inspired, not depraved—is useful) has opened a wound in man's side which only the hope of the vast unformulated remoteness (unexpected life) attenuates. [...] (*FH*, 174; 191*; Char's emphasis)

Yet the heretic's hope is never so naïve as to believe that the proximate future with its solutions and advances is not intertwined with the problem. As René Char and his pathetic companions prepared for liberation from totalitarianism and its hypocritical minions, he knew complacency would never do:

> [...] Here, people [*on*] prepare to demand the abstract; there, they [*on*] blindly repress all that might attenuate the cruelty of the human condition in this century, permitting it to reach the future with a confident step. Already evil everywhere is struggling against its remedy. Ghosts issue repeated advice, repeatedly visiting, ghosts whose empirical soul is a mass of mucus and neuroses. This rain penetrating man to the bone is but hope for aggression, attentive listening to contempt. They [*On*] will rush into amnesia. They [*On*] will forgo discarding, excising, and healing. They [*On*] will suppose that the buried dead have nuts in their pockets and that the tree will someday, fortuitously, sprout. (*FH*, 220; 207–8*)

The heretic no doubt needs to be prepared to reckon with this "*On*"—they who maintain *doxa*—just as Primo Levi had to come to some terms with at least some of the "damaged goods" emerging from the "gray zone."

---

⁶² Similarly to the case of the undecidable "my love" (cf. [page above]), each of these gendered lexical items ("him," "his") could legitimately be translated in the neuter ("it," "its"). "*L'arracher à sa terre d'origine. Le replanter dans le sol présumé harmonieux de l'avenir, compte tenu d'un succès inachevé. Lui faire toucher le progrès sensoriellement. Voilà le secret de mon* habilité."

> Oh life, lend the living, if there is still time, a little of your good subtle sense, without deceptive vanity, and perhaps above all lend them the certitude that you are not as accidental and remorseless as they say. It is not the arrow that is hideous, it is the hook. (ibid.)

Invocation to life: an appeal to our native biopower, that is. A determination to embrace the cleave at the core of both being and being with others, to "support," as Georges Didi-Huberman says of the dual myths of Prometheus and Atlas, "the crushing disparity of the world" (2011a: 108). Visceral ordeal on the one hand; sidereal ordeal on the other (2011a: 86): concomitantly, shared, they constitute the "saxifrage agony" that Char says replaces the stake as torment reserved for the heretic ferryman of hope. "On transparent paths, to the snow, to the earth, to storms," wrote René Daumal in his poem entitled "The Cleave", "I divulge my dual countenance. / I run the pheasants [...] of the forests of younger years, / which are not yet." Michel Foucault's expansive genius for ceaselessly thinking beyond the childhood of thought, beyond the limits apparently presented by the empirical state of the species, was captured in the spritual writings of Gerard Manley Hopkins with the same compelling image of the cleave that Foucault had borrowed from René Char:

> As besides the actual world *there is an infinity of possible worlds*, differing in all degrees of difference from what now is down to the having nothing in common with it but virgin matter, each of which possible worlds and this actual one *are like so many 'cleaves'* or exposed faces of some pomegranate (or other fruit) cut in all directions across: so there is *an infinity of possible strains of action and choice for each possible self in these worlds* [...]. (151)[63]

As for René Char, he doubtless first found confirmed in the fragments of Heraclitus the apparent opposites and mortal enemies compellingly cleaving one to another at a cleft, at what Walter Benjamin had called *ein kritische Punkt*, at what Michel Foucault would call *un point d'hérésie*, at what he himself ended up calling *un partage*. Daring to embrace, indeed to embody the *"mince lacune, point de disparition"* (*OD*, 8), *"accroc minuscule"* (14), the poet and the archaeologist who will emulate him know that the only hope for evolution within the species is a philosophy based on the dialectical ecology of the cleave.

> Heraclitus stresses the exalting alliance of contraries. He sees first of all in them the perfect condition and the indispensable motor for producing harmony. [...] The poet can then see the final result of these

---

[63] Hopkins uses the image of the cleave in a later passage that we cited in Chapter 1, p. 54.

contraries—these punctual and tumultuous mirages—their immanent lineage *personified*, poetry and truth being, as we know, synonymous. (*PF*, xvii; 112–13; Char's emphasis)

Cleaves both stand between and unite—for better or worse, inside and outside—you and me. It is such a cleave operating at the "and" between Stephen Dedalus and Leopold Bloom that James Joyce found mirrored in his beloved Dublin:

> *Snakes of river fog creep slowly. From drains, clefts, cesspools, middens arise on all sides stagnant fumes. A glow leaps in the south beyond the seaward reaches of the river. The navvy, staggering forward cleaves the crowd and lurches towards the tramsiding.* (354)[64]

Surely it is such a cleave which in the conclusion of *The Poetics of Space* left the otherwise placid Gaston Bachelard disturbed after reading Henri Michaux's *L'Espace aux ombres* (*The Shadows' Space*), for if there is something that unnerves the poetically imbued epistemologist, it is an unsettled night, any sense that visions from Goya or Michaux could conceivably be our actual lived reality.[65] In the context of discussing the space of built structures,[66] Casey must be concerned with "[t]he articulation of inside with outside or outside with inside" (2009: 123)—an articulation whose drama is amplified by chiasmatic repetition. This drama of reversibility may become threatening, even, to the body at that place, the body through which courses the threshold dynamics, the body always implicated there, in that space, when Casey agrees with Bachelard, whom he quotes at this conjuncture: "outside and inside are both intimate—they are always ready to be reversed, to exchange their hostility. If there exists a border-line between such an inside and outside, this surface is painful on both sides" (217–18). But then, in analyzing Bachelard's claim, the threatened feeling that courses through the body suddenly dissipates to make way for an heuristic (and altogether correct) description of how "architects often design areas of transition that in some way reflect the size and upright posture of the human body" (2009: 123), thus reassuring it, seemingly. Or, as René Char wrote in *Formal Cleave*,

---

[64] The lyricism and rhythm of this long passage in the "Circe" episode beg us to compare Bloom's unrest to Char's "saxifrage agony."

[65] On this point, one could read the luminous pages in G. Didi-Huberman's *Atlas* (116–21) where he examines and meditates on preparatory studies for *Capricho* 43 (1798) to further his analysis of Aby Warburg's obsession with the Atlas myth. Is it only coincidence that Warburg was under the psychiatric care of Ludwig Binswanger, whose work in French translation was prefaced by Michel Foucault in 1954?

[66] Cf. Heidegger's writings on space and the Nazi notion of *Lebensraum*, and Casey's quote on p. 131.

> The poet must maintain an equal balance between the physical world of waking and the fearful ease of sleep, the lines of knowledge where he lays down the subtle body of the poem, moving indistinctly between these different states of life. (*PF*, VII; 109*)[67]

Michel Foucault and René Char before him knew that what Bachelard found disturbing remains and maintains.

That disturbing remnant is conscious existence itself. We have already seen René Char call for an alliance with other heretics—companions in a pathetic mode to be developed from the incontrovertible given that is "the wall between life and death" (*PF*, xxii; 114–15*). "A new mystery sings" as the cohort steps forth lucidly along the cleave where "a substantive imposition"—whether totalitarianism and its no less egregious partner: the willful amnesia of collaboration—is inseparable from "an objective choice"—a biopower, that is, standing as remainder against biopolitics (*PF*, XXIX; 117*).[68] No more clear and overtly recapitulative an expression of the hope to be had from the cleave formed by essential alliances of humans unafraid to evolve beyond humanity can be found than in the forty-fifth aphorism of *Formal Cleave*:

> The poet is the genesis of a being who projects and a being who retains. From the lover he borrows emptiness, from the beloved, light. This formal couple, this double sentinel, gives him pathetically its voice. (*PF*, XLV; 123)[69]

The dialectic of projection and retention obtained from a will to become one's own "genesis" not only comes from Nietzsche, but lends expansiveness to the construction site of ethics. The "formal couple" of lover (*eromenos*) and beloved (*erastes*) replicates the dialogical hope that Diotima imparted to Socrates according to Plato's *Symposium*. The conceptual force in René Char's use of "the pathetic"—a note so often sounded in *Furor and Mystery*—gains precision here. The pathetic lends free rein to emotion, yet emotion is mastered. "We are fighting on the bridge thrown up between vulnerable being and its ricochet at the wellsprings of formal power" (*FH*, 183; 195*).[70]

---

[67] "*Le poète doit tenir la balance égale entre le monde physique de la veille et l'aisance redoutable du sommeil, les lignes de connaissance dans lesquelles il couche le corps subtil du poème, allant indistinctement de l'un à l'autre de ces états différents de la vie.*"

[68] "*Le poème émerge d'une imposition subjective et d'un choix objectif. / Le poème est une assemblée en mouvement de valeurs originales déterminantes en relations contemporaines avec* quelqu'un que cette circonstance fait premier" (Char's emphasis).

[69] "*Le poète est la genèse d'un être qui projette et d'un être qui retient. À l'amant il emprunte le vide, à la bien-aimée, la lumière. Ce couple formel, cette double sentinelle lui donnent pathétiquement sa voix.*"

[70] "*Nous nous battons sur le pont jeté entre l'être vulnérable et son ricochet aux sources du pouvoir formel.*"

The pathetic promoted by Char leaves room for a pathology of the pathetic: in addition to reason and aside from it, in addition to imagination and aside from it as well; tenderness more than pity; transient as opposed to permanent (*ethos*); stirring (Beckett); each individual committed to pathetic common presence with another is in an emotional state somewhere between the dangers of encroachment in *Einfühlung* or empathy and the wanton irrationality possible in Aristotelian *pathos*.

The cleave out of which the band of lucid resisters operates must be temporal as well as spatial, for their only raw material is the seemingly unrealizable future. We have already seen Char hail the "salvo from the future [that comes in response to] every collapse of proofs" (*PF*, XLIX; 125*) and exhort both himself and his comrades to "place [...] the *diurnal* possible and the *prohibited* possible [...] on the royal way of the hypnotic impossible" (*PF*, XLVII; 123*). This is because "reality," which is the hope that the pathetic hold, "is ahead of the imagination by several minutes." The heretic therefore knows that only subversion will work where conversion always fails.[71] This is the only way forward in "a period of time never recaptured, [a] chasm [...] foreign to the acts of this world" (*FH*, 218; 207*).

The heresy of resistance must never be carried out alone, but always in common with pathetic companions, together in a state of "as-oneness," as Michel Deguy's substantified syllabic cleave of *commun* in *comme-un* illustrates. It is, as W. G. Sebald described "the essence of [Jean] Améry's philosophy [...] resistance without any confidence that it will be effective, resistance *quand même*, out of a principle of solidarity with victims and as a deliberate affront to those who simply let the stream of history sweep them along" (2003: 198). This resistance *despite all*—an adverb dear to Georges Didi-Huberman as he declines case after case of unlikely heroes (heretics) of a new dawn[72]—is, in René Char's words, like "the sea and its shore [...] lying at the bottom of our common thought, a mold in material made equally from the murmur of despair and the certainty of resurrection" (*FH* 192; 197*).[73] The tenuousness of "despite all" mirrors the fragility of the "as-oneness"

---

[71] Cf. Frédéric Gros, 238–43.

[72] He even sees as-oneness in the way Sam Fuller filmed the burials at Falkenau. After reminding his readers that *Figuren* was the Nazi slang term for *Häftlinge*, he writes, "*Voilà pourquoi les morts de Falkenau comme les notables contraints de les enterrer ne sont pas filmés comme des masses mais comme des communautés, ensemble mais un à un, nombreux mais côte à côte, chacun gardant par-devers soi sa dignité*" (Didi-Huberman 2010: 53; his emphasis).

[73] "*Je vois l'espoir, veine d'un fluvial lendemain, décliner dans le geste des êtres qui m'entourent. Les visages que j'aime dépérissent dans les mailles d'une attente qui les ronge comme un acide. Ah, que nous sommes peu aidés et mal encouragés ! La mer et son rivage, ce pas visible, sont un tout scellé par l'ennemi, gisant au fond de la même pensée, moule d'une matière où entrent, à part égale, la rumeur du désespoir et la certitude de résurrection.*"

holding the community of resisters fast together. "Fragility" is the right word if what is understood is strength from an altogether optional coming together, a togetherness altogether mindful of between-ness. "Counter-terror," wrote Char on one of his *Hypnos* leaves, "is a miniscule prospect whose intentions are unknown to us, [...] it is the shadow a few feet away of a brief companion who bends over, worrying that the leather of his belt is going to give... [...] (*FH*, 141; 181*).[74] Yet as tenuous as that hope is, as ephemeral as that counter-terror camaraderie might be, the resulting "as-oneness" fosters action:

> A being you don't notice is a being infinite, likely by his intervention to change our anguish and our burden into an arterial dawn.
> Between innocence and knowledge, love and nothingness, the poet extends his health each day. (*PF*, XXXIV; 119)[75]

It is precisely our ontological betweenness that keeps us mindful of the necessary cleft as we cleave with our comrade, ensuring that the pathetic bond be anything but a clinging or a cloying, perhaps—in vindication of Primo Levi's warning—innoculating empathy from identification. Sounding almost like a passage taken from the work of René Char, here is how Georges Didi-Huberman interprets the main argument in Jean-Luc Nancy's *La Communauté affrontée*:

> *With* speaks of community; *between* prohibits us from from conceiving of it under the auspices of a simple communion or of a substantial unity. That is why it is necessary to think being-together beyond the assembly and rather in terms of the community's intimate confrontation with itself, which is the essence of *partage*. (2012: 105)[76]

These axioms of "as-oneness" with our pathetic companions are borne out in the proof provided by human events. In her address to the Free City of Hamburg upon receiving the Lessing Prize in 1959, Hannah Arendt was

---

[74] "*La contre-terreur c'est ce vallon que peu à peu le brouillard comble, c'est le fugace bruissement des feuilles comme un essaim de fusées engourdies, c'est cette pesanteur bien répartie, c'est cette circulation ouatée d'animaux et d'insectes tirant mille traits sur l'écorce tendre de la nuit, c'est cette graine de luzerne sur la fossette d'un visage caressée, c'est cet incendie de la lune qui ne sera jamais un incendie, c'est un lendemain minuscule dont les intentions nous sont inconnues, c'est un buste aux couleurs vives qui s'est plié en souriant, c'est l'ombre, à quelques pas, d'un bref compagnon accroupi qui pense que le cuir de sa ceinture va céder... Qu'importent alors l'heure et le lieu où le diable nous a fixé rendez-vous!*"
[75] "*Un être qu'on ignore est un être infini, susceptible, en intervenant, de changer notre angoisse et notre fardeau en aurore artérielle. / Entre innocence et connaissance, amour et néant, le poète étend sa santé chaque jour.*"
[76] The passage in Nancy's book that Didi-Huberman comments upon is at 43–7.

most eloquent about such proof and, as though summoning the likes of René Char and Michel Foucault, she assigned "the poet in a very general sense and the historian in a very special sense [...] the task of setting [a] process of narration in motion." Though she doubts that "mastering the past" is ever possible, to the limited extent that it is, it consists of "relating what has happened" in dark times "and of involving us in it." "[W]e are constantly preparing the way for 'poetry,' in the broadest sense, as a human potentiality," Arendt explains, "we are, so to speak, constantly expecting it to erupt in some human being" (21). With a sense of mission as "ferryman of justice," René Char steps up to the challenge:

> Certain epochs of the human condition undergo the frigid assault of an evil that is bolstered by the most dishonorable elements of human nature. At the center of this hurricane, the poet will fill in, by refusal of himself, the meaning of his message, then will join the side of those who, having removed the mask of legitimacy from suffering, assure the eternal return of the stubborn porter, the ferryman of justice. (*PF*, LI; 125*)[77]

Such a vow of self-abnegation foreshadows the ethical preoccupations of the "final" Foucault and that "early" Foucault who prefaced his own translation of Kant's *Anthropology*, ironically cleaving to each other in the sense that Kant was the first modern philosopher to advocate for the adjustment of rules or even the scrapping of old rules and the invention of new ones if the situation demanded it. In any case, "the poet" who, as René Char describes him, "shares in innocence and in poverty the condition of some [and] condemns and rejects the arbitrariness of others" approaches asymptotically that minimal degree of "reality" which Hannah Arendt insisted "must be retained even in a world become inhuman if humanity is not to be reduced to an empty phrase or a phantom" (22). That "bit of humanness," that sliver of hope resides in a type of friendship that Arendt puts to the test of Hitlerism.

> [...] in the case of friendship between a German and a Jew under the conditions of the Third Reich it would scarcely have been a sign of humanness for the friends to have said: Are we not both human beings? [...] In keeping with a humanness that had not lost the solid ground of reality, a humanness in the midst of the reality of persecution, they

---

[77] "Certaines époques de la condition de l'homme subissent l'assaut glacé d'un mal qui prend appui sur les points les plus déshonorés de la nature humaine. Au centre de cet ouragan, le poète complétera par le refus de soi le sens de son message, puis se joindra au parti de ceux qui, ayant ôté à la souffrance son masque de légitimité, assurent le retour éternel de l'entêté portefaix, passeur de justice."

would have had to say to each other: A German and a Jew, and friends. (23)

The commonality that we still call "humanness" for lack not so much of a better term or another concept of ourselves, but for lack of another species to which we might belong—commonality or "as-oneness" is not obtained by the simplistic fiction of collapse in difference but by a certain *indifference* that inheres to friendship:

> One needn't love men to be of real help to them. One needs only desire to ameliorate the expression in their eyes as they contemplate what is more impoverished than they, and to prolong by one second some pleasant moment in their lives [...]. (FH, 135; 179*)[78]

This visceral need to share the labor of resistance with "all of those beings with whom I find myself in serious kinship" (*FH*, 209; 203)—"a marvel common to all" (*PF*, viii; 109*)[79]—succeeds because it is a work-in-progress, because it defies commonplace definitions of facile friendship, because "this constancy persists at the very heart of contradictions and differences" (*FH*, 209; 203)[80], because it abides by Montaigne's difficult axiom in the form of apostrophe, "*Ô mes amis, il n'y a nul amy.*" To turn the zone's devastation towards the aleph's fertility we must exploit common ground, "We must overcome our rage and our disgust, we must insure that they are shared, to elevate and extend our action, our ethics" (*FH*, 100; 167*).[81]

In "*Pour un Prométhée saxifrage*," a poem written "while touching Hölderlin's eolian hand" (*OC*, 399), René Char asserted that "the only struggle takes place in the shadows [and that] victory comes only at the edges" (*OC*, 400). The zone survivor eyes the buddleia and the ailanthus and longs for more congenial flora: the ferns that crop up from the cracks that form as soon as Kilauea's lava cools. René Char, survivor of Nazi terror,

---

[78] "*Il ne faudrait pas aimer les hommes pour leur être d'un réel secours. Seulement désirer rendre meilleure telle expression de leur regard lorsqu'il se pose sur plus appauvri qu'eux, prolonger d'une seconde telle minute agréable de leur vie. À partir de cette démarche et chaque racine traitée, leur respiration se ferait plus sereine. Surtout ne pas entièrement leur supprimer ces sentiers pénibles, à l'effort desquels succède l'évidence de la vérité à travers pleurs et fruits.*"

[79] "*Chacun vit jusqu'au soir qui complète l'amour. Sous l'autorité harmonieuse d'un prodige commun à tous, la destinée particulière s'accomplit jusqu'à la solitude, jusqu'à l'oracle.*"

[80] "*Mon aptitude à arranger ma vie provient de ce que je suis fidèle non à un seul mais à tous les êtres avec lesquels je me découvre en parenté sérieuse. Cette constance persiste au sein des contradictions et des différends. L'humour veut que je conçoive, au cours d'une de ces interruptions de sentiment et de sens littéral, ces êtres ligués dans l'exercice de ma suppression.*"

[81] "*Nous devons surmonter notre rage et notre dégoût, nous devons les faire partager, afin d'élever et d'élargir notre action comme notre morale.*"

eyed the sturdy saxifrage and took heart at its indifference to the ruin wrought by formal enemies. W. G. Sebald reminds us that the narrator of Heinrich Böll's posthumous *Der Engel schweig* (*The Silent Angel*) (1992) "comments that you could tell the date of a building's destruction from the plants growing among the ruins" (2003: 57). The ground upon which an ethics may be built is neither *zone* nor *aleph*: "The purest harvests are sown in soil that does not exist. They eliminate gratitude and are indebted only to spring" (*FH*, 86; 161). If by "zone" one means nameless lands in which equally anonymous indigent souls eke out survival or, worse, the concentration camps to which Giorgio Agamben believes we are all condemned, then such spaces obviously can never be propitious to moral intersubjectivity. As for "aleph," the space or situation is equally untenable: Borges reminds us that it is "one of the points in space that contain all points" (280) and that "Alain de Lille speaks of a sphere whose center is everywhere and circumference nowhere" (283); Heller-Roazen, in discussing none other than Agamben's use of the Hebrew letter as section marker in many of his books, says that it is, among other things, "the forgetting from which all language emerges," that it "guards the place of oblivion at the inception of every alphabet" (25). In that case, it might as well be the forgetting that allowed the U.S. to call the disaster zone of lower Manhattan "Ground Zero."

As for the poet and his acolyte, the archaeologist, they set their eyes on a space fully realizable within our means, a "serene [and] unperforated city [that] lies in front of [them]" and that they can reach with "pathetic companions" surviving in actuality.

> After conferring his treasures (spinning about between two bridges) and abandoning his perspiration, the poet, half of the body, the summit of breath in the unknown, the poet is no longer the reflection of an accomplished fact. Nothing measures him any longer, nor binds him. The serene city, the unperforated city, lies in front of him. (*PF*, LIII; 125*)[82]

The poet uproots the inspirational saxifrage, the archaeologist uncovers the historical irony and transplants them into earth where the fruit of the communal vine might prosper.[83] By striving to maintain and develop our

---

[82] "*Après la remise de ses trésors (tournoyant entre deux points) et l'abandon de ses sueurs, le poète, la moitié du corps, le sommet du souffle dans l'inconnu, le poète n'est plus le reflet d'un fait accompli. Plus rien ne le mesure, ne le lie. La ville sereine, la ville imperforée est devant lui.*"

[83] Cf. "*Debout, croissant dans la durée, le poème, mystère qui intronise. À l'écart, suivant l'allée de la vigne commune, le poète, grand Commenceur, le poète intransitif, quelconque en ses splendeurs intraveineuses, le poète tirant le malheur de son propre abîme, avec la Femme à son côté s'informant du raisin rare*" (*Partage formel*, LIV).

The Cleave Informs: René Char and the Hope of Heresy

heretical attitude and solidarity with our "as-ones," we nurture hope that a contruction site of togetherness may one day (before the extinction of the species) become a propitious cleave between the unliveable zone and the impossible aleph. If we follow the logic of Pascal, from whom Foucault forged the nominal form of *point d'hérésie*, the heretic is a subject tending to contain all subjects—"My inability to fix my life comes from the fact that I am faithful not to one but to all of those beings with whom I find myself in serious kinship" (*FH*, 209; 203). It should be now, in any case, incontrovertably evident that Michel Foucault strictly followed the spirit of René Char's hopeful resistance. Hence, we can now see that Foucault was expressing himself hyperbolically when, in the first pages of *The Order of Things*, he called Borges' table "an atlas of the impossible," for that table "initiates the elaboration of a concept that will be crucial to every dimension of Foucault's thought—from epistemology through esthetics to politics." That table, as Georges Didi-Huberman explains, is a "concept meant to designate a field for operations that is precisely *not* the 'tableau' or the 'commonplace', but the *heterotopia*—a concept easily envisioned on the basis of Goya's or Borges' disparate inventions" (2011a: 69).

Unattainable, the aleph is a horizon at best. But tending, leaning, bending, striving toward it, keeping it in sight is also a "best": the best we can do to leave the zone behind, bringing our "pathetic comrades" with us as we do. This is the life work of the species: the only work worthy of the modifier, "life." Though like the denizens of Dante's (and Beckett's) *purgatorio*, *homo sapiens* makes its appearance in a zone of souls, shadows, and a few fireflies, yet it is—we are—hardwired in hope. And it is when we convert hope into action as the poetry of René Char enjoins, implores us—action however unnoticed, thus insignificant—that we are filling the whole space of our construction site with Beauty.

> In our shadows, there is not one space for Beauty. The whole space is for Beauty (*FH*, 237; 215*).[84]

---

[84] "*Dans nos ténèbres, il n'y a pas une place pour la Beauté. Toute la place est pour la Beauté.*"

Bibliography

Adorno, Theodor. "Der Essay als Form" [1954–8]. Translated as "The Essay as Form" by Shierry Weber Nicholson in *Notes to Literature*, v. I. Edited by Rolf Tiedemann. New York: Columbia University Press, 1991.

Agamben, Giorgio. *Homo sacer. Il potere sovrano et la nuda vita*. Turin: Giulio Einaudi editore, 1995. Translated as *Homo sacer: Sovereign Power and Bare Life* by Daniel Heller-Roazen. Stanford, CA: Stanford University Press, 1998.

Agamben, Giorgio. "Qu'est-ce qu'un camp?" In Giorgio Agamben, *Moyens sans fin: Notes sur la politique*. Paris: Éditions Payot et Rivages (Bibliothèque Rivages), 1995.

Agamben, Giorgio. *Ce qui reste d'Auschwitz*. Translated as *Remnants of Auschwitz: The Witness and the Archive* by Daniel Heller-Roazen. New York: Zone Books, 2002.

Agamben, Giorgio. *L'uso dei corpi. Homo sacer IV, 2*. Neri Pozza, 2014. Translated as *L'Usage des corps. Homo sacer, IV, 2* by Joël Gayraud. Paris: Éditions du Seuil, 2015.

Aitken, Ian, ed. *The Concise Routledge Encyclopedia of the Documentary Film*. [Ryan Smith, "Lacombe, Georges" and Suzanne Langlois, "Zone, La" (France: Lacombe, 1927)].

Aitken, Ian, ed. *Moyens sans fin. Notes sur la politique*. Paris: Bibliothèque Rivages, 1995.

Alazet, Bernard and Christiane Blot-Labarrère, eds. *Marguerite Duras. L'Herne*. Paris: Les Cahiers de l'Herne no. 86, 2005.

Anonyma [Marta Hillers], *Eine Frau im Berlin. Tagebuchaufzeichnungen vom 20. April bis 22. Juni 1945*. Frankfurt am Main: Eichborn AG, 2003 © 2002 Hannelore Marek; translated as Anonymous, *A Woman in Berlin* by James Stern. New York: Harcourt, Brace and Company, 1954, then by Philip Boehm. New York: Metropolitan Books, 2005; and as *Une femme à Berlin. Journal, 20 avril–22 avril 1945* by Françoise Wuilmart. Paris: Gallimard, 2006.

Antelme, Robert. *L'Espèce humaine*. Paris: Éditions de la Cité Universelle, 1947. Translated as *The Human Race* by Jeffrey Haight and Annie Mahler. Marlboro VT: Malboro Press, 1992.

Apollinaire, Guillaume. "Zone" in *Alcools* [1913]. Translated by William Meredith. *Wisconsin Studies in Contemporary Literature* 4 (3) (Autumn 1963): 279–83; Anne Hyde Greet. *Alcools*. Berkeley, University of California Press, 1965; Roger Shattuck. *Selected Writings of Guillaume Apollinaire*. New York, New Directions, 1971; Samuel Beckett. *Zone*. Dublin, Dolmen Press, 1972; Ron Padgett. *Zone: Selected Poems*. New York: New York Review of Books, 2015; and Charlotte Mandell, http://www.charlottemandell.com/Apollinaire.php (accessed January 8, 2017).

Arendt, Hannah. "On Humanity in Dark Times: Thoughts About Lessing" in *Men in Dark Times*. New York: Harcourt, Brace, 1955.

Arendt, Hannah. *Lectures on Kant's Political Philosophy*. Chicago: University of Chicago Press, 1982.

Bachelard, Gaston. *La Poétique de l'espace*. Paris: Presses Universitaires de France, 1957. Translated as *The Poetics of Space* by Maria Jolas. New York: Beacon Press, 1994.

Balibar, Étienne. "'*Ego sum, ego existo*': Descartes au point d'hérésie." *Bulletin de la Société française de Philosophie* LXXXVI (1992): 77–122.

Balibar, Étienne. "'Quasi-Transcendentals': Foucault's Point of Heresy and the Transdisciplinary Function of the Episteme." *Theory, Culture and Society* (September–November 2015): 45–77.

Beckett, Samuel. *"Drunken Boat": A Translation of Arthur Rimbaud's Poem "Le Bateau ivre."* John Knowlson and Felix Leakey, eds. Reading: Whiteknights Press, 1976.

Beckett, Samuel. *Texts for Nothing*. In *The Complete Short Prose, 1929–1989*. New York: Grove Press, 1995.

Beckett, Samuel. *Imagination morte imaginez*. *Les Lettres nouvelles* 13 (October–November 1965): 13–16. Translated by the author as *Imagination Dead Imagine*. *Sunday Times* (November 7, 1965): 48. Reprinted in *The Complete Short Prose: 1929–1989*. New York: Grove Press, 1995.

Benjamin, Walter. Translated as "On Some Motifs in Baudelaire" by Harry Zohn in *Illuminations*: 155–200. New York: Schocken Books, 1968.

Benjamin, Walter. [1923] Translated as "The Task of the Translator" by Harry Zohn in *Illuminations*: 69–82. New York: Schocken Books, 1968.

Benjamin, Walter. *Das Passagen-Werk*. (Rolf Tiedemann, ed.). Berlin: Suhrkamp Verlag, 1982. Translated as *The Arcades Project* by Howard Eiland and Kevin McLaughlin. Cambridge: The Belknap Press of Harvard University Press, 1999.

Blanchot, Maurice. *La Communauté inavouable*. Paris: Les Éditions de Minuit, 1983.

Bogaert, Sophie. "'Trop pour un livre': Théodora ou la réécriture en guerre." In Sylvie Loignon, ed. *Les archives de Marguerite Duras*: 189–97. Grenoble: ULLUG Université Stendhal, 2012.

Borges, Jorge Luís. "Deutsches Requiem" [1949]. Trans. Andrew Hurley. *Collected Fictions*: 229–34. New York: Penguin Books, 1998.

Borges, Jorge Luís. "The Aleph" [1949]. Trans. Andrew Hurley. *Collected Fictions*: 274–86. New York: Penguin Books, 1998.

Boudard, Alphonse. *Les Grands Criminels*. Paris: Le Pré aux Clercs, 1989.

Bourin, André. "'Non, je ne suis pas la femme d'Hiroshima.'" *Les Nouvelles Littéraires* (June 18, 1959): 1, 4.

Carse, Alisa L. "The Moral Contours of Empathy." *Ethical Theory and Moral Practice* 8 (1/2) (April 2005): 169–95.

Casey, Edward S. *Getting Back into Place: Toward a Renewed Understanding of the Place-World* [1993]. 2nd edn. Bloomington: Indiana University Press, 2009.

Casey, Edward S. *The Fate of Place: A Philosophical History*. Berkeley: University of California Press, 1997.

Caws, Mary Ann. *The Presence of René Char*. Princeton, NJ: Princeton University Press, 1976.

Caws, Mary Ann. *René Char*. Boston: G. K. Hall and Co. (Twayne World Authors Series, 428), 1977.

Caws, Mary Ann. *L'œuvre filante de René Char*. Paris: Librairie A.-G. Nizet, 1981.

Ceccaty, René de. "Duras et les autres," *Gai Pied*, June 1981.

Céline, Louis-Ferdinand. *Voyage au bout de la nuit* [Denoël, 1932]. In *Romans, I*: 1–504. Paris: Gallimard (Bibliothèque de la Pléiade, 157), 1981. Translated as *Journey to the End of the Night* by Ralph Manheim. New York: New Directions, 1983.

Céline, Louis-Ferdinand. *Mort à crédit*. In *Romans, I*: 507–1104. Paris: Gallimard (Bibliothèque de la Pléiade, 157), 1981. Translated as *Death on the Installment Plan* by Ralph Manheim. New York: New Directions, 1966.

Char, René. *Œuvres complètes*. Paris: Gallimard (Bibliothèque de la Pléiade, 308), 1983.

Char, René. *Selected Poems*. Ed. Mary Ann Caws. New York: New Directions, 1992.

Char, René. *Dans l'atelier du poète*. Paris: Gallimard (Quarto), 1996.

Char, René. *Furor and Mystery and Other Writings* by Mary Ann Caws and Nancy Kline. Boston: Black Widow Press, 2010. [I indicate translations that I alter with an asterisk after the page reference.]

Char, René. Translated as "Dim Light in the Creuse" by Nancy Naomi Carlson, *Cider Press Review* 14 (1) (July 2012). http://ciderpressreview.com/cpr-14-1/dim-light-in-the-creuse/#.V-aUbjKZMUE (accessed September 24, 2016).

Cohen, Jean-Louis and André Lortie. *Des fortifs au périf. Paris, les seuils de la ville*. Paris: Picard Éditeur; Édition du Pavillon de l'Arsenal, 1991.

Daumal, René. *Poésie noire, poésie blanche*. Paris: Gallimard, 1954.

Deleuze, Gilles. *L'Image-mouvement. Cinéma I*. Paris: Les Éditions de Minuit, 1983. Translated as *Cinema I: The Movement-Image* by Hugh Tomlinson and Barbara Habberjam. Minneapolis: University of Minnesota Press, 1997.

Deleuze, Gilles. *Foucault*. Paris: Les Éditions de Minuit, 1986. Translated as *Foucault* by Seán Hand. Minneapolis: University of Minnesota Press, 1988.

Derrida, Jacques. "'A Self-Unsealing Poetic Text': Poetics and the Politics of Witnessing." In Michael P. Clark, ed. *Revenge of the Aesthetic: The Place of Literature in Theory Today*: 179–207. Berkeley: University of California Press, 2000.

Diderot, Denis. "Vernet" in "*Salon de 1767*." *Œuvres. Tome IV. Esthétique—Théâtre*. Robert Laffont (Bouquins), 594–635.

Didi-Huberman, Georges. "Le Lieu malgré tout." In *Phasmes. Essais sur l'apparition*. Paris: Les Éditions de Minuit, 1998.
Didi-Huberman, Georges. *Remontages du temps subi. L'œil de l'histoire, 2*. Paris: Les Éditions de Minuit, 2010.
Didi-Huberman, Georges. *Atlas ou le gai savoir inquiet. L'œil de l'histoire, 3*. Paris: Les Éditions de Minuit, 2011a.
Didi-Huberman, Georges. *Écorces*. Paris: Les Éditions de Minuit, 2011b.
Didi-Huberman, Georges. *Peuples exposés, peuples figurants. L'œil de l'histoire, 4*. Paris: Les Éditions de Minuit, 2012.
Didi-Huberman, Georges. *Sortir du noir*. Paris: Les Éditions de Minuit, 2015.
Dobbels, Daniel, ed. *On Robert Antelme's The Human Race: Essays and Commentary*. Evanston: Northwestern University Press, 2003.
Duras, Marguerite. *Les Petits Chevaux de Tarquinia* [1953]. In *Œuvres complètes*, v. I. Paris: Gallimard (Pléiade, 572), 2014. Translated as *The Little Horses of Tarquinia* by Peter DuBerg. London, John Calder, 1960. [All references to the French will be to the page numbers in *OC I*.]
Duras, Marguerite. "Les Chantiers" and "Madame Dodin." In *Des journées entières dans les arbres* [1954]. In *Œuvres complètes*, v. I. Paris: Gallimard (Pléiade, 572), 2014. Translated as "Building Sites" and "Madame Dodin" by Anita Barrows in *Whole Days in the Trees*. London: John Calder, 1984. [All references to the French will be to the page numbers in *OC I*.]
Duras, Marguerite. "'Non, je ne suis pas la femme d'Hiroshima.'" *Les Nouvelles Littéraires* 18 (June 1959): 1, 4.
Duras, Marguerite. *Hiroshima mon amour. Scenario et dialogues* [1960]. In *Œuvres complètes*, v. II. Paris: Gallimard (Pléiade, 573), 2011. Translated as *Hiroshima mon amour* by Richard Seaver. New York: Grove Press (Evergreen Original), 1961. [All references to the French will be to the page numbers in *OC II*.]
Duras, Marguerite. *Les Parleuses* [1974]. In *Œuvres complètes*, v. III. Paris: Gallimard (Pléiade, 596), 2014. Translated as *Woman to Woman: Les Parleuses* by Katharine A. Jensen. Lincoln: University of Nebraska Press (European Women Writers Series), 1987. [All references to the French will be to the page numbers in *OC III*.]
Duras, Marguerite. *Les Yeux verts* [1980, 1987]. In *Œuvres complètes*, v. III. Paris: Gallimard (Pléiade, 596), 2014. Translated as *Green Eyes* by Carol Barko. New York: Columbia University Press, 1990. [All references to the French will be to the page numbers in *OC III*.]
Duras, Marguerite. *Outside. Papiers d'un jour* [1981]. In *Œuvres complètes*, v. III. Paris: Gallimard (Pléiade, 596), 2014. Translated as *Outside: Selected Writings* by Arthur Goldhammer. Boston: Beacon Press, 1986. [All references to the French will be to the page numbers in *OC III*.]
Duras, Marguerite. *La Douleur* [1985]. In *Œuvres complètes*, v. IV. Paris: Gallimard (Pléiade, 597), 2014. Translated as *The War: A Memoir* by Barbara Bray. New York: Pantheon Books, 1985. [All references to the French will be to the page numbers in *OC IV*.]

Duras, Marguerite. *Cahiers de la guerre et autres textes*. Paris: P.O.L./Imec, 2006. Translated as *Wartime Writings* by Linda Cloverdale. New York: New Press, 2008.

Duras, Marguerite. *Théodora*. In *Œuvres complètes*, v. IV. Paris: Gallimard (Pléiade, 597), 2014. [All references to the French will be to the page numbers in *OC IV*.]

Duras, Marguerite and Gérard Jarlot. *Une aussi longue absence*. In *Œuvres complètes*, v. II. Paris: Gallimard (Pléiade, 573), 2011. Translated as *Une aussi longue absence* by Barbara Wright. London: Calder and Boyars, 1966. [All references to the French will be to the page numbers in *OC II*.]

Duvoux, Nicolas and Pascal Sévérac. "Citoyen Balibar: Entretien avec Étienne Balibar" (September 28, 2012). Translated as "Citizen Balibar: An Interview with Étienne Balibar." http://www.laviedesidees.fr/Citoyen-Balibar.html (accessed January 8, 2017) and http://www.booksandideas.net/Citizen-Balibar.html (accessed January 8, 2017).

Egan, Moira. *Cleave*. Washington, DC: Washington Writers' Publishing House, 2004, 68.

Elsaesser, Thomas. "Between Erlebnis and Erfahrung: Cinema Experience with Benjamin." *Paragraph* (November 2009): 292–312.

Faulkner, William. *As I Lay Dying* [1930]. In *Novels 1930–1935*: 1–178. New York: The Library of America, 1985.

Faure, Alain. "Classe malpropre, classe dangereuse? Quelques remarques à propos des chiffonniers parisiens au XIXe siècle et de leurs cités." *Recherches* 29 ("L'haleine des faubourgs") (December 1977): 79–102. Translated as "Sordid Class, Dangerous Class? Observations on Parisian Ragpickers and Their cités During the Nineteenth Century" in Shahid Amin and Marcel van der Linden, eds. *Peripheral Labour: Studies in the History of Partial Proletarianism*: 157–76. Cambridge: Cambridge University Press, 1997.

Favreau, Jean-François. *Vertige de l'écriture: Michel Foucault et la littérature, 1954–1970*. Lyon: ENS Éditions, 2012.

Foucault, Michel. "Le 'non' du père" [Introduction] in Ludwig Binswanger, *Le Rêve et l'Existence* (tr. Jacqueline Verdeaux). Brussels, Desclée de Brower, 1954.

Foucault, Michel. *Histoire de la folie à l'âge classique* [1961, 1964]. Translated as *History of Madness* by Jonathan Murphy and Jean Khalfa. New York and London: Routledge, 2006. [abbreviated *HF* and *HM*]

Foucault, Michel. *Naissance de la clinique. Une archéologie du regard médical*. Paris: Presses Universitaires de France, 1963. Translated as *The Birth of the Clinic: An Archaeology of Medical Perception* by A. M. Sheridan Smith. New York: Vintage, 1994. [abbreviated as *NC* and *BC*]

Foucault, Michel. *Les Mots et les choses. Une archéologie des sciences humaines*. Paris: Gallimard, 1966. Translated as *The Order of Things: An Archaeology of the Human Sciences* by Anonymous. New York: Vintage, 1994. [abbreviated as *MC* and *OT*]

Foucault, Michel. *L'Archéologie du savoir*. Paris: Gallimard, 1969. Translated as *The Archaeology of Knowledge* and *The Discourse on Language* by A. M. Sheridan Smith. New York: Vintage, 2010. [abbreviated as *AS* and *AK*]

Foucault, Michel. *L'Ordre du discours: Leçon inaugurale au Collège de France prononcée le 2 décembre 1970*. Paris: Gallimard, 1971. Translated by Ian McLeod as "The Order of Discourse" in Robert Young, ed. *Untying the Text: A Post-Structuralist Reader*. Boston: Routledge and Kegan Paul, 1981, 51–76. Translated by A. M. Sheridan Smith as "The Discourse on Language" in *The Archaeology of Knowledge*, 215–37. [abbreviated as *OD* and *DL*]

Foucault, Michel. *Surveiller et punir. Naissance de la prison*. Paris: Gallimard, 1975. Translated as *Discipline and Punish: The Birth of the Prison* by Alan Sheridan. New York: Vintage, 1995. [abbreviated as *SP* and *DP*]

Foucault, Michel. *Histoire de la sexualité*, v. 1. *La Volonté de savoir* [*The Will to Knowledge*]. Paris: Gallimard, 1976. Translated as *The History of Sexuality*, v. 1: *An Introduction* by Robert Hurley. New York: Vintage, 1990. [abbreviated as *VS* and *WK*]

Foucault, Michel, ed. *Herculine Barbin, dite Alexina B*. Paris: Gallimard ("Vies parallèles"), 1978. Translated as *Herculine Barbin, Being the Recently Discovered Memoirs of a Nineteenth-Century Hermaphrodite*. New York: Pantheon Books, 1980.

Foucault, Michel. *Dits et écrits, I. 1954–1975*. Paris: Gallimard (Quarto), 2001. [abbreviated as *DE I*]

"Préface à la transgression." *Critique* 195-6 "Hommage à Georges Bataille" (August–September 1963): 751–69. In *Dits et écrits* I, 261–78. Translated as "A Preface to Transgression" by Donald F. Bouchard and Sherry Simon. In James D. Faubion, ed. *Aesthetics, Method, and Epistemology: Essential Works of Foucault 1954–1984*. Vol II. New York: The New Press, 1998, 69–87.

"Des espaces autres" [1967], 1571–81. Translated as "Of Other Spaces" *Diacritics* 16 (1) (Spring 1986): 22–7. [On *Le Marteau sans maître*.]

"À propos de Marguerite Duras (entretien avec Hélène Cixous)," 1630–9. Translated as "On Marguerite Duras, with Michel Foucault" by Suzanne Dow in Hélène Cixous, *White Ink: Interviews on Sex, Text and Politics*. Susan Sellers, ed. Stocksfield: Acumen, 2008.

Foucault, Michel. *Dits et écrits, II. 1976–1988*. Paris: Gallimard (Quarto), 2001. [abbreviated as *DE II*]

Fourcaut, Annie, Emmanuel Bellager and Mathieu Flonneau, eds. *Paris/Banlieues. Conflits et solidarités. Historiographie, anthologie, chronologie, 1788–2006*. Paris: Créaphis éditions, 2007.

Fuller, Samuel. *Falkenau*. See Emil Weiss.

Fuller, Samuel. *A Third Face: A Tale of Writing, Fighting, and Filmmaking*. New York: Alfred Knopf, 2002.

Genel, Katia. "Le biopouvoir chez Foucault et Agamben." *Methodos: savoirs et textes* 4 (2004).

Gros, Frédéric. *Marcher, une philosophie* [2009]. Paris: Flammarion (Champs essais), 2011.
Harvey, Robert. "Droit de regard droit. *Film* de Samuel Beckett au regard de *Tu m'*." *Étant donné Marcel Duchamp* 4 (2003): 84–93.
Harvey, Robert. *Witnessness: Beckett, Dante, Levi and the Foundations of Responsibility*. New York and London: Continuum, 2010.
Harvey, Robert. "Hiroshima, ou l'amour de l'ennemi." In Sylvie Loignon, ed. *Les Archives de Marguerite Duras*: 163–71. Grenoble: ELLUG—Université Stendhal (La fabrique de l'œuvre), 2012.
Harvey, Robert. "Un chantier du désir." In Najet Tnani, ed. *Étrangers et étrangeté dans l'œuvre de Marguerite Duras*: 17–23. Rennes: Presses Universitaires de Rennes, 2013.
Harvey, Robert and Hélène Volat. *De l'exception à la règle. USA PATRIOT Act*. Paris: Léo Scheer (Lignes et Manifestes), 2006.
Heidegger, Martin. *Four Seminars: Le Thor 1966, 1968, 1969, Zähringen 1973*. Translated by Andrew Mitchell and François Raffoul. Bloomington and Indianapolis: Indiana University Press, 2003.
Heidegger, Martin. *Der Ursprung des Kunsteswerk in Holzwege* in *Gesamptausgabe*, B. 5. Frankfurt: Vittorio Klostermann, 1950. Translated as "The Origin of the Work of Art" in *Off the Beaten Track* by Cambridge: Cambridge University Press, 2002.
Heller-Roazen, Daniel. *Escolalias: On the Forgetting of Language*. New York: Zone Books, 2005.
Hirsch, Charles-Henry. *Le Tigre et Coquelicot*. Paris: Albin Michel, 1905.
Hopkins, G. W. "Jean Barraqué." *The Musical Times* 107 (1495) (1966): 952–54.
Hopkins, Gerard Manley. *The Sermons and Devotional Writings*. Edited by Christopher Devlin, S. J. London: Oxford University Press, 1959.
Huffer, Lynne. "Foucault's Ethical Ars Erotica." *SubStance* 38 (3) [120] (2009): 125–47.
Joyce, James. *Ulysses* [1922]. Hans Walter Gabler, ed. New York: Random House, 1986.
Kant, Immanuel. *Kritik der Urteilskraft* [1790]. Translated as *Critique of Judgement* by J. H. Bernard. New York: Hafner Press, 1951.
Kelly, Van. "Passages Beyond the Resistance: René Char's *Seuls demeurent* and Its Harmonics in Sembrun and Foucault." *SubStance* 32 (3) [102] (2003): 109–32.
Kline Piore, Nancy. *Lightning: The Poetry of René Char*. Boston: Northeastern University Press, 1981.
Kristeva, Julia. *Soleil noir: Dépression et mélanchoie*. Paris: Gallimard, 1987. Translated as *Black Sun: Depression and Melancholia* by Leon S. Roudiez. New York: Columbia University Press, 1989.
Lacombe, Georges, dir. *La Zone. Au pays des chiffonniers*, 1928, 28 min.
Lawler, James R. *René Char: The Myth and the Poem*. Princeton: Princeton University Press, 1978.
Le Hallé, Guy. *Les Fortifications de Paris*. Paris: Éditions Horvath, 1986.

Levi, Primo. *Se questo è un uomo* [1947]. Translated as *If This Be a Man*. New York: Orion Press, 1959. Aberrantly retitled as *Survival at Auschwitz*. New York: Touchstone, 1996.

Levi, Primo. *I sommersi e i salvati*. Turin: Giulio Einaudi, 1986. Translated as *The Drowned and the Saved* by Raymond Rosenthal. New York: Vintage International, 1989.

Lewin, Christophe. "Le Retour des prisonniers de guerre français (1945)." *Guerres mondiales et conflits contemporains* 147 (La Captivité [1915–54]) (July 1987): 49–79.

Lindon, Mathieu. *Ce qu'aimer veut dire*. Paris: P. O. L., 2011.

Lucretius. *De natura rerum, II*. In John Dryden's *Sylvae or, The Second Part of Poetical Miscellanies*, 1685.

Lyotard, Jean-François. *Discours/figure*. Paris: Klincksieck, 1971. Translated as *Discourse/Figure* by Antony Hudek and Mary Lydon. Minneapolis: University of Minnesota Press, 2011.

Lyotard, Jean-François. *L'Inhumain. Causeries sur le temps*. Paris: Galilée, 1988. Translated as *The Inhuman: Reflections on Time* by Geoffrey Bennington and Rachel Bowlby. Cambridge: Polity Press, 1991.

Lyotard, Jean-François. *Leçons sur l'Analytique du sublime*. (Kant, *Critique de la faculté de juger*, §§23–9). Paris: Galilée, 1991. Translated as *Lessons on the Analytic of the Sublime* by Elizabeth Rottenberg. Stanford: Stanford University Press, 1994.

Lyotard, Jean-François. *Moralités postmodernes*. Paris: Galilée, 1993. Translated as *Postmodern Fables* by Georges Van Den Abbeele. Minneapolis: University of Minnesota Press, 1997.

Lyotard, Jean-François. *Chambre sourde. L'antiesthétique de Malraux*. Paris: Galilée, 1998. Translated as *Soundproof Room: Malraux's Anti-Aesthetics* by Robert Harvey. Stanford, CA: Stanford University Press, 2001.

Lyotard, Jean-François. *Misère de la philosophie*. Paris: Galilée, 2000.

Mascolo, Dionys. *Autour d'un effort de mémoire. Sur une lettre de Robert Antelme*. Paris: Maurice Nadeau, 1987.

Mathieu, Jean-Claude. *La Poésie de René Char, ou le Sel et la Splendeur. II. Poésie et résistance*. Paris: Librairie José Corti, 1985.

Melville, Herman. "Bartleby, The Scrivener" [1853]. In *The Complete Shorter Fiction*. New York: Alfred A. Knopf (Everyman's Library 232), 1997.

Michaux, Henri. *Connaissance par les gouffres* [1961]. In *Œuvres complètes, III*. Paris: Gallimard (Bibliothèque de la Pléiade, 506), 2004. Translated as *Light Through Darkness* by Haakon Chevalier. New York: The Orion Press, 1963.

Miller, J. Hillis. *Topographies*. Stanford, CA: Stanford University Press, 1995.

Milner, Jean-Claude. "Michel Foucault ou le devoir aux rives du temps." *La Règle du jeu* 28 (April 2008): 7–18. Revised version in Jean-Claude Milner, *La Puissance du détail: phrases célèbres et fragments en philosophie*. Paris: Grasset, 2014.

Milner, Jean-Claude. *La Puissance du détail. Phrases célèbres et fragments en philosophie.* Paris: Grasset, 2014.
Montaigne, Michel de. "Des cannibales" [1579–80] in *Œuvres complètes*: 200–13. Paris: Bibliothèque de la Pléiade, 14), 1962. Translated as "On the Cannibals" by M. A. Screech in *The Essays of Michel de Montaigne*: 228–41. Allen Lane, The Penguin Press, 1987.
Müller, Filip. *Eyewitness Auschwitz: Three Years in the Gas Chambers.* New York: Stein and Day, 1979.
Nancy, Jean-Luc. *Le Partage des voix.* Paris: Galilée, 1982.
Nancy, Jean-Luc. *La Communauté affrontée.* Paris: Galilée, 2001.
O'Leary, Timothy. "Foucault, Experience, Literature." *Foucault Studies* 5 (January 2008): 5–25.
O'Leary, Timothy. *Foucault and Fiction: The Experience Book.* London and New York: Continuum, 2009.
Orgeron, Marsha. "Liberating Images? Samuel Fuller's Film of Falkenau Concentration Camp." *Film Quarterly* 60 (2) (Winter 2006): 38–47.
Pascal, Blaise. *Œuvres complètes*, édition Jacques Chevalier. Paris: Gallimard (Bibliothèque de la Pléiade, 34), 1954.
Pingeot, Mazarine, ed. *Marguerite Duras et François Mitterrand, Le bureau de poste de la rue Dupin, et autres entretiens.* Paris: Gallimard, 2006.
Queneau, Raymond. *Le Chiendent* [1933]. Translated as *The Bark Tree* by Barbara Wright. London: Calder and Boyars, 1968.
Queneau, Raymond. *Œuvres complètes*, I. Édition établi par Claude Debon. Paris: Gallimard (Bibliothèque de la Pléiade, 358), 1989.
Rabinow, Paul. "Space, Knowledge, and Power. Interview: Michel Foucault." *Skyline* (March 1982): 16–20.
Rancière, Jacques. *Le Partage du sensible.* Paris: La Fabrique, 2000. Translated as *The Politics of Aesthetics: The Distribution of the Sensible* by Gabriel Rockhill. New York: Continuum, 2004.
Rossellini, Roberto, dir. *Germania anno zero* [*Germany, Year Zero*], 1948, 78 min.
Rotman, Brian. *Becoming Beside Ourselves: The Alphabet, Ghosts, and Distributed Human Being.* Durham: Duke University Press, 2008.
Rousset, David. *L'Univers concentrationnaire.* Paris: Les Éditions de Minuit, 1965. Translated as *The Other Kingdom* by Ramon Guthrie. New York: Howard Fertig Inc., 1982.
Sallis, John. *Topographies.* Bloomington and Indianapolis: Indiana University Press, 2006.
Sardinha, Diogo. *Ordre et temps dans la Philosophie de Foucault.* Paris: L'Harmattan, 2011.
Schwartz, William Leonard. "The Populist School in the French Novel." *The French Review* 4 (6) (May 1931): 473–9.
Sebald, W. G. *Luftkrieg und Literatur.* München: Carl Hanser Verlag, 1999. Translated as *On the Natural History of Destruction* by Anthea Bell. New York: Random House, 2003.

Self, Will. *Cock and Bull*. New York: Vintage, 1992.
Strauss, Claudia. "Is Empathy Gendered and, If So, Why?" *Ethos* 32 (4) (December 2004): 432–57.
Surya, Michel. *L'Autre Blanchot. L'Écriture de jour, l'écriture de nuit*. Paris: Gallimard, 2015.
Uhrig, David. "Blanchot, du 'non-conformisme' au maréchalisme." *Lignes* 43 (2014): 122–39.
Vallier, Jean. *C'était Marguerite Duras. Tome 2, 1946–1996*. Paris: Librairie Arthème Fayard, 2010.
Varda, Agnès, dir. *Sans toit ni loi*. 1985, 105 min.
Varda, Agnès, dir. *Les Glaneurs et la Glaneuse*. 2000, 82 min.
Veyne, Paul. *René Char en ses poèmes*. Paris: Gallimard, 1995.
Veyne, Paul. *Michel Foucault, sa pensée, sa personne*. Paris: Albin Michel, 2008. Translated as *Michel Foucault: His Thought, His Character* by Janet Lloyd. London: Polity Press, 2012.
Ville, Isabelle. *René Char. Une poétique de résistance: être et faire dans les Feuillets d'Hypnos*. Paris: Presses Paris Sorbonne, 2006.
Vinciguerra, Lucien. *La Représentation excessive: Descartes, Leibniz, Locke, Pascal*. Lille: Presses du Septentrion, 2013.
Walsh, Lisa. "Symptomatic Reading: Kristeva on Dura." In Kelly Oliver and S. K. Keltner, eds. *Pyschoanalysis, Aesthetics, and Politics in the Work of Julia Kristeva*, 143–62. Albany: SUNY Press, 2009.
Weiss, Emil, dir. *Falkenau: The Impossible*, 1988, 52 min. [Documentary footage by Samuel Fuller; Pierre Boffety, cinematographer.]
Williams, Bernard. *Ethics and the Limits of Philosophy*. Cambridge: Harvard University Press, 1985.
Wormser-Migot, Olga. *Quand les alliés ouvrirent les portes*. Paris: Robert Laffont, 1965.
Zakaras, Alex. "Isaiah Berlin's Cosmopolitan Ethics." *Political Theory* 32 (4) (August 2004): 495–518.
Zanghi, Filippo. *Zone indécise. Périphéries urbaines et voyage de proximité dans la littérature contemporaine*. Villeneuve-d'Ascq: Presses Universitaires du Septentrion ("Perspectives"), 2014.
Zourabichvili, François. *Deleuze, a Philosophy of the Event*. Edinburgh: Edinburgh University Press, 2012.

Index

The letter *f* after an entry indicates a page that includes a figure.

9/11 112–14

Abensour, Miguel 99
abjection 91–2 *see also* humiliation
Adorno, Theodor 49, 245
   "The Essay as Form" 279–80
Agamben, Giorgio 141, 172, 178–80, 254–5 *see also* zones of indistinction
   biopolitics 245, 248
   camps 182–3, 245, 259–60
   epistemology 258
   Foucault, Michel 181, 259
   Führer's body 183, 190
   Heidegger, Martin 259
   Homo sacer viii, 141, 180–2, 184–5, 240, 259–64
   human guinea pigs 183
   Muselmann 260–2, 277
   Remnants of Auschwitz 260–1
   thresholds 264
Aleph, the 191–2, 290, 291
Algeria 44
Améry, Jean 179–80, 286
   Örtlichkeiten 180
amnesia 51, 159–60
anamnesis 46, 48, 84, 113, 159–60
Andersch, Alfred: *Winterspelt* 154
anonymity 37
Antelme, Marie-Louise 36–7, 68
Antelme, Monique 52
Antelme, Robert 32, 33, 34, 68, 71*f*
   concentration camps 36, 50, 66–8, 69–70, 72–3, 108
   The Human Species 261
   Mascolo, Dionys 106–8
   unimaginable 111

apartness 103–4
Apollinaire, Guillaume:
   "Zone" 148
Arendt, Hannah 65, 194, 228, 287–9
ars erotica 253
Artaud, Antonin 203
as-oneness 286–7, 289, 291
Atget, Eugène vii, 163
   Seven Albums 163
   Zoniers 163–70, 166*f*, 167*f*, 174
atomic bombs 112
Auschwitz extermination camp 59, 61, 70–3, 117–19, 117*f*, 118*f*, 124
   Levi, Primo 216, 260
   Muselmann 260–1
   survival 264

Bachelard, Gaston 60, 195, 201
   The Poetics of Space 60, 201–2, 284–5
Balibar, Étienne 230, 231–4
Barraqué, Jean 206–7
Barrows, Anita 24, 61
Barthes, Roland 244
Bataille, Georges 84 n.16, 132, 178
   transgression 193, 218–19
Baudelaire, Charles 168–70, 178, 180, 280
   "Les Épaves" 273
   Les Fleurs du mal 273
Baudrot, Sylvette 40, 47
Bazin, Philippe 98
beauty 220–1, 291
Beckett, Samuel viii, 111, 127
   Compagnie/Company 91

Film 115, 120, 127
The Unnamable 206, 270
Benjamin, Walter 132–3, 181
   Baudelaire, Charles 168–70, 178
   dialectics 188–9
   images 188–9
   Passagen-Werk (*The Arcades Project*) viii, 80, 129–30, 148, 162, 169–70, 180, 188–9
Berlin 109–10*f*, 111–12
Berlin, Isaiah 97
Bernanos, Georges 110
   Les Grands Cimetières sous la lune 126
between-ness 287
Bichat, Marie François Xavier 209
   General Anatomy 209
Binswanger, Ludwig: *Traum und Existenz* 49, 201–2
biopolitics 181–3, 213–14, 227, 243–7, 252–3, 258–9
   Char, René 248
   Foucault, Michel 181, 213–14, 243–7, 252, 258–9
biopower 213–14, 243–7, 252–3, 258–9
   Char, René 248
   Foucault, Michel 213–14, 243–7, 252, 258–9, 275
Blanchot, Maurice 204, 226
   Le Très-Haut 85
Bloch, Ernst: *Das Prinzip Hoffnung* (*The Principle of Hope*) 245, 264–5
Bloody Week 130
body 257–8 *see also* docile bodies; Führer's body
Bogaert, Sophie 34–5
Böll, Heinrich: *Der Engel schweig* (*The Silent Angel*) 290
Bonaparte, Napoléon 103
Borges, Jorge Luís 217, 290, 291
   The Aleph 191–2
   "Deutsches Requiem" 262
Boubat, Édouard 74

Boulez, Pierre 225
   Le Visage nuptial 225
   Pli selon pli 225
Bourgade, Léontine 51–2 *see also* Fourcade, Léontine
Brainard, Joe: *I Remember* 32
Bram concentration camp vii, 73, 76, 79
bridge 257
brotherhood 274
building sites 61

camps 86–7, 96, 124, 141, 177, 180–4
   see also concentration camps; extermination camps
   Agamben, Giorgio 182–3, 245, 259–60
   human guinea pigs 183
   Muselmann 260–2
   power 265, 266
Camus, Albert: "Neither Executioners Nor Victims" 200
Canetti, Elias 49
Canguilhem, Georges 195
cannibalism 142
Cantaloube-Ferrieu, Lucienne 277
Carse, Alisa 89
Casey, Edward S. 180, 188, 228, 240
   body 257–8
   docile bodies 60
   Heidegger, Martin 257–8
   inside/outside space 284
   sites 27, 61
Caws, Mary Ann 201, 251–2
Céline, Louis-Ferdinand viii, 151–2, 210
   Bagatelles pour un massacre 154
cemeteries vii–viii, 101*f*–7, 113–15, 119–26, 129–31*f*, 138
   Hiroshima 124
   Home of Peace Cemetery, Oakland 101*f*–2
Je suis partout 154
Jews 153, 154

Kraków-Plaszów concentration
  camp 138
language/dialect 156
  in literature 126–9
  Mort à credit (*Death on the
    Installment Plan*) 126, 143,
    153, 154
  Paris 113, 133–8
  Père Lachaise cemetery 113, 138
  racism 154
  Voyage au bout de la nuit (*Journey
    to the End of the Night*) 121–2,
    126, 150–3, 156, 210
  la Zone 133–4, 150–5, 156, 171
Centelles, Agustí vii, 73, 76, 78, 91–2,
  215
chantiers (construction sites) 26–7,
  33, 35
chantiers de la mort 58
Char, René ix, 194, 199–203, 219,
  224–5, 254f
  "*L'âge cassant*" ("The Age of
    Curtness") 268–70
  "*Allégeance*" 271–3
  biopolitics 248
  biopower 248, 275
  commonality 274
  Commune présence 224
  Demi-jour en Creuse (*Half Day on
    the Creuse*) 226
  evil 282
  "*Faim rouge*" (*Red Hunger*)
    251–2
  Feuillets d'Hypnos 201, 262–3f
  formal cleave 246–50, 252
  Furor and Mystery 245, 271–3
  Heidegger, Martin 254f–5
  heresy 238–9, 262–3, 268–70,
    273, 275–7, 280–1
  hope 277–81, 285, 291
  L'Isle-sur-la-Sorgue 252
  "*Le Loriot*" ("The Oriole") 246–7
  love 271–2
  Les Loyaux adversaires 271
  Marteau sans maître 225

  "*Ne s'entend pas*" 278
  "*L'ordre légitime est quelquefois
    inhumain*" 271
  partage 200–1, 251–2
  Partage formel (*Formal Cleave*) ix,
    200, 202, 221, 237–8, 245–7,
    264, 285
  the pathetic 285–6
  poetry 201, 238–9, 279, 283–4,
    288
  politics 274
  "*Pour un Prométhée saxifrage*"
    289–90
  psychoanalysis 251
  Pyrenées 277
  Recherche de la base au sommet
    268
  resistance and 238, 250–3, 275–6,
    286–7
  Sept parcelles de Luberon 239
  Seuls demeurent 200, 249, 278
  subject/predicate relationship
    249–50
  "*Suzerain*" ("Liege Lord") 253
  transgression 251
  Le Visage nuptial 225
charniers (charnel houses) vii, 27,
  32, 33
Chasney, Jasmine 50
Chevalier, Haakon 146
Chevalier, Michel 144
Chomsky, Noam 236
cities 129–30
citizenship 264
Cixous, Hélène 85–6
cleave 54, 196, 218–20, 266, 283–4
  see also partage; der Riß
  Bachelard, Gaston 284
  formal cleave 225, 246–50
  Foucault, Michel ix, 207–13, 225,
    246
  Hopkins, Gerard Manley 54, 196,
    283
  Joyce, James 284
  language 230

Cohen, Jean-Louis 168
Colpi, Henri: *Une aussi longue absence* (*The Long Absence*) 35, 48, 50, 159–60
Comité d'action des intellectuels contre la poursuite de la Guerre d'Algérie 44
comme/commun(e)/comme-un 281 n.58, 286
commemoration 114–15, 138
common 1, 130–1, 173, 281 n.58
common ground vi, 1–2, 138
commonality 274, 289
communism 97–8
community 287
concentration camps 69, 96, 177, 180–1 *see also* camps; extermination camps
    Agamben, Giorgio 245
    Bram concentration camp vii, 73, 76, 79
    Dachau concentration camp 67–9, 108
    Flossenbürg concentration camp, Falkenau vii, 73, 75–7, 92–3, 95–6, 128 *see also Falkenau: The Impossible*
    Kraków-Plaszów concentration camp 138
construction site of desire 53
construction sites 26–7, 60–2, 190 *see also chantiers*
"Construction Sites" (Duras, Marguerite) vi–vii, 24–6, 31, 122–3, 217
    cemeteries 107, 122–3
    chantiers (construction sites) 26–7, 33
    charniers (charnel houses) 33, 57, 107
    concentration/extermination camps 57–60, 90–1
    construction sites 26–7, 56–7
    desire 53–7, 65–6
    dialectic tensions 44–5
    division in unity 125
    docile body 60
    empathy 56–7, 66, 90, 94–5
    eroticism 83
    formlessness 66
    gaze 26, 29, 55–7, 60, 93–4
    gender 27–9
    hotel 32
    laughter 123–4
    love 89–90
    memory 41, 48, 58, 84–5
    morality 56–8
    nature 55, 87
    patriarchy 28, 56
    ravishment and reassurance 88–9
    sharing 90
    silence 82–3
    space of interest 24
    spectacles 87
    sublime 66, 73, 87, 89
    surveillance 94–5
    text of 3–23
    "Théodora" and 90–1
    "thing" 187
    translation and publication of 24, 35, 61
    trauma 88
    voyeurism 56–7, 88
    writing of 42
critique 29–30
Critique 84 n.16, 226

Dachau concentration camp 67–70, 108
D'Anglemont, Alexandre Privat: *Paris anecdote* 165
Dante 272–3, 280
Daumal, René: "The Cleave" 283
death 121–2, 182–3, 252, 273 *see also* cemeteries
Deguy, Michel 248, 281 n.58, 286
Deleuze, Gilles 105, 120
dépôt 136–7
Descartes, René: *Meditation on First Philosophy* 231

desire 270–1, 272–3 *see also* love
Desnos, Robert 122
Destouches, Louis-Ferdinand *see* Céline, Louis-Ferdinand
dialect/slang 150–1, 156
dialectics 80, 84, 99, 186–7
    Benjamin, Walter 188–9
Diderot, Denis: *Salon de 1767* 27
Didi-Huberman, Georges 91–2, 215–16, 240, 286, 291
    community 287
    "The Eye of History" vii, 73, 98
    Falkenau: The Impossible and 93, 96–7
    human/inhuman 98–9
    Images in Spite of All 116–19
    "Opening the Camps, Closing (One's) Eyes: Image, History, Readability" 75–6, 77–8
    partage 287
    Peuples exposés, peuples figurants (*Peoples Exposed, Peoples as Extras*) 98, 130–2
    political/politics and 98
    Remontages du temps subi (*Going Back Over Time Undergone*) 75–6, 77–8
    shared zones 172–3
    Sortir du noir (*Out of Darkness*) 265
    "*Visages en chantier*" 98
dignity 75, 77, 215
discourse 211
Disdéri, André-Adolphe-Eugène 130
    "Communards in Their Coffins" 131*f*–2
distance-without-distance 95–6
docile bodies 60
Dolet, Étienne 275–6
double distance 91–2
drugs 145–6
Duras, Marguerite vi–vii, 28, 31, 71*f*
    Abahn Sabana David 124–5, 192, 216

Algeria 44
L'Amante anglais (*The English Lover*) 74 n.7
amnesia 51, 159–60
apartments 68
Aurélia Steiner series 30, 91
"The Boa" 25, 42
Bourgade, Léontine, story of 51–2, 159
Le bureau de poste de la rue Dupin, et autres entretiens 68–70
"Cahier à Outa" ("Outa's Notebook") 37*f*, 38*f*, 43, 44, 125
cemeteries 126
"Les Chantiers" ("Construction Sites") *see* "Construction Sites"
"Les Chantiers de Monsieur Arié" 58–9, 107, 125
communism 97–8
Delval, Charles (A.D.) 39–41, 48
Des journées entières dans les arbres (*Whole Days in the Trees*) 24, 25, 35, 42, 56, 158
desire 53–4
Détruire, dit-elle (*Destroy, She Said*) 26, 30, 59, 192
dialectics 84, 99
La Douleur (*The War: A Memoir*) 32, 39–40, 46, 67–8
La Femme du Gange (film) 105
"Les Fleurs de l'Algérien" 44
Foucault, Michel 85–6, 192–3, 216
French Resistance 36
Hiroshima 32, 32–3, 37–8, 43, 73
Hiroshima mon amour (film) *see* Hiroshima mon amour
Hôtel de la Poste, Lake Annecy 33
"I Remember" 32, 38, 40, 48
India Song 85
Jarlot, Gérard 47, 48

journalism 44, 47, 51
Judaism 34–5, 97, 125–6
The Lover 29, 31, 53
"Madame Dodin" 25, 42, 157–8
The Malady of Death 53
"Man Makes Do with Fear" 75
The Man Seated in the Corridor 46, 75
memory 30, 32–3, 41–2, 45–6, 48–51, 58, 83–5, 158–9
Moderato cantabile 24, 35–6
"Note on the Images of Encounter" 84
other 119–20
Outside 47
Les Petits Chevaux de Tarquinia (*The Little Horses of Tarquinia*) 26, 55
place/s 185–6, 187
plots 85–6
private life 47, 48, 52, 66–7
Queneau, Raymond 157
ravishment 88–9
La Ravissement de Lol V. Stein (*The Ravishing of Lol Stein*) 24, 53, 88
relationships 39–41, 47, 48 *see also* Antelme, Robert
Shoah 30, 32, 36, 43
spaces 61, 107–8
Le Square 24
"Théodora" 33–5, 58, 59, 90–1
"Théodora Kats" 59
trauma 108
Une aussi longue absence (*The Long Absence*) vii, 35, 44, 48–9, 50–3, 159–60
Un barrage contre le Pacifique (*The Sea Wall*) 26, 56
The Viaducts of Seine-et-Oise 50
La Vie tranquille 157
Yann Andréa Steiner 34, 59
Les Yeux verts (*Green Eyes*) vi–vii, 30–1, 32, 38, 74f–5, 77
Dylan, Bob 48

earthquakes 63–5
Eine Frau in Berlin 108–10, 111
Élie, Amélie 150
Elson, Christopher 281 n.58
Éluard, Paul 202
  Dignes de vivre 202
empathy vi, 73–4
  Berlin, Isaiah and 97
  Compagnie/Company 91
  "Construction Sites" 56–7, 66, 90, 94–5
  Didi-Huberman, Georges and 91–2
  ritual and 93
  sublime and vii, 73–7, 80–1
  vicariousness and 96–7
empirico-transcendental doublet 233–4
Enlightenment, the 87
episteme 231–5, 240
Erfahrung 133, 175
Erlebnis 133, 175
essays 279–80
état des lieux 76–7
evolution 273–4
extermination camps 58 *see also* Auschwitz extermination camp; concentration camps
Muselmann 260–2

Falkenau 76, 92–3, 95–6 *see also Falkenau: The Impossible*; Flossenbürg concentration camp
Falkenau: The Impossible (film) 77, 78, 80, 92–3, 95f, 96–7, 170–1
  cemeteries 115–16
  narration 170–1
Faulkner, William: *As I Lay Dying* 126, 128–9
Favreau, Jean-François 203
film 173–5 *see also Falkenau: The Impossible*; *Hiroshima mon amour*

La Femme du Gange 105
Germania anno zero 111–12
Jaune le soleil 124
Un chien andalou 84
Zazie dans le metro 154
La Zone 147–8, 152, 159–62, 164, 170–1
flora 289–90 *see also* saxifrage
Flossenbürg concentration camp, Falkenau vii, 73, 75–7, 92–3, 95–6, 128 *see also Falkenau: The Impossible*
form/formlessness 221
formal cleave 225, 246–50
Foucault, Anne 189
Foucault, Michel ix–x, 24, 130
　Archaeology of Knowledge 204–5
　ars erotica 253
　Artaud, Antonin 203
　Bachelard, Gaston 201
　Balibar, Étienne 230, 231–4
　Barraqué, Jean 206–7
　biopolitics 181, 213–14, 243–7, 252, 258–9
　biopower 213–14, 243–7, 252, 258–9, 275
　The Birth of the Clinic 92, 196, 208–9, 219
　Blanchot, Maurice 204
　Borges, Jorge Luis 217
　Boulez, Pierre 225
　camps 86–7
　Casey, Edward S. 240
　cemeteries 102–5, 114, 129
　Char, René 194, 199–204, 224–5, 237–8, 245–53, 269–73, 277–8
　Chomsky, Noam 236
　Cixous, Hélène 85–6
　cleave ix, 207–13, 225, 246
　delinquents 86–7
　"Des espaces autres" ("Of Spaces Otherwise") vii–viii, 2, 102–7, 114, 215
　desire 270–1, 272–3
　discourse 211
　Dits et écrits 224
　docile body 60
　Duras, Marguerite 85–6, 192–3, 216
　empirico-transcendental doublet 233–4
　episteme 231–5, 240
　epistemology 258
　family and early life 189–90
　Folie et déraison (dissertation) 199, 204–6, 226, 237–8
　formal cleave 225, 246–7
　Guyotat, Pierre 204
　heresy 227–37, 239, 241
　heterotopias 64, 104–5, 114, 138
　Histoire de la sexualité (*The History of Sexuality*) 92, 102, 141, 153–4, 203, 211, 237, 269–70
　history 193–6, 204–6, 218
　History of Madness 137, 195, 199, 216, 237, 253
　"Hölderlin et la question du père" (Laplanche, Jean) 224
　hope 277–8
　illness and death 269–70
　Kant, Immanuel 220–1
　language 196–7, 201, 219, 229–30, 234–5
　literature 196–204, 217
　madness 216, 226–7, 237, 247, 253
　man 222–4
　Michaux, Henri 203–4
　mirrors 104
　Monnier, Blanche 189–90
　Les Mots et les choses (*The Order of Things*) ix, 102, 102, 207, 219, 221–4, 227–34, 291
　"Omnes et Singulatim" 243–4
　The Order of Discourse 206–7
　outcasts 152, 209
　partage viii–ix, 185–6, 195–200, 204–14, 218, 221–4, 233–8, 240–1

Pascal, Blaise 226–7, 233–6
poetry 201–4
point d'hérésie 227–37, 241, 291
"Preface to Transgression" 197
prison 114
psychoanalysis 252
Q.H.S. 86
Raymond Roussel 196, 203
rémanence 194
resistance 210–11
sexuality 212–13, 227–8, 236–7
shared zones 172
Le Souci de soi (*The Care of the Self*) ix, 203, 236, 253, 259
space/s and 49, 64, 85, 102–7, 114, 138, 185–8, 240
spatialization 208–9
Surveiller et punir (*Discipline and Punish*) 60, 86–7, 102, 136, 211
temporality 193–4, 217
The Use of Pleasure 236
theatre 270
transgression 193–7, 205, 212, 214–21, 223–4, 227–8, 234–5, 240–1
Traum und Existenz (Binswanger, Ludwig) 201–2
trauma 85–6
unthought 207–8
La Veille (Laporte, Roger) 197–8f, 206, 209–10, 217
La Volonté de savoir (*The Will to Knowledge*) 102, 203, 208, 210–13, 227–8, 253, 259, 280
Foucault, Paul 189
Fourcade, Léontine 50, 51
Fourcaut, Annie 135–7
France 82, 124 *see also* Paris
   Hôtel de la Poste, Lake Annecy 33f, 34f
   L'Isle-sur-la-Sorgue 252
   Luberon 238–9f
   Mérindol 238–9
   Montmartre 134
   Nanterre 136, 137
   Puteaux 159
   Saint-Denis 135
   Saint-Jorioz 122
   Saint-Ouen 155–6f
French 229–30
   translating 103
French Resistance, the 36, 68, 238
Freud, Sigmund 251
   Traumdeutung 251
friendship 288–9
Führer's body 183, 190
Fuller, Samuel vii, 73, 75–7, 92–3, 96, 115–16 *see also Falkenau: The Impossible*
narration 170–1

garbage *see* refuse
Gaulle, Charles de 103
gaze, the 60, 219 *see also* "Construction Sites"; the look
General Hospital policy 137
Germania anno zero (film) 111–12
Germany 111–12, 176–7 *see also* the Shoah
   Berlin 109–10f, 111–12
   Hamburg 176
   Nazism 87, 180, 183, 200–1, 250, 262, 265, 288–9 *see also* camps; the Shoah
Gide, André: *La Séquestrée de Poitiers* 189
Goethe, Johann Wolfgang von: *Dichtung und Wahrheit* 73
Göth, Amon 138
Goya, Francisco 272, 280
gray zone 176, 177, 178–9, 181, 261, 263–7
ground 1–2
Ground Zero 112–14, 176, 290
gulfs 146
Guyotat, Pierre 204

Hamburg 176
head shaving 81–2, 83f

Hebrew language 191–2
Heidegger, Martin 60, 254f–5
   Bauen Wohnen Denken ("Building Dwelling Thinking") 257
   Being and Time 255
   bridge 257
   epistemology 258
   Kluft 256–7, 258, 259
   der Riß 255–8, 259
   Der Ursprung des Kunstwerkes ("The Origin of the Work of Art") 255–8
   Vier Seminare (Four Seminars) 254–5
Heller-Roazen, Daniel 191, 290
Hennape, Aschille 137
Heraclitus 254–5, 279, 283
heresy 227–41, 261–3, 273, 274, 280–1
   Char, René 238–9, 262–3, 268–70, 273, 275–7
heretics 238–9, 269, 273, 275–8, 281–2, 291
heterotopias 64, 104–5, 114, 138
   Borges, Jorge Luís 217
   Didi-Huberman, Georges 214, 291
Hilberg, Raul: *The Destruction of the European Jews* 111
Hillers, Martha 111
Hillis Miller, J. 257
Hiroshima 31–3, 37, 43, 49, 61
   cemetery 124
   Ground Zero 112–13, 176
Hiroshima mon amour (Duras, Marguerite) vii, 30, 31–2, 35–50, 59–60
   dialectic tensions 44–5
   division in unity 125
   eroticism 83–4
   head shaving 81–2
   intelligence 187
   Judaism 125–6
   laughter 124
   memory 81–3, 84–5, 158–9
   recollection 45–6
   Resnais, Alain 35–6, 40, 45, 48, 84
   screenplay 35–8, 40–2
   silence 82–3, 84
   subterranean continuity 47–8
Hirsch, Charles-Henry 149
   Le Tigre et Coquelicot 149f–50
history 193–5, 218, 269, 273
Holocaust, the *see* the Shoah
Home of Peace Cemetery, Oakland 101f–2
homo sapiens see man
hope 245, 277–81, 285, 291
Hopkins, Gerard Manley 54, 196, 283
Hôtel de la Poste 33f, 34f
human body 257–8 *see also* Führer's body
human guinea pigs 183
humanity 119, 130–1, 148, 216, 288
   see also man
humanness 288–9
humiliation 78–9, 91–2 *see also* head shaving

images 80, 91–2, 113, 115–20, 188–9
imagination 62, 65, 76, 110–11, 174–5
   Bachelard, Gaston 201
   empathy and 97
imprisonment 189–90
inclusion 181
indignation 75
indistinction *see* zones of indistinction
Innerlichtkeit 274
inside/outside 284
intelligence 187

Jarlot, Gérard 47
   Une aussi longue absence (*The Long Absence*) 48, 52, 159
Jaune le soleil (film) 124
Jews/Judaism 97–8 *see also* Hebrew language; the Shoah

Céline, Louis-Ferdinand 153, 154
Joyce, James: *Ulysses* 93, 126, 127–8, 284
Juillard, Robert 111–12

Kant, Immanuel 205, 220–1, 288
  "The Analytic of the Sublime" 65–6, 73, 78, 80, 87–95, 123, 220–1
  Critique of Judgement vii, 53, 65, 66, 220
  imagination 76
  negative Lust (negative pleasure) 66
  partage 220
  sublime 65–6, 73, 78–80, 87–95, 123, 220–1
Keaton, Buster 120
Kellogg, E. R.: *Falkenau the Impossible* 77
Kelly, Van 252
Kluft 256–7, 258, 259
Kraków-Plaszów concentration camp 138
Kristeva, Julia 42, 54
  Black Sun 81

Lacombe, Georges viii, 147
  La Zone: au pays des chiffoniers 161–2, 164
language/dialect 191–2, 194, 207–8, 218
  Char, René 249
  dialect/slang 150–1, 156
  Foucault, Michel 196–7, 201, 219, 229–30, 234–5
  French 229–30
  Hebrew 191–2
  Roussel, Raymond 196
  subject/predicate relationship 249–50
Laplanche, Jean: *Hölderlin et la question du père* 224
Laporte, Roger: *La Veille* 197–8f, 206, 217

Laub, Dori 70–3
laughter 123–4
Lépine, Louis 136
Levi, Primo 50, 78, 170, 175–6, 216
  gray zone 176, 177, 178–80, 181, 261, 263–7
  Muselmann 260
  Report on Auschwitz (1945–1946) 77
  Se questo e un uomo (If This Be a Man) 77, 179, 181 260, 261
  I sommersi e i salvati (The Drowned and the Saved) 176, 178–9, 261, 263–6
  survival 267, 282
Lifton, Robert Jay 176
limit phenomenon 132–3
L'Isle-sur-la-Sorgue 252
literature 154 *see also* poetry
  cemeteries 126–9
  essays 279–80
  Foucault, Michel 196–204, 217
  trauma and 49–50
  la Zone 147–57
  zones 145–57
look, the 79, 91–2, 174 *see also* the gaze
Loutrel, Pierre 157–8
love 89–90, 271–2 *see also* desire
Luberon 238–9f
Lyotard, Jean-François 24 n.1, 65, 98–9, 146–8
  The Differend 146
  Soundproof Room 147
  zones 146–7

M.N.P.G.D. (*Mouvement national des prisonniers de guerre et déportés*) 68
madness 45, 49, 205–6, 216, 226–7, 237, 247, 253
Malapart, Anne 189
Malle, Louis 154
Malraux, André
  La Condition humaine 195

L'Espoir 126
man 222–3, 273–4 *see also* body; humanity
   commonality of 274
   hope 291
   rights 264
Mandela, Nelson 262, 264
Manhattan 112–14, 176
Marker, Chris
   La Jetée 160
   Le Joli Mai 171
Mascolo, Dionys 32, 52, 67, 70, 71*f*, 72–3
   Antelme, Robert and 106–8
   memoirs of 97–8, 99
Mascolo, Jean 38
Mathieu, Jean-Claude 249–50
Melville, Herman: "Bartleby the Scrivener" viii, 126–7, 129, 148
memory 175–6
   Duras, Marguerite 30, 32–3, 41–2, 45–6, 48–51, 58, 83–5, 158–9
   trauma and 81–2
Mény, Georges: *Professions et Métiers* 166
Mérindol 238–9
Merleau-Ponty, Maurice: *Phenomenology of Perception* 60
Metz, Christian 174–5
Michaux, Henri viii, 145–6, 203–4
   Connaissance par les gouffres (Light Through Darkness) 146
   L'Espace aux ombres (The Shadow's Space) 284
Michelet, Jules 217–18
Milner, Jean-Claude 269–70
mirrors 104, 106
Mitchell, Greg 176
Mitterand, François 32, 68–9 *see also* Morland, François
   Le bureau de poste de la rue Dupin, et autres entretiens 68–70
Monnier, Blanche 189–90

Montaigne, Michel de 142, 289
Montmartre 134
Morland, François 67–8 *see also* Mitterand, François
mouroir 69
Mouvement national des prisonniers de guerre et déportés (M.N.P.G.D.) 68
Müller, Filip 116
Le Mur des Fédérés (the Communards' Wall) 138
Muselmann 260–2, 277

Nagasaki 112–13
namelessness 160
Nancy, Jean-Luc 173, 216, 240
   La Communauté affrontée 287
   Le Partage des voix 195
Nanterre 136, 137
Nazism 87, 180, 183, 200–1, 250, 262, 265, 288–9
negative lust (negative pleasure) 66
Nesbit, Molly: *Atget's Seven Albums* 163–70, 174
New York 112–14
Nietzsche, Friedrich 205, 279–80
   Gaya Scienza 121
   "Truth and Lying" 178
Noack, Ferdinand 133
Nossack, Hans Erich: *Interview mit dem Tode* 49

Oakland 63–4, 101*f*–2
observation 91–3 *see also* the look; the gaze
oneself 106–7
Orgeron, Marsha 93
other 102–3, 119–20
outside/inside 284

parallel lives 189
Paris 121, 130–1, 172 *see also* la Zone
   cemeteries 113, 133–8
   dépôts (workhouses) 136–7

General Hospital policy 137
Père Lachaise cemetery 113, 138
refuse and sewage 136–7
Saint-Ouen 155–6f
stench 136, 137
Thiers wall 144, 150, 171
undesirable people 136–7
Paris Commune 130–1
partage 54, 79, 81, 173 *see also* cleave; *der Riß*
    Agamben, Giorgio 240
    Balibar, Étienne 233
    Caws, Mary Ann 251–2
    Char, René 200–1, 251–2
    Didi-Huberman, Georges 215–16, 287
    Foucault, Michel viii–ix, 185–6, 195–200, 204–14, 218–24, 233–8, 240–1
    Kant, Immanuel 220
    Rancière, Jacques 196
Pascal, Blaise 226–7, 228, 230–2, 233–6, 291
    Lettres provinciales 235
    Pensées 226–7
    unity of opposites 232
pathetic, the 285–6
Père Lachaise Cemetery 113, 138
Perec, Georges: *Je me souviens* 32
photography 78–9, 130–2, 174–5 *see also* images
    la Zone 147–8, 160–1, 162–70, 166f, 167f
"Pierrot le fou" 157–8
Pingeot, Mazarine: *Le bureau de poste de la rue Dupin, et autres entretiens* 68
places 60–1, 76, 185–6, 187 *see also* sites; spaces; zones
Plato: *Symposium* 285
poetry 245, 248–52, 275, 279, 290–1 *see also* literature
    Adorno, Theodor 49, 245
    Arendt, Hannah 288
    Char René 201, 238–9, 279, 288

drugs 203–4
Foucault, Michel 201–4
hope 278
Nazism 200–1
Rimbaud, Arthur 192
point d'hérésie 227–37, 241
political/politics 97–8, 260–1, 274 *see also* biopolitics
political space 173
power 92, 185, 213–14, 227–8 *see also* biopower; humiliation
    camps 265, 266
prison 114
Prometheus 279, 280–1, 283
proper distance 79
psychoanalysis 251, 252
Puteaux 159

Queneau, Raymond viii, 154–7
    Le Chiendent (*The Bark Tree*) 151, 156
    "*Discorde mélodie des terrains d'épandage*" ("Discordant Melody of the Sewage Fields") 155
    Duras, Marguerite 157
    language/dialect 156
    Pierrot mon ami 154, 157
    "Saint-Ouen's Blues" 155
    Zazie dans le metro (film) 154
    la Zone 154–7

racism 154
Rancière, Jacques 216
    partage 196
    Politics of Aesthetics 173
rationalism 97
ravishment and reassurance 88–9
real, the 273
reason 97, 273–4
recollection 45
refuse 136–7, 163–70, 166f, 167f
religion 273–4
rémanence 194
resistance 260–4, 275–6, 277–8, 286

Char, René 238, 250–3, 275–6, 286–7
  Muselmann 277
  the French resistance 36, 68, 238, 276
Resnais, Alain 126
  Hiroshima mon amour 35–6, 40, 45, 48, 84
  Nuit et brouillard (*Night and Fog*) 36
Richmond, Kimball 92, 95–6
Rimbaud, Arthur 192, 268, 270–1
  "*Le dormeur du val*" 252
ritual 93, 96, 115–16
Rockhill, Gabriel 173
Rome 133
Rossellini, Roberto 111–12
  Germania anno zero 111–12
Roussel, Raymond 196

Sade, Marquis de 239
Sagan, Françoise 35
Saint-Denis 135
Saint-Jorioz 122
Saint-Just, Louis-Antoine de 276–7
Saint-Ouen 155–6*f*
Sallis, John 100
  Topographies 64
Sartre, Jean-Paul: *Being and Nothingness* 60
Saussure, Ferdinand de 211–12*f*
saxifrage ix n.1, 275*f*, 290
Schmitt, Carl 181
Schneider, Alan 120
Sebald, W. G. 49–50, 175–7, 180, 286, 290
  Luftkrieg und Literatur (*On the Natural History of Destruction*) 111, 154, 176
sewage 136–7
sexuality 212–13, 227–8, 236–7
shantytowns 146 *see also* la Zone
shared zones 172–3
Shoah, the 30 n.7, 49, 70, 96–7, 111, 175, 177–9, 245 *see also* camps

cemeteries 113, 115, 138
commemoration 115
"Construction Sites" 59
Duras, Marguerite and 30, 32, 36, 43
Führer's body 183
human guinea pigs 183
images 115–19, 117*f*, 118*f*
Muselmann 260–2
Paris 136
power 266
survival testimony 71–3
survivors 59, 177, 179–80, 267, 282 *see also* Antelme, Robert
sites 27, 60–1, 105 *see also* spaces
  building sites 61
  construction sites 26–7, 60–2 *see also* chantiers
slang 150–1, 156
space of interest 2, 24
spaces vi, 2, 76, 104–5, 185, 265 *see also* sites; zones; *zone*
  aleph 290
  apartness 103–4
  Bachelard, Gaston 202
  Casey, Edward S. 180, 188
  cemeteries vii–viii, 101*f*–7, 110, 129, 138
  construction sites 26–7
  crimes 110
  Deleuze, Gilles 120
  Duras, Marguerite 107–8
  Foucault, Michel 49, 64, 85, 102–7, 114, 138, 185–8, 240
  gray zone 176, 177, 178–9, 181, 261, 263–7
  Hiroshima mon amour 43
  home 60
  horror 61
  inside/outside 284
  Levi, Primo 179–80
  oneself 106
  places 60–1, 76
  political space 173
  recollection 45

sharing/dividing 81
sites 27
spaces otherwise 2–3, 64, 133, 139, 172
Stein, Gertrude 64–5
the Shoah 115, 177–9
unimaginable 111
spaces otherwise (*see also* Foucault, Michel) 2–3, 64, 103, 110, 138, 172
   Antelme, Robert 108
   Benjamin, Walter 129–30, 133
   cemeteries 104–6, 114, 119, 122, 129–30
   Deleuze, Gilles 120
   dump 136
   Hiroshima mon amour 124
   imagination 175
   la Zone 155, 172
spatialization 208–9
spectacles 87
Stein, Gertrude 63–4, 70
Stevens, George: *Falkenau the Impossible* 77
structuralism 211–12f
Stunde Null policy 112, 175
subject/predicate relationship 249–50
sublime, the vii, 53
   empathy and vii, 73–7, 80–1
   formlessness 65–6
   humiliation and 78
   Kant, Immanuel 65–6, 73, 78–80, 87–95, 123, 220–1
   ravishment and reassurance 88–9
   Sallis, John 64
superstition 273
surveillance 94–5, 144, 180
survival 59, 261, 264, 267, 274
   Char, René 289–90
   flora 289–90
   Levi, Primo 267, 282
   testimony/narration 71–3, 260
Swift, Jonathan: "A Modest Proposal" 142

temporality 193–4, 217
Thiers, Adolphe 135, 144
Thiers wall 144, 150, 171
"thing" 187
thought/unthought 207–8
thresholds 129–30, 133, 177–8, 264
Tour, Georges de la 276
   Job raillé par sa femme (*Job Mocked by His Wife*) 276f
transgression 193
   Char, René 251
   Foucault, Michel 193–7, 205, 212, 214–21, 223–4, 227–8, 234–5, 240–1
translation
   comme/commun(e)/comme-un 281 n.58
   "Construction Sites" 24, 35, 61
   Eine Frau in Berlin 109
   French 103
   partage 173, 195, 198, 224
trauma 70 *see also* earthquakes
   "Construction Sites" 88
   Duras, Marguerite 108
   Foucault, Michel 85–6
   literature 49–50
   memory 81–2
   substitution 49–50
Turgot 137
Turquet de Mayerne, Louis: *La Monarchie aristodémocratique* 244f

Un chien andalou (film) 84
undesirable people 136–7
unimaginable 111
unity of opposites 232
unthought 207–8
utopias 62, 104

Varda, Agnès
   Les Glaneurs et la Glaneuse (*The Gleaners and I*) 170
   Sans toit ni loi (*Vagabond*) 160
Vercors (Jean Bruller) 265

Veyne, Paul 248
Ville, Isabelle 275
violence 109–10

Weiss, Emil; *Falkenau: The Impossible* see *Falkenau: The Impossible* (film)
Wilson, George 53
witnesses 86
Wittgenstein, Ludwig: *Philosophical Investigations* 249
women 82, 83*f*
    shorn 81–2, 83*f*
    violence 109–10
workhouses 136–7
World War II 245, 246 see also the Shoah
Wormser, Olga 35–7

Zone, la viii, 121, 133, 139, 141–6, 166*f*
    Agamben, Giorgio 183
    Apollinare, Guillaume 147
    Atget, Eugène 163–70, 166*f*, 167*f*
    Benjamin, Walter 148, 168–70
    Céline, Louis-Ferdinand 150–5, 156, 171
    cemeteries 133–4
    Cohen, Jean-Louis 168
    demolition 171–2
    film 147–8, 152, 159–62, 164, 170–1
    Lacombe, Georges 147, 161–2
    language/dialect 150–1, 156
    literature 147–57
    photography 147–8, 160–1, 162–71, 166*f*, 167*f*, 174
    Queneau, Raymond 154–7
    ragpickers 161–70, 167*f* see also zoniers
    surveillance 180
    Thiers wall 144, 150, 171
    Une aussi longue absence (*The Long Absence*) 48, 159–60
    untimeliness 168
zones 142–3, 172, 290 see also zones of indistinction
    Benjamin, Walter 181
    gray zone 176, 177, 178–80, 181, 261, 263–7
    imagination 174
    Levi, Primo 176, 261
    in literature 145–57
    Lyotard, Jean-François 146–7
    shared zones 172–3
zones of indistinction 141, 156–7, 180–4, 190, 259–63
zoniers 142, 152–3, 156, 162
    Benjamin, Walter 168–70
    photography/film 159–71, 167*f*, 174
    relocation 171–2

www.ingramcontent.com/pod-product-compliance
Lightning Source LLC
Chambersburg PA
CBHW052148300426
44115CB00011B/1566